FURNITURE MARKETING

FROM
PRODUCT DEVELOPMENT
TO DISTRIBUTION

RICHARD R. BENNINGTON

Professor of Business
Coordinator, Home Furnishings Marketing Program
High Point College
High Point, North Carolina

FAIRCHILD PUBLICATIONS
NEW YORK

Design by Elaine Golt Gongora
Illustrations by Karen Wiedman

Cover photograph courtesy of:

Blanks Engraving
Dallas, Texas

The Alderman Company
High Point, North Carolina

Standard Book Number: 87005-491-0
Library of Congress Catalog Card Number: 84-81057

Printed in the United States of America

PREFACE

The United States furniture industry is extremely exciting for many reasons. Much of this excitement revolves around the products offered for sale and the many ways that they are marketed. The industry is one of the best examples of the American free enterprise system in action. No one manufacturer or retailer controls a large part of the market as is the case in many other industries. The furniture industry is constantly changing, with older companies moving out and newer or reorganized companies moving in.

To help meet the need for marketing professionals, High Point College inaugurated a bachelor's degree program in home furnishings marketing. The first course in this program was offered in 1979, and currently eight courses related to home furnishings are being offered regularly. In doing research for these courses, it was discovered that no single volume describing the furniture industry was available. Therefore, the project of writing a furniture marketing book was undertaken. This book is intended to be an overview of furniture products and how they are marketed.

In evaluating the possible uses of this book, the following should be considered:

1. This book covers the furniture marketing scene from every vantage point. It, therefore, provides the reader with some perspective about each level of the industry and the interrelationship of each level with every other level.
2. It contains valuable data for everyone involved in the furniture industry; i.e., each element in the distribution flow as well as every experience plateau. That means the student or beginner-trainee, as well as the experienced manufacturer, retailer, and wholesaler. Also, it has value for the small community store owner, the chain executive, advertising person, or anyone needing information about furniture marketing.
3. The book is written emphasizing the consumer-oriented approach to marketing.
4. It is useful as a handy reference book since it contains a wide array of definitions, concepts, sketches of period furniture, and other pertinent data.
5. It fills a conspicuous vacuum in business literature since there is a paucity of definitive works on the furniture industry, and most of these cover only a segment of the industry.

6. It benefits from its resources, especially the input of furniture experts in the heart of the Southern furniture manufacturing region as well as leading retailers who visit the Southern Furniture Market. This business and educational climate gives the book an authority it probably could not have achieved if written elsewhere.

The aim of the book's first chapter is to develop an understanding of the task of marketing by presenting an overview on the subject. This chapter is followed by a description of various furniture products, such as upholstered furniture, case goods, occasional tables, wall systems, summer and casual furniture, and bedding.

Next, a chapter on furniture design is provided to give the reader an overview of a majority of the leading historical furniture design periods and how these designs affect furniture products on the market today. Chapters on product development and furniture manufacturing give an indication of the intricacies of conceiving a marketable product idea and translating this idea into an actual furniture product. The chapter on marketing research and information systems focuses on the information needs of the industry and how these needs are met. The ultimate consumer market chapter outlines many of the factors concerning consumers that marketers need to know to be able to sell consumer furniture products successfully.

The sections that follow are designed to provide an overview of pricing, promotion, and distribution in the furniture industry. Although the book is mainly written to cover residential furniture, a chapter on contract furniture is provided. The chapter on pricing deals with the complexities of arriving at an effective price for a furniture product. The chapters on promotion consider personal selling, advertising, sales promotion, and public relations, and the role each can play in the successful sale of furniture.

Finally, the chapters on distribution are designed to examine the various outlets for the marketing of furniture and how they all fit into the very complex distribution pattern within the industry. The topics of retailing, wholesaling, the wholesale furniture market and the U. S. furniture marketing cycle, physical distribution and inventory management, and international marketing are all considered separately in order to provide an all-inclusive look at furniture distribution.

Space considerations make it impossible to list the many different sources and individuals who provided material for this book. A considerable amount of information came from conversations with furniture professionals, trade publications, furniture brochures, and numerous books on general marketing, retailing, and sales management. I am extremely grateful to the many manufacturers who provided photographs, brochures, and other materials which made my task considerably easier.

Writing this book would not have been possible without the help of Richard Burow, Director of Home Furnishings Marketing at High Point College, who spent countless hours reading and editing the manuscript. In fact, he read most of it two or three times. For his time, energy, encouragement, and enthusiasm, I am extremely grateful.

Much of the insight I gained is the result of having worked with Bassett Furniture Industries, learning their operations. I will always be indebted to Robert Spilman and Joe Meadors of Bassett Furniture Industries for their assistance and willingness to share their knowledge with me.

I am also indebted to the many others who read the chapters and made a variety of comments which were extremely valuable in preparing the manuscript.

Finally, I appreciate the numerous efforts of Irv Black, who has been a great supporter of the High Point College home furnishings program from the beginning, and who helped me secure many of the photographs that are used throughout the book.

I hope, now that the book is complete, that it will serve as a useful tool for anyone desiring to learn about the furniture industry.

Richard R. Bennington
High Point, North Carolina

CONTENTS

CHAPTER 7

THE FURNITURE MANUFACTURING PROCESS 75

CHAPTER 8

MARKETING RESEARCH AND INFORMATION SYSTEMS 92

CHAPTER 9

THE ULTIMATE CONSUMER MARKET 106

CHAPTER 10

PRICING METHODS AND PRACTICES 117

CHAPTER 11

PERSONAL FURNITURE SELLING 128

CHAPTER 1

FURNITURE MARKETING: AN OVERVIEW

"Nothing really happens until the product is sold." This quotation emphasizes the fundamental importance of marketing to business organizations. In fact, successful marketing is essential for survival in the American economic system. The purpose of this chapter is to give an overview of furniture marketing, involving the various activities performed and the environment in which the marketer operates.

WHAT IS MARKETING?

Marketing encompasses all the necessary activities involved in directing the flow of goods and services from where they are conceived and produced to where they are consumed or used. As such, marketing generates the income necessary to keep the business operating. If a person were to be asked, "Why does the average furniture retailer or manufacturer exist?" the answer should be "to make a profit." In order to make a profit, every part of the organization must effectively work together. First, the company must have a salable product. Then, this product must be properly presented to potential customers as something that has value so they will exchange their money or credit for it. In order to accomplish these two objectives, the organization must be marketing oriented. This means the marketing department should be involved in the entire process from product development to the ultimate consumer sale. Thus, the success or failure of marketing is directly related to whether or not the company makes a profit.

FURNITURE MARKETING FUNCTIONS

Several activities or functions under the heading of marketing must be performed by any business organization in the furniture industry.

The *primary furniture marketing functions* are:
- Marketing research
- Merchandising
- Personal selling
- Advertising, sales promotion, publicity, and public relations
- Distribution
- Pricing

Marketing research. The systematic, ongoing search for information relevant to any marketing problem or opportunity. This includes gathering information both inside and outside the company. For the typical furniture company, either in manufacturing or retailing, inside information-gathering involves such activities as keeping accurate sales reports of all types to determine which products are selling, who is selling them, and where they are being sold. Outside market research involves collecting information about what is selling on the retail floor in terms of style, color, shapes, woods, and types of pieces in order to discover emerging trends. It also includes studying competition to determine their areas of success and failure, demographic trends to help determine product or sales opportunities, and the economy to learn more about employment, income, and other factors directly involved in people's ability or willingness to buy furniture. An effective, on-going marketing information network provides management with up-to-date, accurate information upon which decisions can be based.

Merchandising. Planning a product and its customer-attracting attributes, and establishing a competitive price so it can be sold to consumers. The merchandising of furniture begins with product development. The target market is studied so that the product will be designed to have both value and visual appeal for those most likely to buy it. Merchandising also involves telling a persuasive story about the product so consumers can relate to it as something that will satisfy their needs. Finally, merchandising is intimately linked with pricing. In other words, a realistic price must be placed on the product so that it can both compete effectively in the marketplace and provide a profit to the manufacturer and retailer.

Personal selling. The situation in which an individual representing a manufacturer, wholesaler, or retailer attempts to sell furniture, usually on a one-to-one basis, to a dealer or ultimate consumer. This activity is usually essential for the actual sale, as well as such necessary additional functions as the collection of credit information and arrangements for delivery.

Advertising, sales promotion, publicity, and public relations. These activities collectively may be referred to as *nonpersonal selling* because they are normally not performed on a one-to-one basis. However, they still are persuasive forms of communication about a company or its products aimed at creating a favorable climate for the sale of products.

Advertising is paid, nonpersonal communication by a company to an audience through a medium such as direct mail, radio, television, magazines, or newspapers.

Sales promotion consists of miscellaneous activities that supplement or complement a firm's normal marketing effort. Many companies have sporadic or ongoing sales promotion campaigns aimed at consumers, involving such activities as contests, sales incentives, premiums, coupons, and product demonstrations. Sales promotion used by manufacturers or wholesalers aimed at retailers include the furniture markets, cooperative advertising, display assistance, advertising materials, sales training, sales contests, and special quantity purchases.

Editorial news about a company or product intended to benefit the company is called *publicity*. Furniture companies issue news releases, have press conferences, and prepare press kits; officials make speeches, sponsor parties, and conduct showroom tours and other market events to obtain favorable attention from the media.

Public relations may be defined as a deliberate, comprehensive effort to influence favorably a number of "publics," such as customers, government agencies, company employees, and leaders in the local and financial community. Common public relations goals of furniture companies include: obtaining favorable publicity, being identified with education, (e.g., student field trips to furniture companies, company officials as guest speakers in classrooms, etc.), being a good "corporate citizen" of the community, making the business appear to be more "human," being seen as a company that provides fashionable products with good value and quality, and counteracting negative publicity.

Distribution. The development and operation of the network of wholesalers and retailers through which the furniture products flow to the ultimate consumer. While a wide range of distribution channels exists, companies try to develop a distribution strategy compatible with the product and its image. For example, a company with a higher-priced line featuring eighteenth century reproductions might choose to distribute its products through independent furniture retailers offering a complete decorator service. Another company with a lower-priced line in most style categories might choose to distribute through discount department stores.

Pricing. The establishment of a monetary value for a product. Pricing is an integral part of merchandising in the sense that the marketer actually places a value on a product which must be evaluated by a buyer as being either a realistic or unrealistic reflection of the worth of the product.

A number of other activities or functions support the efforts of the furniture marketer on the manufacturing, wholesale, or retail level. All of these supporting functions must be carried out with a marketing orientation in order for the firm to be able to compete in the modern business environment.

These *supporting furniture marketing functions* include:
- Physical distribution
- Financing
- Sales service
- Risk-taking

Physical distribution. Often called *logistics,* this involves transporting and storing products from the time they are manufactured until they reach the ultimate consumer. Both manufacturers and retailers must have sufficient inventory at the right places and at the right times to support the company marketing effort.

Financing. The manner in which the buyer must pay for the product. The method of financing must be designed to allow the buyer to purchase comfortably while, at the same time, ensuring that the seller will be paid as quickly as possible.

Sales service. The group of activities involved in reenforcing the activities of the furniture salesperson. Perhaps the most important aspect is *customer service,* which involves making certain that customer questions are answered quickly and complaints are handled as efficiently as possible. Other activities involve tracing orders, handling necessary correspondence with customers, suppliers or other groups, and working with transportation and warehouse personnel to expedite shipments.

Risk-taking. In the furniture industry, most products are introduced and sold to dealers before they are purchased by the ultimate consumer. Therefore, the manufacturer, wholesaler, and retailer are all taking the risk that the product will be accepted by the ultimate consumer.

PRODUCT VS. CONSUMER APPROACH TO FURNITURE MARKETING

The product-oriented approach to marketing was followed by most marketers in the early days of the furniture industry. This involves focusing on a product that has been designed and produced by a manufacturer and attempting to sell this product to a potential customer or user. As in the case of Henry Ford, who said that a customer could have any color Model T automobile as long as it was black, no attempt is made to discover the needs and wants of the consumer before the product is introduced. This marketing strategy involves selling and promoting products through dealers, and the dealer is simply a means to an end.

The consumer-oriented approach to marketing means focusing on the needs of consumers and producing a product to satisfy these needs. In a company using this type of marketing strategy, the entire organization is built around satisfying the consumer. This means beginning with the development of a product based on an assessment of consumer needs and wants and then marketing through channels that will ensure that the product is sold at the right place at the right time. For this to be accomplished, everyone involved in the company—from production manager to credit manager to sales manager—must be consumer-oriented.

The consumer-oriented approach to marketing recognizes the consumer as the final decision-maker in the marketplace. By providing desired products, furniture marketers can ensure that products will be bought in sufficient quantities for profits to be made.

THE ROLE OF MARKETING MANAGEMENT

Marketing management is the key element in formulating and implementing a successful marketing strategy. In order to be successful, marketing management must efficiently perform five functions:

- Planning
- Organizing
- Staffing
- Directing
- Controlling

Planning. Effective planning should be based on clearly-defined objectives. These objectives should be realistic, precise, and in line with the desired image of the firm in the marketplace. Once these objectives are clearly defined, the planning process can begin.

Planning itself may be conducted on two levels. The first is *strategic planning*, which entails setting an overall, master plan designed to reach the goals of the firm over a period of time. In the furniture industry, key elements in this plan include the annual budget and product planning.

The second level is *short-term planning*, which involves the week-to-week, month-to-month, or even slightly longer tactics designed to ensure the effective marketing of products on an ongoing basis consistent with the objectives of the organization. Many companies in the furniture industry develop marketing plans on a six-month basis. Manufacturers who plan on this schedule take into consideration the sales and trends established at the semiannual Southern furniture markets in North Carolina. Retailers using this same schedule make plans based on the product offerings at these markets.

Organizing. Involves setting up the personnel framework through which plans may be effectively carried out and organizational objectives achieved. This framework involves setting up departments, branches, and other organizational units with clearly defined duties consistent with the strategic plans of the organization. These organizational units should be broken down into individual positions with assigned duties, the authority to act, and the responsibility for making certain that the duties are carried out.

Staffing. The recruitment, selection, and training of the qualified personnel to fill the positions and carry out the plans of the organization. After recruitment and selection of personnel who can do their jobs well, training is essential. The staff must understand the company and its unique image, possibilities and limitations, as well as the products being marketed. Both proper personnel selection and effective training are necessary in order to develop sales and fully utilize production facilities.

Directing. Overseeing the day-to-day operations of the business in a manner that will ensure that plans are carried out and the organizational objectives are reached. Two factors are involved in successfully directing an organization:

1. The adequate communication of instructions to personnel to make sure they carry out their duties efficiently and on time.
2. The effective motivation of personnel to get them to work diligently to implement plans and achieve objectives. This includes setting the proper tone throughout the organization through financial and other incentives.

In a modern business organization, the most effective approach is *participation management*. Everyone in the organization is considered a member of the "company team" and is allowed to contribute to the management of the company. Participation management helps employees develop enthusiasm for the company and provides management with a variety of viewpoints and expertise.

Controlling. Begins with setting meaningful performance standards for accomplishing activities; these performance standards should be measurable and tailored to individual positions. Examples include salespeople meeting a prescribed quota and sales service expense not exceeding a specified percent of gross sales revenue. Once meaningful standards are set up, controlling involves measuring the performance of employees against these standards.

THE MARKETING ENVIRONMENT

The furniture marketer in the United States works within a constantly changing environment that continually affects marketing methods. These environmental factors are largely uncontrollable, but the marketer must react to them. In the furniture industry, the following factors have a constant impact on marketing:

The level of economic activity. Two basic factors that influence how much is spent on home furnishings are the level of economic activity and the level of consumer confidence. Furniture and related items are purchases that may usually be postponed. Therefore, when the level of economic activity falls, the demand for home furnishings historically drops. This means that home furnishings is a cyclical industry, with sales normally rising and falling with the business cycle. A furniture marketer should be constantly aware of the level of employment, disposable income,

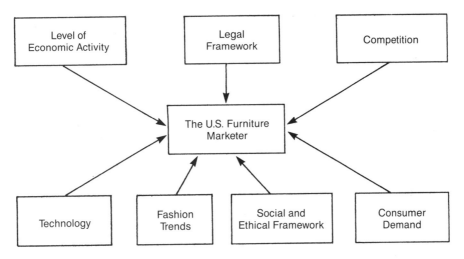

1-1. Forces affecting furniture marketing in the United States

and other economic indicators that have an impact on consumer sentiment and the amount of furniture that will be purchased.

Legal framework. The furniture marketer must operate within a framework of laws and rulings by administrative agencies. Federal laws and administrative rulings must be considered when designing, constructing, and marketing furniture and other home furnishings products. The Flammable Fabrics Act is an example of legislation that affects the production and sale of upholstered furniture. The advertising and sale of all products including home furnishings come under the jurisdiction of the Federal Trade Commission (FTC). Consequently, FTC rulings must be considered in producing advertising and other promotional materials, as well as what is promised in the actual sales transaction. Many states have also been active in regulating the marketplace, which compounds the problem of complying with all the rules and regulations involved in distributing furniture over a wide geographic territory. The marketer must seek the help of trade associations and professionals in the industry in order to know how to comply with all relevant rules and regulations.

Competition. The home furnishings industry, unlike many other industries, is fragmented, with no one company holding a significant market share. In this highly competitive industry, companies are acutely aware of what others are doing. Marketing successes and failures are constantly monitored so that one company can profit from the experience of another.

Technology. Technological advancements must be constantly monitored by the furniture marketer. This involves keeping abreast of all innovations in product design and construction. New man-made fibers and methods of weaving fabrics have provided new materials for upholstered furniture manufacturers. Other innovations have been in component parts and supplies, such as recliner mechanisms, hinges for case-goods doors, and spring units for sleep sofas. These innovations provide more utility and comfort and make new product designs possible.

Other technological breakthroughs involve assembly techniques, different types of machining, and extensive use of computers in all phases of furniture distribution. Manufacturers, wholesalers, and retailers have been able to reduce costs and increase sales by effectively using advancements in technology.

Social and ethical environment. Marketers of furniture should be attuned to the social environment within which they operate. Various social movements, such as consumerism, have affected the marketing of furniture and other products. In part, consumerism is a revolt against shoddy products, false advertising, and deceptive selling practices. It has resulted in the furniture marketer needing to be more aware of the consumer in product design, marketing, quality, and service. Consumer complaints must be handled quickly and effectively before they result in lost sales for the manufacturer or retailer.

Public image is very important, too. Companies that are socially responsible are more likely to develop a positive image which is very helpful in increasing product sales. It is also important to be known as a fair and honest company in order to enjoy a favorable public image from an ethical standpoint.

Fashion trends. The furniture industry is a fashion industry—periodically, new colors and styles become more popular or fashionable, displacing other colors and styles. Managers must be aware of what is popular in the garment industry as well as in home fashions if they are to keep their lines up-to-date. To ignore changes in fashion and consumer tastes will place a company at a competitive disadvantage.

Consumer demand. In the United States, consumers are free to buy or not buy as they wish. Therefore, marketers may spend time and money on technological research to develop a product they feel will sell, only to fail in the marketplace. It should be apparent that by using valid, up-to-date consumer research, chances for success are better because the consumer is the final decision-maker in the marketplace. In evaluating consumer demand, various demographic trends, consumer attitudes, and patterns of consumer behavior should be considered.

SUMMARY

Marketing includes all the necessary activities involved in conceiving a product idea and in profitably moving that product from producer to consumer.

Important primary furniture marketing functions include marketing research, merchandising, personal selling, advertising, sales promotion, publicity, public relations, distribution, and pricing.

Supporting furniture marketing functions include physical distribution, financing, sales service, and risk-taking.

The product-oriented approach to marketing involves focusing on a product and pushing it through a dealer network into the marketplace in an attempt to generate adequate sales and profits.

The consumer-oriented approach to marketing involves focusing on the consumer and designing a product that consumers will find appealing in order to provide the sales and profits necessary to a successful company.

Marketing planning entails defining objectives and formulating both short-term and longer range strategic plans to achieve these objectives.

The marketing management functions include planning, organizing, staffing, directing, and controlling.

The marketer must operate within a framework of uncontrollable environmental factors which include the level of economic activity, the framework of laws and rulings of administrative agencies, competition, technological advancements, social and ethical factors, fashion trends, and consumer demand.

CHAPTER 2

UPHOLSTERED FURNITURE

It has been said that other than clothing and jewelry, furniture is the most personal of our possessions, and this is especially true of upholstered furniture. Because it is covered with fabric, upholstered furniture is often considered to be the most fashionable category of furniture. Fabrics are offered in various colors, designs, and textures so that the consumer can buy the latest in home fashions. The purchase of upholstered furniture is regarded as special and difficult by many people because it creates an impression about the home and the people who live in it.

CLASSIFICATIONS OF UPHOLSTERED FURNITURE

Chairs, sofas, motion chairs, loveseats, sectionals, and sofa beds are the pieces generally classified as upholstered furniture.

UPHOLSTERED CHAIRS

When upholstered furniture is considered, a person usually thinks of living rooms, family rooms, and even bedrooms. Each of these rooms typically contains at least one upholstered stationary chair. Although styles vary, several distinct chair shapes, produced by many manufacturers, have emerged. They have been popular through the years and, although design details such as the type of fabric, skirt treatment, and finish of the exposed wood change from manufacturer to manufacturer, the basic chair shapes do not change drastically.

The specific chair shapes are relatively easy to identify. Two good examples are the wing chair, identified by its prominent, high curved back, and the channel-back chair, distinguished by the deep vertical pleats in the back. Other chair shapes include the club, tub, barrel back, shell, Charles of London, Lawson, spoon back, corner, fan back, and tête-à-tête.

Often, an upholstered chair is accompanied by a matching *ottoman* covered in the same fabric. An ottoman is an upholstered seat or stool, without arms or back, placed in front of an upholstered chair as a footrest.

2-1. Basic upholstered chair shapes

RECLINERS, UPHOLSTERED ROCKERS, AND SWIVEL CHAIRS

Recliners, upholstered rockers, and swivel chairs are usually sold individually and are often not manufactured to match a sofa or other piece of upholstered furniture. These chairs are what most marketers call *motion chairs.* The reason for using this term is quite simple—the chair is constructed to allow for movement and is promoted by emphasizing this feature as well as its comfort.

Recliners are upholstered chairs with adjustable backs and footrests that allow a person to recline at a number of different angles. Beginning with the Morris chair, designed by William Morris in the late nineteenth century, the recliner originally was a bulky chair with a large frame. It had an adjustable back, no footrest, and loose pillows within a wooden frame.

The bulk, extended back, and footrest in the reclining position meant that early recliners required a large area in which to operate. With recent innovations in mechanisms, recliners are being marketed as wall-hugging chairs. The seat is thrust forward allowing the recliner to take up much less space. Innovations in recliner mechanisms that take up less space and allow the disappearance of the footrest make it possible to market a wide range of styles. Even low-profile modern chairs and traditional wing chairs can be adapted to the newer recliner mechanisms.

Upholstered rockers can either be of the conventional type or platform rockers. Conventional rockers accomplish the rocking actions by having the chair rest on exposed wood rockers. Platform rockers rest on a stationary base and the rocking is accomplished by a spring mechanism that attaches the frame to the base.

The most common swivel rocker chairs found in residential furniture are fully upholstered and are attached to a swivel base. The swivel base sits stationarily on the floor, but is constructed to allow the chair frame to both turn from side to side and rock back and forth. Some chairs swivel only, without the rocking feature.

STATIONARY SOFAS AND LOVESEATS

A sofa is the dominant piece of living-room furniture because it is the largest and often the most colorful. In a well-decorated room, the color and fabric of the sofa will coordinate with the colors of the carpet, walls, and draperies. A large variety of sofa styles is available from many different manufacturers. Here again, a number of general shapes of upholstered sofas are popular and readily recognizable. For example, a tuxedo sofa is easily identifiable because of its rectangular shape and arms that are the same height as the back. Other sofa shapes include camel back, Charles of London, Chesterfield, Lawson, and the settee.

These shapes are relatively standard throughout the industry, although individual designers develop their own decorative details in legs, fabric application, contrasting welts, and cushion treatment.

Loveseats are similar in style and shape to sofas, but are shorter and are designed to provide seating space for two people. Larger rooms may contain a sofa and one or two loveseats, while smaller rooms may have a loveseat instead of a sofa. Many manufacturers offer matching sofas, loveseats, and chairs as living or family room groupings.

Camel back   French settee   Lawson

Tuxedo   Charles of London   Chesterfield

2-2. Basic sofa shapes

2-3. This tuxedo sofa and loveseat are upholstered in the same fabric. Many manufacturers also offer matching chairs and ottomans to provide additional options from which to choose when decorating a living room or family room. *(Pearson Furniture, Division of The Lane Company, Inc.)*

2-4. These left arm, right arm, and armless pieces can be placed together to form any configuration that the consumer may desire. For this reason, these pieces are referred to as sectionals, or modular upholstered furniture. Often, they are placed in a U shape, and the matching ottomans are used to form a continuous upholstered unit. *(SilverCraft Furniture Company)*

SECTIONALS

Sectionals, or modular upholstered furniture, offer the consumer an opportunity to group different sizes and shapes of upholstered furniture into the best configuration for the room. Many combinations are available depending on the number of pieces purchased. Sectional or modular pieces come in right arm, left arm, and armless sections. It is quite easy, with the proper pieces, to form an L or U shape. The U shape has been marketed widely by adding matching ottomans to create a continuous upholstered unit.

SOFA BEDS

Many styles of upholstered furniture may be purchased as a sleeper which is a sofa with a concealed spring mechanism and mattress that pulls out to form a queen or full-size bed. Loveseats and chairs that form smaller beds are also available.

Other types of construction allow a piece of upholstered furniture to be converted for use as a bed. For example, a studio couch has two sets of springs—one under the regular sofa spring unit. The bottom set of springs can be pulled out of the rear of the sofa and the detachable seat cushion placed on it to form a double bed. Some companies have introduced upholstered chairs and loveseats that are essentially hinged, upholstered blocks of foam stacked on top of each other; these blocks of foam can open out to form a bed.

Another type of sofa bed that is marketed occasionally is the jack-knife sofa bed. The back and seat are joined by a locking mechanism that, when unlocked, will allow the back to assume a horizontal position level with the seat, making available sleeping room for two people.

Some companies are even producing large ottomans that, through the operation of a variety of mechanisms, form a bed for sleeping.

SELLING FEATURES OF UPHOLSTERED FURNITURE

A number of features of upholstered furniture help to determine whether a product will succeed in the marketplace. Since the purchase of upholstered furniture is extremely personal, many choices are provided to the consumer. The following features are reasons why consumers may or may not buy the upholstered products of a particular manufacturer:

- Color
- Fabric
- Style
- Overall appearance
- Inner construction
- Comfort

COLOR

Upholstered furniture should fit or complement the color scheme of the room. Much upholstered furniture is bought to replace products already owned or to supplement existing furnishings. Therefore, the furniture usually must fit into a decorative scheme already present in the home.

Generally, in buying upholstered furniture, the consumer wants to update or modernize his or her room. Therefore, the upholstered furniture manufacturer must keep up with the latest frame styles as well as fabric colors and textures.

FABRIC

A vast number of fabric choices are on the market today, mainly because the consumer either wants to obtain the proper color or texture or does not want a fabric similar to that on a neighbor's or friend's furniture. To appreciate the diversity of fabrics available for upholstered furniture, one must understand the fibers or yarns that make up the fabrics and the manner in which the fabrics are constructed.

Natural fibers are silk, wool, cotton, and linen. Cotton, especially when treated properly to help prevent staining or soiling, is the most widely used of the natural fibers.

Man-made or *synthetic fibers* are manufactured from chemicals. The man-made fibers most often used in upholstered fabrics are acrylic, nylon, olefin, polyester, and rayon. Many fabrics constructed from man-made fibers are better known by their trade names. For example, polyester is sold under such trade names as Fortrel, Dacron, and Kodel; olefin is sold under such trade names as Herculon and Vectra.

In most cases, fabrics are blends of various fibers. A popular example is a fabric composed of polyester and cotton fibers.

In terms of construction, the two types of fabric most commonly used in upholstering furniture are *woven fabrics* and *nonwoven fabrics*.

Woven fabrics are simply fabrics woven by a machine that interlaces two yarns running at right angles to each other. A number of weaves are popular in upholstered furniture:

1. *Jacquard weaves* are fabrics with differently colored yarns or fibers woven into highly decorative designs. Examples of fabrics woven in this manner are brocades, tapestries, damasks, matelasses, and jacquard velvets. All of these fabrics tend to be relatively formal and are most often found on furniture in the traditional style category.

2. *Pile fabrics* have loops or cut fibers standing up densely from the surface to form a three-dimensional texture called *pile.* Examples of pile fabrics are the various types of velvets and corduroys. Depending on color or design, pile fabrics can be appropriate for traditional or contemporary furniture.

3. *Textured weaves* are fabrics woven from yarns that have been processed to give them more bulk, crimp, stretch, or otherwise alter their hand, appearance, or texture. Such yarns include chenille and taslan. Many of these fabrics convey an informal feeling. Some are constructed to resemble antique, homespun cloth. Other textured weaves are tweeds and twills. Textured weaves are used for family room furniture and both contemporary and Early American styles.

4. *Plain weaves* are fabrics of one color with their character resulting from the type of yarn or fiber used in the weaving process. Examples of various types of fabrics woven in this fashion are muslin and satin. Depending on the texture, plain weaves can be used on formal or informal furniture and with a variety of styles.

5. *Printed fabrics* are fabrics woven so as to provide a flat surface upon which decorative designs are printed. Examples are chintz and polished cottons. These fabrics could be dressy, such as prints correlated with draperies, or casual, such as the prints designed specifically for use on family room or summer and casual furniture. Textured fabrics, such as blends of nylon, rayon, cotton, and polyester fibers, are also printed. Many are rather informal and are used on both Early American and contemporary-styled family room furniture.

Nonwoven fabrics are also important in upholstered furniture. Two examples are:

1. *Vinyls,* which are sheets of vinyl plastic that may or may not be

laminated to a fabric backing, are the most popular nonwoven fabrics. Vinyls are preferred on furniture that is subject to hard usage. Although they are often thought of as "substitute" leather, they can be printed in a variety of patterns. Examples of popular vinyl trade names are Naugahyde and Duran. Vinyls are widely used on office, institutional, and public building furniture.

2. *Flocked fabrics* are made by gluing pieces of cut fibers onto a flat woven cloth base. These fibers form a three-dimensional surface much like pile and are often printed in various designs. Flocked velvet is an example.

Leather is another upholstery material typically used in higher-priced lines. Furniture leather is almost always made from steer hide.

Upholstery fabric, especially woven fabric, is often treated with a fabric finish to make it more resistant to soiling or staining. Trade names of popular fabric finishes are Scotchgard and Teflon.

STYLE

The third selling feature of upholstered furniture is style. Consumers will search for a style of upholstered furniture that will fit into the decor of their homes. Once a person chooses a particular style category, there are many manufacturers with various options from which to choose. In upholstered furniture, the shape of the frame, more than any other feature, determines the style.

OVERALL APPEARANCE

Whether or not a piece of furniture is likely to sell also depends on the overall appearance, which is largely determined by upholstery details and how well a fabric looks on a particular frame. Many people in the furniture industry say that the "marriage" of fabric to frame must be appealing in order for upholstered furniture to sell well. Attention to detail is exhibited by the care the designer takes to make certain that all facets of the design, such as arms, legs, type of skirt treatment, and cushion treatment, blend into an attractive product.

A product that is well-designed, with good proportions, must also be upholstered properly so that all aspects of the product design fit together. Extra care in upholstering, such as matching stripes or plaids and centering fabric designs, is a mark of quality.

INNER CONSTRUCTION

The construction details of upholstered furniture are hidden from the consumer. However, a retail furniture salesperson who has a thorough knowledge of the product and how it is constructed can communicate the features that consumers cannot see. Several hidden features indicate good quality.

The frames used in upholstered furniture often vary in quality. Wood

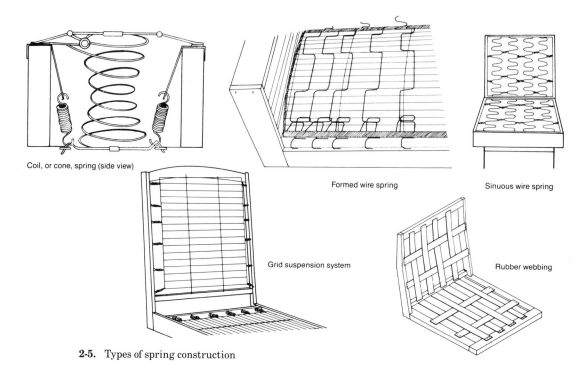

Coil, or cone, spring (side view)

Formed wire spring

Sinuous wire spring

Grid suspension system

Rubber webbing

2-5. Types of spring construction

is the most commonly used material for frames, and the better quality frames are made of kiln-dried hardwood. The hardwood frame components are joined together in various ways such as with dowels and screws. Corner blocks are added for greater strength. Strength also depends on proper gluing methods and properly cut joints that fit well.

The kinds of spring construction used to provide comfort are also a key part of the inner quality. Five basic types of construction are used by most upholstered furniture manufacturers to provide the springing action necessary for comfort. An upholstered furniture manufacturer may use one or more of these types of mechanisms:

1. *The coil or cone spring.* The most expensive and prestigious of the cone or coil spring construction is the use of eight-way, hand-tied double cone springs to provide comfort in a chair or sofa. Basically, it involves fastening the cone springs tightly to the base and expertly tying their tops together with a strong cord. Cone springs may also be manufactured as a unit, tied with steel wire, and attached to the frame. This unitized spring construction has many of the same advantages as hand-tied springs, but costs less.

2. *The sinuous wire spring.* The sinuous wire spring is manufactured in a zigzag shape with both ends of each spring being fastened directly to the upholstered furniture frame. The seat or back springing action is accomplished by having a number of these springs fastened parallel to each other.

3. *The formed wire spring.* The formed wire spring is constructed of wire similar to the sinuous wire spring; however, this spring is formed into long rectangular bends and angles other than the zigzag shape. The formed wire springs are attached directly to the frame like sinuous wire springs.

4. *The grid suspension system.* This system is composed of a wire grid, sometimes covered with paper or plastic-coated wire, which has one side fastened directly to the frame. The other side is connected to the frame by helical springs which provide the springing action.

5. *Rubber webbing.* Instead of having wire springs of any type, some manufacturers use various types of rubber webbing fastened directly to the frame.

Filling material is used to pad the arms, backs, and other areas of the upholstered furniture. The type of materials used and how well the padding is done is another indication of quality and comfort.

Comfort in a piece of upholstered furniture depends primarily on the cushions in the seat and often in the back. In domestic upholstered products, these three types of cushions are most common:

1. A better-quality cushion used by many of the medium-priced to more expensive manufacturers is polyurethane foam, wrapped with layers of polyester fiber and sewn into a muslin cover. This cushion, complete with its muslin cover, will be inserted into the decorative cushion cover.

2. A medium-quality cushion that is widely used is a polyurethane core with polyester bonded or glued on each side. This cushion is inserted into the decorative cushion cover without being sewn into a muslin cover.

3. The less expensive cushions are blocks of polyurethane foam placed directly inside the cushion cover.

Other types of cushions are available, many times as an optional feature, including down and spring down, which are quite expensive. For example, spring down cushions are made by taking a collection of small, individually wrapped coil springs, called a *Marshall unit,* and placing them inside a polyurethane core. This core is wrapped with a mixture of polyurethane and down. The entire unit is sewn into a muslin inner cover and then inserted into the decorative cushion cover.

One final test to determine how well the furniture is upholstered is to determine if the frame can be felt through the fabric. Furniture in which the hard edge of the frame can be felt from the outside is poorly padded and is subject to a more rapid wearing away of the fabric.

COMFORT

The final feature that determines whether a person will purchase a piece of upholstered furniture is comfort.

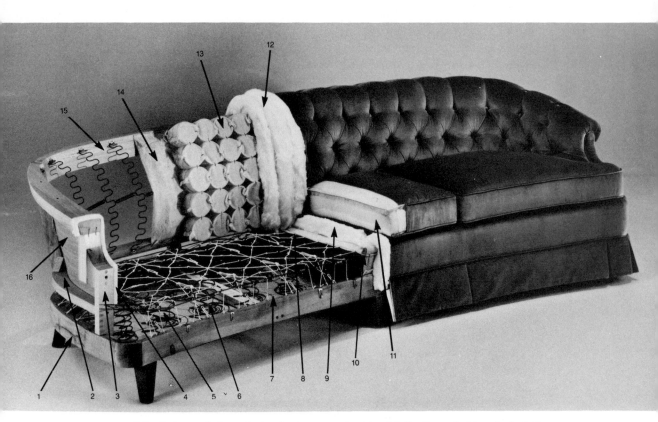

2-6. Cutaway photograph showing inner construction details of an upholstered sofa: **1.** Frame of kiln-dried hardwood. **2.** Corner blocks added for strength. **3.** Glued, double-dowelled joints. **4.** Small edge roll to define and firm arm contour. **5.** Edge wire for shape. **6.** Eight-way, hand-tied coil springs. **7.** Polypropylene webbing base for coil springs. **8.** Polypropylene cover for seat springs. **9.** Fabric-covered deck. **10.** Edge roll to give firmer shape to seat edge. **11.** Multi-layered foam cushion. **12.** Multiple layers of filling materials for comfort. **13.** Marshall unit (individually muslin-wrapped coil springs). **14.** Polypropylene cover over springs. **15.** Sinuous wire springs. **16.** Polypropylene covering inside of arms. *(Pearson Furniture, Division of The Lane Company, Inc.)*

The retail salesperson will normally have the consumer sit on a chair or sofa to see how comfortable it feels. Is it possible for the person to sit with both feet on the floor? How difficult is it for the person to get out of it? Is the seat too narrow or too wide? How soft is the seat and back? These questions must be answered if the shopper is to be satisfied with his or her upholstered furniture purchase.

SUMMARY

Of all furniture products, upholstered furniture is the most subject to fashion trends because of the changes in popularity of colors and fabric textures.

Upholstered furniture includes stationary upholstered chairs, recliners, upholstered rockers, swivel chairs, sofas, loveseats, sectionals, and sofa beds. A number of identifiable chair and sofa shapes have been popular through the years and are produced by many different manufacturers.

Recliners, upholstered rockers, and swivel chairs are most often sold individually rather than as a matching part of a suite of furniture. Recliners are upholstered chairs with adjustable backs and footrests that allow a person to recline at different angles. Newer recliner mechanisms are adaptable to a variety of styles and allow the chairs to be placed closer to the wall than the older models. Upholstered rockers include chairs with exposed wood rockers, platform rockers, and rockers with swivel bases.

Sofas or loveseats are usually the most dominant pieces of living-room furniture because of their large size.

Sectionals, or modular upholstered furniture, provide the consumer with a large degree of flexibility in arranging upholstered furniture in a room.

Sofa beds, or convertible sofas, are available from many manufacturers and are popular with consumers. Some manufacturers offer both stationary and convertible sofa options. Loveseats, chairs, and ottomans that can be converted into beds are also on the market.

Selling features in upholstered furniture include: color, fabric, style, overall appearance, inner construction, and comfort.

Upholstered furniture fabric is woven from natural fibers such as cotton, silk, wool, and linen or from synthetic fibers such as acrylic, nylon, olefin, polyester, and rayon.

Both woven and nonwoven fabrics are used in upholstering furniture. The following types of weaves are popular in upholstered furniture fabrics: jacquard weaves, pile fabrics, textured weaves, plain weaves, and flat woven fabrics that are usually printed. Two types of nonwoven upholstery fabrics are vinyls and flocked fabrics.

Upholstery fabrics are often treated with a commercial treatment such as Scotchgard and Teflon to minimize soiling and staining.

Features that determine the quality of inner construction are the frame, springs, filling, cushions, and the degree of skill and care with which the product is assembled and upholstered.

One of the most important features influencing the purchase of a piece of upholstered furniture is comfort as perceived by the consumer.

CHAPTER 3

CASE GOODS

Throughout history, furniture made from various types of wood has been very popular. Today, wood and simulated wood furniture continues to be important and is known in the industry as that category of furniture called *case goods*.

The word "case," as used in the term "case goods," can be defined as a piece of furniture used for storing or holding various articles in the home. It is a boxlike structure such as a dresser, chest of drawers, china cabinet, or buffet. Since these pieces are most often found in bedrooms and dining rooms, many people refer to furniture found in these rooms as case goods. However, other wood and simulated wood products, such as wall systems and occasional tables, are also made by case-goods manufacturers. To avoid confusion, wood and simulated wood products other than bedroom and dining-room furniture will be discussed in Chapter 4. Chapter 3 will provide an overview of the bedroom and dining-room furniture available from United States manufacturers.

BEDROOM FURNITURE

A grouping of matching pieces of furniture for the bedroom is called a *bedroom suite*. The number of pieces in a bedroom suite may vary from as few as four pieces to as many as it is practical to have in any given bedroom.

A four-piece bedroom suite, typically used in advertising, contains the smallest number of pieces sold together as a suite. It includes a headboard (and possibly a footboard), chest, dresser, and mirror. Other matching pieces can usually be added to make the suite more complete. Most traditional bedroom furniture made by higher quality manufacturers features suites with more matching pieces included.

Other pieces of furniture sold in a bedroom grouping may include a small three-drawer chest, called a *bachelor's chest,* and an *armoire,* which is a tall case piece with doors covering an inner compartment for hanging clothes. One or two bedside tables, bookcases, and a student or corner desk may also be included. Many groupings have a number of pieces that can fit either beside or on top of each other as a wall unit. For example, bookcases or case pieces with drawers or doors are made so that they fit on top of bachelor's chests, bedside tables, or dressers. Sometimes, even bachelor's chests and bedside tables are made to fit on top of each other.

3-1. This six-piece Early American bedroom suite consists of a dresser, frame landscape mirror, four-drawer chest, spindle headboard, and two nightstands. Options include different mirrors, headboards and chests or dressers. *(Bassett Furniture Industries)*

Often, in bedroom furniture designed for teenagers, an effort is made to sell a grouping of furniture as a sleep/study/storage center. Rather than being the usual suite of bedroom furniture, these grouping are called *correlated, modular,* or *wrap groups.* "Correlated" means that the grouping is intentionally designed to fit together to create a personalized living environment. At times, companies correlate case pieces for the bedroom, dining room, and living room. "Modular" means that the pieces may be used separately or can be fitted together in a variety of ways. Finally, the term "wrap group" refers to the fact that the pieces are often used beside each other or on top of each other—so as to "wrap" around the wall as a complete wall unit.

Many suites offer the option of a single, double, or triple dresser. Although probably originally referring to dressers with one, two, or three vertical rows of drawers, these terms now indicate the length of the case pieces.

A variety of mirrors is often offered. Possible choices could be a landscape mirror, twin vertical mirrors, or a triplex mirror which is also called a tri-fold, or wing, mirror.

Landscape mirror

Twin mirrors

Wing, or triplex, mirror

3-2.   Three basic types of mirrors

3-3.   This wrap group features a number of correlated pieces: a corner desk, student desk, dressers, and bookcases to provide the purchaser with a combined sleep/storage/study area. Such a grouping is particularly useful for a teenage student. *(American Drew)*

DINING-ROOM FURNITURE

The options in dining-room furniture include full-size, apartment or con-dominium (sometimes called *junior*), and informal dining furniture or dinettes.

Full-size dining-room suites vary as to number of pieces, depending on manufacturer, retailer, price range, and the needs of the consumer. The minimum full-size dining-room suite consists of a china cabinet (hutch and china base), table, and four side chairs. This grouping of pieces is used mainly for advertising in order to allow the retailer to quote a more attractive price. However, a dining-room suite purchased by most people would probably have more chairs (five side chairs and one armchair) and an optional buffet or server. There could be a choice of two or three different sizes and types of chairs and tables.

An apartment or *condominium dining-room suite* is smaller and de-signed especially for smaller size rooms. In the industry, such a suite is known as a *junior dining-room suite* and usually includes a china cabinet, four side chairs, and a table. The china cabinet is shorter in length, often

3-4. This dining-room suite features a smaller scaled china hutch, which can be used individual-ly or in groups of two or three as shown here *(right)*. The rectangular table can be enlarged to accommodate one or two 18-inch leaves for additional seating space. The suite also includes four cane-back chairs, a mobile server *(rear)*, and a sideboard *(left). (Bassett Furniture Industries, Inc.)*

measuring 48 to 54 inches as opposed to the 60 inches or longer of a full-size dining-room suite. Usually, the table is not an extension table; however, if it does extend, it will do so to a lesser degree.

Informal dining furniture is the grouping commonly known as *dinettes* and *party sets* and is usually composed of a table and four to six chairs. Materials most often used in informal dining tables include wood, wrought iron, chrome, glass, vinyl, and metal with inlaid, laminated tops. Chairs are made of chrome, wood, wrought iron, and aluminum. The seats or backs are often upholstered in vinyl or fabric. Although this category of dining furniture has traditionally been in the lower price brackets, many manufacturers are currently offering more style in higher price ranges.

SELLING FEATURES OF CASE GOODS

Four characteristics that attract customers when purchasing case goods are:

- Quality
- Style
- Overall appearance
- Relative value

QUALITY

The consumer buys furniture based on how well he or she perceives a product will satisfy personal needs. For instance, the product must also have sufficient quality, in the consumer's mind, to be worth the price. There are a number of elements that indicate good quality, and these should be emphasized by the furniture salesperson.

External surface construction. External surface construction is important in providing good quality. Case goods usually are wood or wood-simulated furniture, but some groups are painted or covered with materials such as laminates of different colors.

The following discussion of the usual types of external surface construction is ranked by price from higher priced to lower priced furniture. Individual suites differ, and although this ranking may not be accurate for all manufacturers, it is generally true.

Veneer and solid wood is most likely to be utilized in the higher price brackets, with the exception of Early American pine suites which may be lower in price. Many expensive suites use a combination of solid wood for the pilasters, drawer fronts, parting rails and various external structural pieces, and veneer for the flat surfaces. Since veneer is a very thin layer of wood, it can legitimately be referred to as "all wood."

Veneered panels are a type of plywood construction. Often, these panels provide both beauty and quality by using attractive face veneers and an

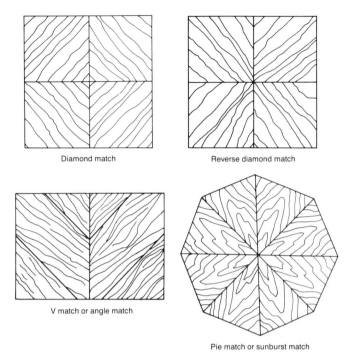

Diamond match   Reverse diamond match

V match or angle match

Pie match or sunburst match

3-5. Types of veneer matches

odd number of plies to prevent the panels from warping. Quality hardwood veneers finish well and when arranged in intricate designs, they give a very interesting appearance to table tops, doors, and other highly visible surfaces. Figure 3-5 shows examples of the ways face veneer may be matched in producing decorative panels.

In most veneered panels, the center ply is much thicker than the other layers to provide added strength. This ply is called the *core* and is at least one-half inch thick. An evidence of quality is whether the core is solid wood or a wood composition material. The composition material is made by grinding wood into very small particles which are glued back together to form a hard board. Depending on the size of the particles, this wood composition material is called *flake core, chipboard, fiber board,* or simply, *particle board.*

A *combination veneer-wood-print furniture* is less expensive because of printing wood grain on particle board. The printed particle board is used for the sides, back panels, and other places that are external but not the most often viewed surfaces. The printing of wood grain is often called *engraving* and is very effective in simulating a solid wood or veneer panel. Large engraved cylinders are used to apply ink to special particle-board panels which are sanded very smooth, are hard, and are not likely to warp or change shape.

Printing has developed into a sophisticated process which can be finished effectively to give a very pleasing appearance to the product. In fact, some manufacturers prefer to print surfaces to simulate woods with very few definite grain characteristics such as maple. By printing such woods, they believe more eye appeal can be created than if the actual wood or veneer is used. Interesting effects can also be created by using slightly different color inks at various stages in the printing process.

In certain suites with this type of surface material, laminated tops are utilized for extra durability. Two trade names of popular laminates used in the industry are Mycarta and Formica.

All-print furniture involves using printed panels for the entire exterior of the case pieces. This furniture is composed primarily of particle board, although laminated tops are used on table dressers, chests of drawers, and other case pieces in many suites.

To create decorative details, plastic overlays are sometimes utilized. These overlays are generally molded from plastics such as polystyrene or polyurethane. They are attached to drawer fronts, doors, or other places where a carved appearance is desired. In some suites, the entire door or drawer front is molded plastic with a carved design.

A *combination of vinyl and print or all-vinyl furniture* is one of the least expensive types of case-goods construction. Vinyl and print furniture has some printed panels with the rest of the particle board covered with a thin layer of vinyl preprinted to give the appearance of wood graining. This vinyl is glued to the outside of the furniture and does not require a separate finishing process. Vinyl is most commonly found in inexpensive occasional tables, stereo cabinets, television stands, and wall units.

Plastic molded furniture is also available. In case goods, molded dining-room chair frames are probably the most common item produced by this process. Either frame components or the entire frame is molded and is finished to match the case pieces. These plastic molded chair frames are usually available in the same lower price range of furniture as that utilizing molded plastic overlays and drawer fronts. Inexpensive, small occasional tables and other smaller pieces of furniture are also made of molded plastic.

Type of wood. The type of wood used in the construction of case goods is an indication of quality. Generally, hardwoods such as cherry, walnut, and oak are more expensive than softwoods such as pine. The same is true of veneers, with some of the rarer decorative hardwood veneers being more expensive than others. Expensive furniture is manufactured with good quality veneers. For example, a suite with cherry or mahogany veneer would normally be much more expensive than a solid pine suite. The type of wood used depends largely on consumer desires at the time. For example, as tastes change, oak furniture may be very popular at one time and walnut at another.

Types of construction joints. This also indicates quality in case goods. While joints are often hard to see after the pieces are assembled and finished, the manner in which the parts are joined together will help determine the strength or weakness of the piece. Joints should be smooth and fit together tightly to ensure that the furniture will provide many years of service.

Examples of joints and methods of strengthening joints used in furniture construction include: mortise-and-tenon joints, corner blocks, dovetail joints, dowel joints, and tongue-and-groove joints.

Mortise and tenon is a strong joint used to join rails to side members in chests and dressers and to join key pieces of chair frames. In a chair, an important joint would be where the side rails and leg stretchers of a chair enter the back post.

Corner blocks help to hold together joints at the point of greatest strain. For example, they strengthen joints where the seat rails of chairs join the posts.

Dovetail joints are considered to be a mark of quality drawer construction. Properly done, this joint "locks" drawer fronts in place, preventing loosening through many years of use.

Dowel joints are very common in furniture joint construction. This type of joint involves gluing a dowel or peg, most often made of hardwood, into

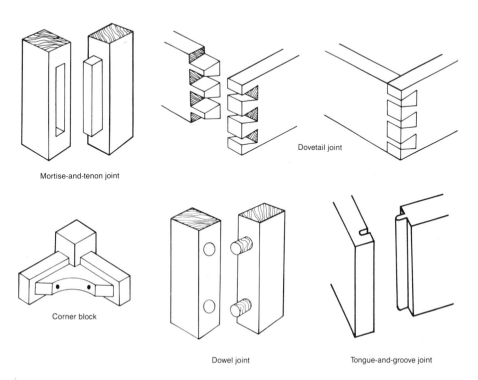

Mortise-and-tenon joint

Dovetail joint

Corner block

Dowel joint

Tongue-and-groove joint

3-6. Basic types of joints used in furniture construction

a predrilled hole to connect two pieces of wood. Often, double dowel construction is used. A better dowel joint is made when dowels have spiral or vertical grooves which hold the glue and make a better bond possible.

Tongue-and-groove joints are used to make a strong flat surface as well as to attach drawer fronts. When glued properly, these joints are very strong.

Overall construction details. Overall construction details other than joint construction are also important evidences of good quality. Examples of important construction features include the type of drawer guides, whether partitions or dust bottoms are used to separate drawers, and the type of hinges used to hang doors. Better-quality furniture will usually have dust protection between drawers and long doors hung with piano-type hinges for added stability.

Figures 3-7 through 3-10 show construction details for selected bedroom and dining-room furniture. The amount of detail and care taken in machining and assembling furniture parts also helps to determine the quality of bedroom and dining-room furniture.

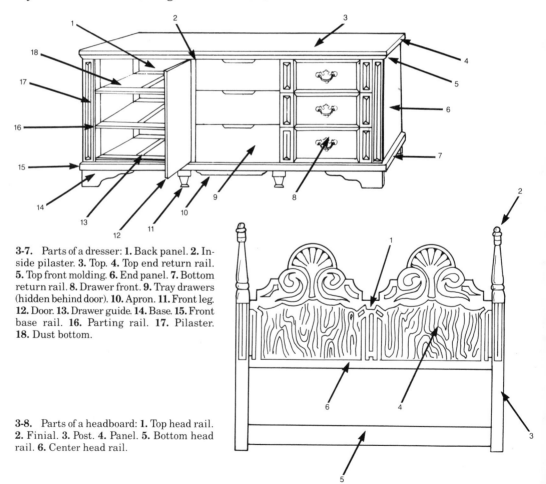

3-7. Parts of a dresser: **1.** Back panel. **2.** Inside pilaster. **3.** Top. **4.** Top end return rail. **5.** Top front molding. **6.** End panel. **7.** Bottom return rail. **8.** Drawer front. **9.** Tray drawers (hidden behind door). **10.** Apron. **11.** Front leg. **12.** Door. **13.** Drawer guide. **14.** Base. **15.** Front base rail. **16.** Parting rail. **17.** Pilaster. **18.** Dust bottom.

3-8. Parts of a headboard: **1.** Top head rail. **2.** Finial. **3.** Post. **4.** Panel. **5.** Bottom head rail. **6.** Center head rail.

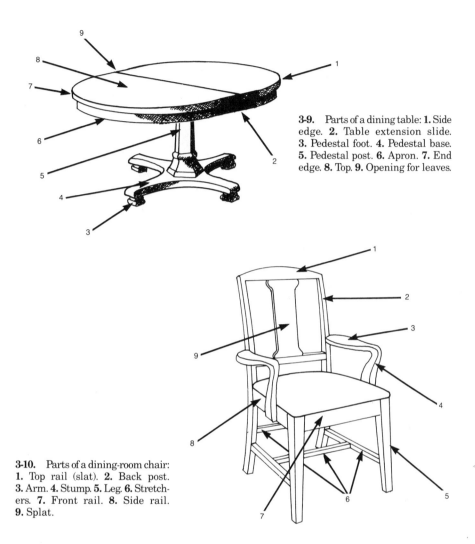

3-9. Parts of a dining table: **1.** Side edge. **2.** Table extension slide. **3.** Pedestal foot. **4.** Pedestal base. **5.** Pedestal post. **6.** Apron. **7.** End edge. **8.** Top. **9.** Opening for leaves.

3-10. Parts of a dining-room chair: **1.** Top rail (slat). **2.** Back post. **3.** Arm. **4.** Stump. **5.** Leg. **6.** Stretchers. **7.** Front rail. **8.** Side rail. **9.** Splat.

STYLE

It cannot be stressed too strongly that furniture is a fashion product and that many people purchase the product because of its style. Countless styles of furniture are available from United States furniture manufacturers. Chapter 5 will provide an overview of the basic styles of furniture as they have developed throughout history. The emphasis is on the style periods that are recognized as distinct and indicative of particular designers or countries.

Although the furniture produced by some companies reflects these design periods in authentic detail, other companies offer their own versions of specific style categories. Their designers borrow ideas from many sources to create a design that combines several style periods.

Some of the considerations as to the salability of a particular suite include how well the style is executed, whether the final design is in balance and, finally, the degree to which the design appeals to consumers.

A term often heard in the furniture industry to describe some very intricate, overdone, or bulky designs is *borax*. This term comes from Kirkman's Borax Soap which was on the market in the early 1900's. This soap came with coupons on the wrapper which could be taken to a redemption center and exchanged for pieces of furniture. The furniture was poorly designed and constructed, so it is from the Kirkman's Borax Soap label that the term borax is derived. However, what is borax furniture to one person could be a desirable product to another.

OVERALL APPEARANCE

The eye appeal of the finished furniture product has a great deal to do with whether it will sell at retail. The two factors that are most important in providing the desired overall appearance of a case-goods piece are *finish* and *hardware*.

The color, depth, and clarity of finish can add definite eye appeal to wood or wood-simulated furniture. Modern furniture finishing processes allow the manufacturer to choose from a wide variety of materials and colors. The number of steps in the finishing process has a definite effect on the final appearance. In general, the number of steps also is reflected in the price range of the furniture.

Stains are applied to the raw wood and dried; and a number of "build" coats, "fill" coats, and "top" coats are added for depth and eye appeal. Some manufacturers hand wipe, sand, highlight, and hand rub at various steps in the finishing process.

Antiquing is important in some styles, and involves such procedures as: (1) spraying the piece with black paint or dye to look like fly specks; (2) cowtailing, which is dipping a stiff, long-bristled brush (cowtail) in black dye or paint and hitting the piece at various places to leave black marks; and (3) distressing the piece with a tool that makes nicks and scratches, thereby creating an antique appearance.

Decorative hardware can also enhance the overall appearance of case goods. The appropriate type of door handle and drawer pull, chosen to fit in with the design of a piece of furniture, can add to its salability. Selecting the right hardware is not a simple task because of the many styles and finishes from which to choose.

Another feature that can add to the overall appearance of furniture is carving and other decorative detail. Carving is done today by carving machines which allow the exact copying of a sample in great detail. Two other methods of adding decorative detail involve using molded plastic components and embossing designs into furniture panels. Molded plastic components attached to doors, drawers, or other external surfaces add a carved look. Embossing, involving the use of a large amount of pressure to make a design imprint in a furniture panel, can also add eye appeal to a piece of furniture.

VALUE

The consumer has a personal view of value which provides motivation to purchase specific products. Evidences of value are the quality, style, and overall appearance compared to the price and the services offered by the retailer. All of these features must be acceptable before the consumer feels the product has sufficient value to be a worthwhile purchase.

SUMMARY

The largest percentage of case goods is bedroom and dining-room furniture.

The name "case goods" comes from the term "case," which means a boxlike structure such as a chest or dresser designed for holding or storing articles in the home.

A four-piece bedroom suite includes a headboard (and possibly footboard), chest, dresser, and mirror. Other bedroom pieces include armoires, bedside tables, bookcases, student desks, corner desks, and wall units. Correlated, modular, or wrap groups are available as bedroom furniture from a number of manufacturers.

A dining-room suite can have as few pieces as a china cabinet, table, and four side chairs. Normally, however, there are at least six chairs (one armchair and five side chairs) and possibly a buffet. Other choices in dining furniture are apartment or condominium (junior) dining-room suites and informal dining furniture (dinettes).

Features that attract consumers to case goods are: quality, style, overall appearance, and relative value.

Elements of relative quality are external surface construction, type of wood, type of joint construction, and overall construction details.

Types of external surface construction include: (1) all veneer and/or all wood; (2) combination of veneer, wood, and print; (3) all print; (4) combination of vinyl and print or all vinyl; and (5) plastic molded furniture.

Typical furniture construction joints include mortise-and-tenon joints, dovetail joints, dowel joints, and tongue-and-groove joints. Corner blocks are often used to strengthen joints.

There are endless varieties of furniture styles on the market with manufacturers providing authentic styles from one or more of the historical style periods and also from original designs.

The overall appearance of a case piece can be enhanced by finish, hardware, and decorative detail, utilizing processes such as carving, embossing, or adding a molded plastic overlay.

CHAPTER 4

OTHER RESIDENTIAL FURNITURE PRODUCTS

O ccasional tables, wall systems, summer and casual furniture, and bedding are important segments of the furniture industry which should be understood by the furniture marketer. Occasional tables and wall systems are manufactured in a similar fashion to case goods and, therefore, are often classified as case goods. Summer and casual furniture is designed for use on the patio, porch, at the fireside, or other areas calling for less formal furniture. Bedding refers to the mattress, box spring, or other foundation upon which a person sleeps.

OCCASIONAL TABLES

An *occasional table* is an accent table that adds style to a room and provides space to hold lamps, books, ash trays, refreshments, or other items. In popular-price brackets, occasional tables are sold in sets, generally for living room or family room use. A set usually consists of two end tables and a coffee or cocktail table.

The end or lamp tables are designed to go at either end of a sofa to hold lamps, books, or other accessories. If one of these tables is enclosed and is round, hexagonal or octagonal with doors opening in the front, it is sometimes referred to as a *commode*.

The terms *coffee table* and *cocktail table* are used interchangeably to mean a larger low table that is usually found in front of a sofa. Although these tables are typically oval or rectangular, some style groups feature tables that are square or round.

Some manufacturers offer additional tables such as a *sofa table,* a long, narrow table designed for use behind a sofa. Therefore, it is the same height as the back of a normal sofa. When used elsewhere in the room, these tables are sometimes called *library tables*.

The predominant table in a set is the cocktail or coffee table because it is in full view, rather than partially hidden by the sofa or lamps and other accessories.

4-1. This French-style grouping of matching occasional tables consists of square lamp or end tables, one with an open shelf *(left)* and the other with a drawer *(right)*, and an oval cocktail table. A design feature on the tops of these tables is the diamond-match veneer. *(Bassett Furniture Industries, Inc.)*

Several manufacturers offer sets of occasional tables that are coordinated with upholstered furniture. These appeal to those consumers who are interested in purchasing a well-coordinated, entire room of furniture.

In traditional furniture styling, there are a number of other occasional tables, many of which have been popular for several years. They may be found between chairs or used as accent pieces at other places throughout the home. Figure 4-2 shows examples of the variety of other types of occasional tables.

Wood and wood-simulated occasional tables have the same types of construction as case goods. Construction materials vary widely, with the more expensive tables made of solid wood and/or veneer and the less expensive tables covered with vinyl or made from molded hard plastic.

Consumers often buy tables to provide interest or a center of attention in a room. For this reason, a wide variety of other materials is used in constructing occasional tables. Inset glass tops, sometimes with cane or other material under the glass, are design features with many manufacturers. Providing greater variety are tables made out of chrome and glass,

French occasional table

Drop-leaf table

Pembroke table

Gate-leg table

Candlestand

Console table

Tilt-top table

Tea table

Folding-top table

Tier table

Nested tables

Piecrust table

Drum table
(with pedestal)

Step table

Trestle table

4-2. Types of occasional tables

wrought iron and glass, or even tubular metal covered with gold and glass. Many of these tables have a relatively high price and are sold only in higher-priced furniture and department stores.

The least expensive tables are usually sold in discount department stores, by mobile-home suppliers, and by dealers who are selling on contract to furnish rooms in hotels and motels. Occasional tables are manufactured both by case-goods manufacturers and companies that specialize in producing tables only.

Often, occasional tables are manufactured and packaged unassembled, or *KD* (knocked down), and are sometimes referred to as ready-to-assemble furniture. By shipping the tables in this manner, freight costs are reduced. Some full-service furniture stores will assemble and check over the tables before they are delivered to the consumer. Other stores consider the ready-to-assemble tables as "take with" or "take home" items and sell the tables in their original cartons. The consumer then takes them home and assembles them. This approach requires that the manufacturer take extra care in designing easy-to-assemble joints that are of satisfactory strength when assembled at home.

WALL SYSTEMS

The category of furniture known as wall systems is comparatively new within the industry. Wall systems are an outgrowth of the desire for more space-saving storage up and around walls for books, television sets, records, and stereo equipment or other electronic equipment. The growth in the sales of wall systems has been stimulated by the electronic generation, the desire for in-home entertainment, and smaller rooms as building becomes more expensive.

The modern wall system is composed of a number of wall units placed together in a variety of ways. The wall units are bookcases, étagères, desks, bars, and enclosed compartments with doors and are designed to be placed side by side to meet the space and storage needs of the consumer. Some smaller wall units are designed to be placed on top of each other. Often, the components of a wall system are deeper than the average bookcase or display cabinet, thus allowing television sets and stereos to fit easily as well as to be hidden behind closed doors.

Wall systems are used by the consumer in living rooms, family rooms, dining rooms, and bedrooms. The styles offered vary, with a wide selection available in traditional, contemporary, and other style categories. Wood and simulated wood are used primarily, with the finishing being similar to that of case goods. In the contemporary style category, there is widespread use of glass in doors and shelves.

Some wall systems have a hinged door concealing a pullout spring-and-mattress mechanism much like a sofa bed. The pullout bed is promoted as an easy way to add an extra bed in a small apartment.

SUMMER AND CASUAL FURNITURE

Included in the category of summer and casual furniture are furniture products designed for use on porches, in sun rooms, on the lawn and/or patio, or as odd pieces throughout the home. A wide variety of materials and styles of summer and casual furniture is offered. In fact, there are furniture markets specializing in only summer and casual furniture, even though these products are also shown at the major furniture markets. Summer and casual furniture can be classified according to the materials from which they are constructed.

WICKER, RATTAN, AND BAMBOO FURNITURE

Wicker, rattan, and bamboo are categories of furniture that require a great deal of handwork and are very popular, especially in warmer climates. Most of the handwork is done in the Orient and Mediterranean countries. The handmade pieces are often imported in sections, with the final assembly and finishing completed in the United States.

Rattan is a very strong, solid vine of the palm family that grows in the jungles of the Philippines, Indonesia, and other Far Eastern countries. It is very practical for making furniture because when placed over heat, it can be bent into many different shapes without splitting or breaking. It also takes stain and various finishing materials quite readily for a very pleasing appearance.

Rattan peel, also called *cane,* is the skin of the rattan furniture. It is woven into intricate designs to be used on case goods, for chair backs and seats, and for a wide variety of other pieces. The larger diameters of the rattan vine are used as the structural members for a variety of types of rattan furniture. Actually, rattan is one of the strongest furniture materials available based on strength per pound.

The inner core of the rattan pole is small in diameter and is more popularly known as *wicker,* or *reed.* It absorbs stain and lacquer readily and is widely used for weaving furniture and accessories. Although other types of woven material are also called wicker, the largest percentage of wicker furniture is made from the core of the rattan pole.

Rattan can be used as the frame of upholstered furniture to create an informal atmosphere. When combined with the right fabric, it is considered quite attractive and fashionable. It is also used for occasional tables, étagères, informal dining tables and chairs, and for furniture often found on porches.

Bamboo is a hollow plant with very pronounced rings that appear periodically on the woody stem. Most of the bamboo used in this country is imported from Far Eastern countries. Because bamboo is difficult to bend, it is usually split in half and used on the edges of table tops, cabinets, and on accessory items. A variety of simulated bamboo made of molded plastic and other materials is used for chair and sofa frames and occasional tables.

4-3. Rattan can be used to accent upholstered sofas and chairs, can be used for screens, and it can be the basic structural material for tables and chairs. This informal dining grouping uses rattan for both strength and durability. (*Tropic Image, Division of Galleon International*)

ALUMINUM FURNITURE

Aluminum frames are widely used in outdoor furniture such as chairs, umbrellas, tables, chaise lounges, and rockers. Outdoor furniture is exposed to all kinds of weather, so it must be sturdy. Because of its light weight, tubular aluminum is a leading frame material for folding outdoor furniture. Vinyl-coated polyester fabrics or brightly-colored straps and webbing are used to add a touch of fashion to aluminum outdoor furniture. Solid bar and cast aluminum, although much heavier, is also sometimes used. Since aluminum is rust free, very little damage (other than a dulling effect because of oxidation) occurs to an aluminum frame when it is exposed to normal weather conditions.

WROUGHT IRON AND STEEL FURNITURE

Wrought iron furniture is bent and formed into beautiful swirls and other designs for casual furniture to be used both inside and outside of the home. It is referred to by some stores as just the right touch for the "room outside" when referring to furnishings for a patio or porch.

Wrought iron is a low carbon steel that can be bent or shaped by hand or machine. It is extremely durable, and when welded and finished properly will hold up to normal use almost indefinitely.

Steel is the heaviest material used in producing casual furniture and may be welded, screwed, or bolted. It is extremely durable when properly finished, and when it has mesh or grill pattern seating, it can be very comfortable. Most steel furniture is protected by a baked enamel finish. Like wrought iron, collections of steel furniture include chairs, ottomans, loveseats, chaise lounges, and tables for indoor as well as outdoor use. Colorful woven fabrics and vinyls are often used for the seat and back cushions.

REDWOOD FURNITURE

Redwood is a popular material for making tables, sofas, chairs, loveseats, chaise lounges, and picnic tables. To prevent splitting and warping, it is specially dried to reduce the moisture content. It is popular because it has a pleasing natural color and is strong and durable. Redwood seating often has cushions covered with brightly colored fabrics. Pure redwood furniture, made from the heart of the redwood tree, has a consistent red color and is resistant to decay and insects. Many manufacturers, however, have groups on the market made of woods such as pine that are dyed or stained to look like redwood. These groups are less expensive than pure redwood furniture.

OTHER MATERIALS USED IN CASUAL FURNITURE

A number of casual furniture pieces are made of kiln-dried hardwood. One of the most consistent favorites is the director's chair, which has a hardwood frame with a canvas seat and back.

Plastics and fiberglass are also used to make a variety of casual furniture. In addition to molded chairs, there are tables, plant stands, bookcases, étagères, and numerous other pieces.

Seating materials include vinyl straps, special types of rubber or foam, and fiberglass. Popular fabrics include polyester duck, vinyl-coated polyester mesh, and cotton. Cotton is especially popular because it is available in bright floral prints.

A variety of filling materials is used in casual furniture cushions. Cushions to be used outdoors need to have filling materials that will dry quickly and will be durable when exposed to the extremes of temperature, sunlight, and rain.

Casual furniture is perceived as being less expensive than a suite of bedroom, dining-room, and living-room furniture. It is purchased on a more sporadic basis. Prime time for the sale of casual and summer furniture is during the spring when the consumer buys in anticipation of enjoying the products throughout the summer.

BEDDING

Bedding is found in virtually all independent furniture stores, conventional department stores, mass merchandise department stores, and most other retail furniture outlets. The term *bedding* refers to the mattress, box spring, or other foundation upon which a person sleeps. In addition to being purchased with a new bedroom suite, it is often purchased as a replacement item, since bedding is a commodity that is subject to wear and tear. In fact, many stores sell bedding faster and more profitably than many categories of furniture. Bedding also requires less floor space than furniture, which makes it a highly profitable item when measured in terms of sales per square foot.

SELLING FEATURES OF BEDDING

Different requirements may exist for bedding for a master bedroom as opposed to bedding for use in a guest bedroom. Price will also be a determinant, as the consumer usually seeks to obtain the best value for the money. The following product features are considered by the consumer when purchasing bedding:

- Size of the units
- Type of mattress
- Foundation
- Ticking

Size of the units. A consideration that will enter into the selection process is the size of the mattress and box spring or other foundation because bedding is usually purchased to accommodate one or two people, to fit a particular bed, or to be adequate for an extra-tall person. Figure 4-4 shows the normal size of bedding offered to the consumer in the United States.

An extra length of 80 inches in twin-size and full-size sets is also often available. These extra-long sets are the same as the length of the queen

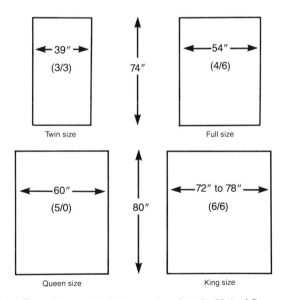

4-4. Typical sizes of bedding marketed in the United States

and king-size sets. Terminology in the industry refers to the width of the four standard sizes, in feet. In other words, a twin-size set is referred to as a 3/3 (3 feet 3 inches, or 39 inches); a full-size set as a 4/6 (4 feet 6 inches, or 54 inches); a queen-size set as a 5/0 (5 feet, or 60 inches); and a king-size set as a 6/6 (6 feet 6 inches). In reality, the king-size set produced by many companies is only 76 inches, or 6 feet 4 inches.

Type of mattress. There are two types of conventional mattresses: *innerspring and foam,* of which there are many variations.

Innerspring mattresses utilize an assembly of coiled wire springs to provide the comfort of the sleeping surface. Various degrees of firmness are provided, depending on the gauge, grade, and resilience of wire used in the coil springs. The firmness and comfort are also determined by the construction of the coils in the innerspring assembly.

The following types of innerspring assemblies are representative of the various innerspring assembly options available from United States mattress manufacturers.

The first is the *Bonnell-type* construction, an all-steel construction most frequently used in less expensive products. It involves hour-glass-shaped coil springs with their edges wired together to form one unit. Helical springs, which are small, closely wound springs, are used to tie together the larger springs, thereby creating a flat surface for the mattress. A newer type is the continuous coil, in which each row of coils is made from a continuous piece of spring wire.

More expensive mattresses may have the *Marshall-type* spring construction. The Marshall unit has cylinder-shaped springs sewn into individual pockets of muslin fabric. With the springs in individual pockets, each one functions independently of all the other springs, providing a great amount of comfort. Here, the amount of firmness is governed by the type of wire used in the springs and the number of coils.

The amount of comfort also results from the amount and type of padding which is placed over the innerspring unit. In many units there is a protector screen at the bottom and top of the coils to provide a more solid surface. Over the screen are two or three layers of padding materials to provide a solid, yet comfortable, feel. This padding may be cotton felt, foam of various types, or a synthetic fiber such as polyester.

Foam mattresses consist of a block of synthetic foam sewn inside the cloth cover or ticking. Different types of synthetic foam, such as polyurethane and latex foam, are used in mattress construction. Mattress manufacturers can make the foam soft, firm, or extra-firm depending on the amount of chemicals used. Characteristics of foam mattresses are that they are lighter than inner-spring mattresses, free of dust and lint, and nonallergenic. Foam mattresses often have layers of different density foam just inside the ticking for extra comfort. Like innerspring units, foam mattresses come in a variety of qualities and price ranges.

Foundation. The proper type of foundation will enhance the comfort provided by a mattress. Therefore, the consumer receives the most comfort and utility from a new mattress when an appropriate foundation is also purchased to go with it.

A popular type of foundation is the *box spring*, which is usually priced the same as the mattress and sold with it as a pair. The box spring is composed of a spring unit covered in a fabric ticking to match the mattress. Better quality box springs often contain coil springs that are padded so the top next to the mattress is smooth and flat. Other box-spring units use different spring mechanisms such as a torsion bar design using steel leaf springs.

The other type of foundation used with conventional mattresses is simply called a *foundation*. It is the same size as a box spring, with a layer of foam on a wooden base and built-up sides. The foam foundation is very firm and is also upholstered to match the mattress.

Ticking. Ticking is the fabric covering the mattress and foundation. Historically, a good quality ticking has been six- or eight-ounce damask. Cotton, rayon, nylon, or polyester are also used. Many mattresses are tufted with buttons on the bottom and top. The buttons are connected by cords passed through the mattress to hold the padding in place. Other mattresses, especially promotionally priced units, are simply covered in a ticking with no particular method for holding the padding in place. Many of the better quality, newer mattresses have a layer of polyurethane foam or other padding material quilted into the ticking for a very soft feel. Flame-retardants must also be present in mattress ticking.

WATER BEDS

Water beds, or flotation sleep systems, have become a popular alternative for many people in the United States. They are now used in one-family homes, condominiums, apartments, and mobile homes. One of the selling features of water beds is the uniform support they provide, which results from the mattress conforming to the shape of the body and eliminating what has been referred to as "uncomfortable pressure points."

The main component of the water-bed sleep system is a water mattress. A number of companies advertise that their water mattresses are 20 millimeters thick, which is about the same thickness as ten normal sheets of paper. Some mattresses have built-in baffles to help reduce the movement of water. A safety liner surrounds the mattress to contain any water that may leak from it. The mattress and liner are contained within a water-bed frame, which is a sturdy, boxlike structure to provide a definite base and shape to the water bed. The frame is then mounted on a pedestal or base, which is a platform designed to raise the water bed to the normal height from the floor. Heaters, made especially for water bed use, are mounted beneath the water-bed mattress and safety liner to raise the temperature of the water to a comfortable level for sleeping.

Although water beds are considerably heavier than conventional bedding, there is no great danger because of their weight; many kitchen appliances weigh more per square inch than water beds.

SUMMARY

An occasional table is an accent piece that adds style to a room and provides space to hold lamps, books, ashtrays, refreshments, or other decorative accessories. A set of three occasional tables being sold at popular prices would likely consist of two end tables and a coffee or cocktail table. A fourth table in such a set could be a sofa table.

Some companies coordinate occasional tables with upholstery to offer a complete matching room of furniture to the consumer. Several recognizable occasional tables have been on the market for a number of years.

Many materials are used in constructing occasional tables, including wood, injection molded plastic, chrome, and glass.

Occasional tables are often shipped KD (knocked down) with assembly being done by the retailer or consumer.

Wall systems provide space up and around the wall to hold electronic equipment of various types, televisions, books, records, and a wide variety of other items. Desk and bar units are also sometimes available. Usually, wall systems are composed of a variety of wall units that can be purchased individually to be placed beside or on top of each other according to the space and storage needs of the customer.

Casual and summer furniture is a category that includes a wide variety of informal furniture used on the porch, patio, and other places around the home.

Major structural materials used in the construction of casual and summer furniture include wicker, rattan, bamboo, aluminum, wrought iron, steel, and redwood. Each has its unique advantages and disadvantages and has a rather informal appearance. Appropriate fabrics also add a colorful element to their appearance. Summer and casual furniture seating materials include vinyl straps, special types of foam, fiberglass, and fabrics such as polyester duck, vinyl-coated polyester mesh, and cotton.

The term "bedding" refers to the mattress, foundation, and/or other surface upon which a person sleeps. Options in bedding include a variety of sizes, mattresses, foundations, ticking, patterns, and colors. Water beds have also become popular as a bedding option.

Standard sizes of bedding are twin or 3/3, full or 4/6, queen or 5/0, and king or 6/6. The two types of conventional mattresses are innerspring and foam. Foundations include box springs and a foam block in a wooden frame, simply called a "foundation." The ticking is the fabric covering of a mattress and foundation.

Water beds are promoted as comfortable sleep systems because they conform to the contour of the body. A water bed consists of the water mattress, safety liner, frame, pedestal or base to raise it to a comfortable height, and heater to raise the water temperature to a comfortable level for sleeping.

CHAPTER 5

FURNITURE DESIGN

Furniture is a product that is purchased both for function and design appeal. In other words, furniture must perform a dual role. For example, a dresser or chest must serve the purpose of providing storage space for various articles and, at the same time, its appearance must also appeal to the consumer. Therefore, furniture is consciously designed to fulfill both functional and aesthetic needs.

WHAT IS A STYLE?

The word *style* refers to products exhibiting particular design characteristics. Styles have traditionally been identified by the name of a designer or school of designers, by reference to a ruling monarch, a country or region of the world, or a particular time in history. Specific styles will be discussed later in this chapter.

In the furniture industry, reference is frequently made to period or style period, the time when various styles were popular. However, for our purposes, the terms *style, period,* and *style period* will be used interchangeably.

WHAT IS FASHION?

A *fashion* is a popularly accepted style. Consumer tastes change, causing fashions to change. For example, Spanish-style furniture may be popular one year and some other style fashionable the next year. A style never changes, but fashions constantly do. Effective furniture marketers and designers must have an appreciation of a variety of styles to keep up with trends and make different style introductions into the market whenever it is desirable.

BASIC AREAS OF FURNITURE STYLES

In reality, one style period flows into another, and many borrow decorative details from each other. This makes the job of identifying individual styles somewhat difficult. Most, however, have at least one or two design details that are unique. An overview of the basic areas of furniture styles will be discussed, followed by a discussion of individual styles. A glossary of common furniture terms is included at the end of this book for purposes of further clarification.

TRADITIONAL

Traditional furniture includes those designed by master designers, cabinet-makers, and manufacturers of the seventeenth, eighteenth, and nineteenth centuries. Much of it was designed for the royalty of Europe. Traditional furniture has been called *court furniture* and is associated with formality and elegance.

Some people limit traditional furniture to England, known by the names of craftsmen, such as Chippendale, Hepplewhite, and Sheraton, or by a reference to particular monarchs, such as William and Mary, Queen Anne, and Victorian. In reality, styles of traditional furniture were also produced in other countries, such as Louis XIV, XV, and XVI in France and Duncan Phyfe in the United States. The term "traditional furniture" usually refers to an original piece or a recognizable reproduction. A recognizable reproduction is one that has sufficient design characteristics of the original to make its origins clear. Although actual sales have fluctuated, many traditional styles have remained popular through the years, and manufacturers producing quality reproductions of these styles have been successful.

COUNTRY OR PROVINCIAL

At the same time that elegant, formal furniture was being produced for royalty, simplified versions were being produced for the masses. This furniture, called *country,* or *provincial,* is less formal and more practical and functional than traditional furniture. French Provincial, Italian Provincial, and Early American or Colonial furniture are examples of country or provincial furniture. Craftsmen in the provinces produced rugged, solid-wood, durable furniture appropriate to country living. Much of it, however, is very well designed and is not crude or rustic.

Today, much of American country furniture is very casual. Country versions of other styles, also, have come to mean less formal furniture that is still recognizable as French, Italian, or some other style.

CONTEMPORARY/MODERN

There is no clear definition to separate contemporary and modern furniture. Although many furniture designers and marketers make such a separation, this seems to be a matter of individual interpretation. Contemporary/modern, as we know it today, had its beginnings in the late nineteenth century and is still developing. It includes a large number of designs made possible by advances in technology and capitalizes on the capabilities of machines.

Clean, simple lines, smooth contours, and the effective use of a variety of materials such as wood, steel, chrome, plastic, and glass, characterize contemporary/modern furniture. Much is light and airy, versatile in its use, and made to be easy to maintain.

SPECIFIC STYLES

The following discussion of specific furniture styles is designed to give a brief description and an overview of design characteristics useful in identifying various styles. Several of the styles flow into each other, and the designers used many similar design characteristics. This often makes it difficult to identify individual pieces. Therefore, each description focuses on those attributes that are most unique or most characteristic of each style.

The designs described here began with Jacobean (about the seventeenth century); however, ideas and decorative details were borrowed from the early Greeks, Romans, and Egyptians. People moved from country to country and some eventually settled in the United States. With each of these moves, they took some furniture and design ideas with them; so in many cases, it is possible to see some influence by one country on the furniture of another.

Charles II cabinet, spiral legs

Wainscot chair

TRADITIONAL ENGLISH FURNITURE STYLES

A number of traditional English furniture styles have enjoyed considerable popularity and have contributed design characteristics to furniture on the market today. The dates given for each style are estimations of the time of their greatest popularity.

JACOBEAN (1603–1688)

Derived from the Latininized form of James, this term refers to the style of architecture and furnishings during the reigns of James I and Charles I, the subsequent commonwealth under the strict control of Oliver Cromwell, the restoration of the monarchy in 1660 under Charles II, and the reign of James II.

The furniture was largely made of oak and had square and rectangular lines. To save space, folding furniture, such as the gate-leg table, was popular. Distinctive Jacobean style characteristics include low relief carvings and spiral turned legs.

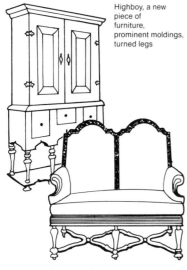

Highboy, a new piece of furniture, prominent moldings, turned legs

Love seat, fully upholstered, turned legs, X-stretchers

WILLIAM AND MARY (1689–1702)

Queen Mary, daughter of James II, was joint ruler of England with her Dutch husband, William of Orange. With their ascendency to the throne came several Dutch craftsmen who were designing and producing furniture with definite Dutch and Flemish influences.

The highboy and lowboy are characteristic of William and Mary styling. Indicative turnings and other design characteristics of this style include the inverted cup, trumpet, bun foot, shaped stretchers placed crosswise between the legs, and double hood used on cabinets and highboys. Upholstered furniture was first introduced during this period. The predominant wood was walnut.

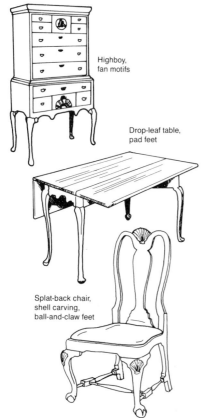

Highboy, fan motifs

Drop-leaf table, pad feet

Splat-back chair, shell carving, ball-and-claw feet

QUEEN ANNE (1702–1714, with this style period lasting even longer)

Although Queen Anne ruled England for only twelve years, the period of furniture bearing her name lasted about forty years. Queen Anne furniture developed from the William and Mary style and is considered one of the most graceful of all styles of furniture.

This period marked several innovations, such as the first popular use of "overstuffed" upholstered furniture. The most popular wood was still walnut. However, near the end of this period, considerable use was made of mahogany. The Queen Anne chair with its distinctive splat back is probably the most recognizable of all the furniture from this period. Cabriole legs (originally designed to resemble a goat's leg in earlier periods) were widely used. The foot of the leg could take a number of forms, such as a hoof, pad, and ball and claw. Shell carvings were widely used on the knees of the cabriole legs and the crests of chairs.

Sideboard with curved front

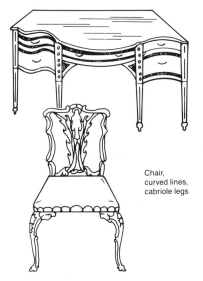

Chair,
curved lines,
cabriole legs

GEORGIAN (1714–1795)

Georgian is a collective term used to describe various styles of furniture produced in England from 1714 until 1795 (the reigns of George I, George II, and much of the reign of George III).

Early Georgian furniture popularized the use of mahogany. Casters and decorative details, such as the scallop shell on cabriole legs and ball-and-claw feet, were used. Middle and late Georgian styles are known by the names of craftsmen and designers such as Chippendale, Hepplewhite, the Adam Brothers, and Sheraton.

Highboy, Chinese
and rococo motifs

Pierced-splat armchair,
cabriole legs,
ball-and-claw feet

CHIPPENDALE (1740–1779)

Thomas Chippendale was the first person other than a king or queen to have a furniture style named for him. He was a designer and cabinet-maker with a talent for successfully combining design elements from other styles. His principal influence came from earlier English, French, and Chinese designs.

Early Chippendale pieces had cabriole legs; later ones had straight legs. Popular decorative details include simulated Chinese bamboo and fretwork. For the first time, the open or pierced splat was used on chairs. Mahogany was the most favored wood.

Chippendale's fame was ensured when he published *The Gentleman and Cabinet-Maker's Director,* which established him firmly in the public eye as an outstanding furniture designer.

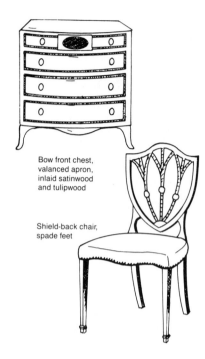

Bow front chest,
valanced apron,
inlaid satinwood
and tulipwood

Shield-back chair,
spade feet

HEPPLEWHITE (1770–1786)

George Hepplewhite was a cabinetmaker influenced greatly by French furniture of the Louis XIV period. His designs were lighter and more graceful than those of Chippendale. His chairs had slender, fluted legs built on a smaller scale. The chair backs were delicate and open, and featured such designs as the shield and interlacing heart patterns.

One of Hepplewhite's better known introductions is the sideboard. His sideboard design featured a serpentine front with concave corner construction. Again, the most favored wood was mahogany. Horsehair stuffing was used in upholstered pieces.

ADAM BROTHERS (1760–1792)

Robert and James Adam were brothers who were educated as architects, but became very successful furniture designers—rather than cabinetmakers like Chippendale and Hepplewhite. Their furniture was characterized by simplicity and delicacy. Chairs had slim, tapered, round or square legs which were often fluted. Tables were long and narrow with decorated side rails.

They also designed highly ornamented sideboards, upholstered sofas, settees, and daybeds. The ornamentation was made with painting, gilding,and inlay. Mahogany and satinwood veneer were the most popular materials used. The designs used on the furniture included animal heads, human figures, disks and ovals, floral swags and pendants, drapery, acanthus, and pineapples.

Console table,
painted, decorated,
reeded legs,
oval medallion

Armchair, carved sycamore,
tapestry cover

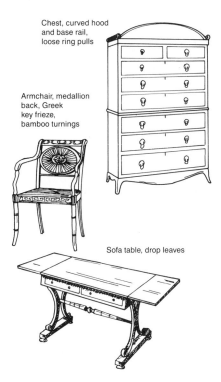

Sideboard, inlaid
mahogany and tulipwood

Vase-back chair,
rectangular lines,
spade feet

Chest, curved hood
and base rail,
loose ring pulls

Armchair, medallion
back, Greek
key frieze,
bamboo turnings

Sofa table, drop leaves

SHERATON (1780–1806)

Thomas Sheraton's influence on furniture design came largely through the publishing of
four books on the subject. The most important,
*The Cabinet-Maker and Upholsterer's Drawing
Book,* probably caused this period to be named
for him. His designs were structurally sound,
but appeared to be slender, refined, and delicate. He was a master of the straight line.

The tapered legs were round, square, or octagonal and were often fluted. His chair backs
generally were rectangular, often with a raised
center portion, and featured delicately carved
openwork with such designs as urns, lyres,
turned posts, and shields. Sheraton made sideboards with straight lines and convex corners
rather than the concave corners designed by
Hepplewhite.

His furniture was made from mahogany,
rosewood, and satinwood with a painted finish.
Inlay and marquetry were used extensively for
decoration. Sheraton designed many tables,
some with pedestal bases and others with drop
leaves.

ENGLISH REGENCY (1793–1830)

English Regency is one of the styles of the late
Georgian period, named for the time when
George IV served as Regent while he was
Prince of Wales. (Actually, English Regency
originated in England before the Prince of
Wales became Regent in 1811 and extended
through his reign which ended in 1830.)

Mahogany, satinwood, and rosewood were
popular. Generally, the furniture was scaled
down to smaller proportions. Elements of
Roman, Greek, Egyptian, Chinese, and Gothic
design were mixed together in this style. Surfaces were flat, often decorated with carving
and relief. Chairs had straight or curved legs
and straight or concave backs. The seats were
often thinly upholstered, although cane was
also used.

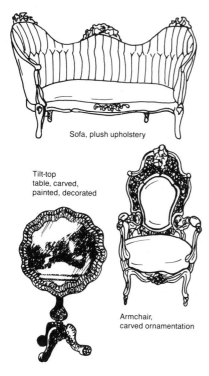

Sofa, plush upholstery

Tilt-top
table, carved,
painted, decorated

Armchair,
carved ornamentation

VICTORIAN (1830–1890)

Named for Queen Victoria, this furniture was large and heavy. Dark finishes and deep shades of upholstery made the furniture relatively formal. Still, the furniture has maintained a considerable degree of popularity through the years.

Characteristic chairs have oval or horseshoe-shaped backs. Walnut and rosewood were the favored woods. Considerable use was made of carved legs and backs of chairs and sofas. It was also common to have inlaid brass, wood, and mother of pearl. Upholstered pieces were often highly tufted. Many occasional tables have marble tops and carved or turned pedestals.

FRENCH FURNITURE STYLES

During many of the same periods when the English were producing distinctive styles of furniture, French craftsmen were also at work creating their own furniture styles. Much of their work was done for three monarchs, Louis XIV, Louis XV, and Louis XVI, giving formal French furniture the name *French Court*.

An overview of the styles of furniture named after these kings provides an introduction to French Court furniture, which continues to influence much of the French-style furniture produced today. Also discussed below are two other French furniture styles: French Provincial and Empire.

LOUIS XIV (1643–1715)

The Louis XIV style of massive, ornate furniture was designed and built primarily to glorify the palace at Versailles. The pieces were highly carved, mostly with straight, severe lines. The Baroque decoration, although lavish and heavy, was completely symmetrical. The carving represented animal forms and mythology. Flat and curved surfaces were made from elaborate marquetry panels, and inlays of such materials as brass, pewter, ivory, and mother of pearl were common. Much of this furniture was painted in vivid colors.

Table desk, bronze hardware

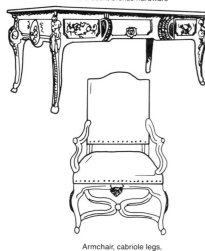

Armchair, cabriole legs,
crossed stretchers

Chest, inlaid design,
bronze hardware, marble top

Armchair, curved lines,
carved, covered in
needlepoint

LOUIS XV (1715–1774)

Encouraged to produce new styles, craftsmen in the court of Louis XV created furniture that was smaller in scale, but very elaborate. Rococo ornamentation was introduced; furniture was often covered with ornate, asymmetrical carvings.

The curved line became dominant. Possessing curved outlines, individual furniture elements flowed into one another, making joints much less obvious. The cabriole leg become the characteristic shape, flowing from table or chair edge to floor in a continuous curve.

For the first time, furniture seating pieces were built for human comfort. Examples of these seating pieces are the fully upholstered armchair, chaise lounge, and small sofa called a "canapé." Woods used were mahogany, walnut, oak, ebony, and chestnut. Painted decoration, marquetry, and inlay of various materials were popular.

Semicircular chest, decorative
veneering and inlay, marble top

Armchair; straight,
round fluted legs
and back posts

LOUIS XVI (1774–1792)

The unearthing of the ruins of Pompeii and Herculaneum renewed an interest in classical Greek and Roman styling. During this period, lines become straight again, in part a reaction against the ornate style of Louis XV.

Styles were refined and elegant; workmanship was excellent. Chair legs were straight, tapered, and fluted. Chair and sofa backs were square or medallion-shaped, with many having padded armrests. Popular woods were mahogany, ebony, tulipwood, rosewood, and fruitwood. Marquetry and black and gold lacquer decorated many of the wood pieces.

Cabinet in
Louis XV style,
panels outlined
in decorative
molding

Chest in Louis XV style
showing court influence

FRENCH PROVINCIAL

At the same time furniture was being designed for the French court, many very fine craftsmen were producing furniture in the provinces. Although all of the periods of French Court furniture influenced French Provincial furniture, the Louis XV style had the most impact.

The graceful, curving lines were interpreted in a more modest way for life in the country. The less-ornate cabriole leg was very popular, although earlier pieces had straight legs. The French took the armoire, which had been used in the Middle Ages to hold armor and/or armaments, and adapted it to hold clothes. Woods native to particular regions, such as oak, walnut, chestnut, ash, and poplar, were used in making French Provincial furniture. Upholstered pieces were designed to be comfortable.

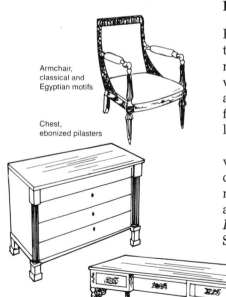

Armchair,
classical and
Egyptian motifs

Chest,
ebonized pilasters

Desk, ebonized wood,
bronze drawer hardware

EMPIRE (1804–1815)

French Empire furniture was created under the rule of Napoleon. Furniture was massive, made from rich woods such as mahogany, rosewood, and ebony. Decoration included brass and gilt with symbols of victory, mythological figures, and Napoleonic emblems such as the letter *N*.

Furniture had a boxlike appearance and severe right angles which featured prominent columns. The French Empire style influenced many designers in England, the United States, and Germany. This style, known as *American Empire,* continued to be popular in the United States until approximately 1840.

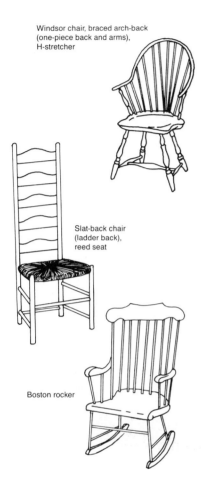

Windsor chair, braced arch-back (one-piece back and arms), H-stretcher

Slat-back chair (ladder back), reed seat

Boston rocker

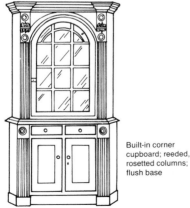

Built-in corner cupboard; reeded, rosetted columns; flush base

AMERICAN FURNITURE STYLES

The style influences, from England and France especially, were exported to America. Many of the settlers brought selected pieces of furniture with them. Other craftsmen came to this country and made furniture after they arrived. Much of the furniture, although influenced by previous styles, was built mainly for function from materials found in the "New World." This furniture has come to be known as Colonial and Early American style. One American furniture designer, Duncan Phyfe, was popular enough to have a furniture style named for him. Eighteenth century American furniture shows the greatest influence of styles from Europe. Following is an overview of these American furniture styles.

COLONIAL AND EARLY AMERICAN FURNITURE (1620–1780)

Colonial and Early American furniture, which might be called *American Provincial* furniture, was produced in the colonies prior to the Revolutionary War. Although the American craftsmen were influenced by the styles of England and France, living conditions forced them to produce simple, functional styles. Native woods such as maple, walnut, and pine were widely used. Chairs had cane or rush seats, often with ladder backs. Trestle tables and benches were popular, as well as simple chests and corner cupboards.

Two distinctly American pieces, the Windsor chair and the rocking chair, are classified as Early American. (Although the Windsor chair was introduced in England, it was most popular in the United States.)

Wooden furniture produced by the Shaker religious sect had a great effect on this category of furniture. The Shakers were excellent craftsmen and they produced well-proportioned, simple, solid wood furniture. More formal pieces, such as the canopy bed, were also produced in America before and after the Revolutionary War.

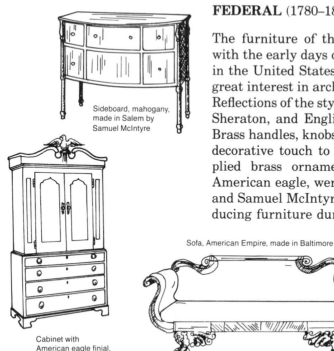

Sideboard, mahogany, made in Salem by Samuel McIntyre

Cabinet with American eagle finial, symbol of the new Republic

FEDERAL (1780–1830)

The furniture of the Federal style coincided with the early days of the Federal government in the United States. This era was marked by great interest in architecture and archaeology. Reflections of the styles of Adam, Hepplewhite, Sheraton, and English Regency are common. Brass handles, knobs, and escutcheons added a decorative touch to better quality pieces. Applied brass ornaments, particularly of the American eagle, were common. Duncan Phyfe and Samuel McIntyre were two craftsmen producing furniture during this period.

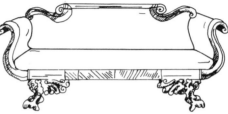

Sofa, American Empire, made in Baltimore

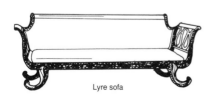

Lyre sofa

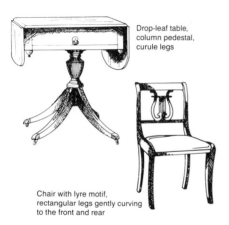

Drop-leaf table, column pedestal, curule legs

Chair with lyre motif, rectangular legs gently curving to the front and rear

DUNCAN PHYFE (1790–1830)

Duncan Phyfe, an immigrant from Scotland, is considered to be America's first great furniture designer. Although his designs fall under the Federal period, his popularity was such that his style is considered a separate category. Various of his pieces were influenced by such styles as Hepplewhite, Sheraton, and Adam.

Duncan Phyfe was successful in combining straight lines and curves to create a readily recognizable style. His decoration consisted of turnings, fluting, reeding, brass tips on table legs, and china and glass knobs. His tables have single lyre or column pedestals and curule feet. (Curule feet extend outward from the pedestal to meet the floor at an angle.) The lyre was also used extensively in his famous lyre sofa and lyre-back chairs. Almost all of his furniture was made of mahogany.

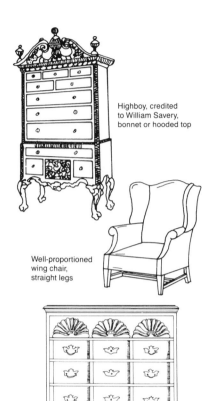

Highboy, credited
to William Savery,
bonnet or hooded top

Well-proportioned
wing chair,
straight legs

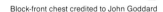

Block-front chest credited to John Goddard

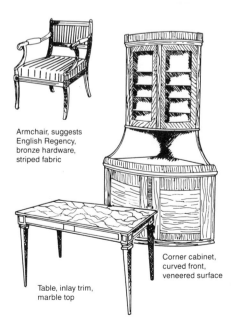

Armchair, suggests
English Regency,
bronze hardware,
striped fabric

Corner cabinet,
curved front,
veneered surface

Table, inlay trim,
marble top

EIGHTEENTH CENTURY AMERICAN

Although it is difficult to assign a definite time period, a style of American furniture more formal than Colonial and Early American furniture developed, and has become known as Eighteenth Century American furniture. This style is also referred to as *American Traditional.*

Famous American craftsmen and designers, such as John Goddard and William Savory, produced well-designed furniture, showing the adaptation of French and English designs. Most of these pieces were produced in New England and Philadelphia. Duncan Phyfe's furniture might also be described as Eighteenth Century American furniture.

Many of the remaining pieces of Eighteenth Century American furniture are adaptations of Queen Anne, Chippendale, and other classic English styles. French styles, particularly Empire, were also adapted for production in America. These styles were often simplified to colonial tastes, and some of the more typical designs, such as the *Newport Shell,* are truly American.

GERMAN

A furniture style introduced in Germany in the early nineteenth century emerged as being particularly significant. The name of this style, Biedermeier, comes from a comic strip character, "Papa Biedermeier," a symbol of middle class comfort and well-being in the home.

BIEDERMEIER (1800–1850)

Biedermeier styling represents a simplified version of Empire with some influence from other styles, particularly Sheraton and Regency. The furniture was largely made of local woods, such as pear and other fruitwoods, walnut, maple, birch, and beech. Details were sometimes painted or carved to represent familiar forms of vegetation. Later examples used more scrollwork and ornamentation.

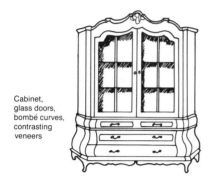

Cabinet, glass doors, bombé curves, contrasting veneers

Table; straight, tapering legs; gilding; low relief carvings; marble top

Commode, bombé curves, decoupage decoration, allegorical vignettes

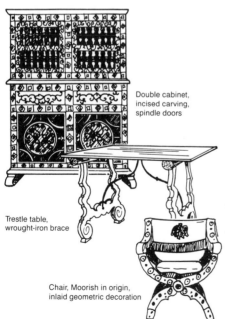

Double cabinet, incised carving, spindle doors

Trestle table, wrought-iron brace

Chair, Moorish in origin, inlaid geometric decoration

ITALIAN

Italian furniture was shaped considerably by the rediscovery of ancient Roman works around the fifteenth century. The furniture that developed during this period was large and stately, with straight, dignified lines classically decorated with such details as dentil moldings and egg-and-dart designs. Later Italian craftsmen were influenced by Renaissance designs from throughout Europe, resulting in more ornate, richly ornamented furniture.

Italian furniture, as we know it today, was influenced by the elegance of French furniture design, much of which has a decidedly rococo flavor. Bombé chests are an interesting example. Other Italian furniture resembles what would have been produced in the Italian provinces and also draws upon English styles such as Adam and Hepplewhite.

SPANISH

The Moors who conquered Spain in the eighth century and lived there nearly 800 years had the most profound effect on Spanish furniture. Although Spain has been greatly influenced by the Renaissance and outside influences since then, the Moorish influence resulted in the development of Spanish as a distinctive style of furniture.

Walnut, oak, pine, chestnut, cedar, and pearwood are popular woods used in Spanish furniture. A liberal use of decorative wrought iron is present on many pieces. Chair legs and arms are often turned and scrolled. The Spanish scroll foot is characteristic, as are decorative nailheads shaped into roses and shells. Finely tooled leather is also used on many pieces.

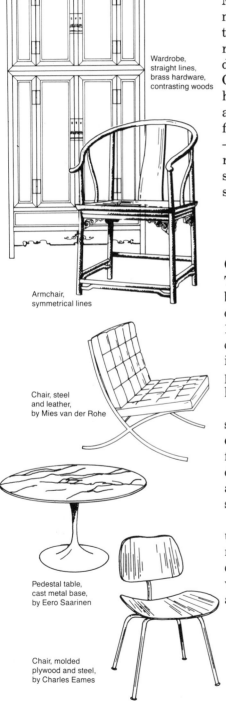

Wardrobe,
straight lines,
brass hardware,
contrasting woods

Armchair,
symmetrical lines

Chair, steel
and leather,
by Mies van der Rohe

Pedestal table,
cast metal base,
by Eero Saarinen

Chair, molded
plywood and steel,
by Charles Eames

ORIENTAL

Most good Oriental furniture is simple and well made. Although the Chinese and other Orientals use straw mats or floor cushions and have relatively little furniture by Western standards, their styling is attractive and popular. Oriental furniture is made of finely polished hardwood. Tables, side chairs, and other pieces are usually lacquered for a deep, luxurious finish. Much use is made of contrasting woods —ebony, rosewood, and teak. Corners are decorated with brass corner brackets. Lines are straight and unbroken, with care taken to ensure that every piece is symmetrical.

CONTEMPORARY/MODERN

This period is generally considered to have begun with the Bauhaus, an influential school of design which was opened in Germany in 1919 and remained in operation until the Nazis closed it in 1933. Furniture designed by those involved with the Bauhaus school, with its emphasis on function and form, looks as if it could have been designed today.

Basically, contemporary furniture is designed by looking ahead rather than back to earlier traditions. It is a continually changing furniture style. Clean lines are distinctive, with designers constantly searching for new materials and new shapes. The emphasis in upholstered furniture is on comfort and utility.

Some contemporary furniture pieces have an ultramodern flair, while others have a less modern look. Much use is made of modern machinery and materials such as chrome, glass, various types of veneers, plywoods, plastics, and vinyl upholstery fabrics.

SUMMARY

A furniture style refers to products exhibiting particular design characteristics. Styles traditionally have been identified by the name of a designer or school of designers, a ruling monarch, a country or region of the world, or a particular time in history.

A fashion is a style that is popularly accepted. Styles remain the same, but they increase and decrease in popularity.

Basic areas of furniture styles include: traditional, country or provincial, and contemporary/modern.

Traditional English furniture styles include: Jacobean, William and Mary, Queen Anne, Georgian, Chippendale, Hepplewhite, Adam Brothers, Sheraton, Regency, and Victorian.

French furniture styles can be divided into these groups: French Court, which was produced for the ruling families; French Provincial, which is the less ornate furniture produced by craftsmen in the French provinces; and Empire, which was introduced during the period when Napoleon ruled France. The three most important styles of French Court furniture are Louis XIV, Louis XV, and Louis XVI.

American furniture styles include Colonial and Early American furniture, Federal, Duncan Phyfe, and an assortment of styles which are today called Eighteenth Century American or American Traditional furniture. Duncan Phyfe is the only American furniture designer to have a style named for him.

Biedermeier is a German style that represents the adaptation of French Empire furniture to reflect a taste for a simpler, yet sturdy design.

Other style categories named for countries or regions are Italian, Spanish, and Oriental.

Contemporary/modern furniture has a "now" look and is designed to use modern machinery and modern construction materials.

CHAPTER 6

PRODUCT DEVELOPMENT

Furniture manufacturers, if they are to be successful, must have the right product at the right place at the right time. This objective not only includes individual pieces, but also the entire assortment of furniture products offered for sale by the manufacturer. In other words, the chances for marketing success are greater if a manufacturer's entire line is well designed and fits together logically. Basically, product development is the group of activities revolving around having the right product available.

WHAT IS A FURNITURE PRODUCT?

The question of what a furniture product is seems very simple on the surface. However, when the definition of a furniture product is thoroughly examined, the question becomes more complex. To be precise, a furniture product is both tangible and intangible, with many features and benefits to satisfy the consumer. It is more than just "something" a furniture company markets. A piece of furniture has a certain style which makes it a form of art. And at the same time, it performs a function. For example, a Queen Anne chair supplies the function of providing support to a person in a sitting position. It also has a decorative splat in the back, cabriole front legs, and rather graceful lines.

Because of its obvious style, a piece of furniture causes anyone seeing it to have a mental image about the product and probably about its owner. For some people, this impression may indicate status; for others, good taste; while others might feel the product to be old-fashioned or out of date. Therefore, buyers are revealing something about themselves when they select furniture.

The product also includes the manufacturer's and retailer's reputation and commitment to service. In other words, a consumer may decide to buy a particular brand or from a particular store because of a good reputation for quality products and the organization's willingness to stand behind them. At other times, a brand may be bought at a particular store because of price or economic comparisons.

If a manufacturer is known for high-priced, high-quality antique reproductions, for example, it would not be good marketing strategy for that

61

company to come out with a group of inexpensive, contemporary occasional tables. The manufacturer produces a complex product that must be appropriate for the company and have the right type of supporting features for its niche in the marketplace.

THE NECESSITY OF FREQUENT PRODUCT INTRODUCTION

Most furniture manufacturers frequently introduce new products into their lines in order to stay competitive in the American home furnishings industry. The number of introductions could vary from a manufacturer of antique reproductions who might introduce two or three small pieces per year to another manufacturer who may change one-fourth of its line semiannually. Other companies come out with new introductions even more often. Although upholstered furniture is often thought of as being the leader in fashion because of changing fabric designs and colors, many manufacturers of case goods also introduce new or different styles regularly. A product introduction is something that is new to the marketplace or new to the company offering it. Although the number of product introductions varies from company to company, they are regarded as necessary for a variety of reasons:

- Style obsolescence
- Furniture product life cycle
- Motivation for retailers and company salespeople
- Expressed needs of retailers
- Company image

STYLE OBSOLESCENCE

As previously discussed, style in furniture refers to the unique design features that give distinctiveness to a product, while fashion is a popularly accepted style in the marketplace at any point in time. In reality, styles increase and decrease in popularity.

The decrease in popularity of a style may be referred to as "style obsolescence." When a style is no longer fashionable, and does not sell, it is said to be obsolete or "out-of-date." Some style obsolescence is planned by manufacturers who introduce new products with different style or design characteristics. Often these new products make consumer goods already on the market appear to be out-of-date or no longer fashionable. Fabrics, colors, finishes, and hardware may all be changed, making many of the styles on the market obsolete. Changing consumer tastes also necessitate the introduction of new products. It is this fashion nature of the industry that creates change and the need for continual development of new products.

FURNITURE PRODUCT LIFE CYCLE

The vast majority of all products, including furniture, go through a life cycle composed of an introduction and a gradual increase in sales volume and profits. Almost always there is a time limit on success because this rise is followed by a decrease in sales volume and profits, when eventually the product is dropped by the manufacturer. Furniture, being a conspicuous, highly designed product, subject to the rise and fall of fashion popularity, usually follows four life cycle stages:

1. Introduction. The product is introduced through market showings and sales photographs brought to retail stores by the manufacturer's representatives. Sales volume gradually increases because floor samples are new and retail sales staffs require time to become familiar with the furniture before they can sell it with the most success. Profits are only starting to appear at this stage; costs of product development, market samples, and other start-up costs must first be recovered.

2. Growth and possible emulation. The product enters the growth stage when the samples are in place on the retail floor, initial sales have taken place, and the cumulative effect of word-of-mouth endorsement by consumers and a well-trained retail sales force cause sales to gain momentum. In this stage, profits begin to be generated because product development costs have been recovered. This stage is also often marked by emulation by other manufacturers. The product is gaining in sales volume and, in the highly competitive furniture industry, this success has undoubtedly been noted by competitors. Therefore, at the next furniture market, other companies may introduce their version of the same basic style to capitalize on consumer demand in that style category. By the end of the growth stage, this emulation has greatly increased the firm's competition. However, profits usually continue at an acceptable level in the growth stage.

3. Maturity. The maturity stage is marked by a leveling-off of sales. Although they may continue at a relatively high level, few additional people, on a percentage basis, remain to be introduced to the particular suite or piece of furniture. Competition is undoubtedly increasing from newer introductions by the manufacturer producing this suite and from other manufacturers. Profits are beginning to decline because of the increased effort it takes to keep the product on retail floors and the retail sales forces interested.

4. Decline. The decline stage is marked by decreased placements on retail floors and decreasing sales. Manufacturers' cuttings are reduced in size and management begins to look for a new introduction to replace the existing style. When the product development process creates a new replacement product, the manfuacturer will try to sell the existing stock of the old style in the warehouse and to discontinue the suite.

The length of product life cycles in the furniture industry is not the same for any two suites or for any two manufacturers. A great deal depends on sales, the relative popularity of the style, price range of the merchandise, and competition within a particular niche of the market.

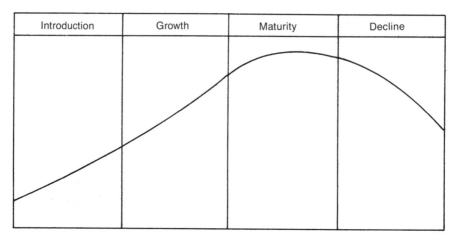

| Introduction | Growth | Maturity | Decline |

6-1. Furniture product life cycle

MOTIVATION FOR RETAILERS AND COMPANY SALESPEOPLE

Periodic new introductions are necessary to keep retailers interested and to convince them that the company is keeping up with fashion trends. In most product style categories, with the exception of antique reproductions, new introductions are important in keeping retailers motivated to feature a firm's products. The changes sometimes involve adding upholstery fabrics, which still indicates to the retailer that the manufacturer is seeking to provide up-to-date salable merchandise.

New introductions also create excitement among company salespeople who like to have something different to talk about when they call on retailers. These introductions give the salespeople new photographs to show and something to sell that the retailer has not seen before.

EXPRESSED NEEDS OF RETAILERS

Sometimes, a key retailer will ask a manufacturer to produce a new product in order to fill a need he has in his store. If the retailer is important enough, the manufacturer may introduce a new product primarily to satisfy this expressed need. Some manufacturers, especially of upholstered furniture, will produce private-label merchandise for large retail accounts. For example, a large, regional department store chain might buy the majority of its upholstered furniture for advertising promotions from a small manufacturer in the area. The merchandise may be developed just for that store and manufactured to its specifications.

COMPANY IMAGE

Some manufacturers have a reputation of being innovative or of having

6-2. After receiving instructions from manufacturing management, the furniture designer prepares sketches for new product introductions. In preparing his sketches, a good designer will consider the manufacturer's niche in the marketplace and its production capabilities.

a product line that is "ahead of the crowd." These companies may introduce new products to keep that image intact. The product introductions may not always follow the strategy of style obsolescence or the decline stages of the furniture product life cycle. However, this reason for making a new product introduction is definitely related to creating excitement among retailers and the company sales force.

PROFESSIONAL PERSONNEL INVOLVED IN PRODUCT DEVELOPMENT

Product development, ideally, is a team project that draws information and assistance from a wide variety of people both inside and outside the furniture manufacturer's organization. Some of this personnel holds other positions; however, the following individuals spend at least the greater portion of their time and energy on product development:
- The furniture designer
- The merchandising manager
- The fabric coordinator
- The sample maker

THE FURNITURE DESIGNER
The furniture designer is the person given the responsibility for taking an intangible idea and designing an actual product from it. Designers are

6-3. These typical sketches were prepared by a furniture designer after consultation with manufacturing management which has given the designer a description of the style considerations it wants in its new products. In these sketches, the designer is presenting his interpretation of the product to be introduced. If these sketches are accepted by management, the designer will next prepare mechanical drawings that can be used by the sample maker to prepare actual samples of the product. *(Norman Hekler Associates)*

skilled individuals who understand design, size, color, and proportion. They must be skilled in drawing sketches of various pieces and then transferring these sketches into mechanical drawings, rendered to scale, which the sample maker can follow in producing mock-ups and sample merchandise. A good designer, who is familiar with a company's production capabilities, can take a relatively brief description of an idea and design a product that the company can manufacture.

The furniture designer may have an independent studio and work for the manufacturer on a freelance basis, contracting to design one or more suites or groups of furniture. Sometimes, manufacturers will invite three or four freelance designers to submit their interpretations of a basic product idea. The manufacturer will then choose the design to be produced from those submitted.

The freelance designer may be paid for the design as soon as the product development is completed. Most often, however, the designer is compensated by a royalty based on sales of the product. This royalty may be one or two percent of sales, paid much like a sales commission. Many designers and manufacturers prefer the royalty method of payment because the designer participates in the product's success or lack of success. Also, the royalty can be added into the cost of the product just like other cost factors.

The other option is to employ a staff designer, who is a regular employee of the company and a member of the marketing team. The staff designer works with many people throughout the organization to ensure that designs are salable and fit into manufacturing capabilities. Small firms usually do not have sufficient design work to keep a full-time designer, so most staff designers are found in medium-to-large furniture manufacturing companies. A large company may employ one or more staff designers and also use freelance designers.

THE MERCHANDISING MANAGER

The merchandising manager supervises the development of the entire product line and has the major responsibility for coordinating the timing of product introductions. Although, in small companies, the merchandising manager may have additional responsibilities, this person heads the product planning committee and is the main liaison with the furniture designer.

The merchandising manager schedules all the events in product development to ensure that introductions will be ready for the furniture market. He or she is in contact with the fabric coordinator or fabric suppliers and other resources, such as hardware and finish suppliers, to ensure that all trends and options are considered.

The merchandising manager also works with furniture market showroom designers to obtain the proper display of market samples and attends premarket sessions with key buyers to consider comments that may lead to helpful changes or product modifications.

THE FABRIC COORDINATOR

Larger upholstered furniture manufacturers often have a fabric coordinator who is responsible for the fabric "look" of the line. The fabric coordinator is responsible for knowing the fabric suppliers, their capabilities, and their lines. This person recommends fabrics to the product planning committee (discussed below) on the basis of value and desired fashion image for the merchandise.

An effective fabric coordinator must also keep up with the latest trends in colors, textures, and weaves. Since the colors in upholstered furniture often follow the colors in women's clothing fashions, the fabric coordinator must be familiar with clothing trends. A well-designed suite, for example, may be a market failure if it is shown in the wrong fabric.

The fabric coordinator must make sure that an adequate selection of

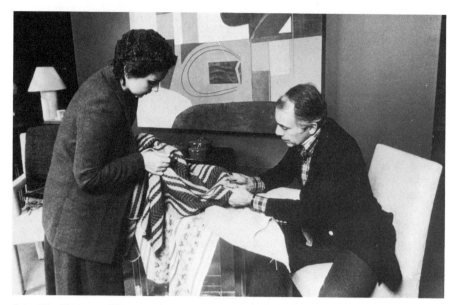

6-4. The fabric coordinator works closely with the furniture designer to ensure a good "marriage" of fabric to frame. Here, the fabric coordinator *(left)*, in consultation with the designer, carefully chooses fabrics that will enhance the appearance of the furniture. Selecting from available fabrics is one of the most important considerations for the consumer in making a decision whether or not to buy the company's furniture.

suitable fabrics is available for retailers to show their customers. He or she must work with furniture market showroom designers to select fabrics for showroom samples that will result in an exciting display.

Most fabric coordinators are also responsible for making certain that all fabric received from suppliers is of acceptable quality, and they also handle complaints and problems.

THE SAMPLE MAKER

Sample makers are very skilled employees who can read mechanical drawings or blueprints and produce mock-ups or samples from them. The sample maker often works away from the main flow of the plant to avoid interfering with production.

In many case-goods plants, the sample room contains a small machine shop where the sample makers lay out the drawings, cut out the pieces, and assemble mock-ups or actual samples. The sample maker makes one piece in a suite first, and if it is approved, proceeds to complete the suite.

In an upholstered furniture manufacturing plant, sample makers assemble the frame according to the specifications of the drawings. They calculate how the fabric must be applied and make the pattern from which the fabric will be cut. Master upholsterers will then complete the prototype sofa or chair.

ORGANIZING FOR NEW PRODUCT INTRODUCTIONS

Because new product introductions are a necessary, frequent occurrence for furniture manufacturers, there should be a separate organization for making as certain as possible that these introductions are on target. The most common organization for new product introduction in the American furniture industry is the product planning committee.

PRODUCT PLANNING COMMITTEE

A product planning committee is composed of a variety of management personnel from within the company and, sometimes, outside members as well. Many companies call this group the *design committee* and its meetings, *design meetings*.

The merchandising manager is normally the committee chairman. The other company committee members have various jobs within the organization, but are called to serve on this committee because of their responsibilities and insight. The company president sits in on at least part of the meetings to provide overall policy decisions. In upholstered furniture manufacturing companies, the fabric coordinator serves on the committee to provide valuable input about fabric and trends in color. If the company has a staff designer or group of designers, one of them will likely serve, which provides a direct dialogue with the person who will draw or direct the drawing of the new introductions. At least one representative of sales management is present to provide input to the new product development.

Other personnel may attend at least some of the committee meetings. For example, a representative of production is often present to give an opinion on how projected designs may fit in with production capabilities. A person from the cost accounting department may be a member to provide cost figures or profit projections. The purchasing agent may occasionally sit in to get information needed to purchase the right type of materials.

The bulk of the work of the committee occurs in the months before new products are to be introduced at the furniture market. The aim is to have the product designed and samples ready to show at market. The committee must discuss such things as the current product offerings, the overall direction of the firm's marketing efforts, styles, price brackets, market share, the company's fashion statement, and various statistics which may include everything from demographics to what type of store is increasing in popularity and what type is decreasing.

Furniture manufacturers differ concerning their attitudes about the makeup of their product planning committees. Following are four options for membership in a product planning committee:

1. An executive panel is one way of saying that only people who work full-time in the home office, except possibly a freelance designer, are allowed in any of the committee meetings. These members solicit ideas from key retailers, salespeople, and others in the marketplace. This solicitation may be through trips to retailers in key cities, rather than bringing them to the home office.

2. Committee with the input of company salespeople involves having salespeople from key sales territories come to the home office to discuss the product line and plans for product introductions. These salespeople go over the entire product line and give their ideas about what should be retained and what should be replaced. They provide insight into what is happening in their sales territories and give their opinions concerning the salability of projected designs.

3. Committee with the input of retailers has much the same objectives as the committee with company salespeople. However, many manufacturers would rather invite key retailers to participate in the committee meetings because they feel the retailers can be more objective. Bringing key retailers to the home office for their input may provide helpful insight as to which designs are likely to sell as well as nurturing a closer relationship between retailer and manufacturer.

4. Committee with consumer input is utilized by a relatively small number of manufacturers. In this approach, consumers are asked their opinions about prototypes of possible product introductions. For example,

6-5. Here, a product planning committee is evaluating a manufacturer's entire product line, based on such variables as price and style. By looking at the entire line, it is easier to see where voids exist or where sales of particular products are declining so that the right product introductions can be made.

a case-goods manufacturer might display ten dressers from suites that are possible introductions. A group of consumers are then brought in and asked their opinions. The responses will be recorded or the consumers will indicate their comments on forms that are provided. Companies using consumer input may also solicit the input of company salespeople or dealers.

SOURCES OF NEW PRODUCT IDEAS

New product ideas come from sources that are as varied as the number of products introduced. However, the following sources of new product ideas are the most common:

Designers. Good furniture designers do not stay at home. They are constantly traveling to see what is selling, to review famous designs on display in museums, or simply to be on the lookout for new ideas. When they know the style and price bracket in which a manufacturer needs an introduction, successful designers will do a considerable amount of research to try to come up with an idea that "fits."

Consumers. At times, consumers will make comments or perhaps write letters giving manufacturers or retailers new product ideas. Simply observing consumers, finding out about their life-styles, and their likes and dislikes, may also reveal new product ideas. For example, a trend of people spending more time at home, along with a trend indicating a rise in the sale of home computers, may signal a demand for desks designed for the use and storage of such products.

Retailers. Even though they may not be invited to participate in product planning committee meetings, retailers can provide a great amount of helpful information. They see what is selling, hear the comments of consumers and, in general, have a feel for what is needed in the marketplace. Many products are introduced in direct response to the expressed needs of retailers.

Product/market analyses. A necessary component of effective product planning is a thorough product/market analysis. This analysis involves a manufacturer reviewing its entire line and noting areas of strength and weakness. All style and price categories should be carefully charted to determine where the company has sufficient market coverage and where new products need to be added. The market, with its inevitable shifts, must be carefully compared to the merchandise being offered by a manufacturer to help the company come up with the right products at the right time.

Competition. Manufacturers are constantly investigating to determine which of the competitive products are drawing the most attention. Many times, the competition has introduced something that uncovers a previously unnoticed demand in the marketplace or creates a different style treatment that seems to be appealing. By carefully studying competition, manufacturers can introduce variations on the same theme which may prove to be successful product introductions.

Manufacturing needs of the company. New introductions are sometimes made to balance production in the manufacturing plants. For example, management in a company with a multiplant operation might need additional work for the dining-room plant. In this case, one or two dining-room suites may be introduced in an attempt to stimulate more work for the dining-room plant. Another example would be the introduction of a suite requiring extensive carving because the carving department needs more work.

Suppliers. Companies that supply various materials to furniture manufacturers are a good source of new product ideas. Examples of such companies are furniture finish suppliers, fabric mills, hardware suppliers, and veneer suppliers. All are watching the industry and are looking for ways to sell more of their materials. For example, a finish supplier may have a new tone or color of wood finish that would provide a successful new product introduction.

PRODUCT DEVELOPMENT CYCLE

The product development cycle in Figure 6-6 reveals typical steps that are followed from the idea stage to scheduling the completed product into full production. The product development cycle differs from manufacturer to manufacturer; however, these steps are representative of those that are taken:

1. **Marketing/design meetings** by the product planning committee are conducted. From these meetings, instructions will be given to the furniture designer as to what pieces, style category, and prices are to be considered in designing the new product.

2. **Prepare sketches.** The designer prepares product sketches as an interpretation of the products desired by the committee. The committee goes over the sketches and selects those it feels has the greatest potential.

3. **Prepare mechanical drawings.** The designer then prepares detailed mechanical drawings of the prototypes. These mechanical drawings are actual size, showing the pieces from top, front, and side views.

4. **Build mock-ups.** The sample maker builds mock-ups from the mechanical drawings, which may be sample dressers or chests with drawer fronts, tops, and sides, but no insides. The mock-ups may be viewed unfinished or finished for a more complete idea of how the product will look. By this time, the upholstery manufacturer will have selected sample fabrics and will have them applied to the new frames.

5. **Product planning committee review.** The product planning committee will review the mock-ups, eliminate those it feels are not salable,

and determine a projected price to be used in discussions with the buyers at premarket reviews.

6. Premarket reviews (for some manufacturers). Manufacturers, whose customers include the larger retail furniture store chains and department stores, invite key buyers to the sample display area at the factory to view their projected offerings. The comments of these retailers may lead to changes in the samples before they are shown at market. Some manufacturers will quote a definite price at premarket, and if the introduction is sufficiently appealing, the buyers may place orders at that time. On occasion, the first cutting may even be sold out during premarket reviews. Premarket showings are generally more important to case-goods manufacturers than upholstery manufacturers.

7. Show samples at market. Completed samples of the pieces that the committee decides to introduce are produced and are shown at the furniture market. A lack of buyer interest at or after the market may still cause a product not to be manufactured.

8. Evaluation of orders after market. Judgment as to whether to produce some items may be withheld until the salespeople have had an opportunity to show them for a few weeks after market. The final decision on actually producing a new product depends on the number of customer orders.

9. Full production. Products with sufficient orders are scheduled for production.

As is apparent, product development is a complex, continuous effort in the United States furniture industry.

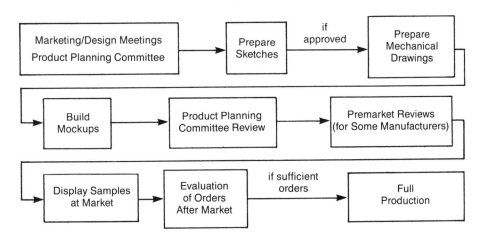

6-6. Product development cycle

SUMMARY

Product development is the group of activities revolving around having the right product available in the marketplace. A furniture product is both tangible and intangible with many features and benefits designed to satisfy the consumer. To be successful, a furniture manufacturer must produce a product that is appropriate for his or her niche in the marketplace.

Product introduction is necessary because of style obsolescence, the furniture product life cycle, motivation for retailers and company salespeople, expressed needs of retailers, and/or company image.

The stages in the furniture product life cycle are introduction, growth and possible emulation, maturity, and decline.

Professional personnel involved in product development include: the furniture designer, merchandising manager, fabric coordinator, and sample maker. A company either may use freelance furniture designers or employ full-time designers on its staff.

The product planning committee is most often used to initiate and approve new product introductions. The options for membership in a product planning committee are: an executive panel, committee with the input of company salespeople, committee with the input of retailers, and committee with consumer input.

Typical sources of new product ideas are: designers, consumers, retailers, product/market analyses, competition, manufacturing needs of the company, and suppliers.

A product development cycle may include: marketing/design meetings by the product planning committee, preparing sketches, preparing mechanical drawings, building mock-ups, product planning committee review, premarket showings (for selected manufacturers), displaying samples at market, evaluation of orders after market, and full production.

In the final analysis, the decision to produce a product depends on the number of customer orders.

CHAPTER 7

THE FURNITURE MANUFACTURING PROCESS

W hy should a furniture marketer be concerned with manufacturing? A basic understanding of furniture manufacturing gives the marketer a knowledge of furniture as a manufactured product. This understanding will help to explain why certain features are possible while others are not. The marketer will gain valuable insights that may lead to more effective personal sales presentations or advertising copy. Understanding furniture manufacturing will also help the marketer answer consumer questions and handle complaints more easily and quickly.

AN OVERVIEW

The furniture manufacturing process is a relatively complex production system involving a combination of people and machinery. Compared to other industries, the furniture industry would be considered by many to be inefficient and not very advanced technologically. It tends to be somewhat of a craft industry, involving a large number of people in many departments. For example, in the preparation of decorative doors and table tops featuring veneer in intricate patterns, a number of skilled people are involved to cut and position the veneer for the desired effect. In upholstering many types of furniture, especially in the upper price categories, skilled upholsterers must be able to handle the intricacies of the many different styles produced by the company. Therefore, furniture manufacturing is a labor-intensive industry requiring a relatively large number of skilled workers.

The large number of people is assisted in many departments by machines to speed up the routine tasks such as sanding, boring holes, and stapling—for example, the upholsterer is assisted by an air pressure staple gun to make the work easier and faster.

The computer has become very important to many furniture manufacturers in preparing lists of material required for a suite of furniture. The specifications of materials necessary to produce a suite of furniture are entered into the computer. The computer then calculates and prints out a listing or bill of materials complete with routing tickets that specify how many of each part are needed and what types of processing each is to undergo. Some companies are even using computers with graphics capabilities to prepare patterns to be used in cutting wood pieces or fabrics.

Newer furniture factories are featuring conveyors, fork-lift trucks, hydraulic lifts, and other labor-saving devices to speed production as well as to make the work easier.

To illustrate the specific production functions, a typical flow chart for the manufacturing of upholstered furniture and case goods (mainly wood or wood-simulated bedroom and dining room furniture) is helpful.

UPHOLSTERED FURNITURE MANUFACTURING

Figure 7-1 is the flow chart for a company manufacturing the complete upholstered product from wooden frame to the finished article.

For upholstered furniture, the manufacturing is normally scheduled by customer order, which means that most companies do not produce items for warehouse stock. The reason is that the retailer or consumer, in most cases, has many fabric choices and there is really no way to second-guess his or her selections. Therefore, very few upholstered furniture manufacturers maintain a significant amount of finished-goods inventory. They do, however, maintain an inventory of the fabrics offered in their line and frame parts so that the frame can be assembled and fabric cut and sewn promptly according to the selection of the customer.

Companies that feature a "quick ship" program often keep either complete or partially assembled frames in stock and have a number of covers already sewn from among the variety of fabrics offered. A "quick ship"

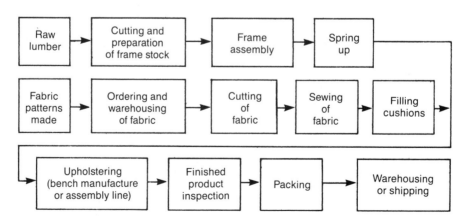

7-1. Flow of upholstered furniture manufacturing

program means the company is promoting a service allowing a retailer to submit an order and have the product completed and shipped within a much shorter time period than is normally required for the upholstered furniture manufacturing cycle.

Although frame assembly and fabric cutting and sewing normally take place simultaneously in different departments, each step needs to be described separately.

Raw lumber. Upholstered furniture frames are primarily produced from hardwood lumber, although plastic and other materials are sometimes used. The raw lumber is received and is normally air- or kiln-dried to reduce the moisture content so that it is less likely to warp or split and is easier to machine. The dried lumber is then sawed into various sizes for maximum yield and smoothed by a planer to make it ready to be cut into the various specified frame parts.

To allow the cutting of large or carved pieces, smaller pieces of wood are glued together to make what is referred to as "glued-up stock." This provides larger sizes of wood pieces than the manufacturer would normally buy. It is usually stronger and less expensive than the same size block of natural wood.

Cutting and preparation of frame stock. Frame stock are those pieces from which the upholstered furniture frame will be built. A quantity of each piece for every frame in the line is cut and prepared so they are available when a particular frame is needed for production. The preparation involves a certain amount of sanding, boring of holes for screws or dowels, and any sawing necessary to ensure that the frame parts will fit together properly. The exposed wooden arms, legs, or other parts are smoothed by sanding more than other frame parts so that they can be finished properly.

Frame assembly. When an order is received, it is scheduled and placed into the flow of production. At this point, a sufficient quantity of necessary frame parts is obtained from inventory to build the number of frames specified in the order. The frames are then assembled, using various techniques to ensure strength and durability. Depending on the company and product price range, the frames may be put together with screws, dowels, nails, staples, and glue, with added reinforcement blocks for strength.

Spring up. Once the frame is assembled and inspected to ensure that the parts fit securely, the springs are installed. The term "spring-up man" refers to the person who installs the springs. The skill required depends on the type of spring mechanisms used. (Various types of springs were discussed in Chapter 2.) The spring-up man installs the springs and checks them for proper configuration and flex to ensure adequate comfort when upholstering is completed. He or she also applies a plain, durable fabric over the springs to serve as a base upon which to lay other filling materials.

Developing fabric cutting patterns. Fabric cutting patterns are developed when a sample is approved for showing at the furniture market. These temporary patterns are transferred to more durable paper or other material when sufficient orders are received to actually place the piece of furniture into production. In designing the pattern, such factors as yield and pattern match must be considered. Yield and pattern match mean the manufacturer is trying to waste as little fabric as possible while taking into consideration potential problems, such as centering large floral designs on cushions or matching stripes and plaids. The paper or cardboard patterns are perforated so that the large multiple layers of cloth can be marked before they are cut. This is done by using dusting powder which goes through the holes in the pattern and marks a cutting line on the fabric.

Ordering and warehousing of fabric. The fabric coordinator or sometimes the purchasing agent is responsible for making certain that enough material is ordered to produce the estimated number of orders. The objective is to have enough—but not too much—fabric in inventory. Fabric is received from the mills in large rolls, usually fifty yards long, and is normally inspected and measured before it goes into the fabric storage area. Rolls with too many defects are returned to the supplier or a credit is requested for the defective yardage. Today, many upholstered furniture manufacturers use computerized inventory control to help balance their fabric inventories.

Cutting of fabric. When customer orders are received, the proper fabrics are requisitioned from inventory and sent to the cutting department, where the fabric is laid out on long, narrow tables to be cut. Often, if there are sufficient orders and the pattern and type of fabric will allow it, many layers of fabric are placed on top of each other to be cut at the same time in order to save costs. The perforated cardboard patterns are laid out on the fabric and the cutting lines are marked. The cutter also inspects the fabric for defects at this time. The cutting is then done quickly and expertly with an electric cutting knife or saw. Fabric is rarely cut with a hand scissors.

Sewing of fabric. The individual pieces that are cut from the layers of fabric are bundled according to what is required for each piece of furniture and are taken to the sewing department. Care is taken to keep all appropriate pieces together and to ensure that all the fabric to be used in upholstering a piece of furniture comes from the same roll of cloth (different dye lots may vary slightly in color).

Several different types of sewing machines are used, depending on the type of sewing to be done. For example, a double-needle sewing machine is used to sew both sides of a zipper at once.

The cushion covers are sewn, and the other types of sewing take place in order to get the cover ready for the upholsterer to apply to the frame.

7-2. This boring-machine operator is boring holes in wooden pieces that will become part of the arm of an upholstered furniture frame. Wooden dowel pins will be used in glueing these pieces onto the remainder of the frame for greater stability. The care that goes into the cutting and preparation of the frame stock is an indicator of relative quality in upholstered furniture.

7-3. Frame assemblers glue and staple the various frame pieces together. Here, a worker is assembling an entire frame using large hydraulic clamps mounted to the top of a table or work bench. These frame assemblers are skilled employees who work rather quickly and are paid based on the number of frames assembled.

7-4. This spray-booth operator is spraying finish on the legs of a completed camel-back sofa frame. Only those portions of the wood that will be exposed after the piece is upholstered will have finish applied to them. In this case, only the legs of this piece will be exposed; therefore, they are the only areas that will be finished during this procedure.

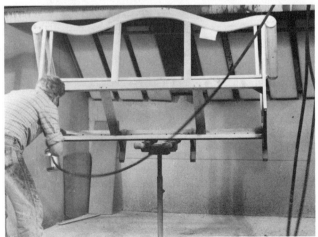

7-5. This spring-up man is hand-tying the tops of hourglass-shaped coil springs to form a level, flexible seating surface. The spring-up process begins when the bottoms of the coil springs are attached to webbing that has been fastened onto the frame. The process ends with the hand-tying of the tops of the springs. Each spring will be tied in eight directions to ensure that the springs will remain upright and level.

7-6. This warehouseman is selecting fabric from inventory to be used in upholstering a sofa or chair according to customer order. Upholstered furniture manufacturers must keep a large stock of fabric in inventory so that orders are filled as quickly as possible without having to wait for shipments from the fabric mill. Here, the warehouseman is using an electric lift which enables him to select fabric from the upper shelves.

7-7. This fabric cutter is using a high-speed rotary saw to cut the pieces to be used in upholstering a sofa or chair. For greater efficiency, he cuts several layers of fabric at one time, using a cardboard pattern that has been prepared to help ensure that all cut pieces are the proper size and shape. Pattern match and yield are primary concerns of the fabric cutter.

7-8. This seamstress is sewing pieces of a cushion cover together. Extreme care must be exercised to help ensure that everything will fit properly in the finished product. Cushion covers are sewn and stuffed in an operation separate from upholstering.

7-9. This upholsterer is applying padding and fabric to a sofa frame. This particular sofa is tufted; therefore, the upholsterer is attaching string to fabric-covered buttons so that they can be secured in their proper place. Sofas such as this may have several layers of filling applied to the frame before the cover is placed on it.

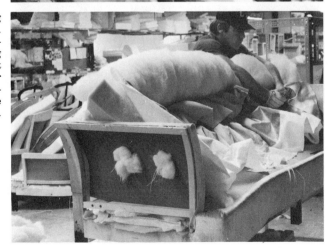

Filling cushions. Cushion inserts, usually foam, are placed inside their covers at this point in production. The cushion covers are normally sewn with a zipper opening in the back of the cover. Most of the cushion units are inserted mechanically with a special machine which has two stainless steel plates that compress the cushion unit so that the cover can be placed over it. Another method of inserting cushions is by a vacuum machine, which compresses foam cushions simply by pulling the air out of the foam and causing it to collapse. While the cushion is collapsed, the cushion cover is applied around it.

Upholstering. Upholstering is applying the filling materials and fabric to the frame. However, the exact job of the upholsterer varies from company to company. In a company that uses the bench manufacturing system, one upholsterer applies the filling and fabric to the entire piece of furniture. Companies using an assembly line method of manufacturing usually break up the upholstery procedure among several people. For example, one person may only upholster the outside of the arms and another may upholster only the inside of the arms. Therefore, the upholstery function is often divided so that there could be several people on the assembly line performing their own special job on the piece.

Regardless of the method of manufacturing, the fabric and filling must be applied properly for the piece of furniture to have an attractive appearance. Therefore, upholstering is an occupation involving considerable skill.

Finished product inspection. Once the upholstering is completed, a quality inspection is made to ensure that no details have been overlooked.

Packing. After it is inspected, the furniture is packed using appropriate packaging for adequate protection. If the merchandise is to be transported by common or contract carrier, it must be packed according to government specifications. It is usually placed in a plastic bag, suitably padded, and then cartoned. Some companies place their furniture in a shrink pack before it is put inside the carton. This process involves attaching the furniture to a heavy cardboard or wooden base, putting a special plastic bag over it, and running it through an oven. The oven shrinks the bag so the furniture is held tight within it to minimize damage.

Warehousing or shipping. After packing, the furniture is sent to the company warehouse or staging area for loading into a truck or railroad freight car. If the furniture is for immediate shipment, shipping tags are applied and the furniture is shipped by the desired method of transportation. Care is taken to ensure that shipping is done properly in order to avoid loss by damage, misdirection, or theft. Merchandise that is not to be shipped immediately is transferred to the company warehouse, where it is held until needed for shipping.

In order to fill orders quickly, some manufacturers maintain warehouse inventories of more popular frames, fabrics, and colors.

CASE-GOODS MANUFACTURING

The manufacturing flow illustrated in Figure 7-10 is typical of bedroom or dining-room manufacturing that involves the entire production process from raw lumber to the finished product. This diagram assumes that the manufacturer has the capability of producing decorative veneer tops, doors, and other veneered furniture parts.

Raw lumber. Raw lumber, often freshly cut from logs, is received from suppliers, graded, measured, and properly stacked in the lumber yard outside the factory for air-drying. Air-drying involves separating each layer of boards with one-inch stacking strips placed at right angles to ensure a flow of air through the stacks of lumber. The time taken to air-dry depends on the kind and thickness of the lumber.

Generally, the lumber may stay in the lumber yard from a few weeks to a few months until it is needed for a cutting that is scheduled for production in the factory. A *cutting* is the term used throughout the industry to refer to a quantity of products, usually of the same style, moving through the factory at the same time. (In other industries, this quantity or grouping of products might be called a job, or job order.) The cuttings vary greatly in size. For example, for one manufacturer a desirable cutting might be five hundred suites, while for another, fifty rocking chairs might be quite sufficient for a worthwhile cutting.

Dry kiln. The amount of moisture that can be removed from lumber during air-drying in the lumber yard is limited. To help ensure that the wood will not warp or split and to make the processing of the wood easier within the factory, the moisture content must be reduced even further. This is accomplished by placing the lumber in a dry kiln under controlled

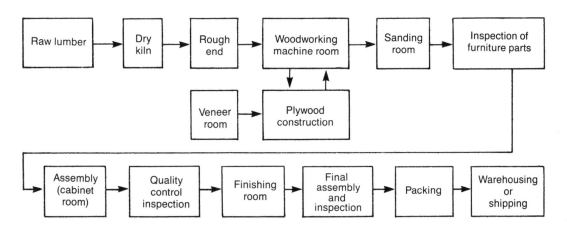

7-10. Flow of case-goods manufacturing

humidity and heating conditions. The dry-kiln operation allows the moisture content to be reduced significantly. One manufacturer reports that the aim of their dry-kiln operation is to reduce moisture content from approximately 20 percent to 6 percent.

Rough end. The term *rough end* refers to the section of the factory where rough lumber is cut and machine processing begins. The amount of kiln-dried lumber needed for a cutting is brought in and cut to dimensions specified by the requirements of the products to be produced in the cutting. The lumber may be cut into square or rectangular pieces needed for posts or may be sawed into strips which will be glued together and used for larger posts or panels.

Woodworking machinery used in the rough end includes *cut-off saws* to cut lumber to the desired length and *rip saws* to cut boards to the appropriate width. In both of these sawing operations, the lumber is cut to obtain the greatest yield and to the requirements of the suites being processed. Examples of other machines found in the rough end are *planers* and *molders*. A planer is a machine with a rapidly turning, horizontal cylinder inlaid with very sharp knives used to smooth the tops and bottoms of boards. A molder has rapidly turning, offset cutting heads which can smooth the sides and round the edges of materials for posts or other parts of the finished product.

The gluing together of pieces to form panels and *dimension stock* (large pieces of wood used to make legs, posts, or other relatively thick parts) may also take place in the rough end. To make panels, pieces are glued together edge to edge. Glued-up dimension stock is made by pieces glued on top of each other. Further processing of the boards, panels, and dimension stock then takes place in the woodworking machine room.

Veneer room. In this section of the factory, veneers are received and cut to the desired size. *Veneers* are thin layers of wood, varying in thickness from ⅛ to ¹⁄₃₂-inch, used for decorative wood surfaces and to make plywood. The cutting is done by a machine with a very sharp knife that is lowered onto the veneer, actually shearing it in a straight line. The veneer slices are spliced or taped together to form sheets of the desired size and design. Splicing involves gluing or sewing veneer slices edge to edge. Veneer to be used on the insides of drawers, doors, or other places where it will not be readily seen is taped or spliced at random. More expensive veneers to be positioned on table tops, door fronts, or other outside areas are often taped or spliced to create a decorative pattern. These more expensive veneers that will be finished as a part of the furniture's design are called *face veneers*.

Plywood construction. Most case-goods construction involves the use of plywood somewhere in the furniture. *Plywood* is actually a sandwich of layers of wood most often made of various grades and types of veneer glued on top of each other.

To help prevent warping, the layers, or *plies*, are glued with the wood grain of each layer running at right angles to the one glued on top of it. As added insurance against warping, plywood is constructed with an odd number of plies. Typical in furniture construction are three- or five-ply plywood with the center layer being a lumber or particle-board core from ½ to ¾-inch thick. The thick lumber cores are some of the panels that were glued up in the rough end. Once the plywood is processed into the desired sheet sizes, it is sent to the woodworking machine room for further processing.

Woodworking machine room. The woodworking machine room, sometimes called the *finish machine room,* is the section of the factory where the wood from the rough end and plywood panels from the plywood construction department are machined to the dimensions specified by the requirements for the finished furniture product.

Although there are many types of woodworking machines in this room, three will illustrate some of the types of machining that take place in this section of the factory. A *band saw* has a continuous, long, thin band of saw-toothed metal that revolves around large wheels. The band saw can be used to cut out intricate designs such as would be required in the base or top of a china cabinet. There are various types of *shapers* in the woodworking machine room. These shapers are used to put decorative edges on many wood pieces such as doors and table tops. *Routers* are machines that use a rotating, side cutting bit to make various types of lines and complex designs which must be cut in flat surfaces of case pieces.

In the woodworking machine room, all machining for joints, holes for screws, dowels or glue, and other types of machining required for proper case-goods construction take place. Once the pieces leave this section of the factory, they are ready for sanding and assembly.

Sanding room. Sanding and polishing take place in the sanding room to remove any marks made in the woodworking machine room and to make the parts smooth in preparation for assembly and finishing. The sanding and polishing are done with a variety of abrasive sandpapers. Rough sanding is done with a coarser sandpaper, followed by polishing with a fine grit or less abrasive sandpaper.

The sanding and polishing are done using various types of machines to sand flat surfaces, edges, and rounded pieces such as posts and legs.

Inspection of furniture parts. At this point in the manufacturing process, the furniture parts are visually inspected to make certain they are properly cut and sanded. Those parts that need additional sanding are returned to the sanding room for further processing. The others are sent on to the cabinet room for assembly. An effective quality-control inspection at this point will more nearly ensure a smoothly running assembly line and fewer product rejects in subsequent departments.

Assembly (cabinet room). The term *cabinet room* is applied to the section of the plant where final assembly takes place. Here, the parts that have been cut and sanded are fitted together to form the end product. The

7-11. These rip saw operators are cutting lengthwise boards that are necessary for the manufacture of case goods. This process ensures that the boards will have a smooth-edged surface necessary for preparing glued-up stock.

7-12. This worker is sanding curved furniture parts so that they will be smooth in preparation for the assembly and finishing operation. Care must be taken because a professionally sanded piece is a mark of quality in furniture construction. *(Bassett Furniture Industries, Inc.)*

7-13. This worker is assembling doors and drawers which will be used in case pieces. Normally, this is done in an operation separate from the assembly line. The doors and drawers are then taken to the assembly line where they can be placed in or on each piece as it passes various work stations. *(Bassett Furniture Industries, Inc.)*

7-14. This assembly-line worker is using a rubber mallet to ensure that the decorative parting rail on this chest-on-chest is fastened securely. He also uses air-driven screw drivers and staple guns to speed the assembly process. These power tools are connected to an overhead line and to a central air compressor by the spring-like hose shown on the left. In this typical assembly-line operation, the worker stays in one place, and the products pass before him on the slatted conveyor belt.

7-15. Quality control people inspect cabinets and bookcases as they approach the end of the assembly line. Touch-up people then sand rough spots, straighten doors, and/or make any other necessary changes before the pieces go to the finishing area. *(Bassett Furniture Industries, Inc.)*

7-16. This spray booth operator is spraying finish on pieces as they move in front of him suspended from an overhead chain conveyor system. There are several steps in most finishing operations so that the pieces will pass several spray booths before the finishing is completed. *(Bassett Furniture Industries, Inc.)*

7-17. The final assembly after the finish has been applied and dried involves workers who put shelves in bookcases or other pieces, attach hardware where needed, put electric light fixtures in the top of china hutches, or perform any other job necessary to make the product complete. This final assembly worker is attaching drawer pulls.

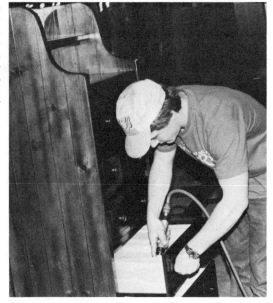

furniture parts are screwed, stapled, and glued to form the piece of furniture. Various worker skills are involved to make certain the furniture is assembled properly and efficiently.

Depending on the factory and the type of furniture being produced, the cabinet room may be set up like an assembly line, with workers assembling the pieces on a conveyor. For example, one worker attaches the left door, the next worker attaches the right door, and so on. The assembly in the cabinet room is complete to the installation of drawer guides and the fitting of drawers into the frame. Only the finishing touches of assembly, such as the installation of decorative hardware and glass, are left to be done after the finishing room.

Quality control inspection. At the end of the assembly operation, the product is inspected for quality to determine if all the procedures have been correctly carried out and the pieces are fitted together tightly. Defective goods are sent to a special area where they are reworked to remove the defect. This area is manned by skilled craftsmen who can reattach loose parts, remove and replace defective parts, and perform other needed operations to ensure that products are transferred to the finishing room in top condition.

Finishing room. The finishing room is normally organized around a conveyor that carries the furniture from spraying operations to rubbing operations required to give the furniture color, gloss, and the "look" needed for it to sell on the retail floor. This "look" is achieved through applying various types of stains, lacquers, varnishes, and other finishing materials. These materials are normally applied to the furniture pieces at various spray booths.

The furniture moves almost continuously from spray booth to spray booth, to drying oven, to workers who wipe off portions of the finishing materials to achieve various design effects. Several steps are often involved, with the exact number depending on the style and price range of the furniture. Less expensive furniture usually requires fewer steps. Normally, a drying operation takes place at the end of the finishing room to ensure maximum hardness and quality of finish.

Final assembly and inspection. At the end of the finishing room, the product is completed except for adding hardware and, in some cases, more rubbing. Before packing, the drawer pulls, door handles, and other hardware are added, plus glass and back panels if required. Some manufacturers send the finished product to the *rub room* where the furniture is "rubbed" with a very fine grade sandpaper and fine textured steel wool, or waxed and buffed for the desired gloss in finish.

The product is now ready for the final inspection before it is packed for storage in the warehouse or for shipment to the retailer. In this process, the quality control inspector determines whether the product is in good enough condition to be sold by the retailer. If so, it is sent to the packing area; otherwise, it is sent to a special area to be reworked.

Packing. Care must be taken in packing case goods so that the product will arrive undamaged. Carefully designed packing materials are a necessity for a quality-minded furniture manufacturing company. Corner pads and a paper or foam blanket are used to properly cushion the product before it is placed in the carton. Then, a carton of sufficient strength to withstand normal shocks and vibrations is placed over the furniture. The furniture must also be placed on a substantial base or skid to help reduce damage.

Warehousing or shipping. In case-goods manufacturing, a finished goods inventory is usually on hand. The amount of inventory depends on whether the company manufactures to inventory or to customer order. Those that manufacture to inventory fill customer orders from the warehouse and, therefore, will need a larger inventory.

The shipping operation itself is extremely important. The shipping clerk is the one who must check the merchandise before it is loaded in order to make certain the right items are being sent. This person should be considered a key employee because careful shipping procedures can save the company money in many ways.

Furniture placed in the warehouse is moved by conveyor belt, forklift, or other merchandise handling system to prelettered or prenumbered locations within the warehouse. An accurate record of the location of each product is maintained to ensure that correct inventory records can be kept and desired items easily retrieved when needed for shipment. Care is taken whenever the merchandise is moved to minimize loss or damage.

SUMMARY

An understanding of furniture manufacturing helps the marketer to gain an appreciation of furniture as a manufactured product and provides facts needed for the preparation of effective sales presentations.

Furniture is basically a craft industry in which people and machinery work together to produce the finished product. There are differences, however; upholstery manufacturing is more labor intensive, and case-goods production is more machine-oriented.

Modern furniture factories are using automation to make production easier and faster.

A typical manufacturing flow for an upholstered furniture company involves the following steps:

Raw lumber—may be air- or kiln-dried to reduce the moisture content of the wood, minimizing warping and splitting.

Cutting and preparation of frame stock—the cutting and preparation of wood parts to be assembled later as a frame for upholstered furniture.

Frame assembly—building the frame from the frame stock.

Spring up—installing the springs in the frame and placing a protective fabric over them.

Developing fabric cutting patterns—allows the cutting of the correct number and sizes of fabric pieces to upholster the furniture.

Ordering and warehousing of fabric—ensures sufficient stock of the various types of fabric necessary to fill customer orders.

Cutting of fabric—laying out numerous layers of fabric on long tables and cutting out the pieces of fabric necessary to upholster a piece of furniture properly.

Sewing of fabric—sewing together the various fabric pieces needed for upholstering, ensuring well-fitting cushion covers and the proper look wherever sewing is required.

Filling cushions—inserting the foam cushion units within their covers.

Upholstering—applying and attaching the filling materials and outer fabric to the frame.

Finished product inspection—inspecting product to make certain the proper level of quality has been achieved.

Packing—proper packing is necessary for shipping.

Warehousing or shipping—shipping the product or storing it in a company warehouse until needed for shipment. Some upholstered furniture manufacturers maintain warehouse inventories of popular frames, fabrics, and colors.

A typical manufacturing flow for a case-goods manufacturer involves the following steps:

Raw lumber—stacked in the lumber yard for air-drying.

Dry kiln—controlling the temperature and moisture of the kiln to reduce the moisture content of wood.

Rough end—where the rough lumber is cut to length, planed, glued into panels or dimension stock, and smoothed ready for machining.

Veneer room—veneer is received, cut to desired sizes, and spliced or taped to proper size and pattern.

Plywood construction—gluing together of thin layers of wood and often a central core to create a panel of proper size.

Woodworking machine room—where the wood pieces are cut to desired specifications.

Sanding room—case-goods parts are sanded and polished.

Inspection of furniture parts—parts are inspected to see if they are properly machined and sanded.

Assembly (cabinet room)—actual assembly of the furniture takes place.

Quality control inspection—checking to determine if the product is assembled properly.

Finishing room—applying stain, lacquer, and/or varnish for desired appearance.

Final assembly and inspection—hardware, glass, and back panels are added. Also final quality inspection; rubbing, polishing, and waxing takes place.

Packing—necessary to avoid damage and loss.

Warehousing or shipping—merchandise is either stored in the warehouse until needed for shipment or shipped immediately to a customer.

CHAPTER 8

MARKETING RESEARCH AND INFORMATION SYSTEMS

Marketing research is the systematic gathering, recording, and analyzing of data concerning problems relating to the marketing of goods and services. As such, it involves searching for information to solve any marketing problem. Just as in any other industry, the furniture marketer needs to define marketing problems and then search for information that can be used effectively to solve those problems.

No decision is any better than the information on which it is based. Therefore, if a marketing manager decides to bring out a new line of expensive furniture based on information stating that after-tax consumer income is rising, when it is old information and no longer true, the product line may fail. If, however, the information is correct, it may be exactly the right time to bring out the new line.

The gathering and use of information should be an ongoing process. Therefore, well-managed organizations establish procedures and systems to provide needed information continuously. Having a marketing information system means that the firm has mandated periodic reporting of information helpful in making marketing decisions. The widespread use of computers by both manufacturing and retailing furniture companies allows the collecting, recording, and analyzing of a larger amount of data than has ever before been possible.

WHY ARE RESEARCH AND INFORMATION IMPORTANT?

Compared to many other industries, furniture companies normally do not have enough profit margin to support the personnel to collect, record, analyze, and interpret a large volume of marketing data. Yet, it is imperative that the modern furniture manufacturer or retailer build workable marketing information procedures into the organization. Through the proper combination of well-formulated computer systems and required reporting procedures, worthwhile information can be generated from normal business operations without spending large sums of money. With correct and current information, the experienced, intuitive furniture marketer increases the chance of making the right decisions. Here are several specific reasons why the availability of accurate, relevant, up-to-date information is necessary:

Shortened time for decision-making. Furniture executives are finding that a shorter time is available for decision-making, a trend projected to continue. Some companies which formerly made new introductions only once a year are now introducing new products twice a year. Others who have traditionally introduced products at the national semiannual furniture markets are now making introductions between markets. Therefore, the entire product development and decision-making process has been greatly speeded up.

Product introductions are only one type of time pressure. Other time pressures have to do with rapid communications, changing economic environments, fluctuating interest rates and other financial considerations, and a changing import and export market situation. These time pressures also have an impact on marketing actions and reactions.

Competitive situation in the furniture industry. The market power in the furniture industry is diffused; no single manufacturer or retailer dominates a significant portion of the industry, although selected manufacturers are very important in particular style or product categories.

Also, consumer brand-name awareness and brand loyalty are quite low in the furniture industry. Consumers are likely to buy from a variety of manufacturers and retailers.

Because of this competitive environment, furniture marketers must be sure they are providing the type of products consumers want. In order to do so, correct information provided by market research is essential.

Complex furniture distribution system. The United States furniture industry has one of the most complex distribution systems of any domestic industry. Furniture may be purchased by the consumer in a variety of ways from a large number of outlets.

The furniture distribution system is made even more complex because several outlets may be handling the products of the same manufacturers. For example, the same manufacturer may be selling to wholesalers, independent furniture stores, department stores, and catalogue outlets that advertise toll-free numbers and sell by telephone.

Only by using correct information about the potential of the various options for furniture distribution can marketers correctly plan sales and marketing strategies.

New products and materials. Technological innovations have occurred in the furniture industry. New machines and production processes are making style adaptations available in price ranges that would have been impossible a few years ago. For example, new recliner and sleep sofa mechanisms are making it possible for these products to have a new look. The older, bulkier mechanisms precluded these products from being offered in many fashionable and popular style categories.

Advanced finishes, filling materials, fabrics, plastics used in case goods, and other new materials are also changing furniture construction and styling. These materials are opening attractive marketing opportunities for manufacturers who can no longer be content with doing things the traditional way. Those who keep using the same materials and methods of construction may find themselves at a competitive disadvantage. The successful furniture manufacturer must be up-to-date on advances in technology.

Furniture purchasing can be postponed. Because a furniture purchase is rarely a matter of necessity, a furniture purchase may be postponed in favor of buying something else or not buying at all. Therefore, furniture marketers must understand consumer motivation and be able to create persuasive sales themes and programs.

Armed with relevant, up-to-date information about consumer values, likes, and dislikes, the progressive furniture marketer will better be able to develop motivating sales programs with a sense of urgency. Also, it is necessary to understand and estimate consumer confidence and disposable income, two factors closely related to furniture purchasing.

Intensely personal nature of a furniture purchase. The purchase of furniture is very personal because furniture is such a conspicuous product, perceived by many people to be a reflection of their individual tastes and personalities. Because of the intensely personal nature of the purchase and the many styles available in the marketplace, the consumer may have a difficult time making a purchase decision.

Knowledge of how the consumer views the purchase decision and of taste and style trends is a valuable asset to the furniture marketer. Such knowledge can result in products that are truly in demand and sales aids that are persuasive. Since people's values and tastes change over time, successful furniture marketers constantly need to keep up with current trends.

Information is a necessary tool for the sales management team. Information must be collected and analyzed in order to evaluate the performance of the sales and marketing people. In judging which salespeople are the most productive, it is necessary to review their respective sales results. Only by comparing actual sales to projected quotas or other performance standards (benchmarks) can management know if the performance of the salesperson is satisfactory.

Other types of essential information are sales by style category, product type, color, fabric weave, or other breakdown which will indicate which products are selling best and generating profits. Such reports can offer valuable evidence on which product categories to reduce and which to increase.

Sales-cost data is also valuable information for the sales management team. All costs, such as the expense involved in hiring, training, and motivating salespeople should be carefully compared to sales. These expenses may reveal places where money is being needlessly wasted. Advertising costs should be compared to sales on an ongoing basis to determine effectiveness and to eliminate ineffective advertising dollars.

Market research information is necessary for accurate sales forecasting. This final point is actually a combination of some of the previous points. A necessary management activity is sales forecasting. Without a sales forecast, meaningful production plans and schedules cannot be made, employees hired, dealers contacted, inventory levels determined, or an advertising campaign instituted. Many types of information should be accumulated and taken into consideration when making an accurate sales forecast.

MANUFACTURER MARKETING RESEARCH AND INFORMATION SYSTEMS

Progressive furniture manufacturers use various types of data to sharpen their marketing focus and enhance their chances of success. To ensure that data will be available, they install marketing information systems that place responsibilities within the organization for the regular reporting of information.

Furniture manufacturers base their decisions both on information available within the firm and on data available from outside sources.

DATA AVAILABLE FROM OUTSIDE SOURCES

Marketing research data can be classified as either *primary* or *secondary*. The advantages of primary data are that it is current and specifically collected for the problem at hand. The disadvantages are that it is costly and time-consuming because it must be specially collected by the company or an outside firm. Furniture manufacturers often do not have sufficient funds to support a specific market research project. Also, the fast-paced nature of the industry does not always allow sufficient time for the research.

The other classification of marketing research data is secondary data, collected and published by sources outside the company for purposes other than the problem at hand. The advantages of using secondary data are that it is inexpensive and readily available. The disadvantage is that it needs to be checked very carefully before use by an organization. First, it should be checked for *impartiality*. The original reason the data was collected should be considered in order to determine if there was a bias in the data collection or reporting. Then, secondary data should be checked for *validity*. Is the data a relevant measure of what management wants to know? And third, the data should be checked for *reliability*. How accurately does the sample data reflect the group from which it was drawn?

Regardless of the disadvantages, a wide variety of valuable information from various sources can be utilized by the furniture marketer:

Government agencies. Several government agencies, especially the United States Department of Commerce, offer information helpful to the marketing of furniture. The Department of Commerce conducts an economic census every five years and a population census every ten years.

The economic census provides the number of establishments, sales, payroll data, value of shipments, and other helpful data about the industry. The population census reflects numbers of people plus information about sizes of families, where they live, and other factors of interest to a furniture marketer. Often, the population statistics reveal significant demographic trends that reveal potential new market opportunities.

The Commerce Department also publishes the *U.S. Industrial Outlook,* which projects trends and activity in the furniture industry, among others, for future years.

Trade associations. A number of trade associations regularly report statistics on the industry. For example, the American Furniture Manufacturers Association (AFMA) regularly reports industry statistics it obtains from its membership. Types of statistics reported include shipments, orders, cancellations, unfilled orders, payroll, and production. This information reflects both the present condition of the industry and relevant trends.

The National Home Furnishings Association (NHFA) provides a large amount of valuable information on furniture retailers. Other trade associations report the relative amounts of various types of woods used in furniture as well as other useful information.

Private organizations. A number of private marketing research organizations, advertising agencies, magazines, and newspapers collect information of various types. Much of it is published in usable form for the furniture manufacturer. A good example is *Sales and Marketing Management* magazine's annual "Survey of Buying Power," which is especially beneficial to furniture manufacturers in the middle- and lower-price categories.

The "Survey of Buying Power" estimates the spending that is likely to take place for mass-distributed products at popular prices in the larger market areas in the United States. These projections give the furniture manufacturer tangible information which can be used for such necessary activities as forecasting sales, preparing sales quotas, and determining size of sales territories.

Wheat, First Securities, Inc., an investment firm, annually publishes a variety of statistics on spending habits, economic forecasts for the furniture industry, and suggested retail price ranges of selected companies' products. This information gives a good overview of the industry and is useful to the furniture marketer.

National magazines and metropolitan newspapers also provide a wide range of statistics, such as circulation and trading area statistics, which help manufacturers to decide where to spend their advertising dollars and how to plan for the distribution of their products.

INTERNALLY GENERATED REPORTS AND RECORDS
A number of internal reports must be generated for the manufacturer to have the data necessary for marketing efficiency. An effective marketing information system will ensure that these reports are available periodically for use in making marketing decisions. The reports that are particularly useful include:

Sales reports. The largest group of reports utilized by most manufacturers in making marketing decisions is the sales report, which may be organized in four ways:

1. *Sales by salesperson and territory.* This report provides information on the performance of each salesperson. Typical items of interest are yearly sales to date, number of accounts, amount of cancellations, percentage of quota sold, and average size of sale. A comparison of sales results to previous points in time helps detect trends.

2. *Sales by suite, piece, color, fabric type, or style category.* This information determines what is selling and what is not. Again, by comparing these sales over time, it is possible to see what is becoming more popular, less popular, or remaining fairly constant.

3. *Placements by suite or piece.* The number of placements on the retailer's sales floor determines the extent of exposure to the consumer. Therefore, manufacturers are interested in knowing how many retail placements have been made for each style or group.

4. *Sales by type or size of dealer.* Is the product being displayed by larger accounts, smaller accounts, catalogue showrooms, independent furniture stores, or some other type of outlet? This information gives manufacturers an idea of how successfully they are reaching those they most want to promote their products.

Inventory reports. Inventory reports give management information on what items or combinations of items are accumulating in warehouses. Future production schedules can thus eliminate shortages and overstocks.

Return and damage reports. This information provides a check on the quality control department and also helps to locate flaws in product design or materials. By promptly taking care of problem areas, the company will enhance its reputation for quality among potential buyers.

Advertising records. The type and costs of advertising should be compared with sales to determine advertising effectiveness. Advertising should result in sales; if this does not happen, changes should be made.
Accounting records. Although not usually considered to be marketing research information, accounting records can yield cost data that may indicate needed changes, such as salespeople's compensation or size and makeup of territories. Cost data necessary for products to be priced properly will also be provided as a necessary starting point to ensure sufficient revenue to cover costs as well as providing enough profit margin.

DATA OBTAINED FROM SALESPEOPLE AND DEALERS

Some manufacturers require their salespeople to complete periodic reports that reveal observations and results as they call on their dealers. These manufacturers ask what the dealers want in terms of products and services, what competing products are on the dealers' floors, and what product voids seem to exist in their trading areas. The manufacturer may informally talk with his or her salespeople periodically to get a better idea of what is going on in the territories, or may set up a formal council of salespeople to advise marketing management.

Marketing managers also talk directly with the retail dealers to get an idea of their problems, observations, and how they can better be served. Most manufacturers have certain key retailers they depend on to give them information. Some manufacturers formalize the process by forming a dealer council to advise them periodically on their products, programs, and policies. Several manufacturers also have either salespeople or retailers as members of their product planning committees.

DATA OBTAINED FROM CONSUMERS

Although consumer research is not widespread in the furniture industry, many manufacturers do try to obtain consumers' opinions. Some hire independent marketing research organizations to get an idea of brand-name awareness, consumer attitudes, and consumer preferences in buying furniture.

A second method of obtaining input from consumers is to solicit their assistance in product development; for example, a panel of consumers may be brought into a room full of samples that the firm is considering and asked for their preferences. Or the panel is simply asked questions which might help in product design—for example: What do you keep in a dresser? What do you place on the dresser top? What do you keep in the first drawer? Second drawer? And so on. Sometimes, the consumers themselves suggest ideas which will help in the design of a useful, marketable product.

Finally, some manufacturers enclose customer questionnaires with their products. This technique is helpful because it allows them to determine who is buying the product. This information often provides ideas which lead to product improvements, resulting in better service to customers.

8-1. *Left:* These consumers are providing data by expressing their opinions about bedroom furniture. By completing the questionnaire distributed by a marketing research firm, they are providing valuable information which can be used by the manufacturer when modifying existing suites or planning new introductions. *Right:* The members of this consumer panel are giving their impressions of advertisements being considered by a case-goods manufacturer. By soliciting input from consumers, manufacturers can be better assured that their ads will generate the desired reaction when viewed by potential customers in the marketplace. *(Thomasville Furniture Industries)*

Over the years, a number of large consumer studies by national marketing research firms have been funded by the entire industry. These have been designed to provide information on consumers, their spending patterns, and other data of interest to all manufacturers or retailers.

RETAIL MARKETING RESEARCH AND INFORMATION SYSTEMS

Successful furniture retailers also base their decisions on several types of marketing research. Again, much of this information is gathered through processing information generated in normal business operations. It merely involves formulating criteria and setting up a marketing information system to make available the needed information.

Retailers, like manufacturers, can profit from using data from both outside and inside the organization.

DATA AVAILABLE FROM OUTSIDE SOURCES

A considerable amount of information is available from outside sources to give retailers trading area statistics and other information that reveals attractive marketing opportunities. These outside sources include:

Lea
LEA INDUSTRIES

1. Where did you purchase your Lea furniture?
   (a) Name of Store_____
   (b) City/State_____

2. What type of store is it? (Check one)
   (a)___Furniture store
   (b)___Warehouse showroom
   (c)___Sears, Penney's, Wards
   (d)___Regular department store
   (e)___Specialty store (like "Sleep Shop," etc.)

3. What were the three most important reasons for choosing this particular furniture?
   Write in "1" for the first, "2" for the second, and "3" for the third most important attraction.
   (a)___Workmanship   (f)___Color
   (b)___Size   (g)___Price
   (c)___Wood used   (h)___Immediately
   (d)___Style   available
   (e)___Finish   (i)___Good brand

4. For what room of the house was the furniture purchased?
   (a)___Living room   (e)___Master bedroom
   (b)___Family room   (f)___Son's room
   (c)___Dining room   (g)___Daughter's room
   (d)___Kitchen/Kitchenette (h)___Other bedroom

5. Are you satisfied with your furniture?
   (a)___Completely satisifed
   (b)___Somewhat satisified
   (c)___Somewhat dissatisified
   (d)___Completely dissatisified

6. If you are dissatisfied with the construction of your furniture, please check the problem area:
   (a)___Quality   (f)___Drawer construction
   (b)___Missing piece (g)___Hardware
   (c)___Finish   (h)___Dents, nicks, and
   (d)___Backing   cracks
   (e)___Parts do not fit (i)___Split wood

7. Please match complaint(s) you checked above to the piece of furniture you purchased by writing the letter of the complaint opposite the piece or pieces listed below:
   (a)___Chest   (f)___Mirror
   (b)___Bed/Headboard (g)___Table
   (c)___Four poster   (h)___Chair
   (d)___Dresser   (i)___Hutch/Desk
   (e)___Night stand   (j)___Desk

8. Please check below any other home furnishings you may have bought around the same time or just after you bought your Lea furniture.

	Same Time	Just After
(a) Other furniture	_____	_____
(b) Carpet	_____	_____
(c) Drapes/Shades	_____	_____

(d) Lamps	_____	_____
(e) Bedspreads/Linens	_____	_____
(f) Art/Wall hangings	_____	_____
(g) Mattress/Boxsprings	_____	_____

   PLEASE TELL US ABOUT YOU AS PURCHASER

9. (a)___Married   (b)___Single

10. Your age:
    (a)___18-34   (c)___45-54
    (b)___35-44   (d)___55 & over

11. Your education:
    (a)___Grade school   (c)___College
    (b)___High school   (d)___Graduate school

    DESCRIBE YOUR HOUSEHOLD (THESE QUESTIONS ARE FOR CLASSIFICATION ONLY)

12. In what type of dwelling do you live?
    (a)___Single-family residence (d)___Condominium
    (b)___Duplex (two-family house) (e)___Other
    (c)___Apartment

13. Do you: (a)___Own   (b)___Rent?

14. Please check number of adults in your household?
    (a)___One   (c)___Three
    (b)___Two   (d)___Four or more

15. Please write in number of children living at home:
    (a)___Under 6 years of age
    (b)___6-11 years of age
    (c)___12 years & over

16. Please check total household income:
    (a)___Under $7,000   (d)___$15,000 - $25,000
    (b)___$7,000 - $10,000   (e)___$25,000 - $35,000
    (c)___$10,000 - $15,000   (f)___$35,000 & over

17. THANK YOU VERY MUCH. Do you have any comments you would care to share with us?

    _____
    _____
    _____
    _____

17. OPTIONAL

    Name_____

    Address_____

    City & State_____Zip_____

8-2. This questionnaire, attached to Lea furniture, helps the manufacturer formulate a customer profile. By filling out and returning forms such as this after their purchase has been delivered, consumers give manufacturers some idea of who is buying their furniture, and why. (*Lea Industries*)

Government agencies. Many retailers use statistics available from government agencies. Some U.S. Department of Commerce publications list the type of information that is collected and disseminated by these agencies. The Census of Business contains "Retail Trade—Subject Reports" and "Retail Trade—Area Statistics." These publications have statistics on the type, location, sales payroll, and size of retail stores, which is helpful information for learning about the competitive retailing environment in an area.

To determine purchasing power in an area, the U.S. Department of Commerce issues a publication entitled "County Business Patterns." It provides information on total employees, total amount of payrolls, and employees by employer size, broken down by state, county, standard metropolitan statistical areas, and industry. This information would be helpful to a retailer contemplating a change in location or opening a branch outlet.

Census tract data from the U. S. Department of Commerce is also useful, helping retailers learn more about their customers from the large amount of demographic information it provides.

Trade associations. Trade association statistics are an excellent source of information for the retailer. Of particular interest is the annual "Operating Experience Report" published by the National Home Furnishings Association (NHFA), a leading association of furniture retailers. It provides average operating statistics by store size and location. Comparisons are provided by product category on profitability, liquidity, sales per square foot, average transaction size, percentage of cash versus credit sales, and percentages of various types of operating expenses. National averages usually cannot be interpreted as absolute standards, but they are useful as guidelines and for comparison purposes. The retailer can compare performance against retailers of similar size and, therefore, identify possible problem areas.

Private organizations. A number of private organizations periodically provide research such as consumer profiles and motivation information. These organizations include marketing research organizations, management consultants, advertising agencies, and various media. A typical study might include a profile of consumers buying various categories of home furnishings.

Various media, such as magazines, radio, television, and newspapers, regularly combine and publish useful data. Some of it includes local shopping patterns and may be used by the retailer to determine who shops where. This data is normally inexpensive, or even free to buyers of advertising space or time.

Other outside sources. Local organizations, such as Chambers of Commerce and retail merchants associations, often compile helpful information for the furniture merchant. Employment information and credit statistics are two types of data available from these organizations.

INTERNALLY GENERATED REPORTS AND RECORDS

Helpful information can also be generated through normal retail business operations. Among the reports that should definitely be prepared and used are the following:

Sales reports. Examples of the types of sales reports that are good management tools include:

1. *Sales by salesperson.* This type of report indicates which salespeople are most productive. It can be utilized in motivating better performance.
2. *Sales by merchandise classification or department.* This report serves a great need in sales analysis. For example, it is helpful in analyzing categories, such as bedroom, dining-room, and living-room upholstery, and the various styles within each. This report format can pinpoint slow-moving items or categories in need of special attention or replacement. It can also reveal changes in consumer tastes and indicate trends.
3. *Sales by store.* Organizations with more than one store can use this report to evaluate and compare the performance of individual stores.

Vendor analysis reports. Vendors should be constantly evaluated to determine their value to the retail store. Their performance should be monitored to determine profitability and turnover on their product and if they are delivering as promised, promptly taking care of customer complaints and, in general, providing good service to the retailer. The sales turnover of their products is especially important and indicates if they are producing the products in demand by consumers.

Retailing management should be aware of what is going on in the warehouse. It is important that merchandise be received and inspected professionally so that it can be delivered in good condition to the customer. Such costs need to be monitored and controlled. If there are recurring problems with a particular manufacturer, actual repair and damage statistics can more effectively get the attention of the vendor involved.

Advertising records. The records indicate the cost effectiveness of the store's advertising. They can show the relative effectiveness of various advertisements, using different media. Advertising expenses by merchandise category should also be monitored.

Customer records. Another valuable source of information is customer records. For example, by sampling charge account customers or cash sales tickets and plotting the addresses of customers, it is possible to determine where they live. It is important for a store to know as much as possible about its customers, who they are and where they reside.

Data obtained from salespeople. Salespeople should be encouraged to provide their input to the marketing operations of the retail store. Often, they hear comments from consumers which can result in improved sales.

```
NHFA SHOPPER INFORMATION PROFILE -- EXIT INTERVIEW

Date/Time: _____ AM PM  Interviewer: _____  Store: _____

1.  Is this your first visit to this location? ( ) YES ( ) NO
    Purpose of visit if learned ( ) "LOOKING" ( ) PURCHASE ( ) SERVICE

2.  What brought you to this store originally? ( ) LOCATION ( ) REFERRAL
    ( ) PREVIOUS PURCHASE ( ) ADVERTISING ( ) SPECIAL EVENT ( ) IMAGE
    If advertising/publicity, what type? ( ) NEWSPAPER ( ) RADIO ( ) TV
    ( ) WINDOW DISPLAYS ( ) STORE EXTERIOR APPEARANCE ( ) SPECIAL EVENT
    ( ) OTHER:

3.  In general, do you like the way the store is arranged and the way in which
    merchandise is displayed? ( ) YES ( ) NO

4.  How could store arrangement and displays be improved?
    a) More room displays? ( ) YES ( ) NO ( ) ABOUT RIGHT
    b) More product group displays? ( ) YES ( ) NO ( ) ABOUT RIGHT
    c) More displays by style? (e.g. "Mediterranean") ( ) YES ( ) NO
       ( ) ABOUT RIGHT
    d) Are items or displays easy to find? ( ) YES ( ) NO ( ) ABOUT RIGHT
    e) Are enough accessories on display? ( ) YES ( ) NO ( ) ABOUT RIGHT

5.  Did you get the information, service or assistance you needed or wanted on
    this visit? ( ) YES ( ) NO ( ) PARTIALLY
    How could this situation have been improved, if any?

6.  Did you find what you were looking for? ( ) YES ( ) NO
    a) If YES, did you purchase it? ( ) YES ( ) NO ( ) MAYBE LATER
    b) If NO, would you mind telling me why not?
    c) What was it you were looking for?

7.  How would you rank this store on the following factors, using GOOD, AVERAGE,
    POOR, and "DON'T KNOW," or "NO OPINION" as your rankings?

                                             GOOD  AVG.  POOR  D.K.  N.O.

    a) Store location & accessibility
    b) Merchandise variety
    c) Price ranges offered
    d) Value for the money
    e) Delivery & service
    f) Quality lines offered
    g) Complaint handling & adjustments
    h) Credit policies & plants
    i) Price-marking system
    j) Friendliness of personnel

8.  What impressed you the most about store?

    What impressed you the least?

9.  Would you recommend this store to a friend? ( ) YES ( ) NO

10. Would you please give us some general information about yourself?
    ( ) Under 25 ( ) 25 to 35 ( ) Over 35
    ( ) Single ( ) Married ( ) Engaged
    ( ) No. children  Ages:
    Occupations: (HIS)_____(HERS)_____
    Where do you live?
    Is that a ( ) HOME ( ) APARTMENT ( ) TOWNHOUSE ( ) CONDOMINIUM?
    Do you ( ) OWN, or ( ) RENT?

THANK YOU FOR YOUR HELP!
```

8-3. The National Home Furnishings Association has prepared this sample exit interview which its members may conduct with their customers. In this way, the retailers will get more information about their shoppers. *(National Home Furnishings Association)*

CUSTOMER EVALUATION CARD				

Questionnaire

	Excellent	Good	Fair	Poor
Our merchandise selection was	☐	☐	☐	☐
Our prices were	☐	☐	☐	☐
Our merchandise quality was	☐	☐	☐	☐

My salesperson was: Yes No

helpful . . . . ☐ ☐

courteous . . . . ☐ ☐

knowledgeable . . . . ☐ ☐

The office staff was: Yes No

helpful . . . . ☐ ☐

courteous . . . . ☐ ☐

efficient . . . . ☐ ☐

The warehouse or delivery staff was: Yes No

helpful . . . . ☐ ☐

courteous . . . . ☐ ☐

efficient . . . . ☐ ☐

Please put my name on your preferred customer list for mailings about sale events. ☐

Telephone No. _____

Name _____

Address _____

City, State _____   ZIP CODE

8-4. This sample customer evaluation card, prepared by the NHFA, allows retailers to poll consumers who buy from them. The card is usually mailed along with the customer's statement or is given to the customer at the time of purchase. The information provided gives the retailer a means of evaluating consumer opinion of the store. *(National Home Furnishings Association)*

They may discover easier ways to close a sale or other techniques that would be helpful to other salespeople in the organization. Information obtained from this source can be used effectively in sale meetings and sales training sessions.

SUMMARY

Marketing research is the systematic gathering, recording, and analyzing of data about problems relating to the marketing of goods and services. Many manufacturers and retailers are setting up marketing information systems to provide needed data on a continual basis.

Marketing research and information are important for a variety of reasons:
- There is a shortened time for decision-making.
- The furniture industry is highly competitive.
- The furniture distribution system is complex.
- Technological developments in production methods and materials have occurred.

- Furniture purchasing can be postponed.
- A furniture purchase is intensely personal.
- It is a necessary tool in management control and decision-making.
- It is necessary for accurate sales forecasting.

Marketing data may be primary (collected for the problem at hand) or secondary (collected prior to that time for some other purpose).

Manufacturers obtain outside data from government agencies, trade associations, and private organizations. They use many internally generated reports and records, such as sales reports, inventory reports, return and damage reports, and advertising records. Manufacturer's sales reports are typically by salesperson and territory, suite, type of piece, fabric type, finish, color, style category, placements by suite or piece, and type or size of dealer. Manufacturers obtain very helpful information from dealers, salespeople, and consumers.

Retailers obtain outside data from the government, trade associations, private organizations, and others. Retailers also use many internally generated reports and records: sales reports, vendor analysis reports, advertising records, and customer records. Retailer sales reports are usually by salesperson, merchandise classification or department, and store. Retailers can also obtain valuable marketing insights from their floor salespeople.

CHAPTER 9

THE ULTIMATE CONSUMER MARKET

The focus throughout the furniture industry is on the ultimate consumer whose purchases determine the profitability of both manufacturers and retailers. Therefore, the consumer must perceive that his or her needs are being met before products are sold and profits made. When manufacturers introduce products and retailers stock them, it is with the hope that the consumer will find them sufficiently attractive to be purchased.

MARKET FORECASTING

Manufacturers and retailers are engaging in market forecasting when they commit themselves to producing or stocking a certain number of suites. While much market forecasting is informal, three components are necessary in generating enough sales for profits to be made. The first component is *people*. In other words, there must be consumers who have a need for the furniture. The second component is *money*. A market cannot generate sales if the people do not have money to spend or cannot qualify for credit. The third component is the *willingness to spend*. People must be willing to exchange their money or credit for the furniture.

The importance of these three components is evident in *Sales and Marketing Management* magazine's annual buying power index for more densely populated areas throughout the United States. This buying power index is based on a weighted average of population, which indicates the number of people; effective buying income, which indicates money available; and retail sales, which indicates a willingness to spend money. The buying power index has been recognized as a valuable tool for sales forecasting by many furniture manufacturers.

MARKET SEGMENTATION

The ultimate consumer market is not a mass of individuals with similar likes and dislikes who buy similar furniture or respond to the same marketing approaches. Rather, the consumer market in the United States is

106

made up of diverse segments, each with its own unique characteristics and requirements.

Successful marketers do not try to sell the entire market, but instead focus their product offerings toward the needs of specific market segments, which become a company's target markets. For a particular company, a worthwhile target market would be a segment that is fairly homogeneous in its need for products and style preferences, and in its probable response to advertising, sales promotion, and personal selling techniques. It must also have a sufficient number of people with purchasing power, as indicated by the availability of money or credit-worthiness and the willingness to purchase.

A manufacturer may appeal to more than one market segment, depending on its size and production and marketing capabilities. Likewise, larger retailers usually appeal to more than one market segment. However, it is impossible for any one manufacturer or retailer to appeal to everyone. It is important for the manufacturer or retailer to have a clear image in the marketplace so that consumers will know what products and services to expect from the company.

Market segmentation is helpful to both the manufacturer and retailer because it provides a clearly defined group that can be carefully studied. By closely looking at these market segments, the manufacturer and retailer can determine the types of products that will appeal to them. Market segmentation allows advertising, personal selling, and sales promotion to be more effective. It also assists the retailer to focus more sharply all of his merchandising activities.

There are a variety of ways to segment a market. The two most widely utilized are *demographics* and *psychographics*. Demographics are the vital statistics of a population—characteristics such as age, sex, occupation, and income which help to describe a target market segment. Psychographics, or life-style analysis, involves segmenting a market based on personality characteristics and the differences in the ways that people live. Terms often referred to in psychographic segmentation include "conformity," "traditional life-style," "sophistication," "contentment," "discontent," "career seeker," and "career achiever." Both demographics and psychographics have an impact on the patterns of consumer purchasing and should be considered by the furniture marketer.

TRENDS IN THE MARKETPLACE

The marketplace does not stay the same for very long. The relative size of various market segments is constantly changing. Therefore, the furniture marketer should consider the various shifts in the marketplace when preparing sales forecasts and making plans. Of particular interest in furniture marketing are demographic and social trends. For example, recent U. S. Department of Commerce figures indicate a rise in the 35–44 age group since 1970, a trend expected to continue until the year 2000. This trend is of particular interest to furniture marketers because this period in the life cycle is one of peak earnings which can be tapped for the purchase of home furnishings. Trends in income, home purchasing, and other demographic factors are also of importance.

Social trends are of concern to the furniture marketer. Changes in the percentage of the population in the various social classes have an impact on the type and price structure of furniture purchased. Marriage, separation, and divorce rates should be noted because these events usually trigger the purchase of additional furniture.

THE FURNITURE BUYING PROCESS

Furniture may be classified as a conspicuous durable product because it is a large item with a definite style which may be observed by anyone entering the home. It is durable because it lasts a relatively long time. Rarely is the purchase of furniture an urgent necessity, meaning that the purchase normally may be postponed a relatively long time. These characteristics have an effect on the furniture buying process, which is divided into a number of definite stages.

9-1. The furniture buying process

Aroused need. An aroused need is the stimulus that causes someone to do something. When considering furniture, this aroused need may be highly conscious or almost unconscious. It may result from going into someone else's home and thinking that his furnishings are better or prettier than one's own furnishings. Or, it might result from a nagging backache incurred by sleeping on a worn-out mattress. Regardless of its origin, the aroused need starts the consumer looking for ways to satisfy the need.

Looking and shopping. This is the second stage in the furniture buying process. Since furniture, for most people, would be considered a specialty consumer product, this stage may be rather lengthy. After all, furniture is a relatively high-priced conspicuous product that reflects the personality of the purchaser and, therefore, its purchase will be given special care and attention.

Looking may consist of taking note of other people's furniture and mentally recording one's likes and dislikes. It can also involve reading home furnishings articles in magazines or newspapers. Or, it might include interviewing three or four interior designers to see if any of them understands the consumer's needs and can help to solve them.

The shopping may begin with looking at advertisements to see which products are available at various stores or what is on sale. Shopping inevitably involves visiting more than one retail furniture store or other

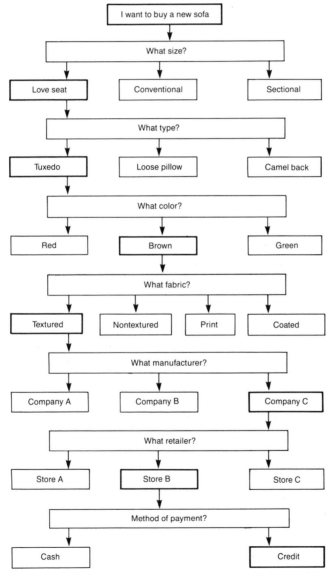

9-2. Buying decision for a sofa

retail outlet selling furniture. Or, it might involve working with an interior designer.

It is at this point that the furniture marketer can begin to make an impact by using well-conceived advertisements. Such ads serve as cues that purchasing the furniture of a particular manufacturer or at a particular store will meet the special needs of the consumer. Having well-designed window displays and a convenient store location are two other ways the retailer may help the consumer with shopping.

Buying decision. The buying decision is really a culmination of many small decisions. Figure 9-2 on page 109 is a simplified illustration of buying a sofa; all the alternatives are not given, but it does indicate some of the decisions required when buying furniture. It is during this process that the furniture retailer can make a difference by providing the right combination of merchandise, information, and services in the store.

Use of the product. This stage in the furniture buying process occurs after the product arrives in the home. The consumer has purchased the furniture to satisfy a need, and the merchandise must satisfy that need if the consumer is to buy again.

The furniture manufacturer should be concerned with how the product is to be used so that it can be designed and constructed to stand up to the demands of the consumer. Valid considerations include who will use it, how it will be used, and when it will be used. For example, a family-room sofa in a household with small children should have a strong frame and be covered with a stain-resistant, durable fabric.

Postpurchase attitudes. These are the feelings that inevitably result from buying and using an article of furniture. It is largely on the basis of these attitudes that the consumer decides whether to use the same retailer or to buy the same brand of furniture. It is to the advantage of the manufacturer and retailer to represent their products fairly and take care of consumer complaints and problems quickly.

FACTORS AFFECTING CONSUMER FURNITURE PURCHASES

A number of factors have an influence on all aspects of the furniture buying process:
- Social influences
- Psychological traits
- Perceptions
- Stage in the life cycle
- Consumer expectations
- Income

SOCIAL INFLUENCES
People are social beings, constantly interacting with each other and with the man-made part of the environment. Since furniture is a conspicuous

product, social influences are present when it is purchased. Several social groups have an influence on the purchase of furniture:

The family has a constant influence on all purchases made by the household, and this is especially true with furniture. A family having twin sons or two sons close together in age might purchase bunk beds to provide sleeping accommodations while taking up a small amount of floor space. A family with no small children might choose living-room upholstery fabric because of its beauty, without necessarily considering durability and stain resistance.

Face-to-face groups are those people with whom one interacts on a daily basis. Face-to-face groups influence furniture purchases because decisions are often made to keep up with the neighbors or, perhaps, to avoid repeating the mistakes of others. Frequently, possibilities are talked over with the members of these groups and advice is solicited before purchases are made.

Social class has an influence on consumer purchasing. Although, comparatively speaking, there are few class distinctions in the United States, the types of products purchased and the outlets patronized vary from social class to social class. The determinants of social class in the United States include occupation and title of the "breadwinner," educational level attained, and the neighborhood in which the family lives. Specific retail outlets tend to cater more to one social class than another, even though two families in different social classes may have the same income. To a lesser degree, the same thing is true with furniture manufacturers.

Reference group influence is also a factor in the purchase of furniture. A reference group is a group to which a person consciously or unconsciously refers when making a purchase decision. In other words, it is human nature for a furniture buyer to measure his or her choices against the choices of others. The reference group may be a face-to-face group, friends or coworkers, or it may be celebrities or members of a group to which the purchaser aspires to belong.

Culture influences the purchase of furniture. The simplest definition of culture is that it is the man-made part of one's environment. It includes the structures of our businesses, methods of distributing furniture, architecture, home furnishings, clothes, and life-cycle activities. The architecture of one's home, for example, certainly influences the type of furnishings purchased.

PSYCHOLOGICAL TRAITS

The attitudes, opinions, and other psychological traits of consumers influence their purchases, including the type of furniture purchased as well as the type of outlet from which it is bought. Some people are essentially positive in nature, while others are fundamentally negative. Some seek pleasure, while others are quiet individuals who prefer rather sedate forms of entertainment. Some are traditional, contented individuals, while others are discontented with their life-styles or station in life.

Home furnishings are considered an extension of an individual's personality, making the purchase of furniture a sensitive issue. It has been widely reported that it is one of the most traumatic events in a person's life. This is primarily because of the personal nature of the purchase, which reflects one's tastes to others, and the diversity of product offerings in the marketplace.

PERCEPTIONS

Perceptions, or the unique way a person looks at products, purchasing alternatives, and life in general, influence the purchasing of furniture. Each person places different values on the home. For example, one person places more emphasis on it and its furnishings than does another. One person may consider home furnishings to be status symbols, while another may consider the main status symbol to be an automobile.

It is possible to identify the unique perceptions of various market segments and to build promotional campaigns to influence favorably individuals within these segments toward the purchase of a company's furniture. The term *perceived value* is sometimes used by marketers to mean that the consumer must perceive that there is sufficient value in buying a particular manufacturer's products from a designated store before the purchase will take place.

STAGE IN THE LIFE CYCLE

The need to buy furniture is not uniform throughout a person's life cycle. In fact, seven stages have been identified as times when people are most likely to buy furniture:

1. Young, single people on their own. When a young person leaves home for the first time, he or she is likely to buy furniture for an apartment. It is usually basic furniture because of a lack of money and, often at this stage, the status symbols are cars, recreation products, or other nonfurniture items.

2. Newly married couples. A considerable amount is spent on furniture in the months before and after a wedding, usually for furniture with an eye toward durability and value. When two people are starting their lives together, furniture is likely to be one of their major expenditures.

3. When children arrive. The arrival of children necessitates the purchase of furniture for the child's room. Many manufacturers are attempting to correlate juvenile furniture with other groups as a way of convincing parents that furniture purchased initially for a child's room can be used for a longer period of time.

4. When the family economic status improves. An improvement in family economic status may be caused by a parent returning to work after the children are in school or old enough to look after themselves, or it may result from a promotion or job change. Regardless of the reason, the family can now afford better furnishings.

5. When the children become teenagers. With small children no longer in the home, furniture has less chance of being bumped into, spilled on, or otherwise damaged. Therefore, families once again are likely to enter the marketplace to replace the furniture that they have had since the children were much younger. By this time, they are probably tired of the old furniture and are ready for a change.

6. When people retire. A common event when people retire is to sell the family home and move into smaller quarters. This may involve a move to a condominium in a Sunbelt state. With this move, the couple is likely, once again, to desire new furniture.

7. Separation and divorce. The rising separation and divorce rate is creating a seventh stage in life for some individuals to purchase furniture. When a household is dissolved, two separate households are created. Therefore, there is an increased demand for furniture by one or both of these households.

Usually, no single marketing strategy will effectively reach all of the life cycle stages. Each requires a separate appeal. Care should be taken to construct a marketing approach that will be effective in each stage of life.

CONSUMER EXPECTATIONS

The purchase of furniture is affected by what consumers expect will happen in the future. Are good or bad economic times ahead? If their expectations are optimistic, they will be more likely to buy.

The expectation of rising prices caused by inflation sometimes has an impact on furniture purchases. If consumers feel that prices are going to rise, they may buy now rather than wait until later when the purchase will cost more.

INCOME

For most consumers, furniture products represent a sizable purchase or one that will absorb a significant amount of current income or, in the case of credit purchases, future income. Therefore, the presence of sufficient income to make the furniture purchase seem affordable is a factor affecting furniture purchases by consumers.

THE FURNITURE MARKETER'S RESPONSIBILITY TO THE CONSUMER

Since furniture is such a personal purchase with a high price tag, consumers expect quality, professional presentation of the product, and someone to listen to their needs and problems. They want someone to present the product fairly and honestly, expecting it to be designed and manufactured at a price they consider to provide good value.

Several potential problems are inherent in the purchase of furniture. First, the consumer is buying a product that is both a work of art and a functional piece of furniture. This means that arms or legs may be attached to a chair at odd angles for a graceful appearance, yet the consumer expects them to hold up well during use in the home.

Second, furniture has been manufactured largely out of two materials, wood and fabric, which contain inherent characteristics that may lead to consumer complaints. Wood is a relatively unstable commodity; it changes shape depending on such conditions as the weather and the amount of moisture in the air. Fabric is subject to deterioration when exposed to wear and will fade or change color under certain conditions.

The third potential problem arises out of misconceptions. The typical purchaser has little experience buying furniture and, therefore, is easy prey for an unscrupulous furniture salesperson who is willing to say almost anything to get a sale.

Fourth, since the purchase of furniture is so complex, with a seemingly endless variety of options, there is a fairly high possibility that the consumer will have misgivings once the furniture is in the home. The chair may be too big or the wrong color. The husband may not like the product the wife picked out. Or the furniture simply looks different than it did in the store. All of these possibilities may lead the consumer to want to return the product.

Fifth, the possibility of real damage or manufacturing defects is high because furniture is a relatively complex product involving numerous materials put together by people and machinery. If quality control is not adequate, or if problems arise beyond the control of the manufacturer, shipper, or retailer, the consumer may be dissatisfied.

There are comparatively few guarantees or formal plans for servicing the furniture products bought by the consumer. Currently, the retailer is the one the consumer most often contacts when demanding answers and service. Today's consumer expects to get a fair hearing regarding questions or complaints arising out of the purchase of furniture.

Complaints regarding defective products or products failing to perform satisfactorily under normal conditions in the home are usually handled informally between the manufacturer and retailer. An attempt is made to find a mutually acceptable solution on a case-by-case basis. Situations not resolved in this manner may be referred to the Furniture Industry Consumer Action Panel for advice and resolution.

FURNITURE INDUSTRY CONSUMER ACTION PANEL

The Furniture Industry Consumer Action Panel (FICAP) is an attempt by the industry to promote good relations between furniture marketers and consumers. Sponsored by the American Furniture Manufacturer's Association, FICAP has been designed to:

- Encourage the industry to meet the highest ethical standards in the sale and promotion of its products.

- Encourage the industry to distribute and utilize consumer education materials.
- Provide advice for the prompt, fair, and equitable resolution of consumer complaints.
- Identify problem areas of consumers with their furniture purchases and to advise the industry accordingly.

The complaint procedure established through FICAP provides for a third party to hear appeals from consumers who have not received a satisfactory resolution of their legitimate complaints from the retailer or manufacturer. The panel, composed of businesspeople, manufacturers, retailers, consumers, and educators, will hear the complaints and, within a reasonable time, issue its opinion as to the solution which it deems to be most fair to all parties involved.

HOW TO BUILD BELIEVABILITY INTO MARKETING PLANS

Regardless of the possibility of dissatisfaction, consumers still desire to buy useful products and to be satisfied with their purchases. Therefore, good furniture marketers should try to build credibility into their marketing plans because believability motivates consumers. There are a number of techniques useful for making marketing materials more believable, including:

1. Presenting straightforward, *honest* advertising, personal sales messages, and sales promotion which indicate how the consumer will personally benefit from using or possessing the product. Consumers are interested in themselves first of all and want to know how they can realistically benefit from the product.
2. Providing product features that back up claimed benefits helps to make messages believable. Benefit claims that cannot be backed up by facts or tangible features sound hollow or unbelievable.
3. Having a long-standing record of continual good customer service gives consumers extra confidence. For example, if a company has been producing products for fifty years, it must have been doing some things right. This point can be promoted and lead to increased sales.
4. Testimonials give believability to sales messages. For example, a famous sports figure endorsing a specific brand of recliner enhances credibility in the minds of certain consumers.

SUMMARY

Satisfying the ultimate consumer is the key to profitability in the furniture industry. Both manufacturers and retailers must correctly forecast sales to consumers in order to be successful and generate adequate profits.

A meaningful market for a specific product is composed of people, money, and the willingness to spend that money.

The ultimate consumer market is composed of many diverse segments so the effective furniture marketer must practice realistic market segmentation. Market segmentation is largely based on demographics, or vital statistics of the population, and psychographics, or life-style analysis. The progressive furniture marketer considers both demographic and social trends when developing marketing plans.

The furniture buying process consists of an aroused need, looking and shopping, the buying decision, use of the product, and postpurchase attitudes.

Nothing happens until the consumer feels an aroused need that causes action. Shopping for furniture includes many activities, from taking note of other people's furnishings to comparing the offerings in various stores. The buying decision is really a culmination of many separate decisions—from what store, to what color, to what payment plan. Use of the product is important in the purchase decision because it determines consumer satisfaction and whether the store will be shopped again or the manufacturer's products purchased a second time.

Factors affecting consumer furniture purchases include social influences, psychological traits, perceptions, stage in the life cycle, consumer expectations, and income.

Social influences that affect consumer furniture purchases are: the family, face-to-face groups, social class, reference groups, and culture.

The consumer is more likely to buy furniture during the following stages in the life cycle: (1) young, single people on their own; (2) newly married couples; (3) when children arrive; (4) when the family economic status improves; (5) when the children become teenagers; (6) when people retire; and (7) separation and divorce.

The consumer expects fairness and honesty from the furniture marketer. However, potential problems may arise because: furniture is a functional art form, composed largely of wood and fabric; the consumer is unskilled and inexperienced in purchasing furniture; there is such a large number of optional products from which to choose that the consumer may change his or her mind; and furniture is a complex product to manufacture.

Most consumer complaints are handled informally by the retailer or the retailer in conjunction with the manufacturer. The Furniture Industry Consumer Action Panel (FICAP) promotes goodwill between the industry and the consumer and hears legitimate complaints between the consumer and the retailer or manufacturer that cannot otherwise be resolved.

The furniture marketer can build believability into sales messages by showing honestly how the products can personally benefit the consumer, backing up claimed benefits with product features, citing a long record of continual service, and using testimonials from satisfied customers or celebrities.

CHAPTER 10

PRICING METHODS AND PRACTICES

Pricing in the furniture industry, as in many other industries, is a sensitive, carefully approached responsibility. When a manufacturer or retailer sets a price for products, the firm's niche in the marketplace, in relation to other manufacturers and retailers, is being set.

Because the furniture industry is highly fragmented, no one manufacturing company has sufficient market power to affect sales in the industry significantly by means of its pricing policies exclusively. The large amount of competition prevents artificially maintained prices from existing in the industry. The same situation is true in furniture retailing because of the large number of outlets where furniture may be purchased by the consumer.

Pricing methods and practices vary widely throughout the industry, depending on costs, management philosophy, and many other factors which will be discussed in detail in this chapter. However, although profit objectives vary, prices are obviously established with the goal of allowing the firm to be satisfactorily profitable.

WHAT IS PRICE?

Although *price* is a commonly used word, the furniture marketer must realize the actual significance of it. In essence, price is value, which means that the seller is expressing in monetary terms the relative worth of the product. Although many factors must be considered in establishing prices, the marketer is really making an educated guess that the product will sell at a given price. Of course, it usually is more than a guess, in that the marketing manager will be knowledgeable about competitors' prices.

Price is an indicator of the relative "want-satisfying" power of a product. A correct price means that the consumer will perceive that the product is worth the asking price and will exchange that amount of money for it. Therefore, price must fit the image of the company and both must be appropriate for the niche in the marketplace the company is attempting to occupy. The products, services, and integrity of the company must support the pricing if the company is to be successful.

The *retail price point* is an important consideration throughout the furniture industry. It is the stated price at retail on a suite or individual piece of furniture. Manufacturers produce and retailers buy to sell at the retail price points where they feel the demand for their products exists.

MANUFACTURERS' CONSIDERATIONS IN PRICING

Although manufacturers offer different products and occupy different niches in the marketplace, there are a number of common considerations or factors that enter the pricing process:

- Pricing objectives
- Complete cost data
- Consumer demand
- Economic factors
- Governmental actions
- Freight charges to dealers
- Discounts and allowances
- Nonprice factors

PRICING OBJECTIVES

Clearly defined objectives are essential to proper price determination. These objectives should be set before the firm decides which products to offer; without a target, the marketing team will be at a loss to know exactly how to establish the price or even what degree of quality and detail to offer in their products. Pricing objectives include a *fiscal* objective based on profit and/or a *marketing* objective that considers the relative position of competing firms.

Target return pricing is an example of a fiscal pricing objective; it sets a prescribed profit figure as a goal. For example, a manufacturer may establish the figure of a 5 percent after-tax profit as the target return. On the basis of estimated costs, demand, and other factors, a price will be established sufficient for the company to pay their taxes and still have 5 percent of its dollar sales volume left over as net profit.

Another objective is simply to match the prices of the competition. *Follow-the-leader pricing* is aimed at keeping the firm's prices in line with the prices of major competitors. This approach avoids a price war and allows the firm to stress the nonprice aspects of its marketing efforts. In other words, many furniture manufacturers match major competitors' prices while trying to gain a competitive advantage by stressing nonprice factors such as styling, service, and quality control.

A related objective is used as a guide by those manufacturers who feel they have better design, name recognition, quality, and service than the immediate competition. These manufacturers simply price 10 percent or so above competition to reflect these features.

Other manufacturers seek to undercut competitors' prices with *penetra-*

tion pricing. Some furniture manufacturers have the objective of consistently lower prices on their products than their competition. With this objective, the manufacturer is emphasizing price and telling the world that the most important aspect of its marketing effort is to have the lowest price in the product category. This objective requires good marketing intelligence to know what other firms are charging for their products. Normally, if the business is based on having lower prices than competitors, the firm must have sufficient volume to compensate for the lower profit margin.

Prestige pricing is placing a higher price on the product to indicate better quality with a prestige image. There must be a considerable amount of good design, quality, and service to back up a prestige price. However, the proper advertising and dealer structure can also help to convince the consumer that the product is worth the higher price. There is a certain amount of "snob appeal" to some consumers when they are able to buy products that others cannot afford.

COMPLETE COST DATA

The manufacturer's pricing objectives must be tempered by the actual costs of doing business. The costs of production, raw materials, administrative support, and marketing the product must be included. Although techniques for cost collection are becoming more sophisticated, many of the costs used in setting prices are still estimates. The furniture industry, to some extent, continues to be a craft industry, making accurate cost collection extremely difficult. In other words, the exact cost of producing a piece of furniture depends on the skill and energy level of the worker. For example, two upholstered chairs produced at the same plant may actually cost different amounts because they were constructed and upholstered by different workers who worked at different rates.

CONSUMER DEMAND

The manufacturer must estimate consumer demand at the various price levels for the type and style of merchandise being sold. This estimate should be based on the best information possible for factors such as income and employment which have an impact on furniture purchasing. This information is then considered by the furniture marketer whose experience and intuition help establish a price for the products. This price must be low enough to allow the retailer and other middlemen involved in the channel of distribution to add their markups and still have a retail price that is considered reasonable by the consumer. The manufacturer must constantly be concerned that the retail price point will not be objectionable to the consumer.

In estimating consumer demand at various price levels, the manufacturer must consider the prices of products with similar style and quality offered by competing firms for two reasons. First, consumer demand may not be sufficient to support any more products in a particular price/style/

product category. A realization of this fact may cause a manufacturer to enter another segment of the market that is less crowded. Second, a firm may be able to justify differences between the price of its product and that of a competing firm. However, unless the manufacturer has a recognized prestige, style, or quality image in the marketplace, there is a limit to the difference consumers will pay for a firm's products. Therefore, the manufacturer must be careful that products are not overpriced in relation to consumer demand as well as competition.

ECONOMIC FACTORS

There are a number of economic factors that must be considered in pricing a product. Since furniture purchases can be postponed, furniture manufacturers must consider the level of employment and income in the economy. If real disposable income is decreasing and unemployment is high, the demand for furniture will probably suffer.

Since demand drops during difficult economic times, many furniture manufacturers tend to price their products at or near the break-even point to capture as large a percentage of existing demand as possible. The emphasis is on providing the best possible value for the stated price. Under these conditions, the manufacturer is not likely to make much profit, but at least the plants will be kept operating.

On the other hand, in good economic times, with rising disposable income, a low level of unemployment, and a positive outlook on behalf of consumers, manufacturers will usually develop products in higher price categories or else price to allow a more satisfactory profit.

The prospect of inflation is another economic factor to be considered in pricing. If consumers expect a certain amount of inflation, they may be less resistant to price increases. Also, manufacturers must consider the likelihood that their suppliers could raise prices on raw materials when establishing prices for any length of time.

GOVERNMENTAL ACTIONS

Laws and government regulations have an impact on product pricing in the furniture industry. Antitrust and related laws forbid conspiracy in setting prices, which is not as relevant in the furniture industry because there are too many producers for any pricing agreements to be effective.

Government regulations also affect costs in the furniture industry, thereby having an impact on the price of the finished product. Everything from packaging requirements enforced by the Interstate Commerce Commission (ICC) to tagging requirements enforced by the Federal Trade Commission (FTC) affect the price of furniture.

Price discrimination has also been outlawed. For example, if a manufacturer makes a quantity discount available to one retailer, this discount must be available to all other retailers in the same trading area who buy in the same quantities.

FREIGHT CHARGES TO DEALERS

The prevailing practice in the furniture industry is to price the products *F.O.B.* (free on board) *Origin* or *F.O.B. Point of Production,* which means that the buyer pays the freight regardless of the type of transportation used to ship the product. Therefore, freight charges add to the retailer's cost of merchandise, and care should be taken to reduce the cost wherever possible. Progressive manufacturers work with retailers to reduce freight charges and thus minimize the price to the consumer.

DISCOUNTS AND ALLOWANCES

A number of discounts and allowances are built into furniture manufacturing pricing structures. These are price concessions designed to encourage wholesalers and retailers to pay promptly, aggressively promote the products, buy in volume, buy slow-moving items, and have defective goods repaired. Examples of discounts and allowances found in the industry include the following:

Trade, or *functional, discounts* are discounts allowed for the middleman's profit and expenses. Such discounts are not as evident in the furniture industry as in many other industries, where issuance of a retail price list is standard practice. Some manufacturers give a trade discount to wholesale furniture distributors who buy and then resell their furniture. For example, a wholesaler might get a 5 percent price reduction from a manufacturer's normal selling price as a trade discount.

Trade discounts are also widespread in selling business, institutional, and public building furniture, where manufacturers publish a retail price list. The dealer gets a price concession from that retail price based on his or her classification and the services rendered. For example, a company might have a 40 percent trade discount for architects and interior designers, a 50 percent trade discount for a nonstocking dealer, and a 50 percent discount plus an extra 10 percent discount for a dealer who stocks merchandise.

Cash discounts are price concessions allowed a customer for paying within a stated period of time. An example would be a sale involving terms of 2/10, n/30, which means that the buyer would get a 2 percent price reduction if he or she paid the bill within ten days. The entire amount of the bill is due within thirty days of the date of the invoice.

Quantity discounts are price reductions given the buyer who buys a specified amount of merchandise. For example, a manufacturer of recliners might have one price for dealers who buy from one to ten chairs at one time, a lower price for dealers who buy from ten to twenty chairs, and a still lower price for dealers who buy more than twenty chairs. These discounts are classified as noncumulative quantity discounts, which means the entire amount must be purchased in a single order to obtain the reduction in price.

A/R	SOLD TO SMITH FURN. CO. MARTINVILLE, VA. 24112		SHIP TO SMITH FURN. CO. MAIN ST MARTINVILLE, VA 24112		DATE 6-2-84	INVOICE NO. 881793
					SALESMAN STONE	

| 6
VENDOR NUMBER | 32456
CUSTOMER ORDER NO. | 1-13
ORDER DATE | DEPT. | NWZ217065
CAR NUMBER | | | | 23497321
ACKNOWLEDGEMENT NO. | COPIES TO |

MARK FOR	QUANTITY	PIECE	DESCRIPTION	UNIT PRICE	TOTAL
			3059		
	3	322	CH HUTCH	$181 50	$ 544 50
			2031		
REMIT TO	3	247	DR DRESSER BASE	278 00	834 00
	3	241	FR MIRROR	62 00	186 00
BASSETT FURNITURE IND.	3	251	CHEST-5DR	230 00	690 00
PO BOX 626	2	119	PANEL HEADBOARD	126 00	252 00
BASSETT, VA. 24055	1	199	CHAIRBACK HEADBOARD	171 00	171 00
PHONE 703-629-7511			3071		
D-U-N-S 312-4617	3	322	CH HUTCH	150 00	450 00
TERMS: 2% 30 DAYS NET 60	3	356	CH BASE	138 00	414 00
FROM DATE OF INVOICE	2	400	RECT. TABLE	115 00	230 00
F.O.B. SHIPPING POINT	1	401	RECT. TABLE	135 00	135 00
LATE PAYMENT CHARGE: 1¼% PER MONTH MINIMUM					

| **ORIGINAL** | | TOTAL $3,906.50 |

10-1. This manufacturer's invoice is sent to the customer (Smith Furniture Co.) as the merchandise leaves the manufacturer's (Bassett Furniture Industries) warehouse or plant. The buyer pays the freight because the merchandise is being shipped F.O.B. shipping point. The terms state that the buyer will get a 2% cash discount if it is paid within 30 days from the date of invoice. Regardless, the entire bill must be paid within 60 days from the date of invoice. If the bill is not paid by that time, the manufacturer will assess a late payment charge of 1½% per month.

Tie-in sales are sometimes offered to retailers as a way of balancing inventory. This technique involves placing an extremely attractive price on good-selling items, but requiring the purchase of other items to obtain that favorable price. For example: a case-goods manufacturer might have a popular, well-designed, pine Early American bedroom suite that dealers are eager to buy. The same manufacturer might also have a maple French bedroom suite that is not as popular, but is in large supply in his warehouse. By using a tie-in sale, the manufacturer might put a very attractive price on the popular pine suite if the dealer buys an equal number of the maple suites.

"Clearance" discounts are price reductions given to a dealer for buying obsolete or slow-moving inventories in large quantities. Many manufacturers only offer such discounts to clearance specialists who buy truckloads of merchandise, mismatches, incomplete suites, and other merchandise offered as a group. The reason for offering the discounts only to clearance specialists is that regular customers might be hesitant to pay full price on later occasions.

Promotional allowances are price concessions provided to compensate the retailer for aggressively advertising or attractively displaying a manufacturer's products. These allowances are sometimes in the form of a cooperative advertising refund. Retailers can receive funds or a credit to their account by proving that they have run advertising prominently featuring the manufacturer's products. Another example of a promotional allowance would be a manufacturer providing funds to help retailers install a manufacturer's gallery in their stores.

Defective goods allowance involves a manufacturer giving the retailer credit for repairing defective merchandise or selling it to the consumer at a discount. Often, the manufacturer would rather give a price reduction to encourage the dealer to keep the merchandise than to have it repacked and shipped back to the factory at the manufacturer's expense. Such a return shipment is expensive and merchandise could be damaged further. It should be noted that these allowances only apply to goods with manufacturer's defects. Claims for merchandise damaged in transit are filed by the retailer, and the recourse is against the carrier if the merchandise was packaged satisfactorily. The title for the merchandise normally passes to the purchaser when it leaves the manufacturer's loading dock.

NONPRICE FACTORS STRESSED BY MANUFACTURERS

Many furniture manufacturers attempt to stress factors other than price in their marketing approach. The manufacturer is trying to give the retailer or wholesaler some reason to buy other than prices that are lower than the competition's. Examples of nonprice factors include:

Design, quality, and workmanship. Manufacturers stressing these product features are indicating to dealers and ultimate consumers that their products represent a good value because of strength of design, good quality control, and a highly skilled, dedicated work force.

Service. Manufacturers stressing service are promoting a well-trained sales force, and they will do everything possible to have the merchandise delivered to the dealer in good condition. They also pledge to take care of customer complaints and problems quickly.

Assortment of products. In this case, the manufacturer is stating that an adequate assortment of products is available to satisfy the needs of the customer. An additional step is to urge the dealer to put a manufacturer-sponsored gallery in the store, with a complete assortment of merchandise that is salable. The assortment of merchandise then becomes the basis for overcoming competition.

Rapid delivery. Some manufacturers advertise prompt delivery on selected merchandise, which typically involves only a portion of their product line. For example, an upholstered furniture manufacturer might select ten frames with twenty possible fabrics and offer only those in the rapid delivery program. In this case, the manufacturer may promise retailers that this group of merchandise will be delivered within two weeks or some other specified time period.

Marketing assistance. Furniture manufacturers may offer many types of marketing assistance to retailers. Such assistance can include advertising, point-of-purchase materials, and sales training for retail floor sales-people. Materials such as advertising mats, color transparencies, video-taped commercials for television, and radio spots may be provided. Point-of-purchase materials such as window signs, descriptive signs to be placed on furniture, and hang tags are other types of marketing assistance. Finally, manufacturers may provide sales training concerning their products and how to best sell them to prospective customers.

RETAILERS' CONSIDERATIONS IN PRICING

Like the manufacturer, it is very important for retailers to properly price their products. The retailer must stock merchandise at a price that fits the store's image. In other words, prices should be in line with what the customer expects to pay at a particular store. A number of considerations affect a retailer's pricing of the products offered at the store:

- Pricing objectives
- Complete cost data
- Economic factors
- Governmental actions
- Psychological pricing policies
- Extra charges
- Nonprice factors stressed by retailers

PRICING OBJECTIVES

The retailer should have pricing objectives clearly stated in writing. Such written objectives will serve as benchmarks to measure the success of the retailer's pricing strategy. Again, as with the manufacturer, the retailer must consider profitability and the relative market position of competing furniture stores.

Target-return pricing involves a figure that reflects the amount of realized gross margin the store wishes to achieve from operations. The realized gross margin is the amount that is left over after the merchandise is purchased and the other costs of doing business are paid. Target-return pricing takes into consideration the average amount of markup that must be maintained throughout the store. Since some merchandise will not sell for the regular price and must be marked down, the initial markup on all the merchandise must be higher than will ultimately be realized on the average.

To match or undercut competition is the objective of many retailers. The objective is to establish the store as a value center so the consumer will feel that the store has better values than the competition. One way of accomplishing this objective is through the use of *loss leaders*. A good loss leader is a product that is readily available in many stores at a price that can be easily compared. Using this strategy, the retailer will choose fifteen to twenty products, cut the markup drastically, and promote them heavily. When consumers see that the store has the lowest prices on these "easy-to-compare" items, they will assume that other products in the store are equivalent values.

Achieving a prestige image is an opposite objective to matching or undercutting competition. The retailer stresses service and usually carries well-known, quality furniture. The layout, display, advertising, and prices must blend satisfactorily to create the proper atmosphere for selling to customers who wish to buy at a prestige store. Many of these stores feature a free decorator service, plus free delivery and setup of furniture in the consumer's home.

COMPLETE COST DATA

Adequate profits cannot be received by the retailer without access to the complete cost data of doing business, including salaries and overhead. In calculating the cost of a product, the freight costs must be added to the manufacturer's invoice price because of furniture sold F.O.B. origin or F.O.B. point of production. The combined merchandise cost is referred to as the *landed-cost of inventory*. It is the true landed-cost that must be used as a basis for markup in a retail furniture store. This markup is fairly high because of the many costs involved. Examples of retail costs are interest rates, salaries of sales and office staffs, warehouse and warehouse personnel, delivery trucks, and items of overhead such as utilities.

Terms such as "a number and ten markup" are common in the industry. A "number markup" means the merchandise price is twice the cost. For example, a table that cost $100 would have a retail price of $200. A number and ten markup would involve the merchandise price being doubled and an extra 10 percent being added.

ECONOMIC FACTORS

The realistic furniture retailer must take into consideration local economic factors in pricing, especially in regard to income and employment levels. Since many furniture retailers have only one or perhaps two stores in a geographic territory, they must be concerned primarily with their local area. It makes no difference that the national economic picture is healthy if the dominant local employer just terminated operations and a sizable percentage of the local population is unemployed.

Again, the expectations of consumers in regard to inflation, as well as future economic conditions, are of interest to the retailer. The threat of inflation may serve as a warning that manufacturers are likely to raise prices and that now is the best time to buy.

GOVERNMENTAL ACTIONS

The federal government regulates pricing at the retail level through the Federal Trade Commission. The advertising of prices is of special interest since it must be done within FTC guidelines. For example, in a special sale on an item using "was-is" pricing, the "was" price must have been the normal selling price for the merchandise in that store for a reasonable period of time on a regular basis.

PSYCHOLOGICAL PRICING POLICIES

Retailers use a number of legitimate pricing strategies that present the pricing in a way that makes it easy for the consumer to buy. These have been called "psychological pricing policies" because the price is presented in such a way that it is the primary reason for the consumer to purchase. Examples of such psychological pricing policies include the following:

Odd pricing is used by many retailers to emphasize that merchandise is available at certain key price points. For example, a store has a sofa priced for $699, which may seem considerably lower to the consumer than if the price were $700.

Combination pricing is utilized by many furniture retailers, especially in the medium- and lower-price brackets. Products are priced by the suite rather than by the piece as is the practice of stores selling higher-priced merchandise. By paying one price for a combination of merchandise, consumers often feel they are getting more for their money. Other types of combination pricing include various techniques, from pricing three occasional tables together to pricing furniture by rooms. An example of the latter would be one price for three rooms of furniture and accessories.

Price-tag discounts involve the retailer using a two-section price tag plainly marked with the regular price and "our" price. The figure quoted as "our" price is lower and plainly shows customers the discount they are getting from buying in that particular store.

EXTRA CHARGES

Furniture stores occasionally have extra charges that are incurred by the consumer. The most common is a finance charge, where the customer pays a carrying charge or interest on credit purchases. Another charge, normally made by retailers in the lower-price brackets, is a delivery charge which becomes necessary because of their discount prices.

NONPRICE FACTORS STRESSED BY RETAILERS

Many furniture retailers try to eliminate the necessity of having "the lowest prices in town" by stressing features other than the price of the merchandise. This type of retail establishment is most often referred to as a "full-service" store, offering a variety of services to help the consumer. Types of services include:

Decorator service. Many retail furniture stores featuring higher-priced merchandise have a home decorator service. These stores have sales personnel and interior designers who can help the consumer select a variety of home furnishings that will blend into an attractive living environment. They will often visit the home and help with the selection of colors, draperies, and wall coverings as well as furniture.

In-stock merchandise. Many consumers want their purchases to be available immediately; they do not want to wait for merchandise to be special ordered. A service some stores offer is that most of the merchandise they carry is in stock, especially if it is featured in advertising.

Free delivery. Some retailers offer free home delivery which can be easily advertised and appeals to many consumers.

Assortment of goods. One of the leading reasons consumers decide to buy at a particular store is because of a large or special assortment of merchandise. For example, a store might advertise "the largest selection of furniture in the county," or "the most carefully selected assortment of furniture in the city." Many stores also seek credibility and the attention of consumers by advertising famous brand names.

SUMMARY

Price is the marketer's expression of what a product is worth in relative terms. In other words, it is an expression of relative value.

A manufacturer's considerations in establishing a price for a product include: pricing objectives, complete cost data, estimates of consumer demand, economic factors, governmental actions, freight charges to dealers, discounts and allowances, and nonprice factors stressed by manufacturers.

The manufacturer's pricing objectives may include achieving a targeted profit, matching competition with follow-the-leader pricing, undercutting competitors with penetration pricing, and/or achieving a better image with prestige pricing.

Discounts and allowances offered by furniture manufacturers include: trade or functional discounts, cash discounts, quantity discounts, tie-in sales, "clearance" discounts, promotional allowances, and defective goods allowances.

Examples of nonprice factors stressed by furniture manufacturers include: design, quality, and workmanship; service; assortment of goods; rapid delivery; and marketing assistance.

A retailer's considerations in establishing a price for a product include: pricing objectives, complete cost data, economic factors, governmental actions, psychological pricing policies, extra charges, and nonprice factors stressed by retailers.

The retailer's pricing objectives may include target-return pricing as to profit, matching or undercutting the competition with loss leaders, and/or portraying a prestige image.

Psychological pricing policies include odd pricing, combination pricing, and price-tag discounts.

Examples of nonprice factors stressed by furniture retailers include: decorator services, in-stock merchandise, free delivery, and assortment of goods.

CHAPTER 11

PERSONAL FURNITURE SELLING

The personal selling of furniture involves presenting the product in a manner that will result in the prospective buyer exchanging money or credit for it. In essence, the job of the salesperson is to facilitate this exchange. The salesperson is the single most critical link between the buyer and seller and has the responsibility of helping the customer make the decision to buy. For example, the retailer needs to feature products that will appeal to the ultimate consumer. Likewise, consumers want furniture that will enhance their living environment and reflect their tastes to all who visit their homes. In both of these examples, the job of the salesperson is to point out how the product will help prospective customers satisfy their needs and solve their decorating problems.

In essence, professional furniture selling is simply effective person-to-person communication. The successful salesperson must understand the customers' problems and needs in order to make a sales presentation in a realistic, honest manner.

BENEFITS OF PERSONAL FURNITURE SELLING

Some of the unique benefits of personal furniture selling that are not found in any other type of product presentation include the following:

Salesperson can make a personal assessment of customer needs. Through personal interaction with the customer, the salesperson can receive feedback that can be invaluable in determining what the customer likes and dislikes. A perceptive manufacturer's representative can note the reaction of a retail buyer to sales photographs and provide reinforcement or explanations where needed. Or an effective retail salesperson can adapt the sales presentation based on customer reaction to products in the store or photographs in suppliers' catalogues.

The assessment of customer needs can take place prior to the actual sales presentation. For example, a retail salesperson often asks a series of questions in order to get a better idea of the interior living environment and be in a better position to help the customer choose the proper sofa, chairs, accessories, or other home furnishings. Occasionally in higher-priced decorator stores, the salesperson may even visit the consumer's home. Manufacturer's representatives can also assist in determining retailers' merchandise needs because they have visited a variety of stores and have a good idea of what styles, colors, and product groupings are most effective.

Selling efforts can be carefully targeted to minimize wasted efforts. In personal furniture selling, it is possible to approach directly those dealers or consumers who are most likely to buy. A good manufacturer's representative will, for example, carefully search for and qualify prospective new accounts. This means that he or she would call on only those retailers or wholesalers where the manufacturer's furniture would logically sell well and who are capable of paying for the merchandise. To take an obvious situation, a manufacturer's salesperson selling high-priced traditional furniture would not call on a store with a poor credit rating that stocks only contemporary furniture. Or a salesperson in a retail store, upon learning that a couple had no children, should not show them juvenile furniture or bunk beds.

The salesperson can make the actual sale. In other words, a completed sale involves filling out forms and working out details such as time and place of delivery. Only a salesperson working closely with a customer can accomplish these tasks.

The salesperson can perform a variety of nonselling activities. In many sales, the customer must be evaluated for credit worthiness before the transaction can be completed. Here, the salesperson can gather the information necessary for the credit manager.

Many manufacturers depend on their salespeople to take care of complaints both from dealers and consumers. A case in point might be a retailer calling the factory to complain that the arm of a dining chair arrived broken. As a way of solving this problem, the manufacturer might have the salesperson check the defective product and help to determine the proper course of action. The same plan of action might be undertaken if a product did not perform satisfactorily in someone's home.

DIFFICULTIES IN ESTABLISHING AN EFFECTIVE SALES FORCE

Two potential problems often present difficulties for managers seeking to establish an effective sales force. The high cost of a sales force and the difficulty of finding good salespeople often offset many of the benefits of personal selling.

Relatively high cost. Good salespeople tend to seek high compensation for their work. In furniture sales on all levels, the better, more experienced salespeople normally move toward organizations providing them with the opportunity to make the most money.

Another factor contributing to high cost is the limited amount of time involved in face-to-face selling efforts. For example, manufacturer's representatives and salespeople for wholesale distributors spend most of their time driving from one account to the next and waiting for buyers to be free to talk with them. This results in very little time each day actually spent in making sales presentations.

The same is true of retail salespeople. A sizeable amount of each day is spent waiting for customers to come into the store. In furniture retailing, it is also hard to always have the right number of salespeople because of the difficulty in predicting the actual number of customers who will visit the store at various times and days.

Difficulty in finding good salespeople. The many options available with each piece of furniture and the wide range of home furnishings products require a rather sophisticated, well-trained salesperson. To be effective in furniture sales, a person must have an appreciation for the product and know the techniques of selling it. Only in this way can the salesperson help the customer make the proper sequence of decisions that will result in a completed sale.

Of equal importance is the need for the furniture salesperson to be dedicated and hard working. Most manufacturer's salespeople must be self-starters who are capable of working long hours independently because their sales territories may be located far from the close supervision of a sales manager. In retailing, the hours are long and holidays are few, so dedication and a willingness to work hard are equally important for retail salespeople.

THE SELLING PROCESS

Several steps must be carried out for sales to be completed on a continual and successful basis. Figure 11-1 shows the chain of events that must occur for a person to successfully sell furniture for either manufacturers or retailers.

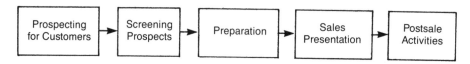

11-1. Steps in the selling process

The chain begins with prospecting (searching) for customers to buy the product. Once the prospective customers have been identified, they must be screened to determine those with a need or desire for the product and the financial ability to make the purchase. The next two steps involve preparing an effective sales presentation and presenting it in a manner that will make it easy for the prospect to buy. The final step in the selling process is to follow up after the sale with proper postsale activities so the customer will be more likely to come back to the manufacturer or retailer when additional furniture is needed.

These steps must be identified and properly completed for personal furniture selling to be effective. The functions of selling for manufacturers and for retailers will be discussed separately.

THE MANUFACTURER'S SALESPERSON

The manufacturer's salesperson, often called the *manufacturer's representative,* usually sells in a prescribed territory the products produced by a company. For example, the manufacturer's representative for a leading upholstered furniture manufacturer might be assigned to sell to dealers in Maryland and Virginia.

The majority of all manufacturer's representatives are independent contractors. They are self-employed business people who have entered into a contractual agreement to sell the manufacturer's products within an assigned territory. The compensation for the independent contractor is a straight commission based on the value of merchandise shipped. For example, the representative may get from 3 to 6 percent of all sales orders in the sales territory that are accepted and shipped.

Because many manufacturers are relatively small, it is a common practice for a manufacturer's representative to sell the products of more than one company. For example, the same salesperson might sell occasional tables for one company, wall units for a second, lamps for a third, and dining-room furniture for a fourth. In this way, a retailer can be offered a variety of products and, at the same time, the representative generates sufficient sales volume to make a living. Those representing large manufacturers normally sell only one line, while those representing smaller manufacturers sell more than one. As independent contractors on straight commission, they pay their own taxes, insurance, and travel expenses.

The other type of manufacturer's salesperson is a regular employee of the company and not an independent contractor. These are individuals who are employed exclusively by one company and receive the same benefits as other company employees. They may be paid in one of three ways: (1) straight commission, (2) straight salary, or (3) a combination of salary and commission or bonus. Here, also, the salesperson is assigned a designated geographic territory.

Regardless of whether a manufacturer's salesperson is an independent contractor or an employee salesperson, personal furniture selling requires more than merely having a good personality. A successful "manufacturer's rep" must be creative and have a good sense of fashion and color to present the product properly. In addition, the representative should have some knowledge of merchandising, advertising, sales promotion, and retailing. Having this knowledge is a distinct advantage in helping the retailer do a better job of presenting the manufacturer's products to the consumer.

Ideally, the manufacturer's representative and the retailer should help each other so that salable products can be offered in a manner conducive to their being purchased by the consumer. With a knowledge of retailing, the manufacturer's salesperson can anticipate many of the problems and opportunities encountered by the retailer and can work to help both of them be more successful.

SELLING FOR A MANUFACTURER

In order to understand the functions of the manufacturer's representative, one must analyze how he or she carries out the selling process. Therefore, prospecting for customers, screening prospects, preparation, sales presentation, and postsale activities will be reviewed separately.

PROSPECTING FOR CUSTOMERS

Prospecting involves searching for potential customers. Unless a manufacturer is in the enviable position of having a presold product with more dealers that want to buy than the manufacturer chooses to sell, the job of prospecting is continual. New accounts are necessary to keep the factories at full capacity and allow for corporate growth. There are a number of sources of customers for the furniture manufacturer:

Current or past customers. The successful furniture manufacturer's representative keeps a file on all the current and past customers in the territory, which allows the rep to call on the stores and inquire about purchases already completed or on order. The file serves to jog the rep's memory and helps create selling opportunities by being able to show a special or personal interest in the retailer's buying activities. For example, a manufacturer's representative might begin his or her sales presentation to the retailer in this way:

> I notice you have dropped our 1042 Early American suite. Many dealers have replaced it with our new 1064 Oak suite. Those who have done so have been pleased with the results. The 1064 has several new features that customers seem to really like, such as solid oak drawer fronts, a carved oak leaf in the center of the dresser door, and polished brass hardware. How about trying three—one for display and two for the warehouse?

Realistically, good record-keeping allows the representative to capitalize on past sales and help to locate problem areas. It is often easier to develop existing customers into larger customers than constantly to try to find new ones.

Furniture markets. New merchandise, special values, and distinctive display at the furniture markets will attract new customers into showrooms. Retailers are usually asked to sign a showroom register book, giving name, store name, and address; this then serves as a contact list for manufacturer's salespeople.

Trade advertising. Trade advertising featuring various products and services is another way to gain the attention of potential new customers. There are a number of trade publications, such as *CompetitivEdge, Professional Furniture Merchant, Furniture Today,* and *HFD/Retailing Home Furnishings,* which are read by retailers and are good media for trade advertisements.

News media and personal observation. News stories of store openings or other furniture store events can provide clues to possible sales opportunities. Stories of personnel changes may also be helpful because a new buyer or manager may be more inclined to purchase a manufacturer's products than was the person leaving the position.

An example of personal observation would be a manufacturer's representative taking notice of the opening of new furniture stores as he or she travels throughout his or her sales territory.

Other sources. Developing lists of retailers may be quite helpful in qualifying prospects. When opening up a new sales territory, a good place to discover what retailers are located in the area is the "Yellow Pages" of the telephone directory. Another valuable source is *Lyon's Red Book,* a listing of home furnishings retailers who have been evaluated by the Lyon's Mercantile Company, a credit reporting agency.

SCREENING PROSPECTS

In order to spend adequate time with those who are most likely to buy, thus leading to a higher percentage of completed sales, it is necessary to screen prospects. Screening is usually based on whether prospects have the money or credit to be "eligible" to buy and have a potential interest in the product involved. In selling for a manufacturer, it is obvious that the major selling efforts should be directed toward those who have adequate credit ratings.

There are two types of strategies in selling to retailers. The first is to sell to everyone who can qualify for credit, and the second is to sell to a smaller number who will promote the product aggressively. Both the manufacturer and representatives should determine which of these selling strategies they prefer so that prospects can be screened accordingly.

Successful manufacturer's representatives also evaluate the store's niche in the marketplace and do not waste time calling on retailers who logically would have no need for their merchandise. Someone selling high-priced eighteenth century reproductions should not waste time calling on a promotionally priced store which handles mainly modern upholstered furniture.

Finally, manufacturer's representatives should focus the majority of their attention on the individuals who have the authority to buy. Although it is good public relations to talk with branch managers even if they do not have the authority to buy, the most time should be spent making sales presentations to the individuals within the organization who do have that authority.

PREPARATION

A key ingredient in successful selling is the careful preparation of the sales presentation. A well-prepared presentation will ensure effective person-to-person communication, which is necessary in establishing the relationships conducive to making repeat sales to retailers. Not only must the manufacturer's representative understand the retailer, but he or she must be able to explain the merits of the product in a way that will convince the retailer that the products are right for the store. Therefore, to be thoroughly prepared, the manufacturer's representative should:

Understand the product being sold. Since the retailer is an expert and will make a purchase decision based on rational buying motives, the manufacturer's representative should know as much as possible about the products being sold and how the products are manufactured. The representative must be able to answer questions and provide information which the retailer, in turn, can translate into benefits that may result in sales to the consumer. It is the responsibility of the manufacturer to provide the field sales force with enough product information to represent the company adequately.

Be thoroughly familiar with the nature and characteristics of the company. Only then can a salesperson fairly represent a manufacturer by truthfully stating with confidence the competitive strengths and capabilities of the firm. An understanding of credit policies is needed so that a representative will not make promises that cannot be kept. Another type of essential information would be delivery policies and procedures. This knowledge will allow the salesperson to commit to a delivery schedule that is achievable.

Understand the competition. Although it is not usually effective to belittle competing products and companies, a knowledge of what the competition offers is extremely helpful. In other words, knowing competing strengths and weaknesses, such as Company A uses stain-repellent fabric and Company B does not, could be used to advantage by Company A's sales force.

Obtain knowledge about the customer. The manufacturer's representative should try to understand the retail store as much as possible. Such facts as styles carried, price brackets, products that are displayed from competing firms, and what the customer has purchased in the past are all very helpful in preparing a sales presentation.

THE SALES PRESENTATION

In a situation where a manufacturer's representative is selling to a retailer, the sales presentation is extremely important. Retailers are busy people, and the presentation will be more effective if the sales points are made quickly and concisely.

A prepared sales presentation can be extremely successful when presented sincerely and professionally. This does not mean that every word is memorized to be recited in exactly the same way to every customer. A well-prepared presentation means that effective sales points are learned so they can be presented clearly and concisely to cover the basic information without wasting the customer's time. At the same time, there is flexibility for the presentation to be tailored to the needs of the specific customer.

Retailers are interested basically in how the products will satisfy the consumer and make their operations more profitable. In order for the retailer to become interested and motivated to purchase the products, the manufacturer's representative often bases the sales presentation on the *"AIDA"* concept. It involves first getting *attention,* which is translated into *interest,* then into *desire,* and finally into *action,* which is expressed by a decision to purchase.

Attention, interest, desire, and action are achieved by effectively telling the value story about a company and its products. It involves a clear, concise presentation of why the products are salable and how they are supported by the services and policies of the manufacturer. Sales aids such as photographs, finish panels, and descriptive brochures help to make the presentation more effective.

It is essential that a climate of mutual respect and trust be developed between a manufacturer's representative and a retail buyer. It will reinforce the sales presentation and ensure that a larger percentage of sales calls will result in action, in the form of completed sales.

POSTSALE ACTIVITIES

Postsale activities by the representative involve keeping in touch with retailers to ensure that they are satisfied with their purchases and that the manufacturer is living up to its commitments. If defective goods are received or delivery dates are missed, the representative should see to it that these problems are corrected.

Other postsale activities involve the representative working with the retailer on advertising, display, and sales training, in order to increase the sales of the manufacturer's products in that store. The representative who regularly stays in contact with the customer after the sale is made will enjoy the confidence of the retailer which should result in repeat sales.

THE RETAIL SALESPERSON

The successful retail furniture salesperson must be a creative and hard-working individual. Although the exact educational requirements depend on the type of store and services offered, retail salespeople must understand the needs and problems consumers have in furnishing their homes. By taking the time to determine why a person is buying furniture, a salesperson can then assist customers in making decisions that will meet their needs and solve their decorating problems.

Retail salespeople are very important to the store. If they cannot relate to the consumer in a way that will result in sales, it would be most difficult for the store to be successful. Salespeople must be well-trained so they thoroughly understand the product and how to sell it. In addition, stores featuring more expensive furniture must have salespeople trained in the basic elements of interior design in order to help the consumer solve a wide variety of decorating problems. Salespeople in all stores must understand color, style, lighting, and how to arrange furniture in the home. They must also understand product features so they can make sales presentations that are helpful to the consumer.

Again, those who work hard and relate well to customers by helping them make the right buying decisions are those who will be successful. In essence, retail furniture selling is a sophisticated type of person-to-person selling. The retail salesperson must be able to understand what benefits consumers expect to obtain from their furniture purchases. These benefits must be explained to consumers and supported by product features that will convince the buyers that the furniture will actually provide these benefits. This type of selling requires that the retail salesperson really knows products and how to sell them.

SELLING FOR A RETAILER

Selling in the retail store is different from selling for a manufacturer. Therefore, an explanation of the retail selling process is vital to an understanding of professional furniture selling in the retail furniture store.

PROSPECTING FOR CUSTOMERS

On the retail level, perceptive salespeople are constantly looking for new prospects and for ways to get current and former customers back into the store. Because people buy furniture at relatively few times during their lives, this search must be energetically pursued day after day. Some of the prospecting methods at the retail level are:

Current or past customers. As in the case of the manufacturer's representative, it is important for retail salespeople to keep good records of what they sell, when, and to whom. This information will allow them to contact customers again to determine if they are satisfied and if they have any other furniture needs. Other reasons for calling customers include advising the customer that a suite is being discontinued and now is the time to add other pieces, that an additional piece of special interest is now in the store, or to personally announce a sale or other special event. The best prospects for future sales are those who have bought in the past, and the salesperson should continue to keep in contact with them.

Local advertising. Retail furniture store advertising should be designed to initiate action now. Sales or other in-store special events are helpful in getting people into the store to buy. Direct mail, newspaper, television, and radio advertising are the usual advertising media which, when used effectively, can draw significant numbers of prospects into the store.

Drawings, contests, and inexpensive "traffic builders." Drawings, contests, and inexpensive merchandise that can be purchased at obvious values by consumers are sales promotional techniques that also draw people into stores. Then, with good sales techniques a considerable number of these people can be motivated to become customers.

Referrals. Often, employees and current or past customers can be encouraged to refer others to a store. One good source of new customers is people who hear about the store from satisfied customers. In other words, the store that takes special efforts to ensure customer satisfaction is really recruiting an "extra sales force"—one person encouraging another to buy where he or she already has satisfactorily bought.

News media. Reading articles about marriage, births, or other events signaling a change in life-style, which could result in the need for furniture, can also be a good way to prospect for customers. For example, newly married couples can be sent coupons giving a percentage reduction off the list price of designated merchandise as a means of soliciting furnishings purchases for their first home. Another way of using an important event to generate goodwill for the store would be to send a small gift to celebrate the announcement of the birth of a new baby.

Walk-ins. Also helpful in attracting new customers is a location where people can easily see the store and its attractive window displays. Therefore, careful market research should be conducted to ensure that the store is in a desirable location. The objective is for a significant number of potential customers to walk or drive to the store because they have noticed it. The possibility that this will happen can be enhanced with a good location, an attractive building, effective signs, and well-designed window displays.

SCREENING PROSPECTS

In retail stores, many salespeople over-analyze their customers and make the mistake of screening out some good prospects based only on their first impression. It is much better to assume that everyone who comes into a store is a potential customer and can successfully be encouraged to buy. A good retail salesperson asks questions and tries to obtain as much information as possible in order to help the customer make an intelligent buying decision. The screening out of a person takes place only when it is determined that the consumer obviously wishes to buy something that is not available in the store or is unable to pay for the purchases.

In most retail stores, especially where salespeople receive a straight commission, a system must be established for determining which salespeople should wait on which customers. Many of these stores use the "up" system, which means that salespeople take turns waiting on customers.

PREPARATION

It is just as important for the retail salesperson to be well-prepared to sell furniture as it is for the manufacturer's representative. The well-prepared salesperson is an authority on furniture who can build confidence in the minds of customers. People like to buy from someone who knows the product being sold and who can answer their questions. In order to be able to answer these questions, the retail salesperson should:

Understand the product and the manufacturer. This includes becoming familiar with product benefits and customer-attracting features, which are usually the reasons why a person buys a product. The retail salesperson can obtain this information by attending training meetings or sales seminars conducted by manufacturers and by reading the information they provide. Many manufacturers provide considerable information and training on how to sell their products.

Retail furniture salespeople should also learn all they can about the manufacturer. It is particularly valuable to know the strengths and weaknesses of a particular manufacturer, which includes how the products are constructed, policies concerning delivery, how defective merchandise is returned, and other helpful information.

Be familiar with the policies and services of the store. The retail salespeople should become thoroughly familiar with the operating policies and services of the store so they can honestly and realistically answer any questions the customer is likely to have. For example, the salesperson may be asked questions such as: Is it possible to special-order merchandise with only a small down payment? Or what is the delivery policy outside the city limits? In other words, it is best for a retail salesperson to promise a customer only something that is possible.

Understand the competition. A good retail salesperson should not sell by being critical of competing retailers. However, it is very helpful to know who the other retailers are in the trading area, their policies, and which lines they carry. It will allow for a more positive response when a customer talks about deals or offers promised by other retailers.

Obtain knowledge about the customer. The retail salesperson should try to learn as much as possible about the needs and problems of customers in order to help them make the decision to buy products they will enjoy using. Of interest would be type of house, size of the family, color schemes, and styles of other furnishings. By understanding these factors, the salesperson is better able to suggest products that will satisfy the needs and solve the decorating problems of the customer.

THE SALES PRESENTATION

In a person-to-person sales situation, the customer has the final choice. The customer may or may not buy, or could choose to buy from someone

11-2. *Left:* After floor samples, manufacturers' catalogues are regarded as the most important sales tool available to the retail furniture salesperson. This salesperson is using a number of manufacturers' catalogues to show the different suites available in a particular style category. In this way, she is able to offer her customer a much larger selection than the merchandise displayed on the sales floor. *(Furnitureland South Inc.) Right:* This customer has decided on the style sofa she wants to buy and is now trying to make a decision about the fabric. The retail salesperson is beginning to fill out the order form. In this situation, the retailer's sofa order from the manufacturer will include the customer's choice of fabric. The many available fabric choices underscore the difficulty of buying upholstered furniture.

else. Therefore, it is necessary to have a carefully prepared sales presentation to be effective on a consistent basis. It ensures that the salesperson covers the necessary points and asks for the order at the proper time.

The retail salesperson also is well-advised to use a modified version of the AIDA concept. The first step in a good sales presentation involves getting the customer's attention. This may be done through sales photographs or catalogues, or pointing out samples on the retail floor. The attention must then be transferred into interest, which can only come from having empathy for the customer and a proper appreciation of the customer's needs and problems.

Next, the salesperson must make the presentation believeable and prove the worth of a product by listing its features, supporting the claim that it is, in fact, the product the consumer should purchase. Hopefully, it will also create desire for the product by the consumer.

Finally, the salesperson should attempt to close the sale by asking the customer to make a buying decision. The closing must be positive and should be reinforced by one or two extra benefits for the transaction to be completed. A closing such as "May we deliver the sofa on Wednesday or Thursday?" is very positive and encourages the customer to make the buying decision.

WHY BE A LOSER WHEN YOU CAN BE A WINNER*

EASY WAYS TO "LOSE" A SALE:	EASY WAYS TO "MAKE" A SALE:
"May I help you?"	"Good morning. Are you looking for bedroom or dining-room furniture?"
Giving fast answers: "$199."	"Reduced $50 from $249. Do you want the chair and the ottoman, or just the chair?"
"When do you want it?"	"We can deliver it Monday or Friday. Which would suit you best?"
"We have it in two colors—green and blue."	"Would you prefer the green or the blue?"
"That dresser's 68-inches long."	"We have this dresser in a 68-inch length. We also have a similar dresser in a 64-inch length. Which size would suit you best?"
"That chest has five drawers."	"We have it in two sizes—a four-drawer and a five-drawer. Which would best suit your needs?"
"You could pay $30 a month for 12 months."	"Would you rather pay $30 a month plus credit charges for 12 months, or $20 a month plus credit charges for 18 months? Which would you prefer?"
Do not tell customers about the furniture's features. They may already know. Do not elaborate on benefits.	Explain the furniture's features. Stress the benefits of the furniture to them and how it will solve their problems.

*Adapted from *Sales Unlimited* by Wyatt Exxum, published by Vaughn-Bassett Furniture Company, Galax, Virginia, 1980.

11-3. These quotations illustrate possible differences between an effective and an ineffective retail sales presentation. To be effective, it is important to give the consumer a choice between two positive options rather than a chance to say "no" as is illustrated under "Easy Ways to 'Lose' a Sale."

POSTSALE ACTIVITIES

The retail salesperson should also be attentive to the customer after the sale, by making certain that damages, delivery problems, and other concerns are taken care of promptly. The satisfied customer can be the best source of future customers.

Stores normally keep a list of customers and send calendars, Christmas cards, or other remembrances, or send advance notice of sales or special promotions designed only for their past customers. Such programs are designed to make the customers feel special and that the store sincerely appreciated their business.

SALES FORCE DEVELOPMENT AND ADMINISTRATION

A successful sales force must be carefully developed and effective administration procedures should be installed for a company to have an even, adequate flow of orders for its products. Steps to be taken are as follows:

1. Analyze the sales responsibility and type of person required.
2. Recruit and select salespeople.
3. Train salespeople.
4. Establish compensation systems.
5. Supervise and control the sales force.
6. Evaluate the sales force.

ANALYZE THE SALES RESPONSIBILITY AND TYPE OF PERSON REQUIRED

Furniture selling, as has been stated earlier, is a relatively sophisticated activity. Therefore, it is necessary to prepare a job description and an outline of the type of person required. This should include the details of the duties and a listing of attributes the person must possess to carry out the job effectively.

Manufacturer's representative's duties include calling on customers to obtain orders, servicing existing accounts, working with freight companies or the company office to ensure on-time delivery, and trying to resolve customer complaints.

The retail salesperson's duties usually include greeting customers, making sales presentations, obtaining credit information, helping with the customer's decorating problems, working with the warehouse to arrange delivery, and helping to keep the sales floor neat and the merchandise properly displayed.

Desired salesperson's attributes often include previous sales experience, education or training, a good appearance, high motivation, and emotional maturity.

The number of sales positions for a manufacturer normally depends on the firm's geographical distribution patterns and how frequently the salespeople are expected to visit the dealers. In a retail organization, the number of sales positions depends on the size of the store, the number of anticipated customers, and the philosophy of management regarding the amount of personal attention it wants individual customers to receive from its salespeople.

RECRUIT AND SELECT SALESPEOPLE

Many furniture manufacturers and retailers hire only experienced salespeople. These companies restrict their recruiting to those who have either proven themselves to be effective salespeople for other furniture companies or for firms in other industries. Other companies recruit people with no sales experience, but who possess the desired attributes and can be trained to become an effective salesperson.

The selection process varies widely from company to company within the furniture industry, but generally they all require the applicant to fill out a personnel application and have a personal interview, usually with the sales manager.

TRAIN SALESPEOPLE

Training usually includes an in-depth study of the product being sold. It is mandatory in selling to understand the product thoroughly. This includes learning the product features and the benefits buyers normally will experience when they purchase the product.

Training also includes learning about company policies, procedures, and what one can and cannot do and promise. By knowing the facts, the salesperson can be more truthful and realistic when making commitments for delivery, credit, advertising allowances, or other services offered by the company.

Finally, training involves learning the techniques of selling. A successful furniture salesperson must know how to establish rapport with a customer, how to make a good sales presentation, and how to close the sale.

ESTABLISH COMPENSATION SYSTEMS

There are a number of compensation systems that may be utilized by furniture manufacturers and retail furniture stores. Each compensation system has a slightly different type of built-in incentive and its own advantages and disadvantages. Realizing this, management should choose and implement the compensation system most compatible with the demands of the sales job in their company.

Straight commission. Historically, the most common method of compensating furniture salespeople is by straight commission, which means that they receive a specified percentage of the sales volume actually delivered to the customer. The commission is usually based on the dollar value of the sales involved. In some cases, it may be based on gross margin.

An example of basing the commission on the gross amount of delivered sales would be a manufacturer's representative who is paid 5 percent of the gross amount of sales dollars. This means that for sales of $10,000 in merchandise, the commission paid will be $500 (if the customer is approved for credit) when the merchandise is shipped. The percentage of commission may vary, depending on whether the merchandise is regular line, closeout, promotion, or, perhaps, sold under a contract.

An example of basing the commission on the gross margin generated would be a retailer who pays his or her sales staff 18 percent of the gross margin on a sale. In this situation, if a salesperson sold a bedroom suite costing $1,000 for a retail price of $2,000, the gross margin generated is $1,000. If the customer is approved for credit and the merchandise delivered, the salesperson would be paid $180 (18 percent of $1,000).

Commission with a drawing account. In this case, the salesperson is paid on straight commission, but receives a specified sum at regular pay intervals even when the commissions are less than that amount. The amount paid in excess of the actual commission must be paid back out of future commissions. For example, a retailer might provide a drawing account of $200 per week for each salesperson. If in a particular week a salesperson's actual commission is only $100, the wages paid will still be $200. However, if the salesperson's actual commission is $350 for the next week, the wages paid would be only $250 ($350 less the $100 paid from the drawing account the previous week). The adjustment can be made at the end of the month, quarter, or year in the case of the manufacturer's salesperson.

Combination salary and commission. This system provides the security of a regular salary plus an incentive in the form of a commission on all sales made. As in straight commission, the commission paid under this plan may be based on gross sales or gross margin. A percentage commission is normally less than that under a straight commission basis. For example, a retail salesperson might receive a salary of $150 per week plus 2 percent commission on gross sales.

Salary plus a bonus or profit sharing. Under this system, all salespersons are paid a straight salary, but have a chance to share in extra compensation if overall sales are at a specified high level. Sometimes, the bonus is based on reaching a certain level of sales or gross margin. This extra compensation often has a direct relationship to profits generated by the group and, depending on the company, may be called a bonus or profit sharing.

Straight salary. Straight salary is compensation paid to salespeople that does not vary from period to period and is not based on the amount of sales. This compensation method inherently has the most security, but the least incentive. A number of companies in the furniture industry pay

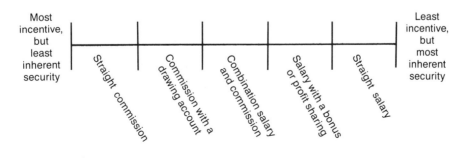

11-4. Types of compensation systems

straight salary because they feel they can get salespeople to perform a variety of functions in addition to selling. Additional duties might include following up on consumer complaints, collecting credit information, and working out delivery details. Also, some executives think that salaried salespeople are more likely to give proper time and attention to each account.

SUPERVISE AND CONTROL THE SALES FORCE

A good portion of the sales manager's time is spent supervising the sales force, which entails motivating them and overseeing the sales effort in order to obtain performance objectives. The compensation plan can help to motivate a sales force, but an energetic, perceptive sales manager is also important. Such a person will make sure that the sales force is on the job, is well-trained, and that customers are treated properly.

The amount of sales supervision varies greatly. For a manufacturer, it will depend on company size and the number of salespeople. A large manufacturer may have regional sales managers, while a smaller manufacturer may only have a single national sales manager.

Similarly, the sales management personnel in the retail store depends on the size of the store. In a small store, the owner or manager will also be the sales manager, while a large store may have a separate sales manager.

EVALUATE THE SALES FORCE

In order to determine how satisfactorily the sales effort is being carried out, sales quotas and other benchmarks are established for measurement purposes. The quotas for manufacturer's representatives may be based on the degree of market penetration and the amount of buying power that is perceived to be in the sales territory. Periodically, the results of the salespeople are measured against their quotas to determine if the sales performance is satisfactory.

Sales reports are also required by many companies to measure the number of calls, amount of orders obtained, cities visited and miles traveled, sales expenses incurred, and new placements on retailers' floors. Also, manufacturer's representatives are often asked to submit reports indicating what retailers are buying from competing firms, comments on the product, and other information useful to the marketing management team.

Although they are slightly different in format, sales reports by retail salespeople are equally important in evaluating their performance.

SUMMARY

Personal furniture selling in the furniture industry is person-to-person communication designed to encourage a buyer to exchange his or her money and/or credit for a furniture product offered for sale.

The benefits of personal furniture selling include the following: (1) the salesperson can make a personal assessment of customer needs; (2) selling efforts can be carefully targeted to minimize wasted efforts; (3) the salesperson can make the actual sale; and (4) the salesperson can perform nonselling activities.

Two difficulties in establishing an effective sales force are high cost and the difficulty of finding good salespeople.

The selling process includes prospecting for customers, screening prospects, preparation, the sale presentation, and postsale activities. For a company to be successful, these steps in the selling process must be completed by both manufacturer's and retailer's salespeople.

Manufacturer's representatives are usually either independent contractors paid on commission or employees paid straight commission, straight salary, or a combination of the two.

Both manufacturer's and retailer's salespeople must be dedicated, hard-working individuals with a complete understanding of their product and company as well as empathy for their customers.

Sources of prospective customers for manufacturers include current or past customers, furniture markets, trade advertising, credit reports, the news media, and personal observation.

Prospects must be screened systematically in order to prevent taking time with those who do not have a legitimate intention to buy or are poor credit risks.

A key ingredient in successful selling is proper preparation, which involves understanding the product being sold, being familiar with the organization offering the product for sale, understanding the competition, and obtaining knowledge about the customers.

The manufacturer's salesperson should use a clear, concise sales presentation to cover the necessary sales points without wasting the customer's time. This sales presentation should attract attention, create interest, and then translate this interest into a desire for the product and a buying commitment.

The manufacturer's salesperson should follow up a sale with appropriate postsale activities to ensure satisfaction and, where possible, to help the retailer with display, sales training, or other activities that will aid retail salespeople to sell the product to the consumer.

Retail salespeople are company employees who are paid either a straight commission, straight salary, or a combination of salary and bonus or commission.

Sources of prospective customers for retailers include current or past customers; local advertising; drawings, contests, and inexpensive "traffic builders"; referrals; the news media; and walk-ins.

An effective retail salesperson should quickly screen prospects and present a properly prepared sales presentation.

Proper preparation for the retail salesperson involves understanding products and manufacturers, being familiar with the policies and services of the store, understanding the competition, and obtaining knowledge about the customer.

The effective sales presentation involves getting the customer's attention, transferring that attention into interest, proving the worth of a product by listing features, creating a desire for the product, and closing by asking the customer to take action by making a buying decision.

An efficient retail salesperson will follow up the sale with appropriate postsale activities, such as working out details concerning delivery, collection of credit information, and other activities helpful to the completion of the retailer's commitment to the customer and to ensuring customer satisfaction.

The steps in sales force development and administration are: (1) analyze the sales responsibility and type of person required; (2) recruit and select; (3) train; (4) establish compensation systems; (5) supervise and control; and (6) evaluate the performance of each person.

CHAPTER 12

ADVERTISING

A key ingredient in selling furniture to dealers and consumers is advertising. It is probably the most noticeable of all the forms of communication with dealers and consumers. Advertising includes the following elements: a nonpersonal communication conveyed through a medium, such as newspapers, television, and magazines, paid by and clearly designated as coming from an identified sponsor.

Consistent with this definition, advertising may be verbal, written, or a combination of verbal and visual presentation, depending on the type of media involved. An advertising medium is any vehicle used to carry the message to its intended audience.

All companies, whether they are manufacturers, wholesalers, or retailers, have unique advertising opportunities based on their distribution, product offerings, media availability, and position in the marketplace. Therefore, it is difficult to generalize about the type of advertising that would be effective for a specific firm, since the types of advertising by manufacturers, wholesalers, and retailers can and should differ. However, effective advertising, regardless of the sponsor, must be carefully planned to reflect the competitive strengths of the firm and the strengths and weaknesses of the media available.

The two most important components of advertising are *media selection* and the *creative message*. Media selection involves choosing the most effective vehicle to carry the advertising message to its intended audience. The creative message is what is spoken, written, drawn, or photographed to create interest in potential customers. This message must be carefully thought out and presented to reach prospects because of the intense competition for their attention.

All advertising, just like other management decisions, should be carefully planned and based on realistic objectives. Although the specific plans will vary from company to company, advertising should be an ongoing, consistent part of a firm's strategic marketing plan designed to create a climate conducive to selling the product. Good advertising has a subtle impact, gaining ground little by little until the cumulative effect results in increased sales. Advertising should be clearly targeted so that it will reach the intended audience and carefully constructed so the audience can relate to the message being conveyed. Only then can advertising truly be effective.

The advertising plan may be composed of several approaches, usually based on a predetermined budget. The advertising plan and budget are normally proposed by the advertising or marketing departments, then approved or revised and approved by top management. The method of budgeting and media options will be discussed generally in this chapter, followed by a separate discussion of advertising by manufacturers and by retailers.

THE ADVERTISING BUDGET

The amount of advertising done by most furniture marketers is determined by the advertising budget, which limits the amount and type of advertising. The most widely used method of determining an advertising budget is by *percentage of sales;* i.e., the budget is based on a percentage of sales forecasted for the year. For example, a retail store might allocate 2 percent of sales for its advertising budget. Companies can use the previous year's figure or can plan for an increased amount of advertising by basing the advertising budget on a projected sales increase.

Another method of establishing an advertising budget is the *objective or task approach;* i.e., focusing on the objectives or tasks to be accomplished. For example, the budget might be based on the costs required to reach a new target market, which often requires an investment beyond the usual percentage devoted to advertising.

MEDIA OPTIONS

Advertisers must choose the proper medium to carry their advertising if they are to be successful. Depending on their message and the impact they wish to make, there are a number of media options from which to choose.

BROADCAST MEDIA

The two major broadcast media are radio and television, which have the following advantages:

1. Some people choose not to read, and broadcasting may be the only way to reach these individuals.
2. On the printed page, the advertiser often has to share space with several other advertisers, whereas on radio and television the advertiser has the exclusive attention of the listener or viewer for a period of time.
3. Selective consumer groups may be reached through the timing of commercials. For example, advertising during afternoon soap operas reaches a different group of consumers than advertising during professional football games.
4. Television has a powerful impact because the advertiser can motivate the consumer both visually and verbally. People also spend a large percentage of their time watching television.

The major disadvantage of broadcast media is that if the impact is not made immediately, the effectiveness of the advertisement is lost forever. The message must be rebroadcast and paid for again if the consumer is to be reached a second time. Specific characteristics of broadcast media include the following:

Radio. Radio is a flexible medium which can be used effectively to segment a local audience. Radio stations usually specialize in their programming to appeal to different groups within the general population.

Television. Television is a medium best known for national and regional viewing audiences. It is possible to reach different groups within these national and regional audiences by the timing of the advertisements. The major disadvantage is that television advertising is too expensive for most furniture marketers. However, the increasing number of local television stations and the availability of cablevision offers furniture marketers the promise of less expensive television advertising. Local television stations and cablevision also allow furniture marketers to choose advertising that more nearly matches their distribution patterns.

PRINT MEDIA

The most often used print media are newspapers, magazines, direct mail, catalogues, circulars, and outdoor advertising. The most important advantages of print media are:

1. Readers have the opportunity to re-read a printed advertisement for clarification or see it again as they go over the publication a second time.
2. Many types of print media allow advertisements with longer explanations and a visual presentation of the product. Generally, print media allows the communication of more information than broadcast media.
3. Coupons or other incentives for action may be used to increase store traffic and stimulate sales. Coupons also allow the marketer to assess the effectiveness of advertisements.
4. It is easier to get across the impact of a reduced price in print than in broadcast media.

Specific characteristics of print media include the following:

Newspapers. Newspapers are an effective medium for advertising furniture because of their large local circulation, flexibility, and timeliness. It has been estimated that almost 90 percent of the adults in the United States are exposed to at least one newspaper regularly. The flexibility comes from the fact that the lead time for preparation and placement of newspaper advertising is short. Advertisements can be run or changed very quickly to announce sales, change themes, alter the selection of merchandise available, or communicate other facts about the store. Newspapers also allow the targeting of an advertisement for specific interest groups when an ad is inserted in the appropriate section of the newspaper.

By using the same logo and layout in all of its advertisements, a furniture retailer can establish an image in the minds of consumers. This continuity of advertising format establishes the credibility of a retailer through newspaper advertising.

Magazines. Magazines provide high-quality printing of furniture photographs, which is very important in showing a persuasive visual presentation of the product. Other than direct mail, magazines give the most specialized coverage of any of the print media. Many magazines cater to special interest groups, which allows advertisers to focus sharply their messages toward their intended market.

Furniture marketers make extensive use of publications that focus on the various aspects of living in the home (often referred to as "shelter" magazines). Typical articles included in shelter magazines are interior decorating, gardening, landscaping, cooking, and how to carry out "do-it-yourself" projects around the home. Even among shelter magazines, there are several with a more narrow appeal, such as those that appeal to people interested primarily in antiques and the country style of living or those that appeal to people who are attracted to contemporary architecture and furnishings.

The main disadvantage of magazine advertising is its inflexibility. The lead times for advertising preparation and placement are long and, normally, the content cannot be changed once the advertisement is accepted for publication. Magazine advertisements are usually expensive to prepare and total costs are often quite high in relation to circulation.

Direct mail. Direct mail provides the most specialized market penetration of any medium because it involves mailing the advertising directly to the sales prospect. Through computerized preparation of letters or other sales messages, the impact can be personalized. These advertisements may be prepared and sent out very quickly to the desired audience. The key to an effective direct-mail campaign is to have well-prepared, motivating advertising messages and materials and up-to-date mailing lists of present and former customers and good prospects. Direct mail offers excellent flexibility in quickly communicating to a target market.

There are two disadvantages which should be noted, however. First, the cost of buying or renting mailing lists is quite high. Second, there is a large throwaway factor, mainly because a company's material usually arrives with a large amount of other direct-mail advertising, and the competition for the attention of the consumer or dealer is intensive.

Catalogues. The most important single form of advertising for most furniture manufacturers is their catalogues. A copy of the catalogue is placed in retail stores and, along with floor samples, becomes the major selling tool of the retail salesperson. Catalogues contain photographs of a manufacturer's entire line of products. Detailed information is provided

12-1. Perhaps the most basic promotional material produced by furniture manufacturers is their product catalogues. By placing catalogues in retail stores, manufacturers have provided a valuable sales tool to retail furniture salespeople. A catalogue is essential for manufacturers who solicit special-order business. It is backed up by other point-of-purchase sales tools such as fabric swatches and finish panels.

about such product features as construction, finish, available sizes of the various pieces, and history of the style. For upholstered furniture lines, the catalogue is supported by fabric swatches, either in the catalogue itself or elsewhere in the store on a separate fabric rack. Companies that have both upholstery and case goods will usually have separate catalogues for each line.

Circulars. Circulars are colorful, printed advertisements featuring a collection of merchandise. They are usually from four to eight pages in length and announce the availability of a new collection or a special price for the merchandise featured in the circular.

The circular has the advantage of being a high-quality advertising piece which can be read and saved by the customer and even carried to the store for reference purposes. It has good impact when inserted in a newspaper because of the quality of printing and the fact that most consumers read it separately from the newspapers. The circular may also be mailed directly to former, present, or potential customers with good results from a cost-effectiveness standpoint.

Outdoor advertising. Billboards, posters, and signs are the most common forms of outdoor advertising. Essentially a retail medium, outdoor advertisements place the name of the store before the public and indicate its location. There is little opportunity to provide lengthy information or a realistic visual presentation of the product, so outdoor advertising has limited use for the furniture marketer. Good quality, visible, readable signs, however, are very important in helping customers locate a particular store. The advantages of outdoor advertising are size, relative low cost per contact, and the fact that it is always there to be seen as the public passes by.

CONSIDERATIONS IN MEDIA SELECTION

Many factors must be considered when selecting media if a furniture advertiser is to achieve the desired impact resulting in a long-term, consistent advertising campaign. These factors include the following:

Objective of the advertisement. Is the advertiser concerned with *frequency* or *reach*? Frequency involves exposing the same people to the message over and over again, while reach involves trying to expose a message to as many different people as possible.

Effectiveness of the media in carrying the message, determined by consideration of the media strengths and weaknesses.

Media circulation. Normally a medium is selected based on the demographics of its circulation. In other words, once an advertiser decides on the intended audience, the media that will best reach that audience at the lowest cost are selected.

Advertising budget. The advertising budget may allow the use of some media and preclude the use of others. A popular way of assessing cost effectiveness is the cost per thousand (CPM) readers, listeners, or viewers. Advertising must be judged on the results obtained, and the media with the lowest cost may not always be the most effective.

Competitive activity. One should analyze what competitors are doing in order to capitalize on their successes and failures.

Continuity. It is wise to develop a plan, become committed to it, and follow it through. In other words, decide ahead of time on the combination of media and how long they will be used.

Prospective customers. A medium or combination of media should be chosen based on what it takes to reach the target audience at the right place and at the right time. This choice involves knowing your selected position in the marketplace, who the prospective customers are, and where, why, and when they are likely to buy.

TYPES	OBJECTIVES
Product	Increase brand-name awareness
Pioneering	Build positive business image
Competitive	Counteract competition
Repetitive or continuity	Increase dealer base
Trade	Increase market showroom attendance
Consumer-oriented	Provide product information
Cooperative	Tell the "quality story"
Contract buyer	Stress manufacturer's services

12-2. Manufacturer-sponsored advertising

TYPES OF ADVERTISING USED BY MANUFACTURERS

Several general types of advertising used by manufacturers should be considered if sales results per dollar expended are to be satisfactory and the goals of the organization achieved.

PRODUCT ADVERTISING

In general, product advertising informs an audience about a product by using techniques designed to improve its sales. Product advertising is very important to the furniture manufacturer, and for clarity three subcategories should be considered:

1. Pioneering product advertising develops demand for a new product. The intent is to stimulate interest in the product rather than a specific brand. For example, the first advertisements for waterbeds had to stimulate a demand by dealers and consumers for waterbeds in lieu of other types of mattresses or sleep systems. Thus, much pioneering product advertising involves selling a concept that is not familiar to the audience.

2. Competitive product advertising emphasizes the merits of a particular brand of furniture or other product. Most advertising is competitive and tries to explain why the offering of a particular firm is the best buy. In other words, a message might stress why Brand X waterbeds are better values than those offered by other waterbed manufacturers.

3. Repetitive or continuity product advertising reinforces earlier advertising and is used when a product and brand have achieved recognition in the marketplace. This advertising is relatively "soft-sell" and simply reminds the consumer or dealer of a firm and its products. Often it is brand-name advertising continually directed toward the consumer or the retailer.

TRADE ADVERTISING

Trade advertising is aimed at those buying furniture for resale. The manufacturer is trying to get wholesalers and retailers to display and sell the manufacturer's furniture products. Key words often utilized in trade advertising are "value" and "profitability." Trade advertising reinforces personal selling by the manufacturer's representative and features those items that the "rep" is not likely to emphasize, such as service, quality, and special financing. In essence, trade advertising is designed to show that a manufacturer's products should be bought because they have value and will add to the profitability of the buyer's organization.

Trade advertising is used extensively in home furnishings trade publications. Periods of peak activity are just before the various furniture markets, and the advertising is designed to get prospective buyers into an advertiser's market showroom. Most of the trade advertising done by manufacturers is aimed toward furniture wholesalers and retailers.

CONSUMER-ORIENTED ADVERTISING

Consumer-oriented advertising is directed to the furniture buyer who is purchasing the product for personal use. In the furniture industry, most of the consumer-oriented advertising is done by retailers; however, manufacturers are involved in a number of ways. Probably the most popular of these is through sharing the media expense of retail advertising or providing art work and other materials for retail ads.

Some manufacturing companies are increasing consumer recognition by advertising in shelter magazines such as *Better Homes and Gardens* and *House Beautiful* or by donating prizes for nationally televised game shows. Other manufacturers have attempted national consumer-oriented advertising campaigns in other types of magazines and on television and radio. However, these efforts have not been widespread, since it is difficult to justify the extra cost in terms of market impact. Also, the distribution pattern of many furniture manufacturers is not wide enough to support national advertising to consumers.

COOPERATIVE ADVERTISING

Cooperative advertising involves manufacturers and retailers combining to pay the media cost of retail advertisements. To qualify for a cooperative advertising program, the products of the manufacturer must be included in the retailer's advertisements. For example, a bedding manufacturer might pay a specified percentage of the cost of a retail advertisement if the store features that manufacturer's brand of bedding.

Often, cooperative advertising funds are made available to retailers through the purchase of a manufacturer's product. A common arrangement is for a certain percentage of the purchase price paid by the retailer to be credited to a cooperative advertising account for that retailer. The retailer can then draw from the account by sending the manufacturer copies of the media invoice and the advertisement that includes the manufacturer's product. In other words, the manufacturer may reimburse the retailer for a portion of the advertising cost (typically up to 50

YOU'LL ♥ LABOR DAY.

$199 up

Enjoy Labor Day as never before. Put your work aside, and put your feet up and your head back in a beautiful, comfortable new Berkline Wallaway® Recliner. And all of the other days of the year will feel like a holiday, too. We have a wide selection from Berkline, originator of close-to-the-wall recliners with patented Feather-Glide® operation, and no handles or levers.

STORE

If you're only promoting recliners at Father's Day and Christmas you are giving up 50 to 65% of your potential. Dealers who promote Berkline Recliners all year report that over 75% of their sales occur at other than Father's Day and Christmas. Get a Berkline 12-month recliner calendar. Special promotions, and retail ads. The Berkline Corporation, Morristown, TN 37814 and Riverside, CA 92507. The fine line between sales and profits.

BERKLINE®

12-3. This trade advertisement for Berkline recliners appeared in trade publications read by furniture retailers. The section of the ad inside the darker border is a consumer ad in which the retailer can insert the name of the store and have it reprinted in his or her local newspaper. There are two advantages to designing this advertisement in this way: (1) It points out the benefits to the store of stocking Berkline recliners year round. (2) It provides an idea of how to promote this product to the consumer.

A Few Old-Fashioned Things A Lane Love Chest Says To A Contemporary Young Woman At Christmas.

"I wasn't even listening when you said you didn't want much for Christmas this year."

"I wanted to give you a Christmas gift you'll be opening for the rest of your life."

"I hope this means as much t   as the Lane chest I received 2(o means to me. (And I still c   e it's been 26 years!)"

"I want you to have a p'   n to when you want to   things you love."

"You've got a life of   though that make   makes me very, ve

"I haven't forgo   you wanted a sp   your special secr

"You're young enough to have a very big future in front of you."

"Even though you're past the stage where I give you little toys, you'll never outgrow the need to keep them."

"I think the girl who has everything should have something to put it in."

"I'm going to love you even more now that you're a woman than I did when you were still a girl."

"I want you to think of me the rest of your life."

"I love you very, very much."

...hat will be filled ...memories."

Lane

| 48" Cedar*, authentic Eastern red cedar | 44" Cherry*, traditional French Provincial | 48" Pin knotty oak*, embossed front rail, self-rising tray | 49" Rustic pine*, Belgium Gros Point upholstered top |

For a catalog showing more Love Chests, write The Lane Co., Dept. AO11, Altavista, Va. 24517.

12-4. This is an example of a consumer-oriented advertisement designed to appear in publications read by ultimate consumers. The manufacturer is presenting evidence of why it is desirable to give a Lane Love Chest to a young woman at Christmas. The ad also provides an opportunity for a direct response by giving, at the bottom, the address where a catalogue may be obtained.

percent) if there are sufficient funds in the cooperative advertising account.

Manufacturers also receive cooperative advertising funds from their suppliers of fabrics, basic chemicals, and other materials. In this case, the furniture manufacturer's advertising states the furniture features the fabric of a particular supplier or uses a certain brand of finishing material. Manufacturers make extensive use of cooperative advertising funds from suppliers in trade advertising.

ADVERTISING TO CONTRACT BUYERS

A wide variety of businesses, such as hotels and motels, hospitals, office buildings, and schools, often gather bids from various furniture suppliers and award contracts for the purchase of multiple units of furniture at one time. Therefore, to solicit this business, manufacturers advertise directly to contract buyers. This advertising makes use of such media as magazines for hotel and motel owners or direct mail to hospital administrators and business managers. The impact is made through promoting functionality and durability, as well as style. Economy, strength, and reliability are other benefits often emphasized. Such advertisements should be carefully developed to appeal to interior designers and architects because these individuals often specify the type of furniture purchased for business use.

ADVERTISING OBJECTIVES OF MANUFACTURERS

The ultimate objective of advertising, regardless of the sponsor, is to increase sales. This overall goal is achieved through specific techniques used by individual manufacturers to pinpoint carefully the creative message of an advertisement. The following objectives are typical of furniture manufacturers:

Increase brand-name awareness. Manufacturers use both consumer-oriented and trade advertising to promote their brand names. Many studies have shown that people are more likely to buy a brand they know or have heard about. The intent of brand-name advertising is to promote the company rather than specific products or their attributes.

Build a positive business image. Advertisements with this objective, aimed at retailers, are stressing the major competitive strengths of the company rather than trying to sell particular products. These strengths help a manufacturer to achieve and maintain an appropriate position in the marketplace.

Counteract competition. Much of the advertising is simply trying to get the retail buyer to switch from one brand to another. A typical advertisement would indicate that the products of one company provide greater value and better service than those of competing companies.

Fresh directions from **THAYER COGGIN INSTITUTIONAL** include the substance of comfort, visual pleasure, and scale for today's office interiors. This series is available arm or armless with optional high back. Choice of natural or dark oak base.

THAYER COGGIN INSTITUTIONAL, INC.
P.O. Box 5867, High Point, N.C. 27262
(919) 883-0111

SHOWROOMS: New York; Dallas; San Francisco; Los Angeles; Chicago, Suite 1173.

TCI

Designed by Milo Baughman

Integral to the TCI design concept is Faultless Chairwear,™ everything between the seat and the floor. Ultra slim Thinline chair control. Twindisk® II dual wheel casters. And a five leg steel base.

Faultless®

FAULTLESS DIVISION / Bliss & Laughlin Industries / Evansville, Indiana 47711

12-5. This advertisement was published in magazines that are read by purchasers of contract furnishings. It is an example of cooperative advertising jointly paid for by Thayer Coggin Institutional, a contract furniture manufacturer, and Faultless Caster Company, a supplier. By using the supplier's name, the manufacturer was able to obtain assistance in covering the cost of the ad.

"Hooker Furniture helps our business grow at Breuner's."

"The John Breuner Company was established in 1856. Today, we're one of the oldest and largest home furnishers in the country.

"We've been doing business with Hooker for many, many years. They're a very consistent supplier of quality merchandise in their mid-price point.

"We carry Hooker furniture in each of our 17 stores in northern California, Nevada and Arizona. Hooker is consistently on time and on target. Their merchandise comes in clean. We have minimal service problems. And it sells.

Duane Holm
Case Goods Buyer
John Breuner Company
San Ramon, California

Jim Cullen
Occasional Buyer

"Their No. 26 Interpretation Group, for instance, is probably the oldest in our line right now. It has been one of our best sellers since the time it came in."

Start doing business with people who generate business. Talk to your Hooker rep, or call us at 1-703-632-2133.

No. 26 Interpretation Wall Unit

for fresh ideas in gracious living

HOOKER

FURNITURE CORPORATION   MARTINSVILLE, VIRGINIA

Showrooms: Atlanta, Dallas, High Point, San Francisco, Seattle.

12-6. This trade advertisement by Hooker Furniture Corporation appeared in a publication read by furniture retailers. It is designed to build a positive business image by stating that representatives of a leader retailer, John Breuner Company, have been happy with Hooker Furniture. This implies that other retailers will also be satisfied if they stock Hooker Furniture. Testimonials of this type tend to make claims made by the manufacturer more believable.

Increase dealer base. By promoting their selection of products and various types of services to dealers, manufacturers attempt to increase the number of dealers handling their products. The emphasis is to show that the manufacturer's product offerings and accompanying services are a desirable combination which will improve retail profitability.

Increase market showroom attendance. By publicizing new introductions, manufacturers hope to increase the number of dealers visiting their market showrooms. Appeals to value and imaginative copy about new introductions are two ways manufacturers advertise to dealers planning to attend the market.

Provide production information. Manufacturers publish catalogues to provide the consumer with information about their product lines. These catalogues also contain information that helps retail salespeople to understand the products better and to make sales presentations more effective. Also, manufacturers use direct-mail advertising to notify retailers about changes in policies, product offerings, or events.

Tell the "quality story." An important step in selling furniture to both retailers and consumers is to show why the product is "worth" the price. In order to make the necessary points, it is necessary to explain the features of the product which evidence good quality. This can be done through product descriptions in catalogues or brochures which can be distributed to the consumer, or by advertising in a variety of print media.

Stress the services offered by the manufacturer. The manufacturer's representative often spends most of his or her time with the retailer explaining the product and its benefits and features. Therefore, it is desirable to supplement the personal selling effort with advertising stressing the services offered by the manufacturer, including special financing, prompt delivery programs, advertising assistance, and point-of-purchase sales materials.

MEDIA USED BY MANUFACTURERS

Television. Because of the cost and difficulty of supporting national advertising with distribution, television has not been widely used by furniture manufacturers. However, some of the larger manufacturers have used television to increase the awareness of their brand name by the public. An example is those manufacturers who donate merchandise to be used as prizes on game shows in return for exposure on national television.

Consumer magazines. Some furniture manufacturers use magazines to reach both consumers and retailers. The bulk of such advertising aimed at consumers is in shelter magazines. Because of the specialized nature of these magazines, it is possible for manufacturers who feature particular style categories to advertise in those magazines that will be read by their target audience. Regional issues of national magazines also allow the furniture advertiser to place advertising that is consistent with geographic distribution patterns and style preferences. Magazine advertising is used primarily by manufacturers attempting to increase brand-name awareness. In addition to advertising placed in shelter magazines, there is some home furnishings advertising in magazines of a more general nature.

Trade publications. Manufacturers also advertise in trade or business magazines and newspapers, which are read primarily by furniture retailers. Their objective is to expose retailers to their products and to supplement the efforts of their field salespeople by emphasizing product features, quality, and service. By announcing new introductions, special purchase plans, or other offers of interest to retailers, trade publication advertising can often secure additional leads for the field sales staff.

As mentioned earlier, one additional objective of selected trade publication advertisements is to attract retailers into market showrooms.

Direct mail. Direct mail is used by manufacturers to communicate with wholesalers and retailers who are current or prospective customers. Direct-mail communication with current customers is especially effective in announcing price changes, changing catalogue photographs, changing fabric swatches, or making other announcements of interest to dealers.

Direct mail includes such materials as computer-generated personalized letters and circulars sent to retailers as a way of encouraging them to buy products. This medium has the advantage of getting information such as price changes or new product offerings to the target audience quickly. Another type of direct-mail advertising used by manufacturers is advertising inserts included with billings or other regular correspondence.

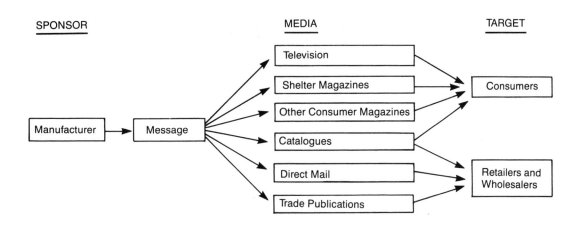

12-7. Media for manufacturer-sponsored advertising

Catalogues. Catalogues of products produced by furniture manufacturers are usually available in retail furniture stores. They contain product photographs and other information such as construction, piece sizes, finishes, and fabric samples which may be used as effective selling tools by retail salespeople. Many upholstered furniture companies also support their catalogues with racks of fabric swatches to be used as sales aids for those customers who wish to select their fabrics and colors. The catalogues and fabric swatches must be updated periodically to support current product offerings effectively.

TYPES OF ADVERTISING USED BY RETAILERS

Although some of the same types of advertising are used by manufacturers and retailers, they are utilized from a different perspective. Advertising by retailers is entirely consumer-oriented, aimed at increasing sales to the consumer.

PRODUCT ADVERTISING

Product advertising by a retailer informs the consumer about a product in order to increase the consumer's interest in purchasing it. These three subcategories of product advertising are used by retailers just as they are by manufacturers:

1. Pioneering product advertising is concerned with developing demand for a new category of product rather than a specific brand. An example would be a retailer encouraging a consumer to buy a "close-to-the-wall" recliner by stressing the benefits of that product rather than a particular brand of recliner.

2. Competitive product advertising is aimed at encouraging the consumer to buy one brand instead of another, and it is widely used by retailers. The benefits of buying Brand A recliners are emphasized to encourage the purchase of that brand over others.

3. Repetitive or continuity product advertising is designed to "remind" consumers to buy a brand-name product with which they are already familiar. By advertising repetitively, the retailer is more likely to be thought of when the consumer is in the "buying mood."

PRICE ADVERTISING

Probably the most common type of retailer advertising is price advertising, which emphasizes the price at which the retail furniture store is offering products. Many furniture retailers take this approach because they feel the best way to get customers into a store is by featuring price appeal. Especially in newspapers, the advertising is prepared so that price stands out prominently.

TYPES	OBJECTIVES

Product
    Pioneering
    Competitive
    Repetitive or continuity
Price
Institutional
Cooperative
	Introduce new products
	Increase customer traffic
	Announce store events
	Announce clearance sales
	Provide information about the retailer

12-8. Retailer-sponsored advertising

INSTITUTIONAL ADVERTISING

Institutional advertising promotes a favorable image about a retail store in general, rather than trying to feature specific products and prices. The intent is to register the name of the retailer in the minds of prospective buyers so that it can be recalled easily. Institutional advertising can provide information about the store or its services. It is indirect, rather than trying to directly stimulate an immediate purchase decision of a particular product.

COOPERATIVE ADVERTISING

Cooperative advertising, with the furniture manufacturer or supplier sharing advertising costs, usually requires the retailer to include the products and name of the manufacturer or supplier in an advertisement. Cooperative advertising funds are important to retailers. Retail advertising is predominately local, and the retailer can get into the local media more often with larger advertisements by using such funds. The more often the name of a retailer appears before the public in persuasive ads, the more likely that consumers will buy from that store.

ADVERTISING OBJECTIVES OF RETAILERS

Retail furniture advertising is primarily aimed at increasing the sales of stores in their market areas. Retailers have a number of objectives in their advertising, including the following:

Introduce new products. Retailers may run advertisements to introduce a new product concept to the area by using pioneering product advertising. Retail advertising also introduces new style trends and announces new brand names being carried by the store.

Increase customer traffic. Often, retailers will run contests to attract new shoppers to their stores. Even though there may be no purchase required to enter, new people will see the store when they come in to register. Free items such as a steak knife may be given away, or other useful items may be available at a special price to increase customer traffic. For example, a household item of obvious value might be sold at a break-even or lower price just to attract people into a store.

Announce store events. Store events such as sales are announced effectively through price advertising in newspapers or circulars. These advertisements may feature a collection of products which have all been placed on sale for a predetermined time period. Other in-store events, such as decorating seminars, visits to the store by celebrities, or other happenings of interest to consumers, may be announced through institutional advertising.

Announce clearance sales. Even though clearance sales are technically in-store events, their wide popularity makes them eligible for special mention. On a periodic basis, retail furniture stores hold clearance sales which must be advertised effectively. The purpose of these sales is to sell old styles and products that have been on the display floor too long. Some stores have what are called "end-of-month" or "EOM" sales to clear out old styles and make room for new offerings.

Provide information about the retailer. Much information about a retail furniture store can be disseminated through advertising. Store hours and location may be announced by a retailer who is moving or changing hours of operation. Methods of financing and interest rates are often featured, as well as warranties, delivery policies, and other consumer services.

MEDIA USED BY RETAILERS

Radio. Radio is used extensively by furniture retailers because it is useful in segmenting a local audience. Because of the large number of people who listen to the radio while driving or conducting other activities, furniture retailers can get their message to a large percentage of consumers in the local area. The major disadvantage is the lack of product visibility.

Radio stations require very short lead times, so advertisements can be placed on the air quickly. This medium is best used by retailers to announce in-store events such as sales or other messages which do not require a lengthy explanation (changes in hours, location, and so on).

Television. Television is being used by larger furniture retailers to make a strong impact in a local or regional market area. Although television has traditionally been too expensive for both furniture manufacturers and retailers, some store owners are using television mainly for institutional advertising and to announce sales and other in-store events. It is a dramatic medium because of the ability to combine a good color and visual image with the spoken word. Manufacturers and retailers sometimes combine their efforts in television advertising—retailers run commercials prepared by manufacturers featuring the retail store's name.

SPONSOR   MEDIA   TARGET

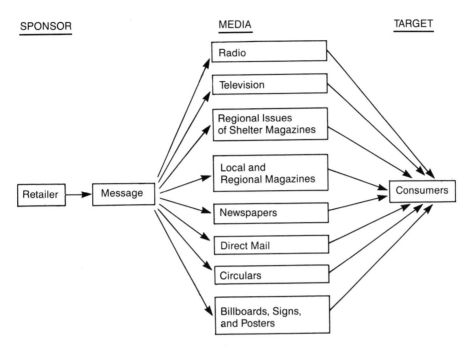

12-9. Retailer-sponsored advertising media

Newspapers. Newspapers are an effective local medium which, like radio, can be used to announce in-store events. Almost exclusively a retailer's medium, newspapers account for most furniture store advertising. Newspapers are the best medium for price advertising because an ad can be inserted quickly and receives intensive local coverage.

Furniture retailers can pinpoint a particular segment of newspaper readers by requesting placement within a certain section of the newspaper. For example, a furniture retailer wanting to appeal to the woman who is interested in making her home fashionable might advertise in the home fashion or women's section of the newspaper. Such incentives as a coupon, which may be clipped out and exchanged for a free item, or a discount off the price of certain products may also be easily included in a newspaper advertisement.

Magazines. The emergence of local and regional magazines offers an opportunity for furniture retail advertising. These magazines tend to be of relatively high quality and most appeal to a well-educated, affluent readership. Therefore, they are best suited for retail stores featuring full service and higher-priced furniture lines.

Regional issues of national magazines offer retailers an opportunity to place advertisements in an issue that will be distributed only in the

BACK TALK

BEMCO POSTURE SERIES :60 RADIO SCRIPT

ANNOUNCER: If you need a good night's sleep, you need to Talk Back.

A little Back Talk will help you discover just the right combination of comfort and support your back needs for a refreshing night's sleep.

Nobody Talks Back better than (store name). And no sleep set talks quality better than our Bemco Posture® Series.

Bedding by Bemco is the label that promises quality.

Posture is the sleep set that delivers.

For example, every Posture sleep set is constructed with three Posture-Frames: two built into every mattress, one built into every box-spring.

This exclusive feature helps your Posture mattress adjust to your weight, your shape, even the position in which you sleep. And it builds years of extra life into every sleep set.

And, because we know that no one mattress is right for all backs, the Bemco Posture Series gives you a choice of four different combinations of luxurious surface softness and deep-down firmness: Posture I, Posture II, Posture III and Posture IV.

Find out which one of them fits your back's idea of comfort.

Come in to (store name) bedding department —and start Talking Back today.

(Store name and address.)

12-10. This suggested sixty-second script is made available by Bemco Bedding to furniture retailers for their own advertising use on local radio. In this advertisement, Bemco is promoting their "Talk Back" advertising campaign. Note that the script is written in such a way that the store name can be easily inserted in a number of places.

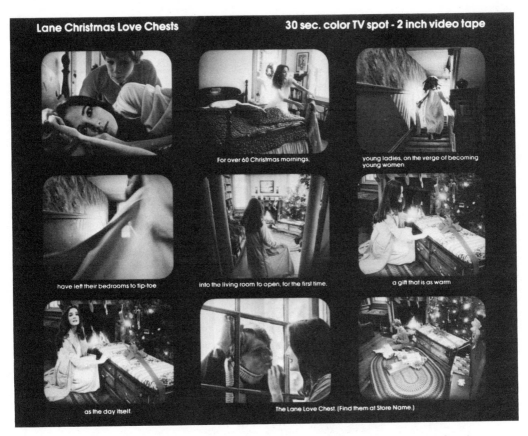

Lane Christmas Love Chests   **30 sec. color TV spot - 2 inch video tape**

For over 60 Christmas mornings.

young ladies, on the verge of becoming young women

have left their bedrooms to tip-toe

into the living room to open, for the first time.

a gift that is as warm

as the day itself.

The Lane Love Chest. (Find them at Store Name.)

12-11. This TV storyboard is contained in a flier that explains the type of television advertising supplied by The Lane Company to their retail furniture dealers. The videotape ad described here is designed to promote Lane Love Chests to consumers as Christmas presents. By using this videotape, the retailer can add his store name at the end, paying for the media time only. The Lane Company paid for the production of the advertisement, which is quite a cost savings for the retailer.

retailers' trading area. Also, some manufacturers run advertisements in regional issues with the names of retailers carrying their products.

Direct mail. Direct-mail advertising to the consumer is popular with many retailers. A well-planned direct-mail campaign by retailers to households in their trading area can generate additional store traffic and profitable extra sales.

As with manufacturers, retail direct mail includes computer-generated personalized letters, circulars, and advertising inserts enclosed with billings or other correspondence. The success of a direct-mail retail advertising campaign depends on an up-to-date mailing list of qualified prospects, including past and present customers.

12-12. The copy, artwork, and layout in this effective retail newspaper advertisement for wall systems activates the selling process, linking consumer needs and reasons to buy in order to create the strongest audience appeal. The ad is designed to catch the reader's *attention*, gain the customer's *interest*, create a *desire* to own the product, and lead to the proper *action*—to come into the store to complete the purchase. It clearly shows the product, its benefits, and how it will meet the consumer's needs and objectives.

12-13. *Facing page:* This ad slick is provided by Lea Industries, a furniture manufacturer, to retailers who stock their merchandise. The ad can be run in newspapers in the same format as shown here, merely by adding the store name and product prices. Often, however, many retailers prefer to do their own layouts, so they will clip out from the ad slick any artwork and copy they want to use and insert it into their own advertising. The sketches and copy are designed in such a way that they can be easily reproduced for newspaper advertising.

0 0
1 1
2 2
3 3
4 4
5 5
6 6
7 7
8 8
9 9

SALE CASUAL OAK CONTEMPORARY

Lea
LEA INDUSTRIES

Progressions

COMPONENT FURNITURE
that offers you
infinite decorating
possibilities!

Contemporary component furniture
that you can bunch along a wall,
stack up to the ceiling, or use as free-
standing units. Use them for open
displays, bookcases, or closed
storage. Re-arrange them to suit your
own interior design plans.

ERNATE LAYOVER ARTWORK
951 BOOKCASE HEADBOARD

ALTERNATE LAYOVER ARTWORK
020 TWIN MIRRORS

ALTERNATE LAYOVER ARTWORK
030 VERTICAL MIRROR

$'000

7-Pc. Component Bedwall

A space-saving arrangement that includes 2 three-drawer units, 2 open
units, and 2 door units spanned with
a light bridge across the top.

- Bookcase Headboard $000
- Platform Bed $000
- Two-Drawer Desk $000
- Desk Chair $000

$'000

4-Pc. Bedroom Grouping

Casual Contemporary design and the
attractive butcher block graining of
Oak solids and veneers combine to
make this master bedroom something special. We include door
dresser, mirror, six-drawer chest and
headboard.

- 2-Drawer Night Stand $000
- Free-standing Open Unit $000

**MAXIMIZE SPACE
WITH YOUR VERY OWN
CAREFULLY PLANNED
STACKABLE COMPONENTS**

Left: Practical, eye-catching storage/
entertainment wall system that's
deep enough for a TV or stereo equipment.

Right: Component units create
generous shelf storage behind a sofa.
Bunched along a wall, a re-
arrangeable grouping features interior lights in the glass-door unit, and
a drop-lid desk/bar.

- Lighted Glass-Door Unit $000
- Narrow Open Unit $000
- Closed Door Unit $000
- Wider Open Unit $000
- Three-Drawer Unit $000
- Drop-Lid Desk/Bar Unit $000
- Narrow Shelf/Drawer Unit $000

STORE NAME furniture

ADDRESS ....
STORE HOURS ....
TELEPHONE ....

LEA NewsAd No. 8101 - 074 "Progressions"

PIECES ILLUSTRATED: 231, 240, 232, 955R or 953 w/951, 673, 342
                      292, 040, 161, 950, 421, 240
                      232, 240, 241, 242, 231
                      243, 232, 241, 123, 242

DEALER PLEASE NOTE: This ad measures 5 col. x 15¼". Your newspaper
can photomechanically reduce or enlarge it without losing detail.

 NEWSPAPER PLEASE NOTE: This ad conforms to recommended ANPA
Advertising Dimension Standards for makeup size adsA. If necessary,
please reproportion to fit your newspaper's ad make-up dimensions.

Circulars. Circulars are widely used by furniture retailers either in direct-mail advertising or as newspaper inserts. Distribution of the circulars by both of these methods can be effective in stimulating sales. If it is properly prepared, a four-color circular vividly can present a collection of products that are either on sale or featured in the store. Circulars make a good impact because they give the customer an idea of what styles and collections of products are available. Most possess good printing quality and make effective use of color.

A circular may be prepared and printed by one retailer independently or collectively by a group of retailers through a voluntary chain or buying service. By joining a voluntary chain or buying service, small retailers can obtain better quality circulars and other advertising materials than they could afford by themselves.

Outdoor advertising. Outdoor advertising is used almost exclusively by retailers as institutional advertising to keep the names of their stores before the public. A good billboard or poster with the right combination of illustration and copy can constantly remind the public about a store and its location. The store sign itself is also a form of outdoor advertising. It should be highly visible, attractive, and easy to read so people can find the store without difficulty.

LEGAL ASPECTS OF ADVERTISING

The Federal Trade Commission (FTC), the agency involved with policing advertising and sales transactions, has issued a number of advertising regulations that concern the furniture marketer. These regulations require accurate, truthful pricing; full disclosure; accurate product descriptions; and the avoidance of misleading terminology. For example:

1. When advertising a reduction in price such as: "This sofa was $899 but now is only $699." The $899 must have been the price that the sofa was offered to the public for a reasonable period of time.
2. When advertising a free or bargain offer such as: "Buy two dining-room chairs and get the third chair free." In making this offer, the retailer must not increase the price of the two chairs that the customer must buy in order to get the third one free.
3. When describing furniture products. Descriptions of products must be done honestly and accurately. For example, an informal dining table with a plastic laminated top should be described as having an "oak-grained plastic top" or another equally accurate description.
4. When credit terms are discussed in an advertisement. The advertised statement "10 percent down and payments of only $20.00 per month" would require additional disclosure of the annual percentage rate of interest, number of payments, and any other

amounts that would be necessary to fully disclose all credit charges to the consumer.

For further information on the legal aspects of advertising, refer to Appendix B, "Advertising Guidelines."

SOURCES OF ADVERTISING ASSISTANCE

Advertising, as already indicated, must be carefully planned. This means it must have the right creative message and media mix to be effective. Therefore, the responsibility for the advertising program must be with someone who is both knowledgeable and creative.

Manufacturers, in many instances, have "in-house" advertising departments or at least someone, usually in the sales department, who is responsible for advertising. The catalogue is generally prepared by people who are company employees, with the photography, swatch making, and printing contracted to outside firms. The remainder of the advertising may be done by company employees or contracted to an advertising agency, or a combination of the two.

An advertising agency may be very helpful because it specializes in creating effective advertising. A full-service agency has a complete staff of commercial artists, creative people to produce copy and layout, and media specialists to recommend the most beneficial media mix. The agency can also help to coordinate the advertising with the requirements of the media in order to avoid confusion and excessive costs.

Retailers, for the most part, do their own advertising. Since the bulk of their advertising will probably be radio and newspaper, it is normally assigned to the owner, store manager, or someone else in management in the organization. Large retailers have separate advertising departments which work directly with local media to coordinate their advertising campaigns. Many retailers make use of drawings, photographs, and sample advertisements provided by manufacturers. If the retailer is a member of a buying service or buys from a wholesaler, good-quality circulars and other advertising materials may be obtained inexpensively or for free from the buying service or wholesaler.

SUMMARY

Advertising is paid communication through a medium by an identified sponsor. Advertising should be an ongoing program planned carefully and based on realistic objectives.

The advertising budget may be based either on a predetermined percentage of present or projected sales, or on the objectives or tasks to be accomplished.

Broadcast media include radio and television. Print media include newspapers, magazines, direct mail, catalogues, circulars, and outdoor advertising.

Considerations in selecting media for furniture advertisements are: objective of the advertisement, effectiveness of the media in carrying the message, media circulation, advertising budget, competitive activity, continuity, and prospective customers.

Types of manufacturer-sponsored advertising include pioneering, competitive, and repetitive or continuity product advertising; trade advertising; consumer-oriented advertising; cooperative advertising; and advertising to contract buyers.

Manufacturers advertise in order to increase sales with such specific objectives as: increasing brand-name awareness, building a positive image, counteracting competition, increasing their retail dealer base, increasing market showroom attendance, providing product information, telling the "quality story," and stressing the services they offer.

Advertising media used by furniture manufacturers include television, consumer magazines, trade publications, direct mail, and catalogues.

Types of retailer-sponsored advertising include pioneering, competitive, and repetitive or continuity product advertising; price advertising; institutional advertising; and cooperative advertising.

Retailers advertise in order to increase sales with such specific objectives as: introducing new products, increasing customer traffic, announcing store events, announcing clearance sales, and providing information about their stores.

Advertising media used by furniture retailers include radio, television, newspapers, magazines, direct mail, circulars, and outdoor advertising.

The Federal Trade Commission has issued a number of regulations that must be observed by the furniture advertiser.

Furniture advertisers either do their own advertising, seek assistance from the media, or employ advertising agencies.

CHAPTER 13

SALES PROMOTION AND PUBLIC RELATIONS

I n addition to advertising, sales promotion is an effective type of nonpersonal communication. It is extremely helpful when the furniture marketer is trying to provide an incentive to encourage potential customers to make a buying decision.

Public relations is closely related to advertising and sales promotion; it is a planned effort to influence the attitudes of various "publics" toward the firm. Sales promotion and public relations will be discussed separately because the furniture marketer should know how each can be used to the best advantage. In the highly competitive home furnishings industry, these tools, along with personal selling and advertising, can greatly help in motivating prospective customers toward a purchase decision.

SALES PROMOTION

Sales promotion techniques are miscellaneous activities that supplement or coordinate the major selling thrust of an organization—activities other than personal selling, advertising, and publicity. In reality, there is a very fine line between sales promotion and many types of advertising. Sales promotion is designed to enhance the effectiveness of personal selling and advertising. It also helps to build a bridge between these two areas.

MANUFACTURER-SPONSORED SALES PROMOTION

Sales promotion has developed as an important selling tool used by manufacturers to gain the attention of both dealers and consumers. Several sales promotion techniques are successful in providing that extra nudge which may result in the purchase of one brand of furniture over others.

SALES PROMOTION OBJECTIVES OF MANUFACTURERS
Sales promotion, like advertising, is designed to sell the product and many of the specific objectives of sales promotion are very close to the objectives

of advertising. Some of the most common sales promotion objectives of furniture manufacturers are:

To obtain placements on retail floors. Here the emphasis is on trying to attract sufficient interest from retailers so they will commit enough funds and floor space to place samples in their stores where they may be seen by consumers.

To increase market showroom attendance. Appropriate sales promotion techniques are used by manufacturers to increase the drawing power of their merchandise displays at the periodic furniture markets.

To obtain buying commitments "now." By offering special credit terms and reduced prices for a limited time period, manufacturers attempt to get dealers to order "now" rather than waiting to see what sells or what the competition has to offer.

To increase brand-name awareness. Sales promotion can be used to get the name of a manufacturer and its products before the public.

To encourage dealers to buy larger quantities. Special price concessions or other sales promotion techniques may result in larger purchases than would normally result from personal selling and advertising.

To reinforce advertising and personal selling. Premiums, point-of-purchase material, and other sales promotion techniques can result in retailers and consumers giving special attention to a company and its products, which supports a company's advertising or personal selling efforts.

SALES PROMOTION TECHNIQUES AIMED AT DEALERS

Most furniture manufacturers actively participate in sales promotion campaigns aimed at retail furniture dealers. Some types of such sales promotion are:

Furniture markets. The wholesale furniture markets are the most obvious type of sales promotion aimed at furniture dealers. This is the major promotional effort used by manufacturers and importers to get dealers to view their offerings in person. Since these markets are so important, they will be discussed extensively in a separate chapter. (See Chapter 16.)

Contests. A wide variety of home furnishings companies, such as bedding or recliner manufacturers have sponsored contests for dealers. In such contests, the store manager or salesperson who sells the most bedding or largest number of recliners in a particular geographic territory could win a grand prize, such as a Carribbean cruise. In other contests, all who sell above a given amount of merchandise might receive an award. Not only can such contests make retailers and their salespeople more enthusiastic about a manufacturer's products, but they also mean the manufacturer will sell a larger volume of products.

Another type of contest could be designed to increase showroom traffic

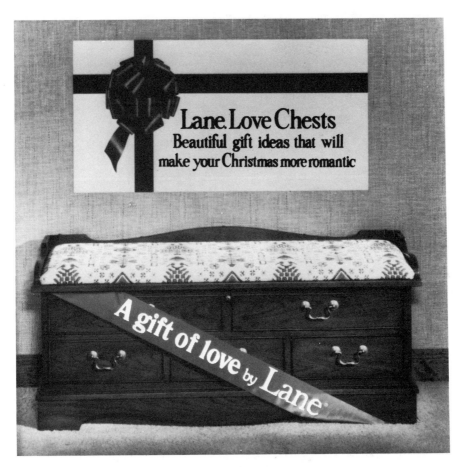

13-1. This sign and banner are examples of point-of-purchase display materials provided by manufacturers to dealers. Note the theme of romance and beautiful gift-giving conveyed by these materials—all part of Lane Love Chests' image which the manufacturer wishes to convey.

at one of the furniture markets. A drawing would be held, and dealers who wished to participate would have to register in the manufacturer's market showroom to be eligible to win.

Point-of-purchase material. Point-of-purchase (POP) material is provided to the dealer to be displayed in retail stores. Examples are posters, banners, streamers, signs, or displays. This material is designed to attract the attention of the retail furniture shopper and to serve as sales aids for the retail furniture salesperson. Signs stating that the store has a particular brand of furniture or bedding may be provided to be easily placed in the store's windows. Display cards explaining graphically how a recliner mechanism works or the materials and construction of a case piece are very effective sales aids for the salesperson on the retail sales floor.

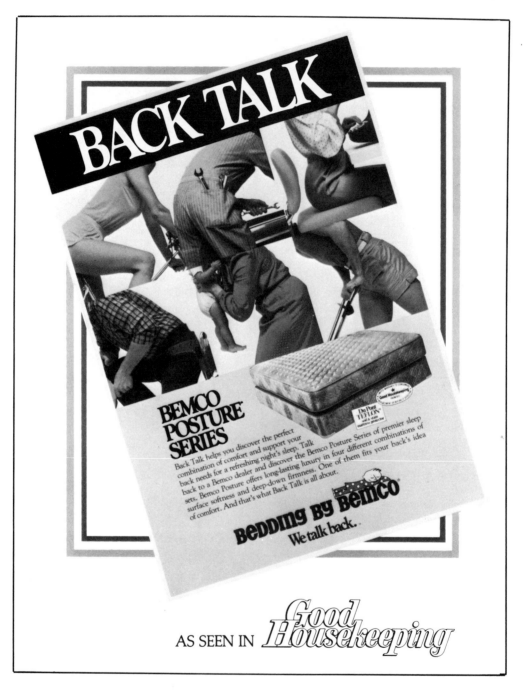

13-2. Bemco Bedding provides retailers with this point-of-purchase display, a cardboard, stand-up sign which is reprinted from one of its *Good Housekeeping* advertisements. The focus is on its "Back Talk" campaign in which the benefits of correct posture and a good night's sleep are emphasized.

Newsletters or periodic bulletins. Manufacturers may cause retailers to be more enthusiastic about selling their products by supplying helpful information about them and news about the company. Of interest also are advertising or display hints which illustrate how dealers in other parts of the country have advertised and sold the manufacturer's products.

Advertising or display allowances and assistance. A number of sales promotion techniques aimed at retailers involve the seller sharing in the cost of advertising or displaying the company's products. (See Chapter 12 for a discussion of shared advertising costs.) As a further incentive to retailers to stock its products, a manufacturer may offer technical assistance in creating attractive retail displays if the retailer agrees to place the manufacturer's products on the sales floor. Various types of advertising assistance are also available from manufacturers. A typical example of such assistance is artwork that can be used in retail newspaper advertising.

Price promotions. Many manufacturers use a variety of price promotions to obtain business when the economy is in a recession or sales are hard to obtain for some other reason. Generous credit terms, such as extending the time period in which a retailer must pay for merchandise, can be an incentive for a dealer to order now rather than wait or shop around. Special prices on selected pieces or groups and quantity discounts may help the dealer to make a buying decision or to order more than would otherwise be the case. Many reduced-price package deals are offered on a one-time basis if the dealer buys a predetermined group or quantity of products.

Advertising specialties. A variety of useful items bearing the name of a manufacturer may be distributed free to current and potential customers, bringing the name of the manufacturer before the retailer on a continual basis. Ideally, an advertising specialty is an item that has a fairly long life and will be used frequently by the dealer. Examples are calendars, pens, pads of paper, ash trays, matches, or even baseball caps or tee shirts bearing the manufacturer's name.

SALES PROMOTION TECHNIQUES AIMED AT CONSUMERS

Most sales promotions sponsored by furniture manufacturers are aimed at retail furniture dealers. However, there are two types of sales promotion by manufacturers designed to reach consumers:

Game show prizes. A relatively inexpensive way to get national exposure for a manufacturer's products is through donations for prizes on televised game shows. The major expense is the cost of the products. Other costs involved are the fee paid to the broker who distributes the photographs and product descriptions to the game show producers and the costs involved in packaging and shipping the products to the television studio or prize recipient. The benefit for the manufacturer is that the company name is mentioned and the product is shown on national television for a fraction of the normal advertising cost for such coverage.

Premiums. Manufacturers may provide a "free" premium for buying certain types of furniture. For example, a dining-room furniture manufacturer might offer to "set the table" with a new six-piece place setting of china with specified dining-room suites purchased within a given time period. Or a television might be provided "free" with the purchase of a name-brand wall system. The promise of this extra merchandise may serve as an incentive to buy now rather than delay the purchase.

RETAILER-SPONSORED SALES PROMOTION

Retailers utilize many types of sales promotion aimed at the consumer. Although some are in connection with the manufacturer, most are sponsored by the retailer. Like the manufacturer, the retailer sponsors sales promotion to increase sales; however, objectives and techniques are somewhat different.

SALES PROMOTION OBJECTIVES OF RETAILERS

When retailers sponsor some type of sales promotion, it is usually with one or more of the following objectives in mind:

To stimulate product trial. Certain types of sales promotion are designed to encourage consumers to try particular products.

To increase store traffic. The object is to get people into the store even though they may not purchase anything. If they visit the store and like what they see, they are likely to come back and buy when they need furniture.

To obtain buying commitments "now." Appropriate sales promotion techniques may be effective in getting the consumer to buy now rather than postponing the purchase.

To establish continuity of purchase. An objective of successful retailers is to "keep them buying." After all, it is easier to get a customer back into the store to buy again than it is to keep having to develop completely new customers.

To reinforce advertising. Sales promotion techniques, such as coupons and sweepstakes, offer the consumer an additional reason to read or listen to an advertisement.

RETAILER SALES PROMOTION TECHNIQUES

Aggressive retailers often use a combination of the following sales promotion techniques to stimulate sales:

Reduced-price promotion. A reduced-price promotion stresses a reduction in the purchase price of a product. It could involve sending out coupons that can be redeemed for a specified percentage reduction in the

13-3. These three direct-mail pieces offer premiums in order to increase store traffic. Crawford's is offering a free turkey baster for coming into the store. On the other side of the direct-mail piece, the store offers a free turkey with a purchase totaling $199 or more. Winner Furniture Co. is making a special mailing to "preferred customers," allowing $100 off any purchase of $399 or more. A necklace is being given away, just for visiting the store. A "treasure hunt" is a device used in another direct-mail piece to which a key is attached. The consumer brings the key to the store in order to try to unlock a "treasure chest" and win a gift. *(Southern Marketing Services)*

purchase price of designated merchandise. Or the retailer might advertise a specific discount to anyone who buys within a particular time period. Giving those who have previously bought merchandise the first chance to buy items on sale can be quite effective.

Of course, the word "sale" is used most often with these promotions. Terms such as "trade-in sale," "red tag sale," or "twelve-hour sale" are commonly used in announcing reduced-price promotions. In each case, the title describes the length of time of the sale, how the sale items are designated, or the method by which savings may be realized.

In-store events or celebrations other than sales. Sales are the most common in-store sales promotion events; however, a number of other events may also be used. Having a local sports figure or personality in the store can be effective. Parents may bring their children to have pictures taken with the celebrity, or they may just come to see for themselves. The tenth anniversary or some other celebration can be used effectively as a sales promotion. These celebrations are usually accompanied by a sale; however, having a party with cake, balloons for the children, and other decorations is usually also included.

Premiums. Steak knives, coffee mugs, or other traffic-building items are examples of premiums that are often free or self-liquidating (i.e., the customer pays a price just sufficient to cover the cost of the merchandise). The self-liquidating premium is usually successful if it is an unquestionably good value.

Contests. Used to get people into a store, contests or drawings may allow shoppers to sign up to win a recliner, sofa, or other prize to be given away by the retail store. Although a purchase is not required to enter, these contests or drawings may get previous or potential customers into the store to see current offerings.

Product demonstrations. It is often effective to have a new product demonstrated in the store, the center of a shopping mall, or some other location where the demonstration can be seen by a large number of people. For example, an exhibit of waterbeds could be on display, giving people an opportunity to lie down on one and actually feel what it is like.

PUBLIC RELATIONS

Public relations is really a management function that involves a conscious effort to influence the attitudes of a number of "publics" toward the firm. Management constantly interacts with several publics and tries to impress them favorably. Examples of such publics are dealers, consumers, government agencies, employees, the press, and leaders in the general and financial communities. It is important that the company have a favorable image because image affects product sales. When consumers hear good things about a retailer or manufacturer, they are more likely to buy products from that organization.

Most furniture manufacturers or retailers are too small to have a separate public relations department or even a person whose only responsibility is public relations. A few manufacturers, however, have their own public relations person and others use an advertising department or agency. In a typical retail organization, the owner or manager handles public relations.

PUBLIC RELATIONS OBJECTIVES OF MANUFACTURERS

Some specific public relations goals of furniture manufacturers serve to illustrate common public relations problems and how to establish a favorable public image:

To receive favorable publicity. The most obvious goal is to receive favorable publicity. By definition, publicity or editorial treatment in magazines and newspapers is news about a company or product which, hopefully, will benefit an organization, but is not paid for by that organization. Both manufacturers and retailers appreciate favorable editorial treatment because it lends credibility to the organization and its product offerings. It is more believable if someone else says something about you than if you say it about yourself. In fact, good publicity is normally more effective than a company's advertising because of the third-party endorsement. Some of the techniques used by furniture manufacturers to obtain favorable publicity are discussed on the following page.

To gain the confidence of the financial community. Furniture manufacturers must be able to borrow money at the most favorable interest rates, which is possible if a company has a good reputation with a variety of potential lenders. Therefore, it is advisable for the officials of furniture manufacturers to provide information to the leaders of the financial community regularly, which will keep them aware of the financial condition of the company.

To gain respect for the organization as a "good citizen." This objective involves being civic-minded and building an image as an active, willing participant in the community. Furniture executives can lend their time as workers in community drives such as the United Way or Community Chest. The fact that individuals within the firm contribute to such funds is further evidence of concern for the community. Company facilities may be used for blood drives by the Red Cross.

Manufacturers sometimes donate merchandise to auctions for charity. For example, if a local educational television station is holding an auction to raise funds, a donation of merchandise would be considered a favorable gesture.

To be identified with education. It lends credibility to a company's image to be identified with education. For example, a manufacturer may make various individuals within the organization available to serve as guest speakers at high schools and colleges. Similarly, it makes a good impression for students to be invited to tour manufacturing plants and offices. Another opportunity open to larger organizations is to pay part or all of employees' educational expenses and to provide scholarship funds.

To make the business more "human." People like to do business with companies that care about people both inside and outside the organization. A plant newspaper may carry news stories about employees to show that the company is interested in them. Retirement dinners and awards for exceptional or long service may be publicized to show employees and the community that the company really does care about its employees.

To counteract negative publicity. At times, companies may be the victims of rumors or negative publicity. For example, a manufacturer might be accused of not employing minorities in sufficient numbers, of polluting the atmosphere, or providing unsafe working conditions. In each of these situations, it is advisable to be aware of what negative rumors exist and plan a positive public relations campaign aimed at acquainting the public with the true circumstances.

To be seen as a company that provides fashionable products with good value and quality. No goodwill ambassador is more effective than a satisfied customer. Therefore, it is important to make certain that products have value in relation to the price charged and that customers are satisfied. This objective can be accomplished by furnishing facts to the press and other interested publics as evidence of the fashion, value, and quality of a firm's products.

TECHNIQUES USED BY MANUFACTURERS TO OBTAIN PUBLICITY

Some of the techniques used by furniture manufacturers to get favorable publicity include the following:

News releases. The most widely used method of obtaining publicity is the news release. This is a relatively short news story about a product, personality, event, or other newsworthy topic sent to selected media. A news release is often accompanied with a photograph or drawing in the hope that the media will find the news release of interest and publish it. Furniture manufacturers often prepare news releases on their new product introductions in the hope that trade publications or consumer magazines will publish the releases or at least mention their products.

Speeches by company executives. Executives of furniture manufacturers look for opportunities to make speeches on occasions such as industry meetings and business seminars. It is good publicity for these executives to share their knowledge with others. An effective, interesting speech is considered by most people as a reflection of an efficient, up-to-date company.

Press kits. At the major furniture markets, manufacturers prepare press kits detailing their offerings, especially the new introductions. Such kits consist of photographs and drawings of major pieces and short, concise descriptions of the product. They should provide interesting details, such as the origin of the design, so that the media will find the product worthy of being featured editorially.

Clip sheets. Clip sheets are short articles and pictures of products on regular newspaper-sized paper which are periodically sent to newspapers. It is easy for the newspaper to clip an article and insert the product picture whenever something is needed on home furnishings or to fill space.

Press conferences. When the company has a major announcement or newsworthy event, an invitation will be sent to newspaper reporters, radio and television program directors, and magazine editors to attend a meeting in which the announcement is made. A packet of information is usually distributed and questions answered.

Market showroom tours. All major manufacturers make one or more people available to show representatives of the press through their showrooms. These guides are knowledgeable and present the product line, especially the new offerings, to the best possible advantage.

Receptions, parties, and other social events. At furniture markets, major manufacturers and market showroom buildings sponsor press parties, receptions, and other events for the representatives of the press. Trade associations of both retailers and manufacturers also invite media representatives to their meetings, parties, and other social events.

PUBLIC RELATIONS OBJECTIVES OF RETAILERS

A positive image is of no less importance to furniture retailers. Although the public relations objectives of retailers are closely related to those of manufacturers, some of these objectives are discussed separately:

To receive favorable publicity. It is important for furniture retailers to receive third-party endorsement. People are most likely to believe information about a retail company if it comes from someone other than an employee of the company. Some of the techniques used by retailers to obtain favorable publicity are presented on page 185.

To gain the confidence of the financial community. Furniture retailers must borrow funds to construct buildings, finance inventories, and purchase needed equipment. Therefore, they also must show potential lenders that they are viable, progressive institutions so that funds can be borrowed at reasonable interest rates. An extra effort must be made to establish a long-term, favorable relationship with the local financial community.

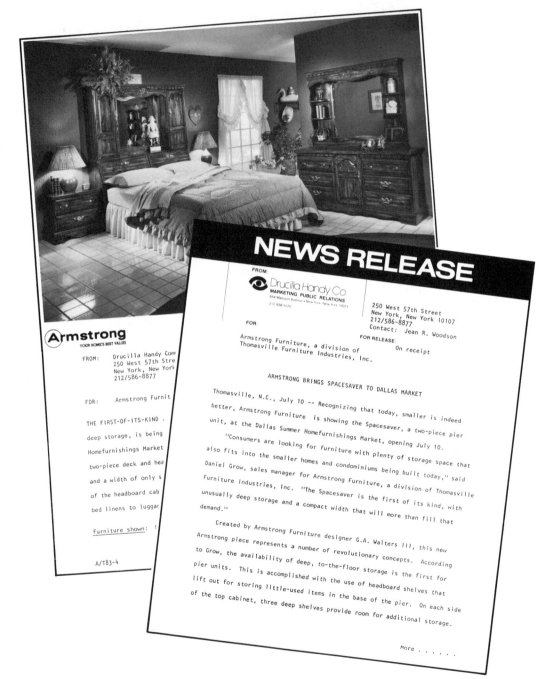

13-4. This news release and product photo plus caption are part of the contents of a press kit which was sent to media editors by a marketing public relations firm for Armstrong Furniture. This material is intended to generate a news story about the product introduction ("Spacesaver," a compact headboard cabinet) in consumer and/or trade publications.

To be a "good citizen." Furniture retailers should be respected members of the community by showing that they are good citizens. For example, retailers can obtain a favorable image by allowing a portion of their warehouse or parking lot to be used as a drop/pick up spot for clothing and articles for the Salvation Army. Other examples of good citizenship may be participating in the United Way or Red Cross blood drives, lending furniture to be used in community theater productions, and donating items to needy families.

To be identified with education. Retailers may be identified with education by placing advertisements in high school or college yearbooks or in athletic and dramatic programs. Another opportunity would be to lend furniture for a school dramatic production in return for a credit in the printed program.

To become known as honest, respectable merchants. People like to do business with retailers they feel are honest and will give them a fair deal. Therefore, it is good public relations not to cut corners or short-change customers. Satisfied customers will tell others about the store just as those who are not satisfied will. Thus, retailers who make an extra effort to ensure honesty and fairness in all their dealings with manufacturers, lenders, customers, and employees will enjoy a favorable public image.

TECHNIQUES USED BY RETAILERS TO OBTAIN PUBLICITY

Examples of techniques used by furniture retailers to get favorable publicity include the following:

News releases. News stories submitted to the press may include such happenings as store openings, promotions, new people hired, and the establishment of close ties with key manufacturers. The objective is to provide stories that newspapers, radio, or other media will find interesting and worthy of being publicized.

Speeches, radio and television appearances. Retail executives, interior designers, or other representatives of the store should seek opportunities to make speeches to such groups as civic clubs and consumer seminars. The same individuals may volunteer to be on television talk shows or perhaps "ask your decorator" radio shows.

Receptions and other in-store events. By inviting members of the press to receptions such as the tenth anniversary celebration, the unveiling of a new addition to the store, or the redecorating of the store, the retailer can encourage favorable comment in local newspapers, radio, and television. Interesting in-store events such as the appearance of local sports figures may also be newsworthy.

Provide a meeting place for clubs. If the store has a home decorating

13-5. One of the major objectives of the public relations efforts of both furniture manufacturers and retailers is to receive favorable publicity. Shown here are examples of some of the feature articles and news items that appeared in various consumer and trade magazines and newspapers. These placements resulted from techniques used by manufacturers and retailers to obtain publicity: news releases, press kits, clip sheets, special events, photographs and captions, press conferences, and so on.

center or some other suitable meeting room, clubs and other local organizations can be invited to hold their meetings at the store. This has the effect of getting a variety of people to see the store, and the mention of the meeting location is also favorable publicity.

Public relations, as can be seen from the illustrations in this chapter, reinforces the marketing efforts of the organization. Its impact is indirect, which means that if consumers have a favorable image of a company, they are more likely to buy from it.

SUMMARY

In addition to advertising, other forms of nonpersonal communication helpful to selling are sales promotion and a progressive public relations program.

Sales promotion involves a wide range of activities undertaken by both manufacturers and retailers to coordinate or supplement a firm's normal selling effort.

Sales promotion objectives of manufacturers include: obtaining placements on retail floors, increasing market showroom attendance, obtaining buying commitments "now," increasing brand-name awareness, increasing quantity purchases by dealers, and reinforcing advertising and personal selling.

Manufacturer sales promotion techniques aimed at dealers include furniture markets, contests, point-of-purchase material, newsletters or periodic bulletins, advertising or display allowances and assistance, price promotions, and advertising specialties.

Manufacturer sales promotion techniques designed for the consumer involve game show prizes and premiums.

Sales promotion objectives of retailers are: to stimulate product trial, to increase store traffic, to obtain buying commitments "now," to establish continuity of purchase, and to reinforce advertising.

Retailer sales promotion techniques are aimed at consumers and include reduced price promotions, in-store events or celebrations other than sales, premiums, contests, and product demonstrations.

Public relations is a conscious effort to influence favorably the attitudes of a number of "publics," such as dealers, consumers, government agencies, employees, the press, and leaders of the local and financial communities, toward the firm. Publicity is news about an organization which is printed or broadcast, but is not paid for by that organization.

Public relations objectives of manufacturers are to receive favorable publicity, to gain the confidence of the financial community, to gain respect for the organization as a "good citizen," to be identified with education, to make the business more "human," to counteract negative publicity, and to be seen as a company that provides fashionable products with good value and quality.

Techniques used by manufacturers to get favorable publicity are news releases, speeches by company executives, press kits, clip sheets, press conferences, market showroom tours, and receptions, parties, and other social events.

Public relations objectives of retailers are to receive favorable publicity, to gain the confidence of the financial community, to be a "good citizen," to be identified with education, and to become known as an honest, respectable merchant with merchandise that is fashionable and a good value.

Techniques used by retailers to get favorable publicity are news releases, speeches, radio and television appearances, receptions and other selected in-store events, and providing a meeting place for clubs.

CHAPTER 14

FURNITURE RETAILING

R etailing has a very simple definition: all sales to the ultimate consumer. But in the furniture industry, distribution is extremely complex, involving a wide variety of retail outlets selling furniture. The situation is further complicated by the fact that many of these retail outlets sell the same brand within a given geographic area.

The consumer can choose from a wide variety of furniture products offered by a large number of manufacturers. Therefore, the retailer must have a carefully planned marketing program in order to be successful.

The profitable retailer must carefully study the market to locate high-potential niches for his or her marketing efforts. In furniture retailing, as in other businesses, it is impossible to be all things to all people. Thus, one of the main components of success is to find a void in the marketplace, formulate a strategy to fill that void, build an effective, workable organization, and then create an image in the minds of consumers of a retail store that has integrity and is worthy of being patronized. Attention to detail is important and customers must be satisfied for sales and profits to be made.

This chapter provides an overview of the complex field of furniture retailing. The following areas will be covered:
- Types of retail outlets
- The various jobs in retailing
- Retail store location criteria
- Merchandising in a retail furniture business
- Retail store operations

TYPES OF FURNITURE RETAILERS IN THE UNITED STATES

To obtain an appreciation for furniture retailing as it exists in the United States, it is helpful to look at the specific retail outlets available to the consumer.

SINGLE-UNIT, FULL-SERVICE FURNITURE STORES
Locally owned, home-operated stores have traditionally represented the largest number of retail furniture outlets. Many are often called "Mom

'n Pop" stores because the owner frequently is the manager and family members are usually involved throughout the organization. The stores may be general merchandise furniture stores or specialty furniture stores.

General merchandise outlets feature a varied selection of furniture and accessories for every room in the house, usually including outdoor furniture. Many of these stores—especially in smaller geographic areas—also offer kitchen appliances, washers and dryers, televisions and stereos, carpeting, and draperies.

Specialty furniture stores feature only one type of furniture product. For example, a store might carry only bedding, seating, or unfinished furniture. In each of these situations, the store would have a complete selection of merchandise within the "special" product category.

Specialty stores usually feature display samples on the floor backed up by one or two in the warehouse. Catalogues are kept up-to-date so desired items not in stock may be ordered from the manufacturer. When merchandise is received it is unpacked, inspected, and "deluxed" before being delivered to the customer. Deluxing involves polishing and touching up scratches, dents, or other minor defects. The merchandise is then delivered to the customer on company-owned trucks or by a contracted delivery service.

Many independent single-unit stores pride themselves in maintaining good communications with customers. They promptly answer questions and aggressively pursue consumer complaints or inquiries with manufacturers or transportation companies. In essence, the foundation of their business is a satisfied customer.

They usually have a credit plan or customer financing relationship with a bank or other lending institution. Depending on the price range and merchandise carried, the store may also offer an interior decorating or design service to help design the complete interior of a customer's home. The layouts of retail furniture stores vary widely, from those comprised entirely of room settings (sometimes called a *showcase store*) to those with a wide variety of merchandise and almost no discernible floor plan.

FULL-SERVICE FURNITURE CHAIN

Many full-service furniture chains operate much like the single-unit store, with similar merchandise and service. The main difference is that the individual units are owned by and operated from a central office using standardized operating procedures. Although the operating procedures vary slightly from store to store, it is normal for the chain to have the same price range of merchandise. The responsibility for buying the stock of merchandise varies greatly from one chain to another, but most have a basic group of merchandise carried by all stores.

DEPARTMENT STORES

Department stores are large retailing establishments which have been

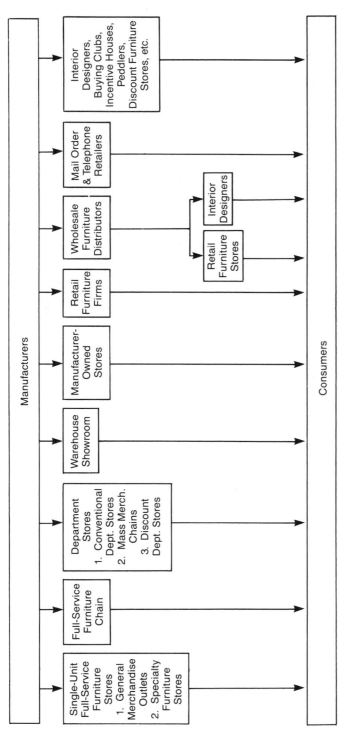

14-1.   Channels of furniture distribution

14-2. This is part of the home furnishings department of a J.C. Penney store. The furniture in this mass merchandising store is arranged by suites and separated at intervals by partial walls and columns. In this way, customers are given an opportunity to view a wide assortment of merchandise without actually walking into the home furnishings department. This allows them to see much of what is available in home furnishings even though they are in the store to shop for other merchandise.

important for many years. Currently, department stores, many of which carry furniture as one of their merchandise departments, are classified in one of three ways: conventional department stores, mass merchandise chains, and discount department stores.

The *conventional department store* is often the community fashion leader and has a wide range of merchandise. The merchandise is organized into separate departments, such as ready-to-wear clothing and accessories, piece goods, appliances, home furnishings, and housewares. The conventional department stores have comparatively higher prices and cater to people in the middle- to upper-income categories. The higher prices are at least partly justified by the wide range of services offered, such as extensive sales assistance, credit, free delivery, and a liberal return policy if the customer is not satisfied.

Some conventional department stores do not carry home furnishings and appliances because of the floor space required to show the product properly and the inability to generate as much profit per square foot as other departments. Many conventional department store chains are made up of clusters of stores. Thus, it is possible to have more than one cluster of stores, each with its own name under the same corporate umbrella.

Mass merchandise chains sell moderately priced merchandise and emphasize quality and durability more than fashion. The three companies that are most representative of this group are Sears, J.C. Penney, and Montgomery Ward. A large percentage of merchandise displayed is under their own brand label, which is often specially manufactured for them according to their own specifications. In home furnishings, they have historically downplayed fashion in favor of durability, function, and consistent quality of merchandise. Again, the mass merchandise chains promote a full-service image.

Discount department stores achieved acceptance by the consumer in the 1950s with the image of selling nationally advertised, branded goods below the manufacturer's suggested retail price. Most discount department stores offer a wide range of merchandise, but usually only a limited amount of furniture. The emphasis is on price appeal, and they offer limited customer service. Therefore, these discount department stores carry largely promotionally priced furniture and often sell single pieces rather than entire suites.

WAREHOUSE SHOWROOMS

A furniture warehouse showroom is just that—a warehouse with a showroom where the customer can see the merchandise. The customer can shop the showroom, decide on a purchase, buy it, and take it home out of the warehouse stock. The emphasis is on high volume, heavy discounting, and instant gratification of the customer's need. The customer can make a purchase decision and not have to wait until the product is made and shipped from the manufacturer.

The furniture warehouse showrooms offer popular styles and popular brands at reasonable prices. Often, because of their sales volume, these retailers have products made by manufacturers especially for them and to their specifications. However, the selection is somewhat limited because they often do business with a limited number of suppliers, and only those products the store has in stock are sold.

RENTAL FURNITURE FIRMS

Companies that rent a wide range of home furnishings are popular, particularly in metropolitan areas. These dealers buy large amounts of furniture, which they rent to various groups of consumers. Renting is popular among such groups as unmarrieds and employees who are transferred quite often. At the end of the lease period, the furniture is often sold as used furniture in the rental firm's outlet store. The majority of these companies feature medium- to low-priced furniture.

MANUFACTURER-OWNED RETAIL STORES

Some furniture manufacturers distribute their products through company-owned stores. This marketing strategy is called *vertical integration* and is practiced by companies who wish to control the distribution of their own products. Some of them also sell accessories and other products that they do not produce themselves. Several manufacturers sell through their own company stores and other retail outlets at the same time.

MAIL ORDER AND TELEPHONE RETAILERS

A number of companies sell furniture by issuing catalogues and soliciting mail-order business. These companies promote quality, often name-brand merchandise, at a very competitive price. Many have toll-free telephone lines for customers to call in their orders and will sell merchandise other than that listed in their catalogues if they have a buying relationship established with the manufacturers involved. While some of these catalogues feature price, others feature fashion, novelty, or hard-to-obtain items.

There are other mail-order retailers who solicit business largely through direct-mail and magazine advertising. These companies carry a limited number of items, many with a novelty appeal. For example, a company might offer four or five imported Oriental accessories for the home.

OTHER RETAIL FURNITURE OUTLETS

Interior designers and *interior design shops* simultaneously sell their services and a wide range of home furnishings. The interior designer is contracted to decorate a home or business and will recommend or specify products in catalogues or wholesale showrooms. Rarely does the interior designer carry a significant amount of merchandise. The emphasis is on image and fashion, with many of the furnishings having a relatively high price. In decorating the interior of a home or business, a designer may recommend or specify products from a large number of suppliers.

Buying clubs require a membership fee. Here, consumers have the opportunity to buy selected furniture as members of the club at a price alleged to be lower than that of regular retail stores. Normally, the selection of furniture offered is limited. These clubs are found mainly in larger metropolitan areas.

Peddlers sell merchandise from the backs of trucks in various sections of the country. A typical situation would involve a peddler buying a truckload of unbranded promotional furniture from a small manufacturer. The load of furniture is then driven to a predetermined city or town where the truck is parked. Some of the furniture is placed outside. The peddler proceeds to sell until the truck is empty.

Discount furniture stores use low prices to attract customers. These stores offer a minimum of service, and very little is spent on store layout and design in an effort to maintain low prices. The customer is generally required to pay by cash or bank charge card.

Incentive houses distribute a significant amount of occasional furniture and accessories. The most successful are trading stamp companies, which allow customers to redeem stamps they obtain through patronizing participating merchants or from contests for merchandise offered in their catalogues.

PERSONNEL IN RETAIL FURNITURE STORES

The furniture industry is a people-related business. Because of the complexity of the product and the difficulty of the consumer in making a decision to buy, all aspects of the business must be well-managed. In order to understand the variety of personnel required to operate retail furniture stores successfully, several positions will be outlined. In general, the larger the store, the more specialized the individual positions.

The *manager* of the retail furniture store is responsible for the five basic management functions of planning, organizing, staffing, directing, and controlling. In reality, the manager of the small- to medium-sized store must be a "jack-of-all-trades," which includes buying and selling merchandise, preparing advertising, supervising personnel, training salespeople, and seeing that displays and facilities are properly maintained. In larger organizations, the manager may not be personally involved in all these areas, but must understand them in order to properly direct the work of others.

The *sales manager* supervises the sales personnel on a day-to-day basis. In larger organizations, the sales manager assumes the responsibility for sales training, plays a key role in hiring salespeople, sets sales quotas and, in general, motivates the salespeople. In most retail stores, the sales manager also sells on the retail floor and helps to handle consumer questions or complaints when they arise.

The *salesperson* sells furniture on the retail floor and, in the case of many smaller stores, also sells appliances and other merchandise. In addition, the salesperson takes care of exchanges and returns, collects the required information for the credit manager, and fills out forms for merchandise which must be ordered from manufacturers. In most stores, the salespeople also help to arrange the display of the merchandise on the floor, tag merchandise, take inventory, and assist with whatever other chores are needed. Stores offering more expensive merchandise and a design service prefer hiring salespeople with training in interior design. Successful salespeople are hard-working individuals who can genuinely sell themselves and their product by helping customers make a good buying decision.

The *furniture buyer* has the responsibility for purchasing merchandise that will sell at the volume necessary to make a profit. A good buyer keeps up with what is in demand by consumers and what competitors are offering for sale, and is constantly researching the industry to determine what products are available. Most buyers attend one or more of the wholesale furniture markets to evaluate personally what various manufacturers have to offer. In medium- and smaller-sized stores, the buyer also sells, helps tag and display furniture, and assists with advertising. In larger stores, especially department stores, the job of furniture buyer is broken down by product category, with one person buying bedding, another buying living-room upholstery, another case goods, or some other breakdown that is effective for that particular organization.

The *merchandise manager,* a key, top-level executive in larger retail stores, is responsible for the overall marketing of the products to the consumer. This person's responsibilities include all buying, displaying, advertising, and selling, although the actual work is delegated to various individuals such as buyers, advertising managers, and salespeople.

The larger department store usually has a *fashion coordinator* who works with the merchandise manager to be sure an appropriate fashion image is being created by the product and its display and advertising. The large department stores also have a *general merchandise manager* who is responsible for the merchandising activities throughout the store and *divisional merchandise managers* who are responsible for specific product areas.

The *advertising manager* supervises all advertising, publicity, and sales promotion for the store. In a very large store, the advertising manager may have a staff including a commercial artist, layout people, and copywriters. Smaller stores, however, work with media, advertising agencies, or freelance artists and advertising professionals to develop ideas and prepare advertising for print and/or broadcast media. In these stores, advertising is usually supervised by the owner, manager, or buyer.

The *credit and collection manager* oversees the credit department, makes approvals for credit, supervises the customer credit records, and makes collections. The credit and collection manager must be customer-oriented and approve credit purchases without taking undue risks. However, the credit manager who takes no risks at all is likely to cause the store to miss valuable sales.

Warehouse personnel are in charge of making certain that merchandise is properly received, inspected, placed into inventory, and retrieved when it is ready to be delivered to a customer or to the sales floor. The *warehouse manager* is in charge of the overall condition of the warehouse and of receiving and shipping goods. The *finisher* and *repairman* "deluxes," repairs, and refinishes merchandise as needed before it is delivered to a customer. Progressive retailers take special care to inspect and repack articles of furniture to ensure customer satisfaction. They also keep the warehouse neat and orderly.

Delivery personnel have the responsibility for delivering furniture to customers. These people should be clean, polite, and courteous because they are usually the last representative of the retail store to be in contact with the customer. Some successful retailers pay a commission on deliveries to ensure that extra care will be taken. In many stores, the delivery personnel also pick up merchandise from suppliers and help in the warehouse.

RETAIL STORE LOCATION

It is important to locate a store where it will be convenient for sufficient numbers of customers. A retail store location decision should involve the following considerations:

- Selecting a trading area
- Selecting a specific site
- Terms of occupancy

SELECTING A TRADING AREA

Furniture stores are predominantly located in towns and cities with enough population of sufficient income to support them. Therefore, in choosing the town or city, population statistics should be examined. Demographic data as published by the U.S. Department of Commerce, local chambers of commerce, and the media give an idea of how many people live in an area and of their specific characteristics.

Local media figures and statistics provided by local chambers of commerce can give needed information on the current competitive retailing situation in terms of shopping centers and furniture stores already in operation. The media information also states who is most likely to shop in various shopping centers and where these shoppers live.

The annual "Survey of Buying Power" conducted by *Sales and Marketing Magazine* gives the "Buying Power Index" for larger metropolitan areas. This index is of value to the furniture retailer because it is a good indication of the buying potential in specific trading areas.

Of interest in assessing the potential for a retail furniture store in a given trading area is the "draw" of the area and of specific business districts or shopping centers within the area. In other words, how far will people commute to shop in the area? For example, a small city surrounded by a rural area may draw shoppers for many miles, while a similar city surrounded by a metropolitan area may draw shoppers from a much smaller area. It is important to know how many total shoppers may patronize a store in the area being considered.

Other factors in considering a particular area for a store location include the following: traffic, congestion, whether or not the area is already saturated with furniture retailers, stability of employment, attitudes of bankers or other lenders in the area, the progressiveness of the area, tax structure, and restrictiveness of local ordinances. For example, stability of employment generally comes from having a diversified industrial base. If an area is dependent on one firm which experiences a downturn in business, the impact can be disastrous to the entire community. The progressiveness of the community is evidenced by the amount of rebuilding and new construction in the area. The attitudes of bankers are important because the retailer may need to borrow funds to build, finance inventories, and buy equipment.

SELECTING A SPECIFIC SITE

Once the trading area has been chosen, the retailer must select a specific site. A promising trading area will obviously contain both good and bad sites, and several considerations determine the difference. Community growth is one factor that should be considered. Some areas expand while others decline, and it is important to locate in an expanding section of the trading area.

Although furniture stores draw customers from a long distance compared with other types of retailers, it is important to consider highway configurations and traffic patterns. A site convenient to enter and exit, with good visibility from major streets or highways, is desirable.

Other factors that should be considered are the location of competing furniture stores, adequacy of parking, and compatibility with existing businesses. The location of competing furniture stores is important because people often like to shop around for furniture, and some smaller retailers like to locate near a very large store to make shopping their store convenient. People normally drive to a furniture store, so parking is important. Also, a store should be compatible with the existing businesses in the area in order to capitalize on the combined draw of a group of stores and to avoid the wrong kind of traffic. For example, a site surrounded by factories would not be a good location for a higher-priced furniture store.

TERMS OF OCCUPANCY

A furniture retailer should get the most favorable terms of occupancy possible to maximize his or her profits. This involves the decision of whether to buy or lease, which should be made based on the relative advantages of these two options.

Buying assures the retailer of permanent occupancy, allows the retailer to rebuild, redecorate, or otherwise make needed changes, as well as to receive the benefit of any rise in property values. On the other hand, leasing requires a smaller investment committed to real estate and provides greater flexibility to make a move if the location decision proves to be incorrect. With leasing, the retailer needs expertise in negotiating the most favorable lease possible. Some retailers obtain advantages by building, selling the building to investors, and then leasing it back for a predetermined period of time.

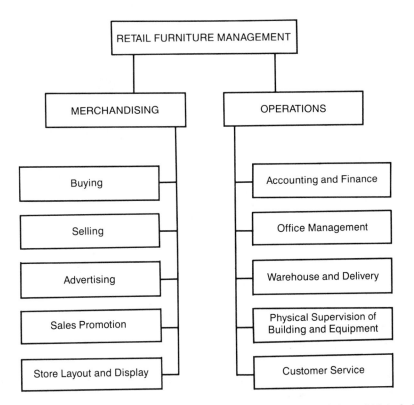

14-3. Retail furniture management is divided into two areas: (1) merchandising, which includes buying, selling, advertising, sales promotion, and store layout and display; and (2) operations, which includes accounting and finance, office management, warehouse and delivery, physical supervision of building and equipment, and customer service.

RETAIL STORE MERCHANDISING

Merchandising includes all the efforts used in selecting, presenting, and selling merchandise to customers. In a retail furniture store, it includes buying, selling, advertising, sales promotion, and store layout and display. All must be done properly for the retail store to be assured of success.

BUYING
The buying function includes buying the right amount of the most salable types of furniture. A phrase that is often quoted in the furniture industry is "merchandise which is bought right is half sold." To be successful, therefore, a buyer must be knowledgeable in many areas. The buyer must know the store and the type of customer who patronizes it, and must keep up with changes in consumer tastes and preferences.

The task of buying includes purchasing merchandise that can be sold at a profit for the best possible price. It means that the buyer must be knowledgeable about product sources and skillful in negotiating the best possible purchase terms.

The buyer must buy the right amount of merchandise for floor samples and back-up stock for the warehouse. The decision is difficult because of the large variety of colors, sizes, and types of pieces available.

Each piece of furniture is called an *SKU (stock-keeping unit)*. A successful buyer must have the right combination of merchandise and at the same time minimize as much as possible the number of SKUs in inventory.

Another factor affecting inventories is the purpose for which merchandise is purchased. For example, merchandise purchased for promotion or a special sale requires a larger number of units than that which is purchased for regular stock.

Retail store management is concerned about inventory turnover which is measured by *turns per year*. This figure is total sales divided by the average value of inventory at retail. For example, a store with total sales of $500,000 would need $250,000 in inventory to accomplish two turns per year. One measure of the performance of a buyer is the number of inventory turns per year.

An expert buyer purchases according to a predetermined plan rather than by what simply looks good or appears to be a "good deal." The entire stock of the store is evaluated and a decision is made concerning what to replace before making a determination to buy something new. Once that decision is made, the buyer then is "open-to-buy" in specific categories. In other words, if the decision is made to discontinue two Early American living-room suites, the store is then "open-to-buy" two new living-room suites in that style category.

SELLING

Good buying and selling go hand-in-hand. The retail sales force must be effective in explaining how the products can benefit the consumer and how they and the store can be helpful in solving home furnishings buying problems. Salespeople must be well-trained, with adequate product knowledge, a thorough understanding of what the store can and cannot do, and good furniture selling techniques. The successful retail person learns to understand consumer motivation and strives to satisfy the needs of customers. In design-oriented stores, it is essential that salespeople be capable of helping customers to decorate the interiors of their homes properly. After all, they are selling more than products, they are selling a beautiful home environment.

The salesperson must be well-motivated and adequately compensated to do an effective selling job on the retail floor. The retail sales force can be compensated by straight commission, commission with a drawing account, a combination salary and commission or bonus, or straight salary. All have their advantages and disadvantages, and managers have different philosophies as to which is best. The objective is to choose a compensation plan that will best fit the type of store and salespeople involved.

ADVERTISING

Most retail furniture store advertising is local in nature. Stores normally use a combination of newspaper, radio, television, and direct mail. Historically, the largest percentage of retail store advertising has been price advertising, in which a reduced price or a percentage reduction in price is featured, often compared to the regular price.

Advertising in the retail store usually must be backed up by merchandise in stock. Exceptions to the requirement for in-stock inventory are those stores which advertise special-order upholstery. Often, good salespeople can "step-up" the customer to a more expensive product by pointing out, using truthful statements, why the more expensive product is better suited to the customer's needs.

Most stores base their advertising budget on a percentage of projected sales. They then plan a campaign to get the most advertising impact for the dollars they have to spend. They sometimes obtain cooperative advertising dollars from manufacturers and other sources.

The advertising is prepared by the store manager, buyer, or a full-time advertising manager, usually in cooperation with the media. Retail advertising can be price advertising, product advertising, institutional advertising, or advertising to introduce some in-store event.

SALES PROMOTION

Sales promotion techniques are designed to create excitement and bring people into the store with occasions such as featuring a local sports figure in the store, having a yearly store birthday or anniversary event, and a twelve-hour, end-of-the-month clearance or special purchase sale. Reduced price promotions are the most often held store events and usually generate considerable interest and traffic.

Other types of sales promotion include premiums, which are small items given away or sold for a price that is an obvious value, having a contest or drawing, or providing some type of combination offer for an attractive price.

STORE LAYOUT AND DISPLAY

The interior of the store must be laid out in such a way that the merchandise is effectively presented to the customer, but suitable for the price range of the merchandise the retailer is offering. A term that applies here is "perceived value." It means that if the store is arranged properly for their selection of merchandise, customers will "perceive" that buying from that particular store has an adequate amount of "value."

14-4.   This is a portion of the sales floor of a retail furniture store in which there is an apparent random placement of furniture. The tables and other occasional pieces against the wall allow the consumer to compare a variety of offerings within the same product category.

Many progressive retailers display their merchandise in room settings or vignettes, completely accessorized, so the consumer can get a better idea of how the furniture will look at home. There are several approaches to how these room settings are arranged. For example, some stores have defined aisles, and others have the room settings arranged more or less at random; some have the style categories mixed together, and others separate the merchandise into style categories.

The main factor in store layout and display is to have a plan that indicates the percentage of square footage or number of room settings to be assigned to each product category. A desirable method of making this determination is basing it on relative sales volume. In a typical store, it could mean that the largest amount of space displays sofas and chairs for living and family rooms, the second largest space displays bedroom furniture, and the third largest space displays dining-room furniture, and then bedding and carpeting.

Store layout and display should create excitement. The store windows and merchandise displayed just inside the front door are important because they should capture the customer's attention and help create a buying mood.

14-5. This retail sales floor, in contrast to the one depicted in Figure 14-4, is organized into room vignettes designed to give consumers an idea of how the furniture and suggested accessories will look in their homes. Many retailers feel that having the furniture organized in this manner enhances the consumer's perceived value of the product as well as encouraging the purchase of the accessory items on display.

14-6. This window display in Abraham and Straus, a Brooklyn-based department store, conveys a very high fashion image. In this realistic, formal dining-room setting, everything is for sale—the furniture, silverware, china, glassware, and rugs, as well as the apparel.

Many retailers devote part of their floor space to a manufacturer-sponsored gallery. The manufacturer furnishes the floor plans and expertise to design the gallery, while providing a number of incentives to the retailer, such as preferential delivery, advertising assistance, periodic special promotions available only to gallery dealers, and more liberal credit terms. In return, the retailer agrees to assign a specified amount of floor space to the gallery, buy a predetermined amount of merchandise, and pay the cost of constructing walls, doors, and other store modifications specified in the gallery plans. The gallery approach results in close ties between the retailer and manufacturer and, in many cases, increases sales dramatically.

RETAIL STORE OPERATIONS

Retail store operations comprise the nonmerchandising functions of the business, such as accounting and finance, office management, customer service, warehouse and delivery, and physical supervision of the building and equipment.

ACCOUNTING AND FINANCE

Adequate record-keeping is the heart of management control in any business. In furniture retailing, records must be kept properly to determine profitability, to detect trends leading toward more or less profits, and to compare the performance of various departments or categories of furniture. Commonly used financial controls are gross margin return on inventory (GMROI), sales per square foot, gross margin percent of net retail sales, and the number of stock turns (at retail). These are the types of controls that determine the success or failure of specific departments, product categories, individual store units in a corporate chain, or the entire organization. A large number of retailers have computer programs to increase their record-keeping capacity, speed up the rate at which reports can be generated and, in general, make office procedures more efficient.

The financing function is extremely important to the furniture retailer. Often, the retailer must borrow to buy or build a building, buy equipment, or finance inventory. The retailer must also manage cash effectively by investing funds when they are not currently needed by the business, taking cash discounts when it is advantageous to do so, and getting the most favorable terms possible from manufacturers.

OFFICE MANAGEMENT

Efficient office management is important in maintaining effective relationships with both manufacturers and customers. The flow of paperwork should be managed so records are available at all times, making information obtainable when needed. When a customer calls about an order, the question can then be answered immediately, or the answer can be found and the customer called back promptly.

Office personnel include the office manager, receptionist, clerical workers, those involved in consumer credit, and computer personnel.

CUSTOMER SERVICE

Customer service involves answering delivery questions and resolving customer complaints. Consumer questions include everything from "When will my furniture be delivered?" to "Can I get a mirror to match the dresser I bought last year?" Every attempt should be made to answer each question honestly and completely.

Customer service also includes taking care of needed correspondence with manufacturers and customers. Consumer complaints should be investigated and immediate action taken where required. Most furniture stores employ a finisher or repairman either full-time or have one on call. One retailer promotes a forty-eight-hour customer service policy—picking up the damaged product, having it repaired, and returning it to the customer within forty-eight hours.

WAREHOUSE AND DELIVERY

Basically, a warehouse is used to:
1. Receive the merchandise.
2. Place the merchandise in stock so that it can be retrieved accurately and promptly.
3. Inspect the merchandise when it is ordered out to be delivered to a customer.
4. Deliver the merchandise to the customer.

These duties must be performed efficiently in order for the selling effort to be properly supported. For example, the warehouse should be constructed with a holding area where the merchandise can be kept until it is accounted for and properly logged into inventory. The merchandise should be stored where it can be retrieved easily. This involves having a locator system, indicating where all the merchandise is stored.

The warehouse should be kept clean and neat with the merchandise stored on the proper type of racks or other storage equipment for the following benefits:
1. Employees feel better about themselves and their work, and will want to do a better job.
2. Damage to the merchandise is minimized.
3. Customers who see the warehouse will be reassured about the type of store from which they are buying.
4. The merchandise will be more easily located and retrieved so the entire operation can run more smoothly.

Merchandise should be inspected thoroughly and "deluxed" before being delivered to the customer. Furniture should be loaded onto the delivery truck with furniture pads and other packing materials to help ensure that it will be in top condition when it is received by the customer. Delivery personnel must be neat, well-dressed, and courteous because they are the last representatives of the store seen by the customer.

PHYSICAL SUPERVISION OF THE BUILDING AND EQUIPMENT

The building should be cleaned and maintained on a regular basis. The restrooms, drinking fountains, and other common areas must be clean; such details are readily noticed by customers.

All equipment should be clean and in good working order. Preventive maintenance usually saves money in the long run. Signs and the exterior of the building should also be well-maintained in order to maintain the image of the store.

SUMMARY

Furniture retailers include single-unit, full-service furniture stores, full-service furniture chains, department stores, warehouse showrooms, furniture rental firms, mail-order and telephone retailers, and manufacturer-owned retail stores.

The single-unit, full-service furniture stores and full-service furniture chains carry a general assortment of furniture for every room in the house or specialize in some category, such as bedding or outdoor furniture. Their services include a decorator service, floor displays, credit, delivery, and a wide selection of merchandise from which to choose.

Full-service furniture chains operate very much like single-unit, full-service furniture stores except that they are owned and operated from a central office.

There are three types of department stores which sell furniture: conventional department stores, mass merchandise chains, and discount department stores. Conventional department stores have comparatively higher prices and cater to people in the middle- to upper-income categories. Mass merchandise chains sell durable, functional merchandise often manufactured to their own specifications and sold under their own brand name. Discount department stores feature price appeal and offer limited customer services.

Warehouse showrooms have merchandise displayed that is available in the warehouse and can be purchased and taken home by the customer in one trip to the store. Rental furniture firms cater to people who would rather rent than buy their home furnishings. Some retail stores are owned by the manufacturers whose furniture they have in stock.

Other retail furniture outlets include interior designers and interior design shops, buying clubs, peddlers, discount furniture stores, and incentive houses.

Personnel found in a retail furniture store may include the manager, sales manager, salespeople, buyer, merchandise manager (and, possibly, fashion coordinator), advertising manager, credit and collection manager, finisher and repairman, warehouse personnel, and delivery personnel.

The manager is responsible for the planning, organizing, staffing, directing, and controlling of the store. The sales manager supervises the sales personnel on a day-to-day basis. The salesperson sells furniture and sometimes appliances and other merchandise on the retail floor. The buyer is responsible for purchasing merchandise that will sell at the volume necessary to make a profit. The merchandise manager is responsible for the overall marketing of the products to the consumer. The advertising manager supervises all advertising, publicity, and sales promotion for the store. The credit and collection manager manages the credit department, makes approvals for credit, supervises customer credit records, and makes collections. Warehouse personnel receive, inspect, place into inventory, and retrieve the merchandise when it is needed. Delivery personnel deliver furniture to customers.

Retail location factors include selecting a trading area, selecting a specific site, and determining the most favorable terms of occupancy.

Furniture store merchandising involves buying, selling, advertising, sales promotion, and store layout and display.

The amount of merchandise in the store is measured by stock-keeping units (SKUs), a term that refers to the number of individual pieces on hand. A measure of effectiveness in retail store management is inventory turnover which is measured by turns per year.

Retail store operations involve accounting and finance, office management, customer service, warehouse and delivery, and physical supervision of the building and equipment.

CHAPTER 15

FURNITURE WHOLESALING

A wholesale furniture sale may be broadly defined as any sale except a sale to the ultimate consumer. This means that sales to business and to firms buying for resale are wholesale sales. In the furniture industry, the organizations that dominate wholesaling are called *wholesale furniture distributors*. Wholesalers serve as a distribution link between manufacturers and retailers. Historically, wholesale furniture distributors have served medium- and small-volume retailers. Many of these companies are members of the National Wholesale Furniture Association (NWFA). This organization has adopted the following code of ethics for wholesale furniture distributors:

1. To encourage the broadest furniture distribution by the wholesaler consistent with sound business principles and the welfare of the industry.
2. To protect the interests of manufacturers from whom we buy, by the concentrated coverage of our fields; and the merchants to whom we sell, by having merchandise readily available for the needs of our trade.
3. To educate the industry and the trade on the proper functions of the wholesale distributor as a relation of mutual trust.
4. To counsel and protect the manufacturer, the merchant, and the consumer against misuse of the word "wholesale" so that the words "common honesty" will govern all our transactions.
5. To cooperate wholeheartedly with other segments of the home furnishings industry to the end that the business welfare of the industry, our own communities, and the public goodwill be served.

As is apparent in this code of ethics, the members of the National Wholesale Furniture Association do not consider companies who also sell to the consumer as legitimate wholesalers.

TYPES OF WHOLESALE FURNITURE DISTRIBUTORS

There are four types of wholesale furniture distributors operating as middlemen between furniture manufacturers and furniture retailers or interior designers:

- Road-selling distributor
- Decorator showroom wholesaler
- Combination road-selling and decorator showroom wholesaler
- Independent sales representative with a warehouse

They are all merchant wholesalers because they buy the merchandise they handle, actually take title to it, and then resell it to retailers or interior designers. Wholesale furniture distributors are different from sales agents, who are independent contractors acting as manufacturers' representatives, because the agents do not take title to the merchandise they are selling. They are acting on behalf of manufacturers under a contractual arrangement to sell merchandise primarily to retailers.

ROAD-SELLING DISTRIBUTOR

The road-selling distributor has a sales force calling upon retailers within a given geographic territory. The sales force sells a stock of merchandise which is stored in the wholesale furniture distributor's warehouse. A majority of the retailers buying from the distributor are medium to small, independent retail stores. Most of the road-selling distributors carry medium- to low-priced merchandise. They sell floor samples to the retailer and carry the backup stock in their own warehouse for delivery as the retailer needs it.

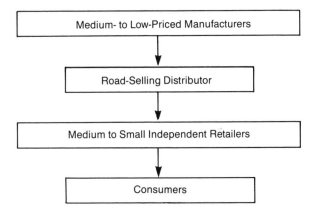

15-1. Wholesale distribution using road-selling distributors

DECORATOR SHOWROOM WHOLESALER

Wholesalers with decorator showrooms cater primarily to interior designers. These wholesalers have very fashionable showrooms where interior designers can bring their clients to see the merchandise. They do not sell to the consumer, but provide display and inventory support for the designer. These showrooms usually carry higher-priced merchandise and aid the interior designer by special ordering merchandise they do not have in stock and assembling the combination of merchandise required to decorate the client's home. Some also employ interior designers for their own staff, which allows them to offer decorative support services to independent interior designers and retailers.

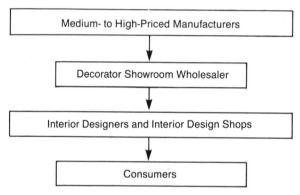

15-2. Wholesale distribution using decorator-showroom wholesalers

COMBINATION ROAD-SELLING AND DECORATOR SHOWROOM WHOLESALER

This organization has an on-the-road sales force selling a collection of furniture to retailers which is available in the warehouse. However, there is also a showroom serving both interior designers and retailers. Many of these wholesalers have an on-the-road sales force selling low- to medium-priced furniture while promoting higher-priced furniture in the showroom. The showroom staff will special-order and assemble desired merchandise.

INDEPENDENT SALES REPRESENTATIVE WITH A WAREHOUSE

Some of the larger, medium- to low-priced manufacturers sell to the independent agents representing them in various geographic territories as well as to retailers. The independent contractor buys merchandise from the manufacturer he represents, has it delivered to his own warehouse or a public warehouse, and then resells it to retailers in his territory. For this manufacturer, the independent sales representative with a warehouse

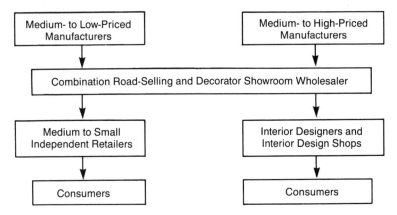

15-3. Wholesale distribution using combination road-selling and decorator-showroom wholesalers

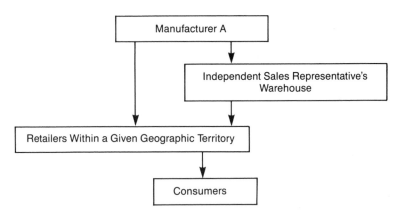

15-4. Wholesale distribution of Manufacturer A's furniture by independent sales representative with a warehouse

provides the same storage function as the road-selling wholesale distributor. He does not provide many of the other services of the wholesaler, such as delivery, because often he has no trucks and very few staff people. Many of these representatives use public warehouses which have delivery trucks and carry out the delivery function. Usually, the sales representative has in his warehouse only a portion of the merchandise offered by the manufacturer, so he is selling both directly from the manufacturer and out of his warehouse.

SERVICES WHOLESALERS PROVIDE FOR RETAILERS

Wholesale furniture distributors can exist profitably within the furniture industry because they provide a number of services which small- and medium-volume retailers would have difficulty providing for themselves.

The typical services provided by wholesale furniture distributors are as follows:

- A nearby inventory
- Competitive prices
- Prompt delivery
- Buying expertise
- Advertising and sales support
- Assortment of merchandise
- Retail floor samples
- Credit
- Showroom facilities

A NEARBY INVENTORY

Inventory is a sizable cost to any retail furniture store. It can be costly in two ways: the funds that are tied up in the merchandise and the mistakes in buying that may be made (especially if in addition to the floor samples, there is a large amount of backup stock in the warehouse).

Using a wholesale furniture distributor can make it possible for the retailer to carry less inventory, thereby reducing costs. For example, the retailer may own only the floor samples and use the wholesaler's warehouse inventory as the backup stock. This program reduces the dollar investment in inventory and can increase the amount of inventory turnover for the retailer. Also, if a buying mistake is made, the retailer has only one floor sample that will not sell rather than the floor sample plus backup stock. Therefore, small retailers can offer a larger supply of merchandise than if they had to "own it all."

The efficient wholesale furniture distributor anticipates the needs of the retailer and assumes the risk of stocking the correct amount, style, color, and assortment of merchandise for his or her retail customers. This service helps keep the retailer from being "out" of merchandise because the wholesaler can fill in needed pieces if, for example, a customer has brought only part of a suite.

COMPETITIVE PRICES

The wholesale furniture distributor is often able to offer the retailer prices that are competitive with the landed cost of merchandise if purchased directly from the manufacturer. The wholesale furniture distributor is often allowed a functional discount from the manufacturer which helps to cover his or her operating costs.

The wholesale furniture distributor also buys for a number of retailers at the same time, so he or she may be able to get a more favorable price than the retailers could get individually. Because of volume purchasing, wholesalers can get merchandise manufactured to their specifications or can obtain special package deals. All of these may result in a cost advantage, especially to the smaller retailer.

By buying in railroad car or truck loads, the wholesaler can get freight rates that are less per unit than would be available to individual retailers. Again, this can result in a more favorable or comparable price to the retailer.

PROMPT DELIVERY

Wholesale furniture distributors offer prompt delivery to their retailers. This is an important competitive advantage because the consumer may be quite willing to wait for three or four days for a purchase, but may not be willing to wait for the next cutting from a manufacturer, which may be in five to six weeks or longer. Prompt delivery by the wholesaler also allows the retailer to offer wider selections of colors, fabrics, and other options than would otherwise be possible while still promising the consumer rapid delivery.

The wholesaler unpacks, inspects, and deluxes the furniture before it is sent out to the customer. Therefore, the retailer does not have to employ a finisher or repairman. The retailer can also get any damaged goods replaced quickly from the wholesaler's warehouse.

BUYING EXPERTISE

Expert buyers are employed by successful wholesale furniture distributors. These buyers shop all the major markets, know suppliers, and how to buy. By furnishing retailers with good information and stocking salable merchandise, the wholesaler prevents the retailer from having to spend the time or incur the expense of attending one or more of the furniture markets.

The wholesale furniture distributor is usually a regional organization that knows the consumer preferences in that area. Therefore, the buyers are able to buy more desirable merchandise at a greater value which is more likely to move quickly off the retail floor.

ADVERTISING AND SALES SUPPORT

The wholesale furniture distributor offers a variety of advertising and sales support services. They normally publish a catalogue of the merchandise available from their warehouse, which is an excellent aid to the retail floor salesperson because the catalogue merchandise greatly extends the choices available to the consumer. Point-of-purchase signs, photographs, fabric swatches, wood samples and other sales aids are available for use inside the store.

Advertising assistance includes such materials as circulars, newspaper inserts, and direct-mail pieces. In each of these cases, the smaller retailers can get colorful and professional advertising material with their names printed prominently for less cost than would be available to them if purchased on their own. The wholesaler can have this material printed for all who buy a selected assortment of merchandise, with only the retailers' names being changed, thereby enjoying reduced per unit costs for volume printing.

The wholesaler's salespeople can work with the local retailer to choose the right advertising materials for the store which includes sharing the experiences of successful noncompeting retailers in other geographic areas.

ASSORTMENT OF MERCHANDISE

The wholesale furniture distributor puts together an assortment of merchandise which he or she feels will sell in a given geographic territory. It is a convenience to the retailer because tables, living-room furniture, dining-room furniture, recliners and other furniture are available from a single distributor. Some wholesalers also include appliances and carpeting in their assortment of merchandise.

Doing business with the wholesaler is an advantage for many retailers, especially when the owner-manager is personally active in all areas of the store; the owner's time is spent with only one salesperson rather than with many. Also, the wholesaler's salespeople usually call more often and regularly than would the manufacturer's representative.

In decorator showrooms, wholesale furniture distributors assemble all the merchandise, from furniture to accessories, needed by an interior designer to decorate a room or home.

RETAIL FLOOR SAMPLES

Wholesale furniture distributors sometimes place samples of various suites on the retailer's sales floor on consignment. These samples are the property of the wholesaler and are not to be sold by the retailer. The retail sales staff can use these samples to sell from, and the retailer can order the suite from the wholesaler, thereby reducing the financial investment of the retailer. This arrangement also ensures the wholesale furniture distributor of a place on the retail floor for his or her merchandise.

CREDIT

Many wholesale furniture distributors provide credit to their customers, which is a distinct advantage for new retailers. Wholesalers may be more likely to grant credit because they are located nearby or are more willing to take chances with new potential customers than are manufacturers. This reduces the financial requirements for the retailer to start or remain in business. With high interest rates, this service can be very attractive.

SHOWROOM FACILITIES

The wholesale furniture distributor with showroom facilities provides the additional service of allowing the retailer to send consumers to see a broader selection of merchandise than may be seen in the retailer's store. Normally the retailer will make arrangements for the consumer to visit the wholesaler's showroom and talk with the sales staff. However, any purchases by the consumer are made through the retailer at retail prices.

SERVICES WHOLESALERS PROVIDE FOR INTERIOR DESIGNERS

Wholesale furniture distributors with decorator showrooms serve interior designers and interior design shops. Since interior designers usually have very little storage and display space for the wide variety of home furnishings they need to offer to the consumer, wholesale furniture distributors can provide a variety of valuable services. Examples of these services are:

- Decorator showroom facilities
- Merchandise in stock
- Special-order service
- Assembly and delivery
- Servicing of products
- Buying expertise
- Competitive prices

DECORATOR SHOWROOM FACILITIES

The wholesaler's showroom serves as the display showroom for interior designers, who plan and select complete rooms of merchandise for a customer from the showroom. They can also bring the customer to the showroom to see the merchandise and better envision how the interior of the home will look when the merchandise is delivered and the decorating completed. The showroom is usually fashionably designed and decorated to appeal to those interested in higher-priced furniture and accessories.

The wholesaler's decorator staff will work with the interior designers and the customer. However, the sale must be made through the designer, not direct to the consumer. At times, the showroom staff will quote the manufacturer's suggested retail prices, but often the customer receives a savings through this arrangement.

Many of the showrooms are located in major metropolitan areas. Designers will come in to select the merchandise for a condominium, house, or other project. The wholesaler's sales staff will then make all the arrangements for assembly and delivery.

MERCHANDISE IN STOCK

The wholesale furniture distributor carries a selection of merchandise in stock. Even though furniture may have to be special-ordered, accessories and other items are often available to be delivered quickly, which allows the designer to add the "finishing touch" to an assignment if it is needed.

SPECIAL-ORDER SERVICE

Merchandise that is not stocked by the wholesaler may be special-ordered for interior designers' needs. This special-order service usually offers an entire group of products manufactured by a large number of firms in the middle- and upper-price categories. It allows the interior designer to have a minimum of paperwork and makes merchandise available from manufacturers who would not otherwise sell directly to individual designers.

ASSEMBLY AND DELIVERY

The wholesale furniture distributor will collect merchandise from a variety of sources and ship them all together at the same time. This service is important because different cutting schedules and shipping procedures will cause merchandise from different manufacturers to arrive at different times. A central collecting and holding warehouse may also ensure that the furnishings will be available as construction or remodeling is completed.

SERVICING OF PRODUCTS

The wholesaler employs finishers or repairmen who unpack, inspect, and repair as required to ensure that products will be delivered to the consumer in excellent condition. If scratches, dents, or other relatively minor problems are noticed before delivery, the wholesaler's service personnel can retouch or refinish the merchandise, making a return to the factory unnecessary. These service people are also available if problems occur after the merchandise is in the home and under a warranty.

BUYING EXPERTISE

The wholesale furniture distributor with a decorator showroom employs expert buyers who keep up with the latest fashion trends and shop the major furniture markets. Such buying expertise helps to ensure that the latest, most fashionable merchandise will be stocked in the decorator showroom.

The wholesaler's buyers use up-to-date purchasing techniques which are helpful in obtaining a good value for the amount of money spent. They also try to get the best combinations of merchandise, which may not be available to individual interior designers.

COMPETITIVE PRICES

An individual interior designer usually needs to buy only one chair, one sofa, or one of any other item. The wholesale furniture distributor, however, is able to buy in volume, which allows him or her to purchase the merchandise at a lower cost per unit. Freight savings can often be obtained by ordering a larger volume of products.

At times, manufacturers will make selected products available only to those who buy a specified minimum amount. Also, manufacturers often make available combinations of merchandise at attractive prices that are contingent on volume purchases to approved customers. Wholesalers are sometimes given a functional discount which retailers or interior designers do not receive. Therefore, through the wholesale furniture distributor, the interior designer has a large selection of merchandise available at prices that are very competitive with those offered directly by the manufacturers.

SERVICES WHOLESALERS PROVIDE FOR MANUFACTURERS

A manufacturer will usually sell to both wholesale furniture distributors and retailers. There are a number of reasons why manufacturers sell all or part of their production through wholesale furniture distributors:

- Carries inventory "on location"
- Reduces manufacturer's financial risks
- Replaces or supplements the manufacturer's sales force
- Handles customer service and delivery in the field
- Provides market information
- Reduces credit risk

CARRIES INVENTORY "ON LOCATION"

The warehouse of the wholesale furniture distributor provides a way for a larger selection of manufacturers' merchandise to be available continually to various locations throughout the United States. This "on location" inventory results in sales of the manufacturer's products that might otherwise go to competitors because the consumer might be unwilling to wait for the merchandise to be shipped from the factory. Even if the retailer or consumer is in no hurry for the merchandise, it can often be shipped from the wholesaler in less time than it would take to ship it from the manufacturer.

Wholesaler distributors with a showroom offer the additional benefit of providing a location where the merchandise can be viewed by retailers, decorators, and consumers. In a sense, this is like having additional market showrooms throughout the United States, without the expense of renting the space.

REDUCES MANUFACTURER'S FINANCIAL RISKS

The wholesale furniture distributors buy and pay for the merchandise they stock in their showrooms and warehouses. With high interest rates and manufacturers having a sizable investment tied up in inventory, it is an advantage to have outlets that buy large amounts of merchandise at one time.

Wholesaler purchases of merchandise reduce inventory risks of all types because the manufacturer eliminates the danger that the merchandise may not sell; be damaged by fire, wind, or some other disaster; or be stolen. By having the merchandise "in the field" owned by the wholesaler, the manufacturer reduces the warehouse inventory that he or she must carry at the factory.

REPLACES OR SUPPLEMENTS
THE MANUFACTURER'S SALES FORCE

The salespeople of the wholesaler are additional representatives selling the manufacturer's products to retailers and interior designers. Some small manufacturers may eliminate the need for a network of manufacturers' sales representatives by selling their entire output to wholesale furniture distributors. At times, these manufacturers may sell and design their merchandise for a group of wholesalers who buy collectively, known as *buying groups*.

Other manufacturers may depend on the wholesaler's sales force to call on the small retailers in certain geographic territories, which frees the manufacturer's representatives to concentrate on the larger retail accounts and to service the wholesalers.

Retailers and interior designers who do not buy large enough amounts to be considered viable accounts for individual manufacturers may buy combinations of products and, therefore, become profitable accounts for wholesale furniture distributors.

HANDLES CUSTOMER SERVICE AND
DELIVERY IN THE FIELD

The prospect of a wholesaler's repairman or finisher taking care of customer complaints has already been mentioned. However, the faster and more efficiently a customer's complaint is handled, the greater the possibility that he or she will remain a satisfied customer. Therefore, it is an advantage to use the wholesaler's repair and finishing services wherever they are available.

By wholesaler handling of deliveries to individual stores and interior designers, the manufacturer may have a less complex delivery problem. It is easier and more economical to deliver to a central wholesaler's warehouse than to a number of retail store locations.

PROVIDES MARKET INFORMATION

The road-selling salespeople of a wholesale furniture distributor call on a variety of retailers in a given territory. This exposure allows them to obtain input from a variety of sources regarding the salability of a manufacturer's products and to pinpoint needs that are not being met. If comments are properly solicited, the wholesale furniture distributor can be a valuable source of market information for the manufacturer.

The wholesale furniture distributor with a decorator showroom can observe purchasing patterns of interior designers and hear their comments concerning the availability of needed merchandise. These wholesalers can provide valuable feedback for the manufacturer.

REDUCES CREDIT RISK

By financing individual retailers and interior designers, the wholesale furniture distributor reduces the number of customer accounts that must be carried by the manufacturer. Because the wholesaler is closer geographically to the retailers and designers he or she serves, the wholesaler is probably in a better position to evaluate them for credit worthiness. The cost of paperwork for evaluating a customer for credit purchases and the cost of administering an account may be lower.

WHY HAVE WHOLESALERS NOT BEEN USED MORE OFTEN?

The majority of furniture sales by manufacturers has historically been directly through their salespeople to retailers. This situation has resulted in the bypassing of wholesale furniture distributors. Some of the reasons why wholesale furniture retailers have not been used more frequently are:

1. *No aggressive wholesaler is available.* There is an uneven geographic distribution of wholesale furniture distributors, with some areas having several and others having none at all. Some of the existing wholesalers have been perceived by manufacturers as not being aggressive enough in promoting their merchandise. Therefore, many manufacturers have historically preferred to go directly to the retailer and/or interior designer rather than relying on the wholesaler to make these contacts.
2. *Manufacturer's desire to control distribution more closely.* Manufacturers often want to control who sells their product. They try to choose retailers whom they feel can create the best selling environment for their products. Many practice selective distribution by selling to only certain retailers in a given geographic area. This also gives manufacturers a chance to work with retail sales and advertising people to obtain the type of promotion and display they feel is best for their products.
3. *Lack of a positive business image by the wholesaler.* Wholesale furniture distributors have suffered from the lack of a positive business image, damaging their relationships with both retailers and manufacturers. They claim that many businesses appearing to be legitimate wholesale furniture distributors have also sold directly to the consumer. Other complaints have been that many wholesalers have not been very progressive in their marketing techniques and have not kept up with fashion and technology trends.

WHOLESALERS' REACTIONS TO BEING BYPASSED

Wholesale furniture distributors have reacted to being bypassed in the furniture distribution process by improving their management practices and trying to police their own organizations. They have been attempting to educate the industry as to their true purpose in the furniture distribution process and are discouraging wholesalers from selling directly to the public.

Many of these wholesalers are now using sophisticated computerized inventory control techniques to ensure they will have optimum inventory levels to serve their customers and maintain their own profitability. They are aggressively soliciting retailers and interior designers, and they are providing effective advertising and other promotional materials.

SUMMARY

The National Wholesale Furniture Association (NWFA) has adopted a code of ethics in an attempt to clarify the purpose of wholesalers within the industry and to improve their public relations.

The types of wholesale furniture distributors include the road-selling distributor, the decorator showroom wholesaler, the combination road-selling and decorator showroom wholesaler, and the independent sales representative with a warehouse.

Wholesalers provide the following services for retailers: a nearby inventory, competitive prices, prompt delivery, buying expertise, advertising and sales support, assortment of merchandise, retail floor samples, credit, and showroom facilities.

Wholesalers offer the following services for interior designers: decorator showroom facilities, merchandise in stock, special-order service, assembly and delivery of merchandise, servicing of products, buying expertise, and competitive prices.

Wholesalers provide the following services for manufacturers: carries inventory "on location," relieves financial requirements by owning the stock, replaces or supplements the manufacturer's sales force, handles customer service and delivery in the field, provides market information, and reduces credit risk.

Reasons why wholesale furniture distributors have not been used more often include: no aggressive wholesaler is available, the manufacturer's desire to control distribution more closely, and the lack of a positive business image.

Wholesalers have reacted to being bypassed by educating the industry as to their true function, by discouraging legitimate wholesalers from selling directly to the public, and by improving their management and marketing techniques.

CHAPTER 16

WHOLESALE FURNITURE MARKETS

The wholesale furniture markets are extremely important to the U.S. furniture industry. It is here that buyers and sellers come together for the purpose of making decisions that determine furniture distribution within the United States and, in some cases, to other countries. The bulk of the production and merchandising planning is governed by the dates of the periodic furniture markets.

WHAT IS A WHOLESALE FURNITURE MARKET?

According to Robert P. Gruenberg, General Manager of the Southern Furniture Market Center in High Point, North Carolina, "Markets provide a contemporary 'wholesale' bazaar on a regularly scheduled basis for the exhibition of a large, bulky product which is not generally purchased from photographs." This refers to the fact that there are large manufacturer showrooms, showing all types of furniture and home furnishings products, open only to retailers and wholesale distributors. It is, in essence, an opportunity for retailers to view products that are too large for manufacturers' sales representatives to carry with them. Markets are held on a regular basis, usually twice a year, in a number of major cities in various parts of the country.

The periodic furniture markets, especially the Southern Furniture Market in North Carolina, serve as the focus of merchandise planning for both manufacturers and retailers. Product development activities are primarily scheduled by the manufacturers so that new introductions will be ready for the opening of the market. Most product development, which includes everything from idea generation to preparation of samples, takes place in the months prior to the furniture market.

Merchandise planning for retailers revolves around the furniture markets because most retailers want to keep up with home fashion trends and purchase new merchandise for their retail floors. Therefore, buyers carefully shop the product offerings of manufacturers and purchase merchandise they think is particularly appropriate for their store in their local

16-1. The 2.3 million square feet of display space at the Southern Furniture Market Center in High Point, North Carolina, accommodates more than 1,300 exhibitors. As shown in this aerial view, the complex, consisting of five buildings, stands on portions of two city blocks. Four of the five buildings are open only for the semi-annual furniture markets held for retailers only. The fifth building is a wholesale shopping center for interior designers to shop both during and between the markets. *(Southern Furniture Market Center)*

trading area. It is the offerings of the manufacturer and the ability to obtain exclusive distribution of selected products in their trading areas that largely determine the selection of merchandise in the retail store. Buyers evaluate the offerings of the various manufacturers based on such factors as value, price, style, and color.

The furniture market is really a sales promotion activity for manufacturers; market exhibits are the way they dramatize their products to retailers. To go one step further, the market also promotes the entire furniture industry. Considerable expense is incurred to enhance the image of home furnishings through the markets. Everything from press releases sent out by the management of the exhibition buildings to the entertaining of media personnel from all over the country by individual manufacturers is designed to create excitement about the industry and the products being offered for sale.

LOCATION AND OPERATION OF MARKETS

The home furnishings industry is the largest user of showroom exhibition space in the United States. There are permanent showroom spaces leased

16-2. In contrast to lavishly decorated permanent manufacturers' showrooms, this furniture market is much like other temporary trade shows. Here, the home furnishings are placed in temporary booths inside a large convention hall, or coliseum. The merchandise is displayed to retail buyers for a short period of time only, and is then removed so that the space can be used for other events, such as automobile, boat, or machinery shows.

for the display of home furnishings in exhibition buildings in Atlanta; Chicago; Dallas; Hickory and High Point, North Carolina; Jamestown, New York; Los Angeles; New York; San Francisco; and Seattle. Private showrooms are also maintained by manufacturers to show their merchandise at the Southern Furniture Market in North Carolina at various geographic locations from Burlington to Lenoir, North Carolina, an area approximately 150 miles long. Often these private showrooms are located near their manufacturing facilities. In addition, temporary home furnishings exhibitions are held in Atlantic City; Boston; Columbus, Ohio; Denver; Miami; Minneapolis; New Orleans; Pittsburgh; and St. Louis. These temporary exhibitions move in, set up, hold market, and move out within a week.

The Southern Furniture Market in North Carolina is also informally known as the "national introductory furniture market." The majority of merchandise is introduced for the first time, and some manufacturers show their entire product line.

The Southern Furniture Market is held in April and October of each year. The market buildings in North Carolina are devoted exclusively to the exhibition of home furnishings. The vast majority of the home furnishings shown in North Carolina are case goods, upholstered furniture, casual furniture, and accessories. Other classifications of furniture are shown, but the space devoted to them is relatively small.

The other furniture markets are referred to as regional furniture markets, which means that the exhibitions are mainly for dealers within the region surrounding the city hosting the event. An important distinction between these regional markets and the North Carolina market is that the cities with the regional markets also host a wide variety of other trade shows and exhibitions.

The largest merchandise mart complex is in Dallas, which includes the Trade Mart, Home Furnishings Mart, Market Hall, Decorative Center, World Trade Center, and the Apparel Center. Dallas and the other regional market cities also exhibit apparel, gifts and decorative accessories, toys, electronic devices, and a wide variety of other products.

The exhibition buildings or merchandise marts provide a place where buyers and sellers can conveniently meet, see the merchandise, and conduct business. The exhibition buildings publish buyer's guides to make market shopping easier. They also provide a variety of other services, from arrangements for transportation and lodging to providing lounges where groups of buyers can relax and compare notes.

Recently, in addition to U.S. manufacturers, a number of importers and foreign manufacturers have shown their merchandise at the markets. International buyers now regularly visit U.S. furniture markets. They are seeking sources who are interested in exporting their products to foreign countries. As an aid to the foreign buyers and sellers, the exhibition buildings and groups of manufacturers provide interpreters and other special services.

In each of the markets, the showrooms are beautifully decorated and accessorized in order to display the furniture in the best possible manner. Considerable expense is incurred in coordinating various aspects of showroom decoration with the products being shown in order to give a very fashionable look. The furniture markets, especially the National Introductory Markets, set the trend in home fashions. The showrooms are closed to the public and are open only to buyers, suppliers to the manufacturers, and the press. The buyers usually register when entering the showroom and are accompanied through the displays by a manufacturer's salesperson.

WHY MANUFACTURERS AND OTHER SELLERS "SHOW" AT MARKET

The majority of the merchandise shown at the various furniture markets is already being produced or consists of samples for which production is planned by manufacturers within the United States. The remaining merchandise is shown by such organizations as importers and representatives of foreign manufacturers. Manufacturers or other sellers display merchandise at the furniture markets because of the opportunity to achieve the following:

1. Make a fashion statement.
2. Collect information upon which to base the decision to produce new offerings.
3. Show all or the major part of their product line properly.
4. Have manufacturing management meet major customers.
5. Expose product offerings to the media.
6. Train the field sales staff on selling the new products and on merchandising introductions.

MAKE A FASHION STATEMENT

The demand for home furnishings is widely diversified with people desiring variety in fabrics, styles, levels of quality, and types of merchandise. Therefore, it is very difficult for any one manufacturer to be "all things to all people."

Successful manufacturers of home furnishings are those who define the segment in the marketplace they want to fill and then develop a marketing program that will create an image as a reliable resource for that type of merchandise. For example, some manufacturers produce traditional-style merchandise with a country flair, others produce merchandise in a contemporary style, while still others produce lower-priced merchandise of obvious value in a number of style categories.

The markets allow the manufacturers to enhance the fashion image of their merchandise. Upholstered furniture companies reveal new fabric treatments including colors, types of fabrics, and new applications of fabric to frame. Case-goods manufacturers try to make their versions of product styles different by varying the finish, drawer configurations, hardware, and other decorative details. All manufacturers want to make a definitive fashion statement in order to convince retailers and the media that the company understands the nature of the demand in its market niche and has the products to satisfy the needs of the consumer.

COLLECT INFORMATION TO PRODUCE NEW OFFERINGS

The feedback from dealers visiting factories prior to market and orders received during and after the market determine whether new introductions will actually be placed into production. In other words, manufacturers bring out a large number of introductions at the market, some of which will not be produced because of lack of orders.

Changes in the new product introductions may be made based on orders received and comments from dealers. For example, if a bedroom suite is presented with a choice of two beds and two mirrors and most orders are placed for one particular bed and mirror, the other alternatives may be dropped. Another change might involve dropping a fabric if it is not popular with buyers.

SHOW PRODUCT LINE

The furniture market provides a showcase for the manufacturer's products, and the setting is controlled so that the furniture is shown to the best advantage. Considerable time and expense are devoted to presenting the complete value and fashion story so that retailers will be motivated to buy.

Furniture is so bulky that it is presented to dealers outside the markets primarily by photographs. Therefore, products are carefully photographed in a beautiful setting for the manufacturer's catalogue. But the market is normally the only chance the manufacturer has to present the products in "real life" to potential buyers.

It is valuable for manufacturers to show all or the major part of their product line. Showing a complete product line gives the dealer a better idea of the production and styling capabilities of each furniture manufacturing company.

Perhaps the most important objective of displaying a product line with new introductions at market is to increase the number of placements of a manufacturer's products on retail sales floors. The sales resulting from these placements over a period of time will usually be much larger than the actual orders placed at market.

HAVE MANUFACTURING MANAGEMENT
MEET MAJOR CUSTOMERS

Customer relationships with retail store executives are enhanced by direct personal contact with manufacturing managers or executive officers. The most convenient way for these managers and executives to meet is at the markets. Such meetings help both manufacturer and retailer to be more willing to make commitments that are mutually beneficial.

By having major customers review the product lines and by answering questions concerning the salability of the merchandise, the manufacturer may be able to make changes that will help to move the products—not only to the retail floor, but to the consumer. An example would be growing product categories that are not being covered sufficiently or other product categories that are declining in popularity and should be reduced or eliminated. The manufacturer may be able to make suggestions as to ways to offer merchandise for effective advertising or promotion by the retailer.

In essence, the furniture industry is a person-to-person industry. Much of the business takes place because one person knows another, which leads to interaction and trust on behalf of both parties.

EXPOSE PRODUCT OFFERINGS TO THE MEDIA

The furniture market provides an opportunity to position the industry and, more specifically, a company and its products in the public eye, which comes largely by means of exposure to print media.

By preparing effective press kits and conducting showroom tours, furniture manufacturers are exposing their product lines to editors of shelter magazines, the trade press, and home fashion editors of newspapers. The intent is that these people will be sufficiently impressed with the fashion statement and product offerings to publish pictures and news stories about what they have seen. It is a part of the sales promotion efforts of the manufacturer and, if done properly, can result in considerable favorable publicity for the company and its products.

TRAIN THE FIELD SALES STAFF
The national introductory furniture market in North Carolina offers manufacturers a good opportunity to train their field sales staff to sell new offerings effectively. All members of the sales staff, whether they are independent contractors or employee salespeople, can be gathered together to review the sales features of the new merchandise. Price lists are provided, product benefits are presented, and questions are answered so that the sales staffs are ready to do an effective job of selling the product in their territories.

Alternative merchandising approaches, such as manufacturers' gallery programs or advertising assistance programs, can also be explained to the sales force. Above all, the sales force must leave a market well-trained and equipped with sales photographs and collateral materials to communicate the new product story to their customers in the important weeks after the market.

WHY RETAILERS AND WHOLESALE DISTRIBUTORS "SHOP THE MARKET"

Considerable effort, time, and expense are spent by the retailers in attending the furniture markets. To get the most out of a market, adequate preparation must be made before going so time will not be wasted. A well-prepared buyer comes with a "to do" list of lines to shop and questions to ask. A buyer wants to shop his or her major suppliers and, as far as time allows, also check out others not currently being bought from to determine if anything is being overlooked.

Buyers from virtually all large retailers and wholesale distributors throughout the country attend the markets, especially the North Carolina market. In addition, a large number of buyers from medium and small retailers also attend. Among the reasons most often given by retailers for attending the markets are the opportunities to:
1. Shop entire product lines.
2. See the newest home fashion trends and product introductions.
3. Meet and work with manufacturing management.
4. See actual product features.
5. Obtain assistance in advertising, sales training, and display.

16-3. These retailers are shopping manufacturers' showrooms during the Southern Furniture Market in North Carolina. In this way, the retailers can examine an entire product line as well as the latest in product introductions.

6. Get commitments to be allowed to buy "first."
7. Coordinate delivery with merchandising plans.
8. Attend many helpful meetings on various topics of interest to retailers.
9. Interact with retailers from other geographic areas.

SHOP ENTIRE PRODUCT LINES

Just as it is important for manufacturers to show their entire product lines, it is important for the retailer to be able to shop that line. It provides an opportunity to see the depth and breadth of product offerings necessary for effective buying decisions.

SEE NEWEST TRENDS AND PRODUCT INTRODUCTIONS

Because of the fashion nature of the home furnishings industry, each year brings a rise in the popularity of certain colors, fabrics, finishes, and styles, and a decline in the popularity of others. As an aid to keeping up with these changes in fashion, the buyer attends the furniture markets. It is the easiest way to determine the fashion statements of the various manufacturers. Buyers are then better equipped to select merchandise that will reflect a progressive fashion image for their stores.

By attending the market, the buyers can see new introductions and determine if they will fit into the merchandising plan of their stores. For instance, technological innovations in recliner or sofa bed mechanisms can best be evaluated if seen in actual operation. New materials and methods of construction can also be better reviewed by actually seeing the product.

MEET AND WORK WITH MANUFACTURING MANAGEMENT

Again, it is very important for the retailer to meet and become better acquainted with manufacturing management. The information buyers need includes delivery schedules and policies, credit and payment terms, advertising and display assistance, point-of-purchase sales aids, and the type of training the manufacturer can provide the retail floor sales force.

Problems can also be discussed more effectively face to face. It is a considerable expense to the retailer to receive merchandise that must be repaired or refinished after it is received in the store. Therefore, retailers are always very interested in discussing quality control problems with the manufacturer.

SEE ACTUAL PRODUCT FEATURES

A buyer can usually make a better buying decision by seeing the actual product than basing the decision on a photograph, finish panel, or fabric swatch brought to his or her office by the manufacturer's representative.

Unless the furniture can actually be seen, there is a considerable amount of subjectivity about how the product will look when it is received and displayed in the store, especially if the manufacturer is a new supplier. Because techniques of photography and printing may be used, which enhance or exaggerate the appearance of the product, flaws or weaknesses in finish or construction may not be noticed.

OBTAIN ASSISTANCE IN ADVERTISING, SALES TRAINING, AND DISPLAY

At the market, retailers can review a large selection of art work for advertising, color transparencies, sample advertisements clipped from newspapers in various geographic areas, and other advertising materials available from the manufacturers. Many manufacturers have a special advertising display area, and the company advertising director will be available to help the retailers plan their advertising of the company's products. The retailer can also review any cooperative advertising programs sponsored by the manufacturer and find out how to qualify for such programs.

The variety of point-of-purchase selling aids offered by the manufacturer is displayed in the advertising area and will usually include signs, scale models, partially upholstered pieces, or other materials designed to make the retail floor salesperson's job easier.

Manufacturers sometimes have programs to show retailers how to display their products in the store and may include diagrams showing how to arrange furniture on the retail floor as well as a complete gallery program. A manufacturer's assistance in setting up a gallery may include everything from having a space planner to developing floor plans to providing a limited amount of funds to help with construction costs.

Retailers are also given details on the sales training aids available from the manufacturer, which may be in the form of slide shows or videotapes showing product benefits and features. The sales representative or some other person from the manufacturer's organization may visit the store for a limited amount of time to conduct training sessions. Manufacturers may also have plant tours and in-house training programs available for dealers and their salespeople.

GET COMMITMENTS TO BE ALLOWED TO BUY "FIRST"

It is perceived to be an advantage to be the "first store in town" to have new introductions which the retail buyer feels is right for his or her store. It is one way of staying ahead of the competition. It also gives the store something new to promote and presents a progressive fashion image to its customers and the community. Some retailers advertise that they shop aggressively for new introductions and, therefore, always carry the latest in home fashions.

COORDINATE DELIVERY WITH MERCHANDISING PLANS

Attending a furniture market gives a retailer the opportunity to confirm delivery dates of merchandise tied to sales or other merchandising events throughout the year. This is especially important in purchasing case goods because of the considerable lead time needed for delivery. Upholstery normally requires less lead time than case goods. Therefore, adequate forward planning for case-goods promotions is especially important.

By getting commitments on delivery dates, the retailer can properly schedule advertising, promotional store events, and the training of salespeople for product arrivals.

ATTEND MEETINGS OF INTEREST

At each market, a variety of educational seminars and other meetings on topics of interest to retailers are held. These meetings are sponsored by groups that include the management of the exhibition buildings, trade associations, and various suppliers. Typical topics would include advertising, display, management techniques, interior design, warehousing, and how to best manage a store's finances. Conscientious retailers who attend these meetings gain valuable ideas that can add to profits.

INTERACT WITH RETAILERS FROM OTHER AREAS

A distinct advantage to many retailers is the opportunity to meet and share experiences with retailers from different geographic areas. Although retailers are reluctant to share secrets of success with competitors, a great deal can be learned from talking with noncompeting retailers. Some retailers meet at every market to share experiences, to discuss what they have seen, and to talk about successes they have had between markets.

BUYING SERVICES

Over the years, medium- and smaller-sized retailers have joined furniture buying services. These buying services offer independent retailers who pay periodic membership fees many of the services individual store units in a corporate chain would receive from the home office. The intent is to serve similar but noncompeting stores. The more progressive of these services provide a complete marketing service which may include:

A *market survey book,* giving details of products the buying service feels its member stores should see at the market, is compiled by the buying service staff through visits to key manufacturers during the premarket period before each national introductory furniture market. Needed information, such as product descriptions, sketches, and an opinion of product value, is provided.

A *core stock list* is published by the buying service as a recommendation of merchandise that should be stocked for promotion purposes. By stocking this core group of merchandise, member stores will be able to participate in circulars, newspaper advertisements, or other promotions offered by the buying service. The core stock is merchandise that can be used for promotion with the stores providing their own individual "step-ups" from there.

A *suggested schedule of promotions* may be provided to member stores as a way of keeping business coming in all year long.

Circulars, newspaper ads, and other advertising materials are provided to members who stock the core group of merchandise. Such materials prominently feature the name of the store and are available to each store for considerably less cost than they would be able to obtain individually.

Market meetings are held during the furniture markets to brief members on what merchandise is available and to give helpful news about the industry or the economy.

A *consulting service* is available to individual members, in person or over the telephone, to provide all types of desired management and marketing information.

Buying service lounges at markets are available to members for relaxing, using the telephone, or talking with members of the buying service staff.

Periodic newsletters and merchandising bulletins are mailed to members to keep them informed about the industry, individual companies, new products, and successful promotions.

Other business services are also provided. For example, packages of computer software programs providing numerous types of management reports are available from some services. By using this software and renting or buying the proper type of equipment, much of the information helpful in the management of furniture stores can easily be provided.

BUYING COOPERATIVES

A buying cooperative is an organization that stocks merchandise in a centrally located warehouse for member stores. To be a member of the cooperative, a store must pay a membership fee. This allows the store to go to the warehouse with its truck to pick up the merchandise that is needed. Theoretically, the warehouse, merchandise, and any profits generated from the operation belong to the members.

The buying cooperative is able to buy in volume, which may result in two types of savings. First, the cost of the merchandise may be less because of volume purchases. Second, freight savings are realized from ordering railroad car or truck-load quantities.

THE U.S. FURNITURE MARKETING CYCLE

Historically, furniture manufacturers in the United States have introduced the majority of their offerings at one of the semiannual wholesale furniture markets. As already discussed, in recent years these introductions have occurred at the Southern Furniture Market in North Carolina. The sequence of steps leading up to the market and the evaluation of orders after the market can be summarized by the term "U.S. Furniture Marketing Cycle." This cycle can be divided into three marketing periods: (1) premarket; (2) the furniture market; and (3) postmarket.

16-4. The U.S. furniture marketing cycle

Premarket is the time when the major case-goods and upholstered manufacturers invite the major retailers and buying services to preview their new introductions. The buyers are shown a prototype of one or more pieces of a possible new introduction. (A prototype is usually a dummy chest with drawer fronts, hardware and sides, but no insides.) The manufacturers obtain a critique from the retailers stating whether they like the suites and what changes should be made. Often, changes are made almost up to market time, based on comments made by retailers.

The premarket review is also a time for the large retailers to obtain exclusive distribution in their trading area of the new introductions they feel are right for them. In the furniture industry, large competitors in a given market area prefer not to carry the same styles or suites, even though they carry the same brand of merchandise. Therefore, if one large retailer has agreed to buy a particular suite in a geographic territory, the manufacturer will try to allow him or her to sell it exclusively, at least for an initial period of time.

The *furniture market* is where the merchandise is actually presented to all buyers and the media. It is also the first time retailers see the complete suites of new merchandise. Teams of buyers shop the lines, compare notes, and begin to decide on their final product lineups and purchases.

Postmarket is the period of about six weeks after the market which usually determines the success of new introductions. A large percentage of orders are not actually placed at market. The buyers want to go back to the store, think over what they have seen compared to their "open-to-buy," and then submit the orders. Other companies submit "HFC" or "hold for confirmation" orders at market. These HFC orders put the ordering process on hold until the buyers get back to the stores and talk to the merchandise managers or owners.

The manufacturer's sales representative does a large percentage of his or her most meaningful work during the postmarket period. Manufacturers make certain that their sales representatives leave the market with adequate photographs and fabric swatches to make a presentation of the new products in the dealer's store. They try to see the dealers who did not come to market to tell them what they missed and call on those who put them off or did not commit themselves at market. This period is very important because it is a time when orders should be high and new introductions survive or are dropped.

SUMMARY

The furniture markets provide a wholesale bazaar, on a regularly scheduled basis, for the exhibition of a large, bulky product which is not easily purchased from photographs. The furniture markets are a manufacturer's major promotion tool for displaying and selling his or her merchandise.

There are permanent showroom spaces in Atlanta; Chicago; Dallas; and in an area of 150 miles stretching from Burlington to Lenoir, North Carolina; Jamestown, New York; Los Angeles; New York; San Francisco; and Seattle. Temporary home furnishings exhibitions are held in Atlantic City; Boston; Columbus, Ohio; Denver; Miami; Minneapolis; New Orleans;

Pittsburgh; and St. Louis. The Southern Furniture Market in North Carolina is the national introductory furniture market and the remainder are basically regional furniture markets.

A manufacturer "shows" at market to:

1. Make a fashion statement.
2. Determine dealer reactions upon which to base the decision to produce new offerings.
3. Display all or the major part of a company's line.
4. Allow manufacturing management to meet major customers.
5. Expose product offerings to the media.
6. Train the field sales staff on selling the new products and on merchandising introductions.

A retailer or wholesaler "shops the market" to:

1. Be able to review entire product lines.
2. See the newest home fashion trends and product introductions.
3. Meet and work with manufacturing management.
4. See actual product features and technological advances.
5. Obtain assistance in advertising, sales training, and display.
6. Get commitments to be allowed to buy a style "first" or exclusively for his or her trading area.
7. Coordinate delivery with merchandising plans.
8. Attend educational meetings on topics of interest to retailers.
9. Trade information with retailers from other geographic areas.

Buying services are groups of independent, noncompeting furniture stores who join to obtain a number of buying and merchandising services that they cannot usually afford to provide for themselves. These services usually include a market survey book, core stock list, suggested schedule of promotions, circulars, newspaper ads, other advertising materials, market meetings, consulting services, lounges for the use of members at market, periodic newsletters, and merchandising bulletins.

Buying cooperatives involve member stores cooperatively renting a warehouse, buying merchandise in truck load or railroad car lots, and having the merchandise available when it is needed.

The U.S. furniture marketing cycle includes premarket, furniture market, and postmarket. Premarket is the period when key accounts review new offerings, make comments on design and construction, and commit themselves to the purchase of desired styles or suites. Market is the actual display of the furniture to all dealers, large and small. Postmarket is the period of about six weeks after market when a large percentage of orders are placed and the manufacturer's representative presents the new merchandise to the dealer in his or her store.

CHAPTER 17

PHYSICAL DISTRIBUTION AND INVENTORY MANAGEMENT

O verall marketing efficiency can be greatly enhanced by having the proper amount of inventory at the right places when it is needed. The title of this chapter, "Physical Distribution and Inventory Management," is significant because the marketing effort must be supported by transportation and storage, the two components of physical distribution. Inventory management must also be considered because having too little inventory available will result in lost sales, and the cost of stocking too much inventory erodes profits.

It is important to establish a workable physical distribution and inventory management system that will ensure optimum inventory levels throughout the channel of distribution. The manufacturer and retailer must both be concerned about the costs of physical distribution because controlling the costs of transportation and storage has a direct effect on the final price paid by the consumer. The key is to have an economical system of physical distribution and inventory management that will also be efficient and effective.

PHYSICAL DISTRIBUTION AND INVENTORY MANAGEMENT CONSIDERATIONS OF MANUFACTURERS

Although much emphasis is placed on the transportation of the finished product, the furniture manufacturer must also be concerned with achieving economies in ordering and transporting inbound shipments of raw materials and component parts. Many of the cost-saving techniques such as combining shipments, thereby paying only truck load or car load freight rates, for completed furniture as well as inbound shipments of materials and supplies will be discussed. In fact, if the transportation costs of materials and supplies are added to those for shipping the product to the consumer, the total transportation cost assignable to one piece of furniture is on the average greater than the labor cost incurred in manufacturing that piece.

The manufacturer has three types of inventory that should be closely monitored to avoid excessive costs. They are:

1. Raw materials that have not had any processing or assembly done on them.
2. Work-in-process, which are products that are partially manufactured but not yet completed.
3. Finished goods that are completed and ready for shipment to the customer.

All of these inventories must be closely monitored to ensure that management is minimizing the costs involved. However, this chapter will concentrate on the storage, transportation, and inventory control of finished furniture products.

From the manufacturing standpoint, the considerations are as follows:

- Warehousing possibilities and philosophies
- Inventory management systems
- Order entry and processing system
- Packaging and materials handling
- Considerations affecting transportation
- Transportation alternatives

WAREHOUSING POSSIBILITIES AND PHILOSOPHIES

The philosophy of management concerning how they can best serve their dealers largely determines what and how much manufacturers will store in company warehouses. This philosophy also largely determines how production is scheduled. For example, management must decide whether they are going to manufacture to their warehouse or to customer orders.

Manufacturers that produce to their warehouse schedule cuttings in order to have a continuous and well-balanced supply of furniture items in their warehouse. This inventory is then shipped as it is ordered by retailers or wholesalers.

Manufacturers who produce to customer order from the retailer have a different way of scheduling production. They schedule according to the receipt of customer orders, and the products are shipped from the factory to the retailer or wholesaler and then to the consumer.

A company manufacturing to the warehouse may have an easier time scheduling production, but it must have a larger warehouse and more money tied up in inventory than a company that manufactures to customer order. Therefore, it is more common in normal economic times to manufacture to customer order. Upholstered furniture manufacturers are more likely to produce to customer orders and case-goods manufacturers usually maintain a finished goods inventory.

Another manufacturing approach affecting warehousing requirements and costs is that some manufacturers choose to store component parts rather than finished merchandise. An upholstered furniture manufacturer might assemble a variety of frames and have a variety of fabrics already cut. The products are stored in this unassembled fashion until customer orders are received. Upon approval of the order, the upholstering is completed and the product is packaged and shipped.

INVENTORY MANAGEMENT SYSTEM

Manufacturers who warehouse finished goods inventories normally promote the fact that they have merchandise in stock and will ship whenever an item is needed by customers. It is desirable for these companies to have an effective inventory management system to help reduce storage costs and, at the same time, be able to fill customer orders quickly. Examples of inventory costs include:

The funds invested in the goods. If the firm has its own funds tied up in inventory, it is losing the revenue that might otherwise be derived from the use of these funds. This cost can be even greater if the firm has borrowed the capital invested in the inventory because of the interest charges that must be paid.

Direct and indirect warehousing expenses. Furniture is a large, bulky product requiring a relatively large amount of storage space. Therefore, the cost of constructing or renting a building large enough to store a sufficient supply of furniture is very high. Utilities, salaries of warehouse personnel, and other expenses also must be considered.

Insurance. Furniture is a valuable commodity and the owner must be adequately protected by insurance.

Obsolescence. Since furniture is a fashion product, merchandise in storage may become out-of-date and less salable due to changes in consumer style preferences. To sell it then requires substantially reduced prices.

Many manufacturers have installed computerized inventory control systems that maintain a continuous count on all items stored. Such systems require all goods to be entered in the computer when they are brought into the warehouse. Likewise, they must be subtracted from inventory when they are shipped to a customer. The speed and accuracy of a well-designed computerized inventory control system can be very effective for furniture manufacturers.

ORDER ENTRY AND PROCESSING SYSTEM

A progressive furniture manufacturer must have an effective order entry and processing system to back up his or her physical distribution and marketing efforts. Computerized order processing is proving to be the most effective approach for larger companies.

The order processing system receives orders, checks the customer for credit worthiness, determines the availability of merchandise, and schedules the order for shipment. This type of system can be extremely costly unless it is well-planned and implemented. It should also be able to fill customer orders as rapidly as possible for maximum customer satisfaction. Checks should be built into the system to help ensure that the correct merchandise is sent to the right people. Merchandise should not leave the manufacturer's warehouse unless it has the proper tag or other documents that authorize shipment and help cut down on theft losses.

PACKAGING AND MATERIALS HANDLING

Furniture must be packaged properly if it is to be shipped by contract or common carrier. This packaging must conform to a number of government-approved packaging specifications, called "F" specifications. There are a large number of these regulations which involve such factors as the type of packaging material, how it is applied to the furniture, and the type of base upon which the furniture sits. If a manufacturer does not package his or her products in compliance with these specifications, the carrier can refuse to transport the products or can assess extra freight charges.

Therefore, the manufacturer is very careful to provide acceptable packaging. Many either have their own packaging test laboratories or use the testing laboratories of packaging materials manufacturers that simulate various transportation conditions.

17-1. This manufacturer is using the shrink-pack method of packing upholstered furniture, whereby it is securely anchored within an outer carton. This process involves encasing the piece in a plastic bag which also goes around its sturdy cardboard base. It then passes through an oven that shrinks the plastic over the furniture. Once this is done, the furniture is placed in large cardboard cartons, which are then placed in a storage or holding area as shown in the background.

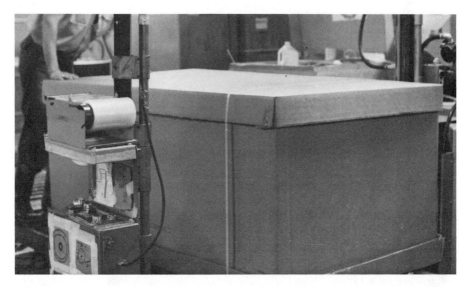

17-2. This machine is placing metal bands around a carton of furniture to help ensure that the product will be stored safely until it is unpacked by the retailer for display or for delivery to a customer. These cartons are tested to determine their effectiveness in protecting the furniture and to meet government regulations.

17-3. The use of this fork-lift truck aids in the efficient movement of a considerable amount of cartoned merchandise at one time in the manufacturing plant, warehouse, or other storage facility. This results in a considerable cost savings as well as reduction in damage to the merchandise.

A manufacturer's exact packaging expense is determined by the volume of materials utilized and the size of the products being shipped. It is apparent that it is relatively expensive to package furniture properly.

Furniture shipped by a manufacturer's own trucks does not have to be packaged in conformity to government regulations. By using this method of transportation, a considerable savings can be incurred, because the furniture can often be blanket-wrapped or paper-wrapped if care is taken in packing the truck. Blanket wrapping involves using furniture pads much like those used by household moving companies. Upholstered furniture shipped on company trucks is sometimes paper-wrapped, which simply involves placing heavy paper and plastic around the furniture.

Proper materials handling procedures must be utilized by the manufacturer because much of the damage to furniture is caused by improper handling. It is also evident that the less each piece is handled, the less likely that the furniture will sustain damage. Most warehouses have conveyors and fork-lift trucks to facilitate the movement of merchandise. Warehouse personnel must be carefully trained so they will know how to best handle furniture and minimize damage to the product.

CONSIDERATIONS AFFECTING TRANSPORTATION

Manufacturers primarily ship furniture by either truck or rail. In the furniture industry, transportation is different than in many other industries because the retailer or wholesaler pays for the freight, but the manufacturer makes the arrangements. There are several considerations that affect the type of transportation selected:

Retailer's instructions. The retailer who is ordering the furniture may have a preference as to how he wishes the shipment to be sent. It is possible that he may say ship "best way," which is not very definite since this might mean the fastest or the most economical or, perhaps, the transportation method on which there is the least chance of damage. Therefore, it is important that there be a clear understanding between buyer and seller as to which transportation alternatives are preferred.

Distance to customers. In general, rail transportation is cheaper for long distances than truck transportation. Although freight rates vary, it may be advantageous to consider a combination of rail and truck transportation, such as piggyback freight, depending on the distance between buyer and seller.

Size of order. The freight charge is less expensive per piece if the customer buys a truckload or carload of merchandise. Smaller shipments are usually shipped more economically if they are combined with other shipments bound for the same geographic location.

Time constraints. Some methods of transportation require a longer transit time than others. Therefore, in situations where the buyer needs a piece of furniture quickly, a more rapid method of transportation may be chosen even though it may be more expensive.

Geographic location of the customer. Transportation alternatives are not uniform all over the United States. Some areas are not served by rail transportation, which prohibits using that alternative. Other geographic areas, such as Vermont, New Hampshire, and Maine, buy relatively small amounts of furniture, which reduces the possibilities of consolidating the shipments of several manufacturers to get lower freight rates. On the other hand, an area like California would be receiving much more merchandise, and the opportunity for consolidation is greater. Some manufacturers have located factories close to the markets to reduce the problems and costs involved in long transportation distances.

TRANSPORTATION ALTERNATIVES

The manufacturer has a number of available alternatives from which to choose in shipping his or her furniture products. These alternatives should be evaluated based on the wishes of the retailer, distance to the customer, order size, allowable waiting time, and customer's geographic location. These alternatives include:

Manufacturer's own trucks. A considerable number of companies, especially upholstered furniture manufacturers, ship products to customers on their own trucks, because upholstered furniture carries one of the highest railroad freight rates. Therefore, transportation on a manufacturer's own trucks reduces the costs paid by the retailer. Many private truck deliveries are to the geographic regions near the factories. It is rare for a manufacturer to ship a large volume of merchandise in his or her own trucks across the country. Usually, the retailer pays for delivery on a manufacturer's trucks, although the amount charged is often less than would be charged by a common or contract carrier. A manufacturer using his or her own trucks is called a *private carrier.*

Outside trucking company. There are a number of trucking companies that haul furniture. In fact, there are some contract carriers that primarily handle furniture and have trailers built especially for that purpose. These outside trucking companies are either common or contract carriers. A trucking company that is a *common carrier* maintains a regular schedule and accepts most shipments from the general public without discrimination. A trucking company that is a *contract carrier,* on the other hand, enters into a contract with one or more shippers to haul the specialized merchandise for an agreed sum. The specific services and length of time required will vary from contract to contract.

Shipment by truck has obvious advantages over rail transportation. Highways lead to almost all customers, while railroads are not uniformly distributed across the country. Trucks can also deliver directly to the customer's loading dock.

It is less expensive to ship full truck loads because this avoids paying the "less-than-truck load" *(LTL)* rates. It is also less costly to ship to one or more stores in a relatively close geographic territory on the same truck if the combined shipment fills the truck. The truck will deliver to more than one store in the destination area for a stop-off fee for each store. This arrangement is called a *stop truck,* and the stop-off fees are lower than LTL rates.

Railroad shipping. Railroads operate most efficiently with completely filled boxcars. A full or "solid" boxcar is charged a car load *(CL)* rate, which is the cheapest way to ship long distances if there are no tight time constraints. Of course, it is less costly than the "less-than-car load" *(LCL)* rates. A solid boxcar can be from one manufacturer or consolidated from several manufacturers. The disadvantage of railroad transportation is the loading and unloading required; most retailers and some manufacturers are not located on a rail siding. It is also possible to receive some savings by having the car stop at more than one destination. This arrangement is called a *stop-car* or *stopover car* and is more expensive than if it were going to one destination, but less expensive than paying the LCL rates.

Piggyback freight. It is possible to achieve a more favorable freight cost arrangement by shipping piggyback. The piggyback arrangement is a combination of truck and rail transportation involving furniture being loaded into a truck trailer that is then transported on a railroad flatcar for the longest portion of the trip. When the train gets to its destination, a truck tractor picks up the trailer and delivers the merchandise. The piggyback arrangement over long distances combines the economies of rail transportation with the flexibility of truck transportation. Damage to merchandise may be less because it is only handled twice—once to load the trailer and once to unload it at the destination.

Combining shipments with others. Shippers of furniture can at times obtain favorable freight rates by combining their shipments with those of other companies. A combination arrangement allows small shippers to achieve lower freight rates than they could by shipping individually. It should be pointed out, however, that combining freight frequently takes longer than an individual manufacturer shipping independently. Transit time includes the entire time from shipper's dock to buyer's dock, some of which may be warehouse time. There are three ways of cooperating with others to combine shipments:

1. *Join a shipper's association.* A shipper's association is a group of shippers who band together for the purpose of consolidating freight to achieve lower rates. Manufacturers or retailers could form a shipper's association, but a firm must be a member of the association to ship through it. In essence, the shipper's association accepts smaller shipments from its members, consolidates them, and presents the larger load to the carrier. The lower rates are then passed onto the member shippers.

2. *Use a freight forwarder.* A freight forwarder is an independent, profit-making company that consolidates shipments of many

small shippers into larger-volume, more economical shipping quantities. These companies receive a flat fee for transportation to a particular location and make all the shipping arrangements. Some forwarders have their own delivery equipment for local store or home delivery, but a forwarder has no long-haul equipment. They make their profits largely from the difference between the large-volume freight rates they obtain and the rates they quote their shipper customers. At times, the freight forwarder may offer a relatively short transit time because he or she is able to combine furniture with other types of freight. In international sales, freight forwarders can be invaluable; they will make all the arrangements and work out the best freight rates using a variety of transportation methods.

3. *Work with a consolidation agent.* A consolidation agent combines smaller shipments into larger, more economical quantities, but unlike the freight forwarder, does not quote a flat fee. The consolidation agent works on a per transaction basis and tries to make the best arrangements for each shipment. Consolidation agents are particularly active in arranging piggyback shipments.

PHYSICAL DISTRIBUTION AND INVENTORY MANAGEMENT CONSIDERATIONS OF RETAILERS

Retailers must consider how incoming merchandise is transported and stored because the costs involved are a significant part of their cost of doing business. Making the proper decisions on warehousing and storage, as well as having the optimum amount of inventory available for immediate delivery to customers, can help to ensure profitable operations. There are a number of factors that have an impact on the retailer's decisions in regard to physical distribution and inventory management:

- Economic conditions
- Warehousing possibilities and philosophies
- Storage considerations
- Inventory management
- Inbound transportation
- Delivery alternatives

ECONOMIC CONDITIONS

The prevailing economic conditions in the local market area affect how much merchandise a retailer will stock in his store and warehouse and how much merchandise he will buy at one time. If economic conditions are healthy and the retailer is optimistic about having a high level of sales to the consumer, he will order in large quantities to get lower freight rates and quantity discounts, resulting in a larger amount of furniture being stocked at the retail level. If the reverse is true and the local economic conditions are poor, the retailer will prefer to carry less inventory and order smaller quantities even if higher freight rates are incurred.

Interest rates are also a factor in determining the amount of furniture that is purchased and kept in inventory by those dealers who must finance their purchases from outside sources. Higher interest rates will cause smaller purchases and smaller amounts of inventory in order to minimize finance charges.

WAREHOUSING POSSIBILITIES AND PHILOSOPHIES

There are a number of warehousing options open to a retailer depending on which brand of furniture he chooses to sell and his philosophy of doing business. Each retailer should choose an option which fits his niche in the market and the expectations of his customers. These warehousing options include:

Let the manufacturer warehouse. Some retailers prefer to let the manufacturer warehouse the bulk of their inventory. These companies do business with manufacturers who maintain a constant inventory of their best-selling groups in their warehouses. Other retailers in the higher price categories who special order merchandise also usually prefer to let the manufacturer warehouse the inventory.

Have regional distribution centers (RDCs). Retail furniture store chains and department stores frequently have regional distribution centers that serve the branch stores within a given geographic territory. These regional dsitribution centers are large warehouses located next to railroad sidings and close to highways where inventory can be kept for a number of stores within the surrounding area. Many stores sell from floor samples and have the merchandise delivered directly from the regional distribution center to the consumer on company trucks. This eliminates the need for a large amount of warehouse space at each store location.

Have inventory "on location" at the store. Some retailers prefer to have a fairly complete selection of inventory in a warehouse adjoining or near the store. These stores can fill customer orders quickly, although they must allow sufficient time to inspect and deluxe the furniture properly before it is delivered. Warehouse showrooms advertise that consumers can buy and take the furniture with them. To support this claim, they maintain an adequate inventory to back up their floor samples at each store location.

Use a wholesale furniture distributor. Wholesale furniture distributors, especially those with over-the-road sales forces, have large warehouses and maintain inventory within the local geographic area. A considerable number of retailers prefer to buy at least part of their inventory from these wholesale furniture distributors. By using the wholesaler as his warehouse, the retailer can reduce the amount of funds tied up in inventory and still get delivery quickly. Buying only from the wholesaler does restrict the number and selection of items the store has available, and often the retailer will supplement his floor display with stock not carried by the wholesaler.

STORAGE CONSIDERATIONS

There are a number of considerations that must be taken into account if the retailer is to have an efficient, economical warehousing operation. These considerations apply even if he decides to let the manufacturer or wholesale furniture distributor warehouse most of his merchandise because it is usually necessary for a retailer to have his own small warehousing and staging operation. The following should be considered in operating a successful retail store warehouse:

Receiving procedures. Proper and careful receiving of merchandise is crucial because any visible damage to the furniture packaging should be noted before the trucking company leaves the premises. These notations are extremely important in filing claims for damage. Proper receiving procedures are also necessary to prevent theft and maintain accurate warehouse inventory records.

Inventory retrieval and preparation for delivery. It is important when a customer buys furniture that the merchandise is retrieved from the warehouse quickly and is properly prepared for delivery. By establishing proper procedures, merchandise can be retrieved from storage, removed from shipping cartons, and inspected by the warehouse crew. The furniture should be properly deluxed, or suitably touched up and polished, so it will be in the best possible condition when it is delivered to the customer. This should include a quality inspection to ensure that all hardware is in place and other needed adjustments are made. As in receiving, proper documentation must be presented before merchandise can be moved out of the warehouse to prevent theft or customers receiving the wrong items.

Materials handling. Modern retail furniture warehouses use fork-lift trucks and other automated equipment to move furniture throughout the warehouse. This reduces the number of accidents and the amount of damage to the furniture.

Storage facilities. An efficient retail warehouse has well-constructed racks or bins where furniture may be stored conveniently to maximize the use of warehouse floor space. The racks or bins are conveniently and logically arranged so furniture can be stored and retrieved easily. There should be a logical arrangement to the warehouse so that store personnel will always know where the merchandise is located. The warehouse should be kept clean and neat, giving the warehouse personnel pride in their work and making their working environment conducive to good working habits.

Suburban Colonial Shoppes Ltd

M 37252

SOLD TO _____
ADDRESS _____ APT. _____
CITY _____ STATE _____ ZIP _____
TEL. NO. _____ P.O.B. TEL. NO. _____
2 MAIN CROSS STREETS _____
PRESENT ADDRESS

DATE _____ / _____ / 19 _____ DELIVERY DAY

FOR DELIVERY INFORMATION TEL. 516 691-8800
FOR SERVICE INFORMATION TEL. 516 691-8803
BETWEEN 10:00 A.M. & 4:00 P.M. MON. THRU FRI. ONLY.

DELIVERY COPY

QUAN.	LOT NO.	F. #	ART. NO.	ARTICLE	DESCRIPTION	FINISH	CODE	EACH	AMOUNT
Quantity		This is the factory	This is the style number of the piece you are looking for	This is what the piece is.	This lets you know what the piece looks like.		this is the location of the piece you are looking for		
	This is the receiving number that you are looking for								

FABRICS ARE NOT GUARANTEED AGAINST WEARING FADING SHRINKING.

RESPONSIBILITY FOR THE SIZE OF ITEMS SELECTED REMAIN WITH THE BUYER. PRICES DO NOT INCLUDE ADDITIONAL COSTS DUE TO SPECIAL RIGGING NECESSARY TO COMPLETE DELIVERY. THIS SALES AGREEMENT MAY NOT BE CHANGED ORALLY.

READ BEFORE SIGNING
THIS SPECIAL ORDER NOT SUBJECT TO CANCELLATION.
NO RESPONSIBILITY CAN BE ASSUMED FOR DELAYS IN DELIVERY DUE TO STRIKES, ACCIDENTS OR DELAYS BEYOND OUR CONTROL.
IF BUYER DEFAULTS ON THIS CONTRACT, SELLER WILL BE ENTITLED TO 20% OF THE TOTAL PURCHASE PRICE AS LIQUIDATED DAMAGES.

TM

DELIVERY C.O.D.

SALES TAX
D.C.

SALE # _____ SPECIAL INSTRUCTIONS

M 37252

CERTIFIED OR CASHIER'S CHECK ONLY ON DELIVERY OR PICKUP.

CASH | TOTAL
CHECK | DEPOSIT
C.O.D. | BALANCE

SALESMAN

RECEIVED ABOVE MERCHANDISE IN GOOD CONDITION BY

PURCHASER'S SIGNATURE

17-4. This delivery or warehouse copy of a retail customer invoice explains to the delivery people the quantity, receiving number, factory or vendor number, style, description, and location in the warehouse of the merchandise ordered.

Costs inherent in storage. There are a number of costs inherent whenever merchandise is stored in a retail store warehouse. These include:

- Funds tied up in the inventory
- Costs of running the warehouse, which include such expenses as salaries of the warehouse crew, utilities, and rent if the store does not own the warehouse
- Insurance on the merchandise in inventory
- Risk of product obsolescence due to style preference changes or other factors.

17-5. Merchandise is stored in this completely racked warehouse, owned by a retail furniture chain, until it is needed for delivery to the ultimate consumer. The multi-tiered racks allow the storage of a large amount of merchandise in one warehouse.

INVENTORY MANAGEMENT

The profitable furniture retailer has a workable, efficient inventory management system to ensure an adequate supply, but not an oversupply, of salable merchandise in the store and warehouse. It is important not to run out of popular items, especially sale items, because being out of key merchandise usually results in lost sales.

An important part of an inventory management system is to have adequate ordering procedures. If a store orders the optimum quantity each time, the paper work and transportation costs will be less than ordering in uneconomic quantities.

Finally, a good inventory management system requires an effective inventory control system to ensure that management will know what is in the warehouse and can keep the stock moving. A good inventory control system will point out inventory imbalances, which can be reduced or eliminated through proper reordering or putting merchandise on sale to get rid of overstocked items.

INBOUND TRANSPORTATION

Retail management must be concerned with the inbound transportation charges incurred in obtaining merchandise from manufacturers or wholesalers in order to reduce the landed cost and be more profitable.

A retail store should select a carrier to transport merchandise to it based on cost-effectiveness over a period of time. Key components of making this decision are rates, transit times, damage rates, and claims ratios. The carrier with the lowest freight rates might not be the cheapest over time because it might have a high damage rate and poor claims ratio. It is the retailer's responsibility to file claims with the carrier for damage incurred during transit, and he or she must consider a carrier's record of taking care of these claims.

DELIVERY ALTERNATIVES

Finally, the furniture retailer must have a low-cost, efficient means of delivering furniture to consumers. It must be done effectively because delivery personnel are the last people to see the consumer and they should leave a good impression. They must also deliver the furniture in good condition to avoid customer problems and complaints. There are two delivery alternatives: using company-owned trucks and using a contracted delivery service.

Using company-owned trucks. In this case, the company has the responsibility of maintaining the trucks in good condition. The trucks should be painted to match the image of the store, and delivery personnel should be neatly dressed and courteous. Because it is expensive to operate trucks, care should be taken to schedule deliveries to save time and operating expenses. To ensure that the merchandise is delivered properly, some stores pay a commission to delivery personnel if the job is done well and there are no complaints.

Using a contracted delivery service. Some retailers, especially in major metropolitan areas, contract with a private delivery service to deliver furniture. The store owner is relieved of the responsibility of owning and maintaining a fleet of delivery trucks. An accepted way to compensate the delivery service is based on the value of the merchandise being delivered. For example: a delivery service might be paid 3½ or 4 percent of the total retail value of the merchandise. Also, some delivery services have their own warehouses and will store merchandise for retail stores.

SUMMARY

Physical distribution and inventory management is concerned with having the right amount of inventory at the right places when it is needed. It involves transportation, storage, and inventory control.

Physical distribution and inventory management considerations of manufacturers include their method and philosophy of warehousing, inventory management system, order processing system, packaging and materials handling, and transportation alternatives. Manufacturers normally either manufacture to have a constant inventory on hand or manufacture to customer order.

Storage costs of furniture manufacturers include: funds invested in the goods, direct and indirect warehousing expenses, insurance, and obsolescence.

Furniture shipped by common or contract carrier must be packaged according to government-approved "F" specifications, while furniture shipped on a company's own trucks does not.

Considerations in choosing a method of shipping from manufacturer to retailer or wholesaler include: retailer's instructions, distance from manufacturer to customer, size of order, time constraints, and geographic location of the customer.

Alternatives in shipping furniture to retailers or wholesalers include using the manufacturer's own trucks, outside trucking companies, railroad, piggyback railroad freight, and combining shipments with others. Manufacturers or retailers can combine their shipments with those of others by joining a shipper's association, using a freight forwarder, or working with a consolidation agent.

Larger volume shipments are more economical because truck load (TL) and car load (CL) freight rates are less costly than "less-than-truck load" (LTL) or "less-than-car load" (LCL) rates.

Physical distribution and inventory management considerations of retailers include: economic conditions, warehousing possibilities and philosophies, storage considerations, inventory management, inbound transportation, and delivery alternatives.

A retailer's warehousing options include: letting the manufacturer warehouse, having regional distribution centers (RDCs), having inventory at the store, and using a wholesale furniture distributor.

Retail warehouse storage considerations include receiving procedures, inventory retrieval and preparation for delivery, materials handling, physical storage facilities, and the costs inherent in storage.

Costs inherent in a retail warehousing operation include: (1) funds tied up in inventory; (2) monetary costs of running the warehouse; (3) insurance on the inventory; and (4) risk of product obsolescence.

A retail store should investigate to determine which method of inbound transportation is most cost effective over time.

Retail deliveries may be made using company trucks or contracting with a professional delivery service.

CHAPTER 18

INTERNATIONAL FURNITURE MARKETING

Historically, exports of furniture from the United States have been relatively small, even though the United States has only about 5 percent of the world population. There are a few stumbling blocks that have kept most manufacturers from pursuing the export market more aggressively:

1. The domestic furniture industry is relatively small in relation to the U.S. market. Manufacturers have not had to export because there has been an ample market for furniture within the United States.
2. It is extremely expensive to ship furniture because furniture products are so bulky.
3. The type of furniture that is demanded is different in other countries than in the United States. Reasons include different tastes in style and proportion as well as different space or storage requirements.
4. The process of conducting business involving different currencies, languages, and cultures is relatively complicated.

Recently, however, an increasing number of manufacturers and retailers have been selling furniture outside the United States. Although there are many reasons for this increased number of exports, three are especially significant:

1. U.S. furniture executives have begun to realize that there are buyers outside the country who genuinely want U.S. furniture and are able to pay for it.
2. The cyclical nature of the home furnishings industry is causing some furniture executives to consider international marketing as a way of stabilizing their business. If there were a recession in the United States and products were not selling well, other countries might be experiencing growth and prosperity, resulting in needed sales there.
3. Some U.S. manufacturers are beginning to look at the numbers of potential customers outside the United States and viewing the international market as a major growth opportunity.

ALTERNATIVE INTERNATIONAL MARKETING STRATEGIES

The success of international furniture marketing depends greatly on proper planning and the particular strategy used to enter the foreign market. There are a number of strategies that can be utilized:

Contract with manufacturers' representatives or agents. These individuals are independent contractors who sell the finished products to retailers and/or wholesalers in the foreign market. The relationship of the agent to the manufacturer is very much the same as the independent contractor operating within the United States. They are paid on a commission basis and operate within a designated geographic territory.

Sell to foreign furniture distributors. Foreign distributors buy furniture and then they resell it to retailers and other dealers in their countries. Some of these distributors stock merchandise and others do not. Regardless, the advantage of the distributor is that he or she takes title to the merchandise and assumes responsibility for marketing it.

Sell directly to large foreign retailers. Large, well-established firms are sometimes able to sell directly to foreign retailers. An example would be a well-known manufacturer of higher-priced merchandise establishing an agreement with a prominent retailer in a country for the retailer to handle his or her line exclusively in a city or sometimes for the entire country.

Export through an export management company. An export management company (EMC) markets American-made products in foreign countries. The EMC may buy the merchandise or may represent the manufacturer and be compensated with a salary, commission, or a combination retainer and commission. Regardless, the EMC handles all aspects of marketing from selling to delivery.

Sell to buying offices located overseas or in the United States. Manufacturers may sell large groups of merchandise to buying offices representing foreign governments, large private corporations, export/import trading companies, or groups of foreign buyers.

Export furniture parts to foreign manufacturers. As in many other industries, American furniture manufacturers may sell furniture parts, such as semifinished hardwood furniture components, to foreign manufacturers who complete the manufacturing and market the finished goods in selected overseas countries.

License the sale of the product. Well-known manufacturers may license a foreign manufacturer to make and market products using the American brand name and expertise in a foreign country or group of countries. The American company is usually compensated with a percentage of the sales revenue.

Enter a joint-venture arrangement with a foreign company. In a joint venture, an American manufacturer and a foreign company sign an agreement to jointly produce, warehouse, or market a particular brand or type of furniture within a particular territory.

Export jointly in combination with other U.S. firms. There are situations where it is mutually advantageous for a number of U.S. firms to export their products together. These combinations are strictly governed by the federal government and any agreement must conform to existing laws.

STEPS IN EXPORTING

There are a number of steps in setting up and operating a meaningful export division:

- Choose target markets
- Select the marketing strategy needed to enter the target markets successfully
- Design products and promotions "for export"
- Appoint someone within the company whose main duty is to manage the export function
- Personally visit the overseas market

CHOOSE TARGET MARKETS

Foreign markets are even more diverse than markets within the United States. Therefore, it is necessary to determine which countries have the most potential for buying the type of furniture sold by a particular manufacturer.

To determine market potential, the relative opportunities of each possible market must be explored, which includes market size and growth rate for various types of furniture. Sales are made where the money is available, so the per-capita income and distribution of income are important. The number of wealthy people should also be considered by upper-end manufacturers.

In evaluating the attractiveness of a particular country as a market, a manufacturer should look at local consumption patterns, distribution channels available, and the political constraints placed on imports to that country.

Hopefully, after evaluating all aspects of the country's demand for the category of furniture being sold, the company can agree on a number of high-potential target markets.

SELECT MARKETING STRATEGY NEEDED TO ENTER TARGET MARKETS SUCCESSFULLY

It is extremely advantageous to find another manufacturer or other seller with experience in exporting who can provide information on the pitfalls of selling to the target market. The company may want to implement one or more of the strategies discussed earlier, but the observations of other exporters are extremely valuable.

It is necessary to have someone handling the export transactions who knows the specific country well and can represent the company effectively.

DESIGN PRODUCTS AND PROMOTIONS "FOR EXPORT"

Many of the products which sell well in the United States are not in demand in other countries. A bedroom suite in the United States might be quite acceptable if it consisted of a bed, headboard, mirror, dresser, and five-drawer chest. However, in a foreign country, to be salable the bedroom suite might have to consist of a complete bed (headboard, side rails, and footboard), two night stands, and a large wardrobe.

Similarly, advertising and sales aids that are effective in this country may not attract attention in another country. The advertising or sales promotion might actually offend the foreign retailer or consumer. The promotional materials must be adaptable to being translated meaningfully into the other language. Product dimensions in feet and inches must be translated into metric measurements for products to be salable in other countries.

APPOINT SOMEONE WITHIN THE COMPANY WHOSE MAIN DUTY IS TO MANAGE THE EXPORT FUNCTION

The export market is quite different, and special management attention is required for the firm to be successful. Even if an export management company is making the actual arrangements, a contact person needs to be at the factory to make sure the sales effort is backed up with production and delivery.

PERSONALLY VISIT THE OVERSEAS MARKET

In order to appreciate the demands of foreign retailers and consumers, it is highly desirable for a company representative to visit the overseas market personally. It is the only way to get a good idea of competition from furniture manufacturers in other countries.

The manufacturer can also evaluate how effectively the company is being represented by the manufacturer's agent, distributor, or export management company. A foreign sales representative who on the surface appears to be quite effective might have rather poor relations with retailers in the foreign country.

Another advantage of personally visiting the foreign market is that the manufacturer can get feedback from retailers and consumers about his or her products. Service or quality-control problems may be detected and, hopefully, solved quickly to avoid damaging customer relations. Retailer and consumer feedback may give valuable product ideas as to changes that can be made easily and profitably. Retailers, for example, may rather receive certain items unassembled because of a shortage of warehouse space, which would be no major problem for the manufacturer and would result in savings on freight costs.

OTHER CONSIDERATIONS IN INTERNATIONAL TRADE

Selling to a variety of foreign countries is more complicated than selling within the United States. Personnel with expertise in international marketing must be in charge of selling to foreign countries. Other factors that must be considered when engaging in international trade include:

- Currency fluctuations
- Different languages and cultures
- Different transportation and distribution systems
- Financial considerations
- Political considerations
- Economic considerations

CURRENCY FLUCTUATIONS

Prices and quotations are important because of fluctuating exchange rates between the U.S. dollar and the currencies of foreign countries. If the same price were quoted that would be charged in the U.S. and there were an unfavorable fluctuation in exchange rates before the merchandise is shipped, a loss may be incurred on the sale.

DIFFERENT LANGUAGES AND CULTURES

A knowledge of the language and culture is extremely important in exporting effectively to another country. The manufacturer needs to know whether advertising, product names, descriptions, and other materials will be as persuasive in the foreign country as they have been in the U.S. Often brand names, product names, and advertising slogans may be ineffective, negative, or even obscene when translated into foreign languages.

Much of the correspondence with foreign buyers should be conducted in their language for two reasons: First, not everyone in the customer's organization speaks English; and second, translating correspondence and sales documents into their language shows genuine interest and concern for the buyers.

As has been stated earlier, product requirements differ from country to country. Therefore, a knowledge of the culture involved may prevent costly mistakes which result from exporting products to a country where the consumers would not buy or use them. A knowledge of business customs can be extremely valuable. For example, in some countries business appointments must always be made in advance, while in others this is not as important.

18-1. This freighter is transporting containers of furniture from the United States to a number of foreign countries. The containers are transported to the dock on flat-bed tractor-trailers. The detachable containers are then loaded onto the ship using an extremely large crane. *(Virginia Ports Authority)*

DIFFERENT TRANSPORTATION AND DISTRIBUTION SYSTEMS

In many foreign countries, transportation and distribution systems are different from those in the United States. Because ocean transportation is often involved, containerized freight is commonly used. Containerized freight involves loading the shipment into a large container, usually made of metal, with the merchandise remaining unopened in the container from the time it leaves the shipper until it arrives at its destination.

Manufacturers often secure the services of a freight forwarder who takes shipments from several small shippers and combines them to fill a complete container. Freight forwarders also help the shipper choose the best routes and methods of distribution.

There are different types of wholesalers and retailers in foreign countries and different distribution strategies. American manufacturers must solicit the help of those who understand how furniture is distributed most effectively in a foreign country if they are to be successful in getting their furniture into the outlets where it is most likely to be seen and bought.

FINANCIAL CONSIDERATIONS

The financial considerations of international trade include establishing selling prices and developing a procedure whereby payment will be received. In quoting, several items such as freight, insurance, tariffs, customs charges, commissions, and turnover or sales taxes need to be added to the price desired by the manufacturer. Therefore, a determination must be made as to whether, with the added charges, the furniture can be profitably sold in the foreign country. Prices can be quoted in a number of ways, and the effective marketer will check with customers to see which they prefer.

The method of payment is negotiated prior to the shipment of goods. The following are possible ways payment can be made:

Cash deposit in advance protects the shipper because payment is received before shipment is made. The shipper may request all or part of the money under this arrangement. This is a good method if there is an unsteady political or economic situation or if the buyer has a poor credit rating.

Open account involves the buyer simply agreeing to pay by some predetermined future date. There is no negotiable instrument forcing the buyer to pay. If the buyer subsequently refuses to pay, then both the purchase price and merchandise are lost.

A *sight draft* involves money being made payable at the sight of the completed documents. Realistically, this means that a U.S. or foreign bank, acting as an intermediary, releases the documents and merchandise to the buyer in the foreign country when payment is made. The seller retains title until the buyer pays for the merchandise in his or her own country.

A *time draft* or *acceptance draft* allows the buyer a predetermined amount of time to pay as in the case of the *open account*. The difference between a time draft and an open account is that with the former there is a document that can be used for legal collection purposes.

An *irrevocable letter of credit* is a safe, commonly used method of payment. Either a U.S. or foreign bank agrees to make payment to the seller after certain conditions are met. A description of merchandise to be shipped is included and the time period in which shipment must be made is stated. If the described merchandise is shipped by the date agreed upon and the proper documents are presented, the shipper receives payment.

POLITICAL CONSIDERATIONS

Political considerations include laws and regulations enacted by the government and the overall philosophy and stability of that government. Tariffs, for example, are at times enacted to protect local industry. These tariffs (or taxes) can make U.S. products equal in price or more expensive than furniture produced within another country. Other countries establish import quotas, which limit the number of designated items that can be brought into a country.

Licensing requirements also apply to furniture being sold in many foreign countries. This involves having to secure licenses to sell within a country and paying fees for doing so. A common requirement is that any company wanting to sell merchandise inside the country must do it through a local distributor. In some other countries, it may be necessary to form specified cooperative arrangements with local businesses.

The political situation in certain countries should be evaluated very carefully. If it is so unstable that the government may change or business become nationalized, it is possible for a U.S. manufacturer to face the problems of confiscated merchandise and unpaid invoices.

ECONOMIC CONSIDERATIONS

A primary consideration is the amount of economic development currently existing within the country. Are there enough people with the proper type of housing and sufficient money to need and afford U.S. furniture?

As in the United States, if the country is experiencing prosperity, it is easier to sell furniture than if the country is in a recession or depression.

The export guide in Figure 18-2, prepared by The Port Authority of New York and New Jersey, summarizes the steps required in a representative export transaction.

The common export documents required in selling U.S. products in foreign countries are summarized in the listing in Figure 18-3, prepared by The Port Authority of New York and New Jersey.

OPPORTUNITIES TO PROMOTE U.S. FURNITURE PRODUCTS TO FOREIGN BUYERS

There are a number of other ways by which U.S. furniture manufacturers can expose foreign buyers to their merchandise:

1. *Foreign buyers attending U.S. furniture markets* and traveling throughout the U.S. are potential sources for sales. These buyers would not spend the time or money to come to the United States if they were not interested in U.S. furniture.
2. *International trade shows,* which are very similar in intent to the wholesale furniture markets in the United States, are another avenue. International trade shows are held in Cologne, Paris, Milan, and Brussels. At these shows, U.S. companies can display their products for buyers from all over the world.
3. *U.S. Department of Commerce Export Development Office exhibitions* have permanent product exhibit facilities in selected overseas locations. A number of major exhibitions are held each year in these facilities, some of which are open to the display of furniture. This same office may also organize exhibitions of U.S. products in locations outside these facilities.

Export Guide

Cargo moves on paper!
The part you play is shown in the following steps.

Prepared by **THE PORT AUTHORITY**
OF NEW YORK & NEW JERSEY
One World Trade Center
New York, New York 10048

Shipper

1 Prepares Domestic Bill of Lading for movement of cargo to pier, and sends copy to his forwarder in the New York - New Jersey Port, along with packing list.

2 Checks Bill of Lading:
✓ number of packages
✓ marks and numbers
✓ description of cargo
✓ foreign destination
✓ gross weights of each package shipped
✓ local party to be notified

3 Marks cargo plainly, to show:
• gross and net weights
• cubic measurement
• foreign destination
• identification marks
• country of origin

Motor Carrier

4 Secures interchange agreement with steamship company on containers.

5 Accepts cargo for transit to the Port of New York-New Jersey.

6 Advises freight forwarder or shipper's local representative of cargo's arrival in the port.

7 Obtains the following information from forwarder or representative:
• name of vessel
• sailing date
• pier numbe. and location
• location of any special permits needed to clear hazardous or oversize cargo for acceptance by ocean terminal.

8 Obtains Dock Receipt from forwarder or other representative to accompany cargo

9 Contacts terminal operator to make appointment for special handling or equipment, if required, at least 24 hours before delivery.

Forwarder

10 Provides Dock Receipt and special permits, if any, to delivering motor carrier.

11 Checks Dock Receipt for completeness:
✓ name of shipper
✓ name of vessel
✓ ports of loading and discharge
✓ number and type of packages
✓ description of cargo
✓ gross weight, dimensions, and cubic measurement of each package
✓ marks and numbers
✓ shipper's export declaration number, if required.

Driver

12 Moves his truck on line upon arrival at pier.

Terminal Operator

13 Issues pass to driver at gate house.

14 Checks driver's papers:
✓ Dock Receipt
✓ Permits

15 Calls driver for unloading.

16 Assigns driver a checker and an unloading spot.

Driver

17 Unloads his vehicle (using extra pier labor is optional, at rates specified in the Terminal Conference tariff.)

18 Obtains signed copy of Dock Receipt, and receipt for extra labor, if used.

Terminal Operator

19 Retains original of Dock Receipt.

Driver

20 Surrenders gate pass at gate house.

Terminal Operator

21 Forwards Dock Receipt to steamship company

Steamship Company

22 Issues Ocean Bill of Lading to shipper or his agent.

18-2. This "Export Guide," prepared by The Port Authority of New York and New Jersey, gives the steps required in exporting products from the United States. Not only does it state what is involved in each step, it also indicates which individual or organization should carry it out.

Common Export Documents

Prepared by **THE PORT AUTHORITY OF NEW YORK & NEW JERSEY**
One World Trade Center,
New York, New York 10048

1. Ocean Bill-of-Lading

A receipt for the cargo and a contract for transportation between a shipper and the ocean carrier. It may also be used an an instrument of ownership which can be bought, sold or traded while the goods are in transit. To be used in this manner, it must be a negotiable "Order" Bill-of-Lading. Abbreviations: Blading, B/L.

A *clean Bill-of-Lading* is issued when the shipment is received in good order. If damage or a shortage is noted, a clean bill-of-lading will not be issued. An *On Board Bill-of-Lading* certifies that the cargo has been placed aboard the named vessel and is signed by the master of the vessel or his representative. On letter of credit transactions, an On Board Bill-of-Lading is usually necessary for the shipper to obtain payment from the bank. When all Bills-of-Lading are processed a *ships manifest* is prepared by the steamship line. This summarizes all cargo aboard the vessel by port of loading and discharge.

Inland Bill-of-Lading—Also known as a waybill on rail or the "pro forma" bill-of-lading in trucking. It is used to document the transportation of the goods between the port and the point of origin or destination. It should contain information such as marks, numbers, steamship line, etc. to match with a dock receipt. Abbreviate "pro" or "pro ticket", waybill.

2. Dock Receipt

Used to transfer accountability for the cargo between domestic and international carriers at the ocean terminal. This is the document, prepared by the shipper or forwarder, which the ocean carrier signs and returns to the delivering inland carrier, acknowledging receipt of the cargo.

3. Delivery Instructions

Provides specific information to the inland carrier concerning the arrangement made by the forwarder to deliver the merchandise to a particular pier or steamship line. Not to be confused with *Delivery Order* which is used for import cargo.

4. Export Declaration

Required by the U.S. Department of Commerce to control exports and act as a source document for export statistics. It includes complete particulars on the shipment. Common abbreviation is Export Dec.

5. Letter of Credit

A financial document issued by a bank at the request of the consignee guaranteeing payment to the shipper for cargo if certain terms and conditions are fulfilled. Normally it contains a brief description of the goods, documents required, a shipping date, and an expiration date after which payment will no longer be made.

6. Consular Invoice

Required by some countries, this document is used to control and identify goods shipped to them. It usually must be prepared on special forms and may require legalization by their Consul.

7. Commercial Invoice

A bill for the goods from the seller to the buyer. It is often used by governments to determine the true value of goods for the assessment of customs duties. It is also used in the preparation of consular documentation. Governments using the commercial invoice to control imports often specify its form, content, number of copies, language to be used, etc.

8. Certificate of Origin

A document which is used to assure the buying country precisely in which country the goods were produced. The certification of the origin of the merchandise is usually performed by a recognized Chamber of Commerce.

9. Insurance Certificate

Assures the consignee that insurance is provided to cover loss or damage to the cargo while in transit.

10. Transmittal Letter

A list of the particulars of the shipment and a record of the documents being transmitted together with instructions for disposition of documents. Any special instructions are also included.

18-3. This listing describes the documents normally required when exporting products from the United States. A furniture company engaged in exporting must know how to use these documents properly in order to carry out the export sales transaction.

4. *Trade missions* are tours by representatives of U.S. firms, organized by the U.S. Department of Commerce, which visit selected countries interested in promoting the product. Arrangements are made for the U.S. representatives to talk with foreign buyers at each stop.

THE EFFECT OF IMPORTING ON THE U.S. FURNITURE INDUSTRY

The prospect of exporting has been discussed extensively and is a major marketing thrust of some U.S. furniture corporations. On the other hand, imports already have an impact on the U.S. furniture industry. The following are three ways that imports are affecting the industry:

1. *Novel and/or inexpensive items are imported.* Many unusual, handmade or antique items are being imported. These may be one-of-a-kind pieces of accessory items, which are very expensive or simply unusual. Because of low labor costs in particular parts of the world, it is possible to import home furnishing items from these countries at very attractive prices. These items are offered for sale by numerous retailers throughout the United States.
2. *Furniture supplies are imported.* Some types of supplies used in the manufacture of furniture are imported, ranging from hinges and fabric to hand-painted wood panels. These items are imported for a variety of reasons, such as cost, availability of technology, and amount of hand labor required.
3. *Raw materials not available domestically are imported.* Several types of raw materials used in furniture manufacturing are not grown or produced in the U.S., such as silk from India, rattan from Indonesia, and exotic veneers from Europe and South America. All serve a purpose in the design and construction of certain pieces of furniture.

SUMMARY

Historically, U.S. furniture manufacturers have not tried to sell their products in other countries because of: (1) the relatively large American demand for furniture; (2) the shipping costs involved; (3) the type of furniture demanded in other countries is different than that demanded in the United States; and (4) business transactions involving different languages, currencies, and cultures are relatively complicated.

Only recently have furniture manufacturers begun to explore the prospect of exporting furniture produced in the United States to other countries. Reasons for this increase in exports include: (1) the realization that there is a demand for U.S. furniture in other countries; (2) an attempt to stabilize cyclical furniture sales; and (3) companies are beginning to realize that the numbers of consumers outside the United States represent a sizable growth market.

Alternative marketing strategies include: exporting directly to buyers in foreign countries; exporting through an export management company; selling to buying offices overseas or in the United States; exporting furniture parts to foreign manufacturers; licensing the sale of the product; entering a joint venture arrangement with a foreign company; or exporting jointly in combination with other U.S. firms.

Methods that may be used to export finished products directly to buyers in foreign countries are to contract with manufacturers' representatives or manufacturers' agents, sell to foreign furniture distributors, or sell directly to large furniture retailers.

Steps in exporting are: choose target markets; select the marketing strategy desired to enter the target markets successfully; design products and promotions for export; appoint someone within the company whose main duty is managing exports; and personally visit the overseas markets.

Other factors to be considered in international trade include currency fluctuations, different languages and cultures, different transportation and distribution systems, financial considerations, political considerations, and economic considerations.

Common ways that payment may be made are cash deposit in advance, an open account, a sight draft, a time draft or acceptance draft, or an irrevocable letter of credit.

U.S. furniture may be promoted internationally in the following ways: (1) to foreign buyers attending U.S. furniture markets; (2) at international trade shows; (3) at U.S. Department of Commerce Export Development Office exhibitions; and (4) through trade missions.

The following items affecting the U.S. furniture industry are being imported: (1) novel and/or inexpensive items; (2) furniture supplies; and (3) raw materials not available domestically.

CHAPTER 19

CONTRACT FURNITURE

Furniture designed for use by businesses, institutions, or in public buildings is commonly referred to as *contract furniture* because it is often purchased under a contract. For example, a contract is involved in the construction of a new public building or office building. The architect or owner selects an interior designer to specify the type and variety of furnishings for the building. The specifications are often described in a bid request and various suppliers bid for the contract to provide the buildings' furnishings.

In addition to large contract purchases, this furniture is sold in smaller quantities to furnish an office, a waiting room, or perhaps a school library. It is common for a specifier such as an interior designer to be involved.

Some companies that produce home furnishings for the consumer also sell under contract or have a contract division. However, most companies that produce business, institutional, or public building furniture specialize in that type of furniture only.

TYPES OF CONTRACT FURNITURE

There are five categories of contract furniture, which illustrates the diversity of this segment of the industry:
- Office furniture
- Hotel/motel furniture
- Hospital/health care furniture
- School/library furniture
- Furniture produced for government purchase

Manufacturers tend to specialize within one of these categories, although some companies produce in more than one. Furniture in each of these categories has its own standards and specifications based on its intended use.

OFFICE FURNITURE

Office furniture includes a variety of furnishings found in an office, from a credenza to a filing cabinet to a desk and chair. Office furniture has more exact specifications than furniture for the home because it must be easy to use, yet very durable. Drawers must accommodate standard paper and file sizes. There are also relatively standard configurations of drawers and constructions of credenzas and desks.

Office furniture is designed to meet the needs of the person using it and to reflect the relative status of the office holder within the organization. The furnishings of a receptionist's office, for example, would be different from the furnishings of a psychiatrist's office because of the different requirements of each. The furnishings of the sales manager's office would not be as elaborate as the office of the chairman of the board of directors because of obvious status differences. This status is reflected in what is sometimes referred to as the "rug rank." This term is derived from organizations in which a person must move up to a certain level before he or she can have different, often more luxurious, office carpeting. Doctors, lawyers, and other professionals use relatively elaborate office furnishings.

Office furnishings are usually constructed of wood or simulated wood, steel with wood or simulated wood panels, or entirely of steel. Within each of these types of construction there is a great difference in quality. Although wood office furniture has traditionally been the most prestigious, there are several brands of steel with wood or simulated wood panels and steel office furniture that are of very high quality.

HOTEL/MOTEL FURNITURE

Hotel/motel furniture includes furnishings for guest rooms and the common areas of hotels and motels such as the lobbies and restaurants. The emphasis is on functional furniture that is durable. Although the furnishings reflect the type of clientele to which the hotel or motel caters, the furnishings are usually the same for all of the guest rooms. There are identical headboards, chairs, tables, dressers, and other furnishings which are bought under a contract according to the specifications of the architect or designer.

There is a greater variety in the furnishings of common areas. Lobbies often contain a variety of upholstered furniture. Chairs and tables are usually identical within a restaurant and are purchased to meet specifications for comfortable seating for dining. For example, the seats of restaurant chairs are a bit higher than those of office chairs.

Chairs, sofas, and other seating pieces in lobbies, lounges, and bars are chosen with the objective of making customers as comfortable as possible to prolong their stay. Durable fabrics that are soil resistant and that will maintain their appearance while being subjected to constant use are necessary.

HOSPITAL/HEALTH CARE FURNITURE

Hospital/health care furniture includes the furnishings found in hospitals and medical offices. There are special needs for furnishings in patients' rooms, operating rooms, and other areas of hospitals. The design of hospital/health care furniture is based on the function the furniture

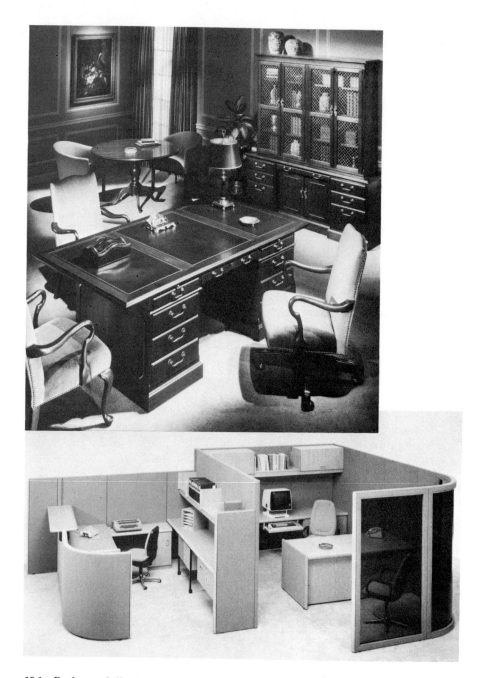

19-1. Producers of office furniture manufacture a wide variety of products. Not only do they produce furniture for all levels of management, they also manufacture a wide range of styles. The very traditional grouping of office furnishings *(top)* would most likely be purchased for the private offices of top management. In contrast, the grouping at the bottom consists of modern modular office furnishings that may be used by lower-level management or clerical employees. *(Alma Desk Company)*

is to perform. Obviously, the needs of furniture for the hospital lobby are different from the furniture in patients' rooms. Chairs in patients' rooms are designed with special feet to keep them from slipping when a patient is sitting down or getting up.

Some hospital seating is made with detachable arms and seats so a damaged part can be replaced without having to reupholster or replace the entire chair, loveseat, or sofa. Extensive use is made of vinyl fabrics, and there are spaces between seats and backs for ease of cleaning and sterilizing.

SCHOOL/LIBRARY FURNITURE

School/library furniture is often referred to as *institutional furniture,* and there are unique design requirements for this furniture. School desks are designed to fit different size students, with larger desks being specified for older children. There are requirements for durability and ease of studying or note-taking.

Libraries contain a variety of furnishings, including tables and chairs, book shelves, and study carrells. The book shelves are adjustable to accommodate books of various sizes. The furnishings for libraries, like most other business, institutional, and public building furniture, are specified when the building is constructed or remodeled.

FURNITURE PRODUCED FOR GOVERNMENT PURCHASE

Various levels of government buy a wide variety of furnishings for government offices and buildings. This furniture is considered a separate category because the federal government has unique specifications for different projects and buildings. The government employs purchasing agents, architects, and space planners who specify what types of furnishings are needed for various projects. Rather than use office furniture and other types of furniture in standard sizes, the government invites manufacturers to bid for the opportunity to manufacture furniture to government specifications. The manufacturers that are allowed to bid must also be on an approved list.

DISTRIBUTION CHANNELS

OFFICE FURNITURE

There are several alternatives available for the distribution of office furniture, including the following:

Full-service office furniture stores or dealers represent the major distribution category for office furniture. These dealers may sell only office furniture; furniture and office equipment; or furniture, office equipment, and office supplies. Such stores normally display a large amount of merchandise. They have a professional sales force to work with the buyer, architect, or designer. The furniture is ordered, received by the store, assembled, and installed in the office by the store's installation crew. The dealer, who is the last point of contact with the customer, has professional installers who, for example, can adjust the chairs to the heights of the people who will be using them. Office furniture manufacturers depend on these dealers to take care of consumer complaints and servicing needs.

Office furniture manufacturers often have showrooms in major cities around the country, with a professional sales staff to support the dealers. These showrooms are visited by architects, designers, and other specifiers in order to view the products being offered. The specifiers may come to the showrooms on their own or be sent by a dealer.

Direct sales to the user do occur in the industry. They are usually large sales and are referred to as *national accounts*. A company like General Motors could purchase such a large volume of furniture that it would be advantageous to both the manufacturer and General Motors to deal directly with each other. In this case, the manufacturer's sales force does the selling, but the manufacturer often contracts with a dealer located near the customer to do the actual installation. The manufacturer normally does not have an installation crew out in the field to service customers adequately. Often, these large purchasers have skilled purchasing agents or other specifiers on their staffs who specify the amount and type of office furnishings to be purchased.

Jobbers, who are catalogue houses with a warehouse and no showroom, are the middlemen in many office furniture sales. The jobber is a wholesaler who buys what is needed for a sale rather than keeping merchandise in stock. He may buy selected items from several manufacturers, assemble them in his warehouse, and when all the merchandise is received, install it in the purchaser's office. The jobber usually has a smaller operation with a smaller sales force than the retail office furniture store. These organizations often advertise lower prices because they have less overhead than retail office furniture stores.

Specifiers are involved in a large percentage of office furniture transactions. They are architects, interior designers, or space planners who specify or recommend what type of furniture the user should purchase.

The specifiers interview the customer, determine his furniture needs, and prepare the specifications based on their research. In higher levels of management, interior designers interview the executive, find out something about his or her personality, and then recommend furnishings with which the executive will be comfortable. One executive might prefer his co-workers to gather close around him for meetings in his office. In this case, the specifier would probably suggest a conference desk, which is an executive desk with an overhanging top so that chairs can be pulled up in front and to the sides for working space. Another executive might prefer people to work farther from him and would rather have conferences in a separate room; the specifier would plan accordingly.

Furniture rental companies. Some companies and individuals prefer to rent their office furniture rather than purchase it. It may be a company policy or because an office is being opened only temporarily in a certain location. Attorneys or other professionals just starting business may prefer to rent their furnishings in order to have a completely furnished office with a comparatively small initial investment.

Furniture rental companies that offer office furniture feature products from various manufacturers. They usually provide a complete selection, including accessories, from pictures to hang on the walls to lamps and ashtrays.

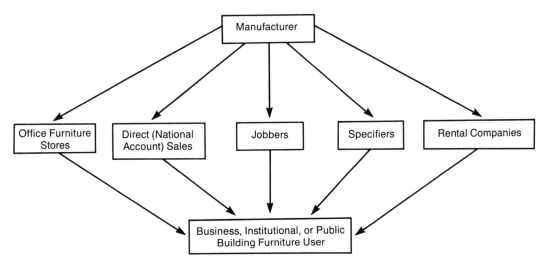

19-2. Distribution channels for office furniture

HOTEL/MOTEL FURNITURE

Hotel and motel furniture is bought in comparatively large quantities under a contract containing product specifications. Examples of distribution alternatives for hotel and motel furniture are as follows:

Wholesale furniture dealers who sell hotel and motel furniture are found throughout the United States. Many of these dealers also sell office and institutional furniture, but others specialize only in hotels, motels, and restaurants. They are full-service furniture distributors with professional sales and design staffs to assist the purchaser in selecting the right type of furnishings for the hotel or motel. They represent a variety of manufacturers and help to arrange delivery schedules to fit in with construction deadlines or other time schedules. They also have professional crews for installing the furniture in the hotel or motel and to provide any needed servicing.

A typical hotel or motel furniture sale will involve purchasing furniture from a variety of manufacturers. One manufacturer may supply the case pieces in the guest rooms, another may supply the bedding, and a third may supply the furniture for the public areas.

Direct sales from the manufacturer to the hotel or motel also occur in the industry. This usually involves large projects, which again are called *national accounts.* Many large hotel or motel chains have their own designers or specifiers and use sufficient quantities to justify buying direct from the manufacturer. In fact, such chains often can require that products be manufactured to their specifications.

Jobbers also sell a variety of furnishings to hotels, motels, and restaurants. These firms, like those selling office furniture, have warehouses but no showroom and sell, to a large extent, out of catalogues. They have a comparatively lower overhead, but will assemble and install the products they sell. Like the wholesale dealer, they work with architects or other specifiers.

Specifiers are involved in a large percentage of hotel and motel furniture purchases. These specifiers might be employed in the architect's office, on the staff of the hotel or motel, or independently. The independent specifiers are interior designers retained by either the owner or architect to decorate the interior of the new facility. The specifiers work very closely with manufacturers, dealers, or jobbers.

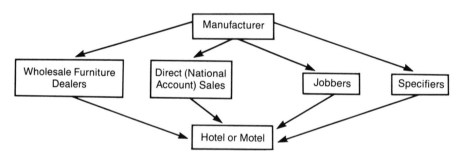

19-3. Distribution channels for hotel/motel furniture

HOSPITAL/HEALTH CARE FURNITURE

As indicated earlier, the requirements for hospital and medical care furnishings are very different from those of other types of furniture. The distribution channels for hospital/health care furniture are as follows:

Wholesale hospital/medical supply dealers specialize in providing hospital and medical care furniture and supplies from a variety of manufacturers. These dealers only handle this type of merchandise, and some manufacturers only produce furniture for hospital and medical care facilities. They have specially trained sales staffs to work with hospital buyers or specifiers on large projects.

Direct (national account) sales also occur in the hospital/medical care field. They could involve a national hospital chain or hospitals forming a group that buys together in large quantities. The manufacturer's sales force works directly with the purchasing agent or specifier representing the hospital chain or group of independent hospitals.

Specifiers are involved in a large percentage of hospital/health care furniture purchases. These specifiers are skilled in the special requirements for furniture to be used in hospitals and other medical care facilities. They may work for architects, work independently, or work for large purchasers of medical equipment and furniture. Regardless of whether the furniture is purchased through dealers or direct from the manufacturer, specifiers are retained when large quantities are needed for new hospital buildings or large refurbishing projects.

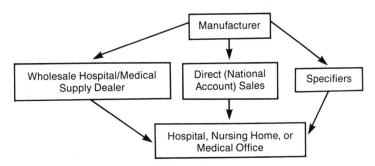

19-4. Distribution channels for hospital/health care furniture

SCHOOL/LIBRARY FURNITURE

As indicated earlier, this category of furniture is often referred to as institutional furniture and may be distributed through wholesale dealers or direct sales from the manufacturer to users, jobbers, and specifiers.

Wholesale dealers handling institutional furniture often handle office furniture, and, sometimes, hotel and motel furniture. A full-service dealer will have a professional sales staff to assist the purchasing agent in choosing the right amount and type of furniture for the school or library. The retail sales staffs of all dealers involved in business, institutional, or public building furniture are basically trained by the manufacturers. Since the manufacturers conduct the research and design the products for specific purposes, they are logically responsible for training the various sales forces in their product functions and capabilities.

Direct sales to large national accounts are also made in the school/library/institutional furniture field. Although the purchaser can make selections for catalogues, in many cases the buyer will visit the manufacturer's showroom when he or she is involved in a large project to make selections.

Jobbers, with operations very similar to those selling office or hotel/motel furniture, are found distributing school/library furniture. These operations, similar to jobbers handling other types of contract furniture, might suitably be called "nonstocking dealers."

Specifiers are normally involved in the sale of institutional furniture to large new construction or remodeling projects. As in the other categories of contract furniture, these individuals are knowledgeable about the requirements of specialized furniture for schools and libraries.

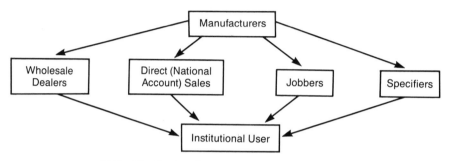

19-5. Distribution channels for school/library furniture

FURNITURE PRODUCED FOR GOVERNMENT PURCHASE

Since the government acts as its own specifier and the furniture must usually be produced to its specifications, the purchases of government furniture are accomplished through competitive bidding by dealers or directly by the manufacturer. In order for a dealer to bid, he must have a good working relationship with a manufacturer to ensure that the specified type of merchandise can be provided within any time constraints imposed by the government contract.

Regardless of whether the dealer or manufacturer is submitting the bid, considerable time is involved in working on the specifications and making certain that the supplier can comply with government regulations. Some manufacturers who solicit a considerable amount of government business have specially trained people managing the government programs.

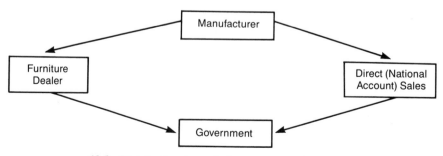

19-6. Distribution channels for selling to the government

ADVERTISING, SALES PROMOTION, AND PUBLIC RELATIONS

The manufacturers of business, institutional, and public building furniture show their products at periodic trade shows for contract furniture. These trade shows are somewhat like the residential furniture markets in that purchasing agents, architects, interior designers, and space planners can evaluate the products that are displayed in the showrooms.

Advertising for contract furniture is concentrated largely in trade publications and direct mail. There are publications related to offices, hospitals, and hotels and motels. Manufacturers place both institutional and product advertising in these publications, and direct-mail advertising also is used to reach potential purchasers within the industry. Service, durability, ease of cleaning, fashion, and value are stressed in this type of advertising.

Public relations techniques, as discussed in Chapter 13, are largely the same as those used by residential furniture manufacturers and retailers.

SUMMARY

Furniture designed for use by businesses, institutions, or in public buildings comprises the category commonly referred to as contract furniture. This furniture is normally purchased in relatively large quantities under a contractual agreement.

Many companies producing contract furniture specialize within one category of that business. The five categories of contract furniture are: (1) office furniture; (2) hotel/motel furniture; (3) hospital/health care furniture; (5) school/library furniture; and (5) furniture produced for government purchase.

Distribution channels for office furniture include full-service stores, direct (national account) sales, jobbers, specifiers, and furniture rental companies.

Distribution channels for hotel and motel furniture include wholesale furniture dealers, direct (national account) sales, jobbers, and specifiers.

Distribution channels for hospital and health care furniture include wholesale hospital/medical supply dealers, direct (national account) sales, and specifiers.

Distribution channels for school/library furniture include wholesale dealers, direct (national account) sales, jobbers, and specifiers.

Distribution channels for selling to the government include furniture dealers or direct (national account) sales. Government contracts normally require furniture to be manufactured to their specifications.

Major sales promotion events in the field of contract furniture are the periodic trade shows. Advertisers in this field primarily use trade publications and direct mail as their advertising media.

APPENDIX A
TRADE AND PROFESSIONAL
ASSOCIATIONS

The following trade and professional associations serve the furniture industry in a number of ways. They carry out research and provide information which is of help to both furniture manufacturers and retailers. Many issue publications that contain articles, educational materials, and other helpful information for those in the industry.

American Furniture Manufacturers
Association
P.O. Box HP-7
High Point, North Carolina 27261

American Innerspring
Manufacturers
1918 N. Parkway
Memphis, Tennessee 38112

American Society of Furniture
Designers
P.O. Box 1792
High Point, North Carolina 27261

American Society of Interior
Designers
1430 Broadway
New York, New York 10018

American Textile Manufacturers
Institute, Inc.
1101 Connecticut Avenue, N.W.
Suite 300
Washington, D.C. 20036

Appalachian Hardwood
Manufacturers, Inc.
P.O. Box 427
High Point, North Carolina 27261

Business and Institutional Furniture
Manufacturers Association
2335 Burton S.E.
Grand Rapids, Michigan 49506

Church Furniture Manufacturers
Association
Box 2436
High Point, North Carolina 27261

Contract Furnishings Council
1109 Merchandise Mart
Chicago, Illinois 60654

Cotton Inc.
4505 Creedmoor Road
Raleigh, North Carolina 27612

Fine Hardwoods/American Walnut
Association
5603 West Raymond Street
Indianapolis, Indiana 46241

Flexible Polyurethane Foam
Manufacturers
Box 465
Southfield, Michigan 48031

Forest Products Research Society
2801 Marshall Court
Madison, Wisconsin 53705

Furniture Factories Marketing
Association of the South
Box 5687
High Point, North Carolina 27262

Furniture Industry Consumer
Advisory Panel
P.O. Box 951
High Point, North Carolina 27261

Furniture Manufacturers
Association of Grand Rapids
220 Lyon Street, N.W.
Grand Rapids, Michigan 49503

Furniture Rental Association of
America
50 West Broad Street
Suite 1325
Columbus, Ohio 43215

Hardwood Dimension Manufacturers
Association
3813 Hillsboro Road
P.O. Box 15721
Nashville, Tennessee 37215

Hardwood Plywood Manufacturers
Association
P.O. Box 2789
Reston, Virginia 22090

Hardwood Research Council
P.O. Box 131
Asheville, North Carolina 28802

Interior Design Society
405 Merchandise Mart
Chicago, Illinois 60654

International Association of Rattan
Manufacturers and Importers
454 Fairman Road
Lexington, Kentucky 40505

International Home Furnishings
Representatives Association
518 Davis Street
Evanston, Illinois 60201

Juvenile Products Manufacturers
Association
66 East Main Street
Moorestown, New Jersey 08057

National Association of Bedding
Manufacturers
1150 17th Street, N.W.
Suite 200
Washington, D.C. 20036

National Association of Decorative
Fabrics Distributors
5940 W. Touhy Avenue
Chicago, Illinois 60648

National Association of Mirror
Manufacturers
5101 Wisconsin Avenue N.W.
Suite 504
Washington, D.C. 20016

National Cotton Batting Institute
1918 North Parkway
Memphis, Tennessee 38112

National Forest Products Association
1619 Massachusetts Avenue N.W.
Washington, D.C. 20036

National Furniture Traffic
Conference
335 East Broadway
Gardner, Massachusetts 01440

National Furniture Warehousemen's
Association
222 West Adams
Chicago, Illinois 60606

National Hardwood Lumber
Association
332 South Michigan Avenue
Chicago, Illinois 60604

National Home Fashions
League, Inc.
107 World Trade Center
Dallas, Texas 75258

National Home Furnishings
Association, Inc.
405 Merchandise Mart
Chicago, Illinois 60654

National Office Products Association
301 North Fairfax Street
Alexandria, Virginia 22314

National Particleboard Association
2306 Perkins Place
Silver Spring, Maryland 20910

National School Supply and
Equipment Association
1500 Wilson Boulevard
Arlington, Virginia 22209

National Wholesale Furniture
Association
Box 1792
High Point, North Carolina 27261

Northeastern Lumber Manufacturers
Association
Four Fundy Road
Falmouth, Maine 04105

Northern Hardwood and Pine
Manufacturers Association
Northern Building
Suite 501
Green Bay, Wisconsin 54301

Northwest Hardwood Association
1303 Terminal Sales Building
Portland, Oregon 97205

Society of the Plastics Industry
355 Lexington Avenue
New York, New York 10017

Southeastern Lumber Manufacturers
Association
P.O. Box 1606
Forest Park, Georgia 30050

Southern Forest Products
Association
P.O. Box 52468
New Orleans, Louisiana 70152

Southern Hardwood Lumber
Manufacturers Association
805 Sterick Building
Memphis, Tennessee 38103

Southern Hardwood Square
Association
c/o Adams, Johnson and McQueen
Drawer 900
Clinton, North Carolina 28328

Southern Home Furnishings
Association
Box 1249
High Point, North Carolina 27261

Summer and Casual Furniture
Manufacturers Association
Box 2436
High Point, North Carolina 27261

Upholstered Furniture Action
Council
P.O. Box 2436
High Point, North Carolina 27261

Urethane Institute, Society of the
Plastics Industry
355 Lexington Avenue
New York, New York 10017

Waterbed Manufacturers Association
1411 West Olympic Boulevard
Suite 304
Los Angeles, California 90015

Western Wood Products Association
Yeon Building
Portland, Oregon 97204

Woodworking Machinery
Distributors Association
1900 Arch Street
Philadelphia, Pennsylvania 19103

Woodworking Machinery
Manufacturers of America
1900 Arch Street
Philadelphia, Pennsylvania 19103

APPENDIX B
ADVERTISING GUIDELINES

These guidelines, based on Federal Trade Commission regulations, were prepared by the National Home Furnishings Association to meet standards for truth in advertising. They are included as a reference to anyone wishing to advertise home furnishings products. (Reprinted with permission of the National Home Furnishings Association.)

Practices and Terminology

A number of the advertising regulations enforced by the Federal Trade Commission concern practices and terminology used by a majority of stores. Among these are price comparisons, bargain offers and use of the word "free" and similar terms.

Former price comparisons. Advertising a reduction from a store's former price is legitimate when the former price is the store's "normal" price: the actual price at which the product was offered to the public on a regular basis for a reasonably substantial period of time.

Descriptive terms such as "regularly," "usually," "reduced to," "sale" and "save," along with statements of savings expressed as fractions, percentages or dollar amounts, are permissible when the amount listed as the former price is actually the "normal" price.

The term "sale" may be used in price comparisons when the amount of reduction from the former price is reasonable and significant. However, it is considered misleading when an item is advertised as "reduced to $990" when the former price was $1,000.

Comparisons with other retail prices. If an advertiser compares his prices to the higher prices being charged for the same product by other retailers, he must make certain that a number of retailers in his trading area are actually offering the same article for sale at the higher price. One or two isolated cases are not enough evidence to support the claim that the higher price quoted is the typical price being charged in the area.

Comparisons with similar merchandise. Comparing prices of advertised merchandise with prices of similar merchandise offered by competitors is permissible when:

1) the product being offered by other stores is of an essentially similar grade and quality to that being advertised and

2) the higher price for the comparable merchandise is actually the price offered by a reasonable number of retailers in the trading area. In these circumstances, the advertiser must prove

that the higher price actually represents the typical price being charged in the area and he must also establish that the merchandise sold by competitors is of "comparable value with that of the advertised goods."

Comparisons with manufacturers' prices. A manufacturer's suggested or list price may be quoted as a point of comparison only when the manufacturer's price is the one at which a substantial number of sales are being made in the advertiser's trading area.

Before quoting a comparison with a suggested or list price, a retailer must determine that the manufacturer's price is actually being charged by principal outlets within his trading area. The requirement does not include discounters who never offer merchandise at manufacturers' suggested prices. If there are no other outlets in the trading area that carry a particular manufacturer's products, a retailer cannot advertise his prices in comparison with the manufacturer's suggested price.

Wholesale and factory price listings. Retailers should never advertise a retail price as a "wholesale" or "factory" price. These terms can be used only when the price offered to the public is actually the same amount which the wholesaler or factory charges the retailer for the merchandise. In addition, retailers should neither state no imply that they are wholesalers, wholesale distributors or that they own or control a factory when this is not the case.

Comparatives for imperfect merchandise. Stores should not advertise imperfect or irregular merchandise or seconds at a reduced price without disclosing that the higher comparative price listed refers to the price of the merchandise if perfect.

Advertising "free" and bargain offers. In advertising, "Two-for-One" sales, "One Cent" sales, "Buy One—Get One Free" sales and other similar promotions, terms and conditions of the offer must be clearly stated. When making this type of offer, the advertiser must not increase the regular price of the merchandise that the customer must buy in order to receive "bargain" or "free"

275

items. The retailer also must not decrease quantity or lower quality of purchased goods in order to compensate for the value of "free" and bargain offers.

The term "regular" price means the normal selling price at which the merchandise is offered to the public for a reasonably substantial (30 days) period of time prior to the "free" offer. For products or services that fluctuate in price, "regular" price means the lowest price at which any substantial sales were made during the 30 days prior to the free offer.

Avoid "Bait and Switch"

The Federal Trade Commission defines bait and switch advertising as "an alluring but insincere offer to sell a product or service which the advertiser does not intend or want to sell." Bait and switch regulations apply not only to advertisements but also to a retailer's behavior after a customer enters the store.

No advertisement should appear when the offer is not a bona fide effort to sell the advertised product. No statement or illustration should be used that creates a false impression of the grade, quality, make, value, size, color, currentness of model, usability or origin of the product.

The advertiser should not discourage the customer from buying the advertised product. The retailer must not:

- refuse to show, demonstrate or sell the product in accordance with the terms of the offer;
- disparage the product or any aspect of it (credit terms, availability of service, repairs or parts, warranty);
- fail to have a sufficient quantity in the store to meet reasonably anticipated demands, unless the advertisement clearly discloses that supplies are limited or available only in certain outlets;
- refuse to take orders for the product;
- show or demonstrate a product that is defective, unusable or impractical;
- use a sales plan or method of compensation for salespeople designed to prevent or discourage them from selling the advertised product.

Once a sale is made, the advertiser is prohibited from attempting to switch the customer to another product. He must not:

- accept a deposit for the advertised product, then switch the customer to a higher-priced product;
- fail to deliver the advertised product within a reasonable time or to make a refund;
- disparage the product or any aspect of it;
- deliver a defective, unusable or impractical product that cannot perform in the manner represented in the advertisement.

Describe furniture accurately

Home furnishings products must be described properly and accurately, both in advertising and on any materials used to tag or label the merchandise. All "material facts" that influence a customer's decision to buy must be disclosed. This includes information on product utility, construction, composition, durability, design, style, origin and quality. The Federal Trade Commission requires disclosures for chairs, tables, desks, cabinets, sofas, beds, chests and mirror frames. Not covered are pictures, lamps, clocks, rugs, draperies and appliances.

Disclosures in advertisements must be made clearly, conspicuously and in close relationship to the copy or illustration which needs clarification.

Manufacturers' tags. When descriptive information appears on tags or labels provided by manufacturers, retailers are prohibited from defacing, obliterating or changing the meaning of the "material facts." A retailer may, however, substitute his own label or tag as long as all the "material facts" are retained. In all cases, information must remain attached to the product until purchased by the customer.

Descriptions of wood. Names of woods may be used to indicate that all exposed surfaces are constructed of that type of wood. A "walnut" table, therefore, means that all exposed surfaces of the table are made of solid walnut. If more than one type of solid wood is used, all names should appear on any disclosure. The terms "hardwood" and "softwood" may also be used. Veneers should be mentioned along with the type of wood (mahogany veneered construction) used in the veneer.

Whenever a wood product appears to be something it is not, the fact must be disclosed. Exposed surfaces made of plastic or other materials which appear to be wood must be identified and color or grain finishes must be described to indicate the wood tone of the finish. Examples: "walnut grained plastic tops;" "maple finish on birch solids and veneers."

Leather and leather imitations. Whenever a product is not made of genuine leather, the fact should be disclosed by stating "imitation leather" or by identifying the composition of the product (vinyl covering, fabric-backed vinyl). A disclosure should also be made when a trade name such as "Durahyde" describes a simulation of the genuine product.

Outer coverings and fillings. If fiber content is mentioned in advertising, each fiber should be identified in order of weight. When ads mention the composition of filling materials, a complete description (shredded urethane foam, latex foam rubber) must be made.

Describing origin, condition. Although it is misleading to call an American-made chair of Spanish design "Spanish," terms such as "Spanish influence," "Danish style" and "Italian design" may be used. The FTC considers that names such as "French Provincial" and "Mediterranean" are recognizable to consumers without disclosure of the country in which they are manufactured.

A retailer may not advertise or otherwise represent a product as "new" unless it is, in fact, new and has never been used.

Terms such as "floor sample" and "demonstration model" may not be used to describe furniture that has been used, traded in, repossessed or previously rented. The term "discontinued" may be used when the manufacturer has dropped the line or when the retailer will no longer carry an item after clearing out existing inventory.

Credit advertising disclosures

Terms of specific credit plans may be advertised only when the advertiser "usually and customarily" offers such credit plans.

In relation to credit disclosures, an advertisement is considered as any commercial message in any newspaper, catalog, magazine, leaflet, flyer, on radio, television, or public address system, in direct mail literature or other printed material, on any interior or exterior sign or window display, in any point-of-transaction literature or price tag.

Separate requirements are in effect for revolving (open end) and installment (closed end) credit plans.

Revolving credit plans. Creditors may advertise only those terms that actually are or will be arranged or offered. Trigger terms that require additional disclosures are:

- circumstances under which a finance charge might be imposed;
- amount of any charge, other than a finance charge, that might be imposed (for example, a late charge) in connection with the credit plan;
- The fact that a security interest is involved.

If any of the trigger terms is used, then you must also disclose:

- any minimum, fixed or similar charge that could be imposed;
- The "Annual Percentage Rate," using that term.

General terms avoid disclosure. In advertising revolving credit plans, there are a number of general terms that can be used without triggering full disclosure requirements of the Truth-in-Lending law. General terms include:

- Just say "Charge it."
- Use our convenient charge plan.
- Your first installment begins in May. (Do not substitute the word "payment" for "installment" unless a monthly payment is specified).
- Put all your purchases on a 30-day, no-carrying-charge account.
- Charge accounts available.

Installment credit plans. Creditors may advertise only those terms that actually are or will be arranged or offered.

Creditors must state a finance charge as an "Annual Percentage Rate," using that term.

Trigger terms which require additional disclosures are:

- the amount or percentage of any down payment;
- the number of payments or period of repayment;
- the amount of any payment;
- The amount of any finance charge.

If *any* of the above trigger terms is used, then you must also disclose:

- the amount or percentage of the down payment;
- the terms of repayment;
- The "Annual Percentage Rate," using that term.

No disclosure necessary. There are also some general terms that can be used in ads for installment credit without triggering full disclosure:

- Use our convenient credit plans.
- Terms to fit your budget.
- Monthly payments.
- Liberal budget terms.
- Financing available at 00% annual percentage rate. (The annual percentage rate is one specific credit term that may be advertised without triggering further disclosures.)
- A new bedroom suite can be within your budget with one of our three credit plans.
- Take 90 days to pay with no finance charges added—pay only one-third in 30 days, one-third in 60 days, balance in 90 days.
- On-the-spot financing.
- Arrange low terms for instant credit.
- 90 days (three payments) same as cash.
- Store financing, you deal only with me.

Multi-page advertisements. All required credit advertising disclosures may be stated together in only one place in a catalog or multi-page advertisement as long as the advertising disclosures required are set forth clearly and conspicuously in a credit-terms table and provided that any statement of "triggering" credit terms on other pages refers to the page(s) on which the table of credit terms appears.

Warranty advertising

No warranty should be offered in advertisements unless the warrantor intends to honor the warranty, and unless the warranty accurately represents the capabilities of the product being advertised.

At a minimum, warranty advertisements must include:

- a designation as either a "Limited Warranty" or a "Full (statement of duration) Warranty;"
- an identification of the warrantor;
- an identification of the product, parts, characteristics or properties that are either covered or excluded from the warranty;
- the duration of the warranty;
- a statement of the costs or charges to consumer (charges for parts, labor, shipping);
- an explanation of what the warrantor will do to honor the warranty (e.g., repair, replacement or refund), and

- a statement identifying any other major terms, conditions or restrictions (coverage restricted to original purchaser, customer must return product to factory, customer must retain original packaging).

Prorated adjustments. If the value of the warranted merchandise is prorated, all terms and conditions must be given. This includes time periods, the manner in which the warrantor will prorate the merchandise and the price on which the prorated adjustment will be based if the price is different from the actual purchase price.

Lifetime warranties. Consumers assume that the phrase "Lifetime Guarantee" refers to the life of the purchaser. Any other "lifetime" (life of the product, life of another product in which the warranted merchandise is installed) must be identified. If the warranty is intended to cover only the original owner for as long as he owns the product, the term

"lifetime" may not be used. In these circumstances, the warranty should indicate the duration (e.g., "as long as you own it").

Savings guaranteed. Ads that claim a savings guarantee ("Lowest price in town") must include a clear and conspicuous disclosure of what the warrantor will do if the savings are not realized, together with any time or other limitations the warrantor may impose.

Satisfaction guaranteed. Simple statements such as "Your Satisfaction Guaranteed" are not considered to be written warranties under the law and therefore do not require disclosure of specific terms. Any conditions or limitations on such statements must, however, be disclosed in the ad. Full disclosure is required only when such statements have specific limits on duration, apply only to certain products or have other conditions or limitations.

GLOSSARY OF FURNITURE PRODUCT TERMS

A

acrylic Synthetic polymer fiber made from natural materials, such as coal, air, water, petroleum, and limestone. Fibers are strong, durable, and resistant to strong sunlight. They make soft, bulky, wool-like fabrics and carpets. Trademarks include *Acrilan, Creslan, Orlon,* and *Zefran.*

Adam brothers Scottish architect/designers, brothers Robert (1728–1792) and James (1732–1794) based much of their styling on the classic lines of the Greeks and Romans. Their neoclassic designs made much use of medallion, urn, and garland carvings. They used straight lines with tapering legs ornamented with painting, gilding, and inlay work. Their furniture is also recognized by its heavy outline.

angle match See V MATCH.

antique satin See SATIN, ANTIQUE.

antiquing Process of making wood or fabric look old and used. Can be done by application of an antique finish, artificial weathering, distressing, etc.

apartment dining furniture Smaller size dining table and chairs (normally four) with optional matching china cabinet and, perhaps, buffet. Often purchased for use in apartments and condominiums. Also called *condominium dining furniture* or *junior dining furniture.*

apron Board placed at right angles to the underside of a table top or seat of a chair, extending between the tops of legs. On case furniture, the perpendicular face below the lowest drawer between bracket feet. Also called a *skirt.*

armoire Tall, movable wardrobe or cupboard. Often sold as a bedroom piece, usually instead of a chest of drawers. Derived from French word for storage cabinet for armor.

arm pad Upholstered part of the wooden arms of a chair, serving as armrests.

arm rail Curved horizontal part of a chair, continuous across the back and arms.

arm stump The vertical element that supports the front part of a chair arm.

arrow back Name given to chairs with three or more arrow spindles in back. Seen in work of Sheraton, American Federal designers, and in some Windsor chairs.

arrow spindle A decorative, flattened spindle resembling an arrow, used in American Federal and Sheraton furniture, especially backs of chairs, beds, and settees. It also appeared in some Windsor chairs. Also see SPINDLE.

ash A strong wood, several native varieties of which are used for furniture. *White ash* is a hard wood of great strength and toughness, usually used in unexposed parts of upholstered furniture. *Black ash* is softer and lighter in weight than white ash. *Brown ash* is burled and used for veneers. Besides these American varieties, more costly European, or English, and Japanese ash are used for veneers and inlays.

B

bachelor's chest A small-scaled chest of drawers, originally used to hold small items of male apparel.

backplate Decorative metal backing for hardware pull or pendant.

bail handle Metal drawer handle or pull that hangs downward in a reversed arch or half-moon shape from pins attached to a backplate.

balance match See CENTER MATCH.

ball-and-claw foot A furniture foot in the shape of a bird or animal claw grasping a ball.

bamboo Tropical woody plant characterized by hollow stems and regularly recurring knotty rings, generally used for casual furniture. In late 18th and early 19th centuries, turnings of other wood made to look like bamboo became popular.

banding See EDGING.

band sawn A serpentine shaping, achieved by a high-speed, thin banded saw.

banister back A late 17th-century English or American wooden chair type with split, turned spindles or flat bars for the uprights of the chair back.

banquette An upholstered bench or settee.

bar cart A mobile table and cabinet for storing and serving liquor, similar to a tea cart.

Barcelona chair *(1)* Stainless steel 20th-century chair designed by Ludwig Mies van der Rohe. The front legs curve up and back to support the chair back and the rear legs sweep forward to support the seat. Seat and back are usually tufted leather pads. *(2)* Elaborate antique ladder-back armchair of late 17th-century Spain.

barefaced tenon A shaped piece used in joinery of furniture in which tenon has only one angled edge, rather than the usual two.

Baroque A style of art and architecture which originated in Italy in the late 16th century and prevailed throughout Europe by the 17th and 18th centuries; generally characterized by exaggerated scale, dramatic movement of line, curves, and brilliant ornamentation. The furniture and decoration of the Louis XIV period is the expression of the Baroque in France.

barrel chair Upholstered chair with a silhouette suggesting a half-barrel sliced vertically.

base Bottom or foundation of a piece of furniture.

base rail Wood trim at bottom edge and above legs of chair or sofa. Also wood trim at bottom edge of dresser, chest, or other case piece directly above legs or flush to floor.

Bauhaus Influential school of architecture, design, and art from 1919 to 1933, first directed by Walter Gropius in Germany. Spread the philosophy that function should be the basis of design and that art and craft, including technology, are inseparable. Considered by some to be founder of modern furniture style with its straight lines and stress on function.

bedding All sleeping equipment including mattresses, box springs, water beds, etc.

bed rails Strips of wood or metal used in pairs to connect headboard of a bed to footboard, forming the frame to support the springs and/or mattress.

bentwood Steam-softened wood molded into curving shapes for structural parts of chairs and other pieces.

bergère French-style armchair with closed, upholstered sides, high back, and loose seat cushion, originated in Louis XV period and still manufactured.

Biedermeier An early 19th century style developed by German craftsmen, derived largely from French Empire. It emphasized convenience, and was simple in line, modest in size, and restrained in decoration, having painted rather than carved motifs on flat surfaces, often in black and gold. Nonetheless aimed for a deluxe effect; employed architectural forms and classical ornament; used mahogany and fruitwood, and rich fabrics. Named for imaginary character in magazine who typified the middle-class German.

birch A light brown, fine-grained American wood. It is strong and hard, easy to work, and can take a natural finish or be stained to simulate mahogany, walnut, and more expensive woods. European birch is similar but less available.

bird's eye Mottled figure in wood grain suggesting a bird's eye, mostly in maple.

blanket chest Low storage chest with hinged lid and often a lower drawer, serving also as a bench.

bleaching A method of chemically treating wood to provide a lighter, more uniform color. "Blonde" mahogany and walnut are bleached woods.

blistering In wood finishing, a defect caused by formation of bubbles on surface of finished work after film is dry.

block foot Cube-shaped base of an untapered square leg.

block front A furniture front divided into three vertical panels; center panel is concave or recessed between the two convex or advancing side panels. Used in 18th-century American chests, highboys, etc. Also called *tub front.*

boatswain's chair Sometimes spelled "bosun's," it is similar to a captain's chair, but is smaller scaled and has half-arms.

bombé Bulging, convex front and sides of case furniture. Bombé-type cabinets and chests are characteristic of Louis XV, late 18th-century Italian, and Baroque pieces.

Bonnell-type innerspring construction An all-steel innerspring construction used in less expensive mattresses, involving hour-glass shaped coil springs wired together and connected with small helical springs.

bonnet top Rounded, hat-shaped top or hood normally found on tall 17th and 18th-century English and American case pieces such as highboys and secretaries.

bookcase headboard A headboard for a bed with space to store books, radios, clocks, and other small items.

book match Method of veneer matching where pairs of adjacent slices of veneer, as they are cut from the log, are opened up like the pages of a book. This produces a mirror image of the veneer grain pattern.

borax A slang expression for furniture that is usually badly styled, poorly constructed and finished, and flashy. Term comes from furniture obtained through saving Kirkman's Borax Soap wrappers.

Boston rocker Early 19th-century American rocking chair with solid wood seat that curves up in back and down in front; wide scrolled top rail, over a high spindle back.

bouclé A plain or twill weave with small, regularly spaced loops and flat, irregular surfaces produced by using specially twisted yarns. Can be made of wool, rayon, silk, cotton, or linen. Rough texture is well-suited to contemporary furniture upholstery.

bow back Windsor-type chair with rounded top rail continuing down either side to the arms and the seat.

bow front Case front with a single convex curve.

box match A veneering pattern similar to the diamond match, but angled to create a series of consecutive squares radiating out from the center.

box pleat In upholstery, a fold of fabric to the left, followed by a fold to the right, stitched in place.

box seat Dining-room seat cushion having welt on top forming a boxlike shape.

boxspring An upholstered support for a mattress, made of springs mounted on a wood or metal frame, covered with ticking to match the mattress.

brace block Piece of wood or metal fitted into an angle of a piece of furniture to add strength or rigidity, as at the corners under a table top or between the leg and seat of a chair.

breakfront A bookcase or china cabinet with a center section on a different plane from the two end sections, characteristic of 18th-century American and English case furniture.

Breuer, Marcel Hungarian-born architect (1902–71) of Bauhaus school who in the 1920's developed tubular metal, cantilevered chairs which became the prototype of many later modern designs.

Brewster chair Early New England chair with heavy turned posts, many spindles, and a rush seat. Named after William Brewster, a 17th-century leader of the Pilgrims of Plymouth, Massachusetts.

brocade A rich jacquard-woven fabric with interwoven design of raised patterns. It has an embossed appearance. Sometimes it has contrasting surfaces, colors, gold or silver threads.

broken pediment An architectural element frequently used on 18th-century English furniture atop cabinets, bookcases, curio cabinets, corner cabinets, highboys, etc. The triangular pediment is interrupted at its apex and the open, central area often filled with a decorative urn, finial, shell, etc.

buffet French term referring to sideboard used to store china, silver, and linens. Top surface used as counter for serving. Unlike sideboard, usually has drawers as well as doors.

bunching chest Chest designed to fit flush against another on either side so that it can be used in multiples.

bun foot Furniture support resembling a slightly flattened ball. Also called *Flemish foot.*

bunk bed Twin beds mounted one above the other.

bureau In the U.S., a low chest of drawers, generally used in a bedroom with a mirror; a dresser. In 18th-century England, a writing desk or table with drawers.

burl Dome-like growth of a tree; source of decorative veneer with mottled pattern, produced by slicing cross-sections of the abnormal, wartlike tree appendages. Sometimes called *burr.*

burlap A plain weave of cotton, jute, or hemp, coarse and loosely woven, used to cover springs in upholstered furniture and occasionally as webbing.

burr See BURL.

butterfly match See REVERSE DIAMOND MATCH.

butterfly table Early American drop-leaf table with leaves supported by swinging brackets suggesting butterfly wings.

butt hinge A simple hinge with two leaves. When attached to a door and vertical frame, the pin joint is visible.

butt joint A type of joint where wood ends meet perpendicularly at right angles without overlapping or notching.

butt match Veneer arrangement similar to book match, but joined end-to-end in a continuous strip. Also called *end match.*

C

cabinet room In furniture manufacture, the shop where shaped and sanded parts are put together.

cabriole A double-curved furniture leg, arching outward at the top ("knee"), inward near the foot ("ankle"), which swings out again. Very popular during Queen Anne, Chippendale, and Louis XV periods, and on French furniture being produced today.

camel back Chair back with a top rail curved up in the center. Also a curved-back sofa with a hump in center. Often used by Chippendale and Hepplewhite.

campaign chest A fairly low, small chest of drawers with metal reinforcement at corners and inset brass pulls. Name derives from portable chests used by the military.

canapé Small French sofa, usually with exposed wood back and arm rail. Name came from a canopied 17th-century seat for two.

candlestand A light table used for candles, vases, or other small ornaments, usually with a tripod pedestal.

cane Rattan and other reedlike plants split into thin strips and woven for chair seats, backs, and side panels; elastic and comfortable. Also used for decorative insets.

canopy Covering over a bed or other piece of furniture, suspended by posts; generally a wood frame with fabric.

capital Uppermost member of a column, usually decorated.

captain's chair Wooden chair with low, rounded back rail supported by spindles; usually has arm rests; has turned legs braced by stretchers.

card table A small folding table used for playing cards and other games. Originated in the 17th century, especially popular during the William and Mary and Queen Anne periods. Some early card tables had depressions for holding candles and money.

case Any piece designed for storage or as a receptacle, from the ordinary box through the chest to the highboy and secretary. Evolved from a box made of planks to one of lighter panels framed to give rigidity with lightness, then to smaller movable boxes, or drawers, within a larger box. Also referred to as a *case piece* or the plural, *case goods*.

case goods Term used in the furniture industry for pieces that are wood and not upholstered, especially those used in the dining-room and bedroom. The name comes from chests, dressers, and other pieces that resemble cases, i.e., used for storage.

casters Small wheels mounted in a swivel frame attached to base or legs to facilitate moving a piece of furniture.

cedar chest Chest made of clear wood for storage of woolens and furs as protection against moths.

cedar, red Fragrant wood used mainly to line chests, closets, and drawers for protection against moths.

cellarette *(1)* Liquor storage cabinet. *(2)* Deep drawer for bottles and glasses in a buffet.

center match Arrangement of two veneer sheets of uniform size, matched in the center on a single face. Also called *balance match.*

chairback Headboard. Refers to an open headboard style of a bed resembling the back of a dining-room chair.

chaise lounge An upholstered chair with a very elongated seat supported by extra legs, used for reclining. Also made with lightweight aluminum frame for outdoor use. Also spelled *chaise longue.*

chamfer The edge of a corner that is beveled or angled off.

channel back Type of upholstered back for chair or sofa, with rows of vertical tufting.

Charles of London sofa A heavily upholstered, 20th-century sofa with flat, massive, low armrests, barely rising above the T-pillows that are set next to them. The *Charles of London chair,* also a 20th century design, has the same generally massive look.

check Small crack that may appear in lumber because of imperfect seasoning or drying. Separation of grain lengthwise, usually occurring through the growth rings.

checkerboard match Arrangement of small squares of veneer with their grain lines alternating in direction, producing a checkerboard effect.

checking In wood finishing, a state of disintegration in which cracks appear in the furniture coating.

chenille A type of yarn that has short, cut fibers protruding from it. Fabrics woven from this yarn have a plushlike or "furry" surface appearance. Can be made of cotton, silk, rayon, etc. Used as upholstery, drapery, and bedspreads.

cherry, black A fine-grained, light reddish-brown hardwood, structurally strong and highly decorative. Has a straight grain and is satiny. Grown mainly in Pennsylvania and West Virginia.

chest A piece of case furniture intended for storage. Originally, a trunklike box with hinged lid. The addition of drawers led to development of *chest of drawers.*

chesterfield Large, overstuffed sofa with closed, upholstered arms that are usually roll-over arms of same height as back.

chest-on-chest Chest of drawers in two sections, a smaller unit placed on top of a larger.

cheval mirror A full-length, swinging mirror hung between two posts anchored by a cross beam.

Smaller versions, often with drawers in base, are used atop chest or dressers.

chiffonier French term for a high, narrow chest of drawers for bedroom use.

china cabinet A display cabinet, usually with glass sides and front for displaying china. Also called a *china closet*. Often composed of two sections, with the bottom referred to as a *china base*, and the top called the *china hutch*.

chinoiserie Lacquered and/or painted decoration of Chinese-style motifs as interpreted by European designers. Grew out of great interest in Oriental objects from 17th to 19th centuries.

chintz Plain weave cotton fabric with a glaze finish giving a soft, lustrous appearance. Usually has a printed design. Used for upholstery, fabric, slipcovers, and drapery.

chipcore See PARTICLE BOARD.

Chippendale, Thomas English cabinetmaker (1718–79). While he was a master designer and carver, primarily he adapted, modified, and even copied many modes, but always with characteristic distinction. He emphasized richly carved mahogany, free use of curves, complex rococo scrolls, claw-and-ball foot cabriole legs, swelling fronts and sides on case pieces. His chairs have pierced back splats, with arms curved and flared at the ends. Chinese Chippendale was his adaptation of Chinese designs. His work is part of the Georgian period.

chipping In wood finishing, a defect developing when dried film of finishing material separates as flakes from surface underneath.

claw-and-ball foot See BALL-AND-CLAW FOOT.

cleat Strip of wood or other material fastened across a structural member or joint to give strength.

club chair Low-slung lounge or easy chair with squared back and arms, loose seat cushion. May or may not be skirted, and the type of arm may vary with period or style.

club foot Thick, outward-extending end of an 18th-century furniture leg; sometimes having a thick, flat base.

cockfight chair Small, caster-mounted reading chair straddled by its occupant who faces the back and rests his arms on the wide, flat, deeply-curved back rail. So named because it was used for viewing sporting events such as cockfighting.

cocktail table Low table used in front of a sofa to hold refreshments, ashtrays, magazines, etc. Also called a *coffee table*.

coffee table See COCKTAIL TABLE.

coil springs Tapering, cone-shaped, resilient wire springs used in construction of upholstered furniture, mattresses, and boxsprings. Also called *cone springs*.

Colonial American See EARLY AMERICAN.

comb back Windsor chair back with center spindles rising higher than the others to hold another rail and form a headrest, thus resembling woman's old-fashioned comb.

commode Low, small chest or enclosed table generally used against a wall and fitted with drawers and/or doors.

condominium dining furniture See APARTMENT DINING FURNITURE.

cone springs See COIL SPRINGS.

console Narrow, shelflike table attached to a wall by a bracket and usually supported by legs in front only. Term used loosely for any wall table.

contemporary Literally "of our day." Present-day furniture style as opposed to "traditional" which refers to a conventional past period or antique style. Compare with MODERN.

contract furniture Furniture normally purchased under a contract. Refers to furniture designed and purchased for heavy use in nonresidential interiors, such as offices, schools, libraries, hospitals, other medical care facilities, hotels, motels, public buildings, or for use by the government. Must be strong enough to withstand exposure to wear-and-tear over extended periods.

convertible sofa A sofa that unfolds into a bed. When folded, it resembles a sofa complete with cushions; people sit on top of the folded mattress. Used mainly in small areas for sitting during the day and sleeping at night.

coordinated grouping Group of furniture pieces of the same design or closely related in material, color, and style.

corduroy A strong, cut pile fabric with ridges or cords in the pile which run lengthwise, giving a ridged, velvety quality.

core In cabinetry, the innermost layer of plywood or veneered sections for cases. May be sawn lumber with grain at right angles to that of veneer or other wood affixed to it. May also consist of particle board.

corner block In furniture making, a triangular wood block used in the concealed structure under table tops, inside cases, and at points of stress on upholstered furniture frames for added strength.

corner chair Designed to fit into a corner, the square seat is diagonally set and the back extends across two adjoining sides. Thus, the chair has a leg in front, one in back, and one at either side.

corner cupboard   Three-sided cabinet designed to fit into a corner.

cornice   Top horizontal molding of a piece of furniture.

correlated grouping   Matching suite pieces that can be grouped to form sets which allow a choice of configurations in a room. An example is bedroom furniture with a variety of desks, chests, and bookcases.

cotton   A popular, natural fiber that is versatile and makes a good upholstery fabric. It blends well and lends its good characteristics (durability, high absorbency, good abrasion resistance, excellent pilling resistance, etc.) to other fibers in a mixture. Often blended with rayon, Dacron, or wool.

couch   Backless, upholstered lounge chair used for sitting and reclining, with supports and cushions at one or both ends. In common usage, often confused with sofa or settee.

country   Style of furniture that is usually heavy in scale and weighty in appearance. Could be any one of several style categories, i.e., French, English, Early American. Also called *Provincial.*

court furniture   Formal, elegant, traditional furniture much of which was originally designed for European royalty.

courting chair   See LOVE SEAT.

cracking   Defect in finish. Advanced stage of checking or crazing, where breaks in the film are deep enough to expose underlying surface.

cradle   Baby's bed mounted on rockers or hung from a bar in order to swing gently.

crawling   Defect in finish leaving uncoated areas where adhesion to surface was poor and coating has pulled together while wet.

credenza   Small buffet or sideboard used for serving, storage, or display.

crewel work   Type of embroidery employing loosely twisted worsted yarn on a fairly plain background such as unbleached linen or cotton.

crib   Infant's bed with enclosed sides, usually raised off the ground on tall legs.

crossbanding   *(1)* Veneer banding in which one layer of veneer runs at a right angle to the next layer in order to offset shrinking, swelling, and warping. *(2)* A narrow band of veneer used as a frame or border.

cross rail   Horizontal rail in chair back.

cross stretchers   Intersecting X-shaped leg stretchers, generally straight, but sometimes curved.

crotch   V-shaped figure attained when veneer is cut from joint of tree trunk and limb.

crystalling   In wood finishing, defect caused by drying of varnish or other material into rough crystalline surface.

cupboard   A storage cabinet with shelves and doors, often built-in.

D

Dacron   Trademark name for a polyester fiber manufactured by Du Pont. A crisp, strong, resilient fiber; combines well with cotton, linen, and wool.

dado joint   See RABBET JOINT.

damask   Firm, glossy, patterned fabric with jacquard weave. Similar to brocade, but flatter. Can be in one- or two-color designs. Weave of the pattern differs from that of background. Pattern is made visible by effect of light striking portions of fabric in different weaves. Originally made of silk, now woven in cotton, rayon, linen, silk, wool, or a combination.

Danish modern   Furniture style of mid-20th century, derived from designs developed in Denmark, with clean lines, and walnut or walnut finishes predominating. Upholstered pieces generally have open-arm construction in wood.

davenport   Sofa with padded arms and back, named for a Boston upholsterer.

davenport table   Long, narrow table, generally placed behind a sofa.

daybed   Couch with low head and footboards, usually placed lengthwise along a wall. Used for resting in daytime.

deck chair   Folding wood-frame chair with canvas seat, back, and leg rest.

deacon's bench   Long wooden bench with back (usually with spindles) and arms. An Early American piece, it probably had its origins in early New England churches.

delamination   Defect resulting from separation of laminated plastic from core stock, or of piles in plywood because adhesive fails to hold.

denim   A firm, heavy, twill-weave cotton fabric. The filler yarns are usually white with colored warp yarns. The filler yarns give the fabric its traditional whitish cast.

dentil molding   Molding or inlay pattern made up of small, projecting, regularly spaced rectangular blocks.

diamond match   Four pieces of straight-grained wood veneer are cut diagonally and are joined to meet in a central diamond shape. Increasingly larger diamond shapes emanate from the central point.

dinette   Small-scaled dining furniture, often made of metal. Originally designed for kitchen use, but also used in small dining areas. Also referred to as *informal dining furniture.*

Directoire   French style following the French Revolution (1799–1804) when classical ornamentation found even greater favor and was superimposed on the already classic lines of Louis XVI style. Influenced by Greek, Roman, and Egyptian design, it was simple and graceful.

director's chair   Scissors-folding, wood arm chair with canvas sling seat and back, so named because of its long-time use by movie directors.

distressing   An antiquing process to make new woods look old and used, done by hand during furniture manufacturing with the use of small surface marks and indentations.

divan   Originally, upholstered couch without arms or back, for reclining. In current usage, a sofa or couch.

double dresser   A chest-on-chest unit with two tiers of drawers, usually three drawers in each tier. Also called a *double chest.*

dovetail   A type of joint generally used to join the front and sides of a drawer by having wedge-shaped projections on one piece of wood interlock with alternating grooves in the other piece.

dowel   A round wooden pin, peg, or rod that is fitted into holes in two pieces of wood to hold them together.

down   Soft, fluffy feathers from very young birds, or from under the ordinary feathers of older birds or fowls. Used for stuffing pillows, cushions, and upholstered chair backs.

drawer guide   Strips of wood or metal placed under the center or on the outside of drawers to serve as a track on which they are drawn back and forth. Also called a *drawer slide.*

draw table   A three-leaved, refectory-like table. The two end leaves rest under the center one. When these two end pieces are drawn out from under the large central table surface, the center leaf falls down into the opening thus created, and the two end leaves make a large, continuous flush surface with the central leaf.

dresser   Long chest of drawers, usually with a mirror. Also called a *bureau.*

dressing table   Table with mirror and drawers to hold cosmetics.

drop-front desk   Hinged desk front which conceals drawers and compartments when closed and falls forward to form a writing surface when open.

drop-leaf table   Type of table with hinged leaf which folds down to shorten or up to lengthen surface.

drop seat   See SCOOP SEAT.

drum table   Pedestal-based round table with deep apron, generally holding drawers.

dry sink   Early American low, two-door wooden cupboard with zinc- or copper-lined open basin in the top, behind which rises a backboard. The forerunner of today's kitchen sink, it is currently used as a planter, bar, etc.

dull-rubbed finish   Treatment of stain, filler, shellac, undercoat, light varnish, pumice stone rub, and final light finish of parafin oil, which gives a soft natural sheen to woods, popular when fashion and taste stress natural qualities.

Duncan Phyfe   See PHYFE, DUNCAN.

dust panel   Thin board between two drawers in a chest to exclude dust. Also called *dust bottom* or *dust board.*

E

Early American   Loosely used term for furniture of early America, both antique and reproduction, reflecting many European influences, but chiefly English, blended with informal interpretations of American colonial design. Characterized by straightforward design, sturdiness, and simplicity, use of locally abundant woods, especially pine, birch, maple, and oak.

easy chair   A roomy, comfortable, upholstered chair of any style or period, which is made for ease and relaxation.

ebony   Costly, hard, dense, heavy, tropical brown-black wood with a fine grain. Takes a high polish. Used for veneers and inlays.

edging   Method of protecting veneer panel by applying a thin strip of solid wood or metal at the edge of the panel. Used on tabletop, drawer fronts, etc. Also called *banding.*

Elizabethan   See TUDOR-ELIZABETHAN.

elm   Strong, tough, native wood which looks well stained and polished. It is light brownish-red with dark brown ring marks and a strong figure. Has good joining qualities and holds nails well.

embossed   Decorated with a raised design produced on a surface by hammering, stamping, pressing, or molding. Can provide carved wood effects.

embroidery   The art of decorating a fabric with a raised design or pattern worked out with a needle and thread, either by hand or machine. The design may be of one or more colors, and a great variety of stitches or combinations of stitches may be employed.

Empire   Style of design and decoration first instituted in France during the reign of Napoleon. Popular from roughly 1804–1820, the style spread to England, where it influenced designers such as Sheraton, to the U.S., where it influenced Duncan Phyfe, and to Germany and Austria, where the Biedermeier style evolved. Classic Greek and Roman forms were revived to emphasize Napoleonic grandeur, symbols of imperial pomp being added to traditional classic motifs, such as wreaths, swags, festoons, laurel branches, mythological figures, and lions, as well as the emblems of the bee, the crown, and the letter N. Symmetry was an essential. Bronze, gilt, and brass were chief ornaments. Staple wood was mahogany; however, highly polished rosewood and ebony were used. Fabrics bore the same symbols and were made in hard textures and strong shades of green, yellow, blue, and red.

enamel finish   On wood, a coating of paint brushed and sometimes rubbed to a high gloss.

end match   See BUTT MATCH.

end panel   Side of a case piece of furniture.

end table   Small side table, used at the end of a sofa or beside a chair.

English Regency   See REGENCY ENGLISH.

engraving   *(1)* A relief effect in furniture made by incising lines into veneer and then filling with bleach. *(2)* A printing process in which the appearance of wood grain is reproduced onto smooth panels (often particle board). Normally used on less expensive furniture; an engraved, simulated wood finish is often simply referred to as "print."

escutcheon   Shield-shaped metal plate, often ornamented, used around a keyhole or as a backplate for a handle, doorknob, or pull.

étagère   Hanging or standing open shelves for displaying books or "whatnots."

exposed wood   That part of a frame of an upholstered chair or sofa which has been finished and which can be seen because it is not covered with a fabric.

extension table   A tabletop that separates in the center, and extends outward in both directions. Additional leaves are then added in the open space created.

F

fan-back chair   A chair or settee with a fanlike motif, either upright or reversed, for the chair back.

fashion   A popularly accepted prevailing custom or style of dress, home furnishings, etiquette, procedure, etc.

Federal   American period of architecture, furniture, art, and decoration from about 1780–1830. Although things English were basically rejected immediately after Revolution, American designers were still under the influence of English cabinetmakers, but now in slightly different fashion. Symbols of nationalism—the new Federal eagle, stars, arrows—were widely used as decorative motifs. Duncan Phyfe is the leading American furniture designer of this period.

felt   A material made by matting and interlocking under heat and pressure, woolen and other fibers. It has no weave or pattern.

fiber   The fundamental unit used in the fabrication of textile yarns and fabrics by interlacing in a variety of methods, including weaving, knitting, braiding, felting, and twisting.

fiberboard   See PARTICLE BOARD.

fiberfill   Soft, synthetic material used as cushioning in upholstered furniture, bedding, and comforters. Polyester fibers are most commonly used. Usually wrapped around foam for upholstery.

fiddle back   *(1)* Queen Anne type of American chair with violin-shaped splat back. *(2)* Figure in veneer shaped like the back of a violin, most often in maple and mahogany with wavy grain.

figure   Variations in color and texture appearing in wood cut across the grain, causing rings, rays, knots, irregularities. Variations appearing in wood cut along the grain are called the *pattern*.

filigree Ornamental openwork of delicate or intricate design, usually done in gold or silver wire.

filler *(1)* Any soft material used to stuff bedding and upholstered furniture. *(2)* In wood finishing, a substance applied to grain of wood to fill pores or irregularities before finishing or polishing.

filling yarn In woven fabric, the yarn that runs from selvage to selvage at right angles to the warp. Also called *weft* or *woof.* Each yarn of the filling is called a *pick, shot, shoot,* or *shute.*

finger joint Movable joint made by cutting two board ends into matching fingerlike projections to fit together.

finial A terminal decoration on a post or other upright. Among the shapes used are pineapples, urns, knobs, clusters of foilage, etc.

finish *(1)* In cabinetry, a treatment applied to wood to protect the surface, to make it more durable and resistant to stains and burns, to accentuate the natural grain, to lighten or deepen the color, to make a dull or glossy surface appearance, or to change the color completely as by painting, lacquering, polishing, antiquing, distressing, etc. Finish is applied to furniture with the use of stains, oil, shellac, varnish, wax, paint, or lacquer. *(2)* In fabrics, the treatment given to produce a desired surface effect or to add resistance to soil, stains, or wrinkles, such as napping, embossing, glazing, waterproofing, durable press, etc. The finish sometimes contributes to the "feel" or "hand" of the fabric.

fire screen An ornamental screen set in front of an open fireplace to keep sparks from flying into the room, or to provide protection from intense heat.

fireside chair Originally, a wing-back chair designed to allow warm air to circulate around occupant's back and ward off drafts. Today, used for any comfortable chair used by a fireside.

fittings Furniture hardware, such as hinges and drawer pulls.

flat-cut veneer A combination straight-grain and heart figure veneer produced by slicing half of a log directly through the center or heart.

Flemish foot See BUN FOOT.

flip-top table Table with a hinged double top which opens either like a book supported on a gate-leg, or by swiveling the top to opposite axis.

flotation sleep system See WATER BED.

flock Short fibrous particles applied by various processes to the surface of fabric, paper, or wood to give the appearance and feel of velvet or suede. The technique for decorating with flock is called *flocking.*

fluting Vertical grooves repeating along columns, furniture legs, table aprons, etc.

foam rubber Latex, the sap of the rubber tree, whipped with air to create a light, porous rubber composition. The firmness of the foam rubber depends on the air content. Used for mattresses, pillows, upholstery, filling etc. Several types of synthetic foams are also used for these purposes.

foot Bottom element of a leg of piece of furniture, or one of the cubes or spheres on which furniture without legs rests.

footboard Supporting piece at the foot end of a bed, sometimes decorative.

footrail The lower supporting stretcher between two legs of a chair or table.

footstool Low bench or stool serving as the footrest with a chair.

formed wire spring A spring with long rectangular bends attached to the frame of upholstered furniture to provide the springing action or "give" for comfort.

foundation The surface upon which a mattress rests in a bed. Commonly used foundations include box springs, solid foam, and plywood.

fourposter Bed with corner posts at head and foot extended upward above the sleeping surface.

four-way match Veneer pattern produced by the combination of book matches and butt matches.

frame Supporting structure of a piece of furniture. The wood, metal, or plastic structure that provides shape and support to upholstered furniture.

French Court Term for formal French furniture created for the courts of Louis XIV, Louis XV, and Louis XVI.

French Empire See EMPIRE.

French Provincial Furniture of the French provinces. The term is usually associated with simplified furniture of the Louis XV or rococo style. However, plain furniture was made in the provinces in all times and styles, usually of walnut, oak, or fruit-wood. Designs varied from province to province and local styles of decorations were used. *Provincial furniture* is simpler in line than the prevailing high fashion and is rarely veneered or decorated with marquetry or ornate carving.

fretwork Interlaced ornamental woodwork, usually in a complicated, repeating, geometric pattern. Often used in backs of chairs, beds, or in china cabinet doors.

frieze Heavy pile upholstery and drapery fabric with rows of uncut loops. Usually made of mohair, wool, cotton, or man-made fibers. Designs and patterns may be created by shearing the loops at different levels or by contrasts of cut or uncut loops in the pile. Also spelled *frisé*.

fruitwood Wood coming from trees grown for fruit, such as cherry, apple, and pear. Also used today to refer to light, honey-brown finish applied to surfaces of other woods to simulate fruitwood and allow the natural grain to show through.

full-size mattress Mattress usually 54 inches in width and 74 inches in length. Sometimes referred to as a *4/6*.

functional furniture Utilitarian furniture in which the function is most important and the aesthetics secondary. Also, term is used for specific pieces, such as convertible sofas, which can serve more than one purpose.

G

gallery Small railing bordering tops of tables, chests, or cabinets.

game table Table designed for playing cards, chess, backgammon, or other games.

gate-leg table Drop-leaf table with supporting legs that swing in and out like a gate. Also called a *swing-leg table*.

Georgian Furniture designed during most of the period covering the reigns of the Georges in England (1714 to about 1795). Often divided into three periods: Early, Middle, and Late Georgian. Some of the notable designers include the Adam brothers, Chippendale, Hepplewhite, and Sheraton. Mahogany and satinwood were the most popular woods. Features were the cabriole leg, pedestal base, the elaborate foot, pediment, column. Ornaments were largely neoclassic motifs.

gilding Method of ornamenting furniture, accessories, and architectural details with gold leaf or gold dust.

glazed doors Cabinet doors with glass panels, frequently with lattice work.

gloss Degree of shine, sheen, or luster of dried film coating of a finish.

Gothic The style of the Middle Ages in Europe from about 1150–1500. The only European style not based on classical forms. Gothic furniture that survives is that for the church and for the rich—heavy and massive, made of oak, the common wood, and iron, the usual hardware for both strength and decoration. The chest is the major article, having served for transport of foods, storage, seats, tables, even beds. Furniture decoration consisted largely of carving and followed architectural forms, especially pointed arches, but also heavy tracery and moldings.

grain Variations in color and texture made by the size and arrangement of cells and pores of a living tree, and revealed when wood is cut through the trunk in an essentially horizontal direction. Most marked grain characteristic is caused by the annual growth rings. Woods are classified in three types: *fine-grained* (e.g., birch, cherry, maple); *medium-grained* (e.g., walnut, mahogany); and *coarse-grained* (e.g., oak, chestnut).

grandfather's clock A floor-standing clock with a wood case which consists of a hood, a waist, and a base. The pendulum and the weights are protected inside the clock, which usually stands over six feet high.

grandmother's clock A smaller-scaled and more refined version of the grandfather's clock.

gray goods Fabrics just off the loom or knitting machine and in an unfinished state. Also called *greige goods*.

Greek Revival Renewal of interest in Greek designs in 18th and 19th century, stimulated by contemporary archeological excavations at Pompeii and Herculaneum, which influenced English, French, and American architecture and furniture.

green lumber Wood that is not ready for use because it is not thoroughly dried and seasoned.

greige goods See GRAY GOODS.

grid suspension system Wire mesh fastened to upholstered furniture frame on one side and fastened with helical springs on the other side as a springing mechanism.

grille Metal latticework, usually brass, often used on cabinet doors in place of or behind glass.

gum Hardwood from a wide range of the U.S. *Red gum* is the heartwood; it is hard, straight, fine-grained; often used for cabinetmaking because of its attractive figure; reddish-brown with dark streaks. The sapwood, called *sap gum*, is plain, watery, not strong; it is used for plywood and woodwork to be painted.

H

hackberry Native American wood, yellowish, heavy, coarse-grained, moderately hard, resembles elm. Used extensively for upholstered furniture frames and table legs.

half turning Turned part, split in half lengthwise, thus creating two half-round moldings. Applied to cabinets, cupboards, etc.

hall tree A hat and/or coat rack made of metal or wood turnings. It is a floor-standing unit with upturned arms at the top to hold hats and coats, sometimes with umbrella rack in base.

hand The touch or feel of a fabric to the hand, its tactile qualities, including softness, resilience, firmness, and delicacy.

hand tied In upholstery, type of construction having spring coils laced with twine by hand.

hardware In cabinetry, metal handles, pulls, escutcheons, hinges, decorative push plates, etc. Also called *mounts*.

hardwood General term for the lumber of broadleafed or deciduous trees in contrast to evergreen or coniferous trees, which are termed *softwoods*. The name has no real connection with the hardness of the wood. The furniture hardwoods are porous, and include oak, walnut, mahogany, beech, maple, and gum.

harvest table Long, narrow, rectangular table with hinged drop-leaf sides, straight legs. Usually 18th-century American.

hassock Stuffed cushion used for a footstool or ottoman.

headboard Panel rising above mattress at head of bed; often supports the bed rails. Compare with FOOTBOARD.

heartwood Inner core of mature tree trunk comprising the earliest grown annual rings, no longer carrying sap. Usually darker in color than sapwood.

heaving In wood finishing, a defect caused by partial softening of the undercoat, which raises the surface of the top film.

helical springs Spiraling springs used in mattresses, box springs, or in upholstered furniture.

Hepplewhite, George An 18th-century English designer and cabinetmaker (died 1786) whose neoclassic furniture was marked by lightness of construction, elegant curvilinear forms, and perfection of workmanship. Distinguishing marks include straight, fluted legs with spade feet, curved fronts, concave corners, and low backs; favored motifs include wheat ears, three-feathered Prince of Wales crest, ribbon, fine swags, lyre, honeysuckle, and urn shapes. Special contributions are his shield-back chair and his development of the sideboard. Wrote *The Cabinet-Maker and Upholsterer's Guide* (published in 1788).

herringbone match Two V-match veneer or wood panels butted together to form a series of horizontal valleys and peaks.

hickory Native American wood of the walnut family. Hard, tough, and heavy. Reddish-brown in the heartwood and pale yellow in the sapwood. Often used for rustic furniture and bent and molded plywood.

hideaway bed See MURPHY BED and TRUNDLE BED.

highboy Tall chest of four or five drawers, on legs, with a cornice or pediment crown.

high-gloss finish Wood treatment that follows all steps in dull-rubbed finish, with an additional rubbing with rottenstone and linseed oil usually applied with a soft cloth.

highlight In wood finishing, the effect produced by wiping stain from the high points of turned or carved members or edges, to produce an appearance of age and use.

high-riser An armless and backless couch, usually 75 inches long by 30 inches to 36 inches wide, with another slightly shorter and narrower mattress on a collapsed frame beneath it. The under-unit can be pulled out and raised level with the upper mattress to sleep two people. When the under-unit is not in use, the high-riser takes up the space of an ordinary couch.

high-tech A term describing furniture and furnishings that are, or appear to be, constructed of factory or industrial parts and pieces: grids, pipes, metal stampings, expanded metals, vacuum-formed elements, etc. The design and its elements suggest commercial or heavy-duty use, although adapted to the home, office, or retail store.

hinge Metal device of two parts called *leaves*, fitted with rings called *knuckles*, through which a pin can pass, and on which they pivot, permitting the turning of a door, lid, or other panel fastened to one of the leaves. There are many types, including *butt hinge, double-acting hinge, H-hinge, HL-hinge, pivot* or *pin hinge, surface hinge*. Hinges may be very decorative.

Hitchcock chair Small American chair first made by Lambert Hitchcock of Connecticut (1795–1852), with oval-turned top rail, splayed front legs, rush or caned seat. Usually black, painted with fruit or flower stencil on the back top rail.

Hollywood bed   A bed without a footboard, the spring and mattress set on a metal bed-frame unit, often equipped with casters. A headboard can be attached to the frame, or the headboard can be attached to the wall, and the frame then hooked on to it. The size varies from twin to king size. Period and style are determined by the choice of headboard.

homespun   Originally a fabric loomed by hand at home, but now the name of a loose, coarsely woven, power-loomed fabric that uses textured and bulky yarns to create a handwoven look.

hood   A shaped top on cabinet work.

hoop back   Style of chair with uprights and top rail forming one continuous curve. Appears in Queen Anne period, and used by Hepplewhite.

hope chest   Storage chest, traditional for bride's trousseau and linens. American term for *marriage chest.*

H-stretcher   Arrangement of bracing stretchers of a chair, connected in middle by a member forming an H-shape, as in Windsor and Chippendale chairs.

hutch   A top cupboard usually placed above buffet or sideboard for display of plates, cups, and utensils—often of Early American styling. Cupboard may be left completely open or have doors on two sides with open shelving area in the middle. Term is used by many to refer to the top part of any china cabinet made in two parts.

I

incised   Engraved or carved decoration cut into a surface.

inlay   A technique in which a design is cut out of the surface to be decorated and then filled in, flush with the surface, with other contrasting materials cut to fit exactly into these openings. The contrast of color or materials creates the decoration. The inserts may be of wood veneer, metals, shells, ivory, etc.

innerspring mattress   Mattress with a center core of springs for buoyancy and resilience. Surrounding the springs is a protective pad. A tough, fabric-like ticking encases the whole unit.

interrupted arch   See BROKEN PEDIMENT.

Italian   Throughout modern history, greatly varying styles of Italian furniture have been produced. During the years of the Renaissance (which lasted from approximately 1350–1600), furniture was large in scale, straight in line, and relatively simple and uncomfortable. Eventually, Italian furniture become more elaborate. Decoration, both painted and carved, based on Greek and Roman styles and motifs, was extensively developed, including the use of ivory, metals, and marble. By the end of the period, exaggerated scale and form transformed the prevailing style into the Baroque. In the late 18th century, as a result of the rediscovery of Pompeii, a renewed interest in Greek and Roman antique designs inspired an Italian neoclassic style, popular especially in France and England. Italian-style furniture produced most recently has been incorrectly called *Italian Provincial.* Actually, it is a simplified version of Louis XVI and French Directoire furniture adapted to present tastes and modern production techniques.

J

jack-knife sofa bed   See SOFA BED.

Jacobean   The period 1603–1688 in English architecture and art. The reigns of English kings James I (1603–1625) and Charles I (1625–1649) and the time of the Commonwealth (1649–1660) are termed *Early Jacobean.* In furniture, it was a time of relative simplicity and smaller pieces, with small melon-bulb turnings, less pronounced curves, straight legs, and flatter carving. The gate-leg table was developed. The time of the Commonwealth and Cromwell favored more severe furniture, largely oak, with ornamentation simplified. Developments included padding on chair backs as well as seats. *Late Jacobean,* after the Restoration of the monarchy in Britain, covers the reigns of Charles II (1660–1685) and James II (1685–1688). Walnut grew popular and Baroque lavishness was expressed in spiral turnings, carved crowns, upholstering in fine silks, tapestries, velvets, brocades, embroideries. Huge beds, wing chairs, coil seats, desks, and bureaus were developed.

jacquard weave   A weave with intricate, multicolored patterns produced on the type of loom created by Joseph-Marie Jacquard in the early 19th century which allows the mechanical production of fabric design. Damasks, tapestries, and brocades, used on both traditional and contemporary furniture, are all jacquard weaves.

joint   In furniture making, the junction at which two pieces of lumber unite to form a support or make a closure.

junior dining furniture   See APARTMENT DINING FURNITURE.

K

kas Early American cabinet of Dutch origin. Large two-door wardrobe or armoire elaborately painted with fruit designs symbolic of fertility, sometimes having drawers, and used to store household possessions.

KD See KNOCKED DOWN.

kettle base A bombé base; bulging front and sides of a case piece, similar to a kettle.

kettle front Bulging front of a case piece, often seen in 18th-century secretaries. Also called *bombé front.*

kick pleat Inverted pleat of fabric used at corners of skirts of upholstered pieces.

kidney Popular shape for the top of a piece of furniture, oval with concave cutout in front like a kidney bean, especially frequent in 18th-century desks, dressing tables, and benches.

kiln dried Wood that has been dried in a control-heated chamber, as opposed to *air dried,* which is more likely to warp because the drying is less even.

king-size mattress Mattress usually 72 inches to 78 inches wide by 76 inches to 78 inches long. Referred to as *6/6,* although many are only 76 inches wide.

knee Upper part of cabriole leg which has a swelling, outward curve; often carved.

kneehole Feature of a desk or dressing table providing open space in front to make room for the user's legs. Also called *knee space.*

kneehole desk See PEDESTAL DESK.

kneehole panel See MODESTY PANEL.

knife pleat In upholstery, single-edge pleats turned in one direction, usually narrower than box pleats. Also called *side pleat.*

knits Fabrics formed by knitting, the interlocking of loops of yarn rather than interlacing two sets of yarn as in weaving. Lengthwise rows or chains of loops are known as *wales* and crosswise rows of loops are the *courses.*

knocked down (KD) Furniture shipped from the factory in parts to be assembled by the retailer or consumer. Also called *ready-to-assemble furniture.*

"knock off" Expression within the industry to refer to an obvious copy of a popular design which is reproduced and sold at a lower price.

knot In lumber or veneer, a round or oval interruption in grain, where a branch grew.

knuckle carving Carved front end of arms of Chippendale chairs resembling the knuckles of the human hand.

L

lacquer A colored or opaque varnish made of shellac dissolved in alcohol, sometimes with pigment added. *Chinese* or *Japanese lacquer* is a hard varnish made from the sap of a sumac tree. It has a shiny, lustrous quality.

ladder back Type of chair with back posts joined by a series of horizontal rails, resembling a ladder, used instead of a vertical splat.

lamination Process of bonding together layers of wood, plastic, fabric, and/or paper by simultaneous application of heat and pressure.

landscape mirror A mirror designed to be displayed horizontally rather than vertically.

latex See FOAM RUBBER.

lathe In cabinetry, an instrument for holding a rotating piece of wood or dowel against a tool that shapes it to make a wood turning.

lattice An openwork crisscross or fretwork made of thin, flat strips of wood or metal. Usually found in chairs and headboards. Also called *latticework.*

Lawson couch A simple, usually skirted, sofa or loveseat, with rollover arms that are usually mid-height between the seat and the top of the straight sofa back. A *Lawson chair* is similar in shape, but seats only one person.

leaf *(1)* A board or panel used as a table-top extension. Some leaves are hinged to the table surface and must be raised to a horizontal position, as in a Pembroke or gate-leg table. Other leaves are drawn out from beneath the table surface, as in the draw table. In other tables, the top can be separated and extended so leaves can be placed in the opening. *(2)* Decorative motif, either realistic or conventionalized in form, such as a laurel leaf.

leather Skin of animals prepared by tanning or a similar process, used for upholstery fabric. Steer hide is almost always used. It is about one-quarter inch thick and split, or sliced, five times. The three middle slices are generally used for upholstery.

leg A furniture support. The leg of a chair usually starts at the seat rail and ends in a foot. Leg designs vary with periods and styles of decoration.

library table Large table with drawers and space for books, often on pedestal base, permitting kneehole space.

linen press Cupboard or chest of drawers designed to hold household linens. Name derives from a board-and-screw device originally used to smooth dampened linens, often made part of the chest.

lining In drapery and upholstery, a fabric used to back up the fine face fabric. It gives additional weight and body and may also serve as an insulating agent or protect the face fabric from sun's rays, etc.

link fabric Strong net of wire links used as a foundation for bedsprings, cots, gliders, sofa beds, or studio couches.

Louis XIII Period in France of the late Renaissance (1610–1643). Rich, overpowering furniture was made, especially in walnut and ebony. Cabinets had geometric panels and deep moldings. New developments were the buffet with drawers below, the bureau, expanding-top tables, and upholstery. Gilt or silver nail-heads were used for upholstery, either close together or in a decorative pattern. Furniture legs were turned, with much detail; H-stretchers appeared.

Louis XIV The period of the Baroque style in France (1643–1715). Furniture was enormous in scale, very elaborate, but generally rectangular in shape. Carving was rich, using all known animal forms of nature and mythology and an endless variety of leaves and floral motifs. Musical instruments, weapons, even agricultural implements were much in favor. Spectacular marquetry using tortoise shell, brass, pewter, ivory, and mother-of-pearl was developed. Pieces were liberally painted, often with strong colors, and often gilded or silvered. The console table appeared. Designs of seating pieces reached a new height, with rich upholstery, including the first fully upholstered easy chair and sofa. While chair backs were straight, legs were scrolled or made of turned balusters.

Louis XV The period of the rococo style in France (1715–1774). A period of gaiety and frivolity, furniture was made as ornamental as possible, and more comfortable and intimate. Symmetry, right angles, and straight lines were avoided; curves became dominant. The commode, chiffonier with many drawers, and secretary made their appearance. Designers developed flowers, shells, and musical instruments for decoration. Marquetry, inlay, and painted surfaces continued to be popular, along with mahogany and fruitwoods; and for veneers, rosewood, satinwood, and tulip. Varnishes were highly developed. Features included the cabriole leg, short and flaring arm, broad chair back, ornate framing, metal appliqué, marble, onyx, alabaster, many mirrors, and special-purpose tables for dressing and writing. Tapestry, brocade, and velvet dominated upholstery.

Louis XVI Known as the neoclassic period or classic revival (1775–1793), furniture and decoration saw a return to straight lines, moderation, and simplicity. Contemporary excavations of Greek and Roman ruins pointed the way to a renewed use of classical architectural forms and ornamentation in symmetrical placement. The straight leg returned in column form; sofas were long, supported by straight legs; beds smaller and less ornate, with wood showing. Mahogany was the main wood, but ebony returned to favor, along with walnut, rosewood, and satinwood.

lounge chair Any roomy, comfortable, upholstered chair in which one can relax. May be of any style or period.

love seat An upholstered settee for two persons. It first became popular in the Louis XIV period in France and in the Queen Anne period in England. The double seat is also called a *courting chair.*

lowboy A low chest of drawers on high legs, for serving.

lyre Harp-type stringed instrument used as a decorative motif for chair backs, table pedestals, sofas, etc., during many periods, but especially popular in traditional English and American furniture styles, such as Adam, Hepplewhite, and Duncan Phyfe.

M

machine room In furniture manufacture, the area where wood is fashioned into shapes by tools and machines, including moulders, shapers, turners, routers, and tenoners, before sanding.

mahogany One of the most widely used furniture woods, this hardwood is noted for its strength and durability. Easy to work, it does not warp easily, takes a high polish, and is noted for its reddish-brown color, handsome grain, and its richness which mellows with age. There are three general types: *African,* from the west coast of Africa; *tropical American,* including *Peruvian* and *Brazilian;* and *West Indian,* the best of which is imported from the Dominican Republic as *Spanish mahogany.*

maple A hard, strong, light-colored wood similar to birch, from northeastern U.S. and Canada. Straight-grained maple is excellent for interior finishes. *Bird's-eye maple* is curly-grained, swirled, blistered, and/or quilted and used as a decorative veneering material. Also called *sugar maple.*

marquetry Pattern made by setting contrasting materials into a veneered surface. The resulting decoration is flush and level. Usually, the material set in is finely grained, interestingly colored woods, but tortoise shell, horn, metal, and mother-of-pearl are also used.

Marshall unit Type of spring construction, with cylinder-shaped springs in individual muslin-covered pockets, as the core of a mattress or upholstered piece, permitting independent coil action and support.

matelassé A fabric with an embossed pattern which resembles quilting or a raised quilted design. Matelassé can be imitated by stitching or embossing. Usually heavyweight, used for upholstery. From the French for padded, or cushioned.

mate's chair Captain's chair without arms.

mattress A fully filled pillow or pad covered with ticking and placed over the springs or slats of a bed frame for comfort and softness. Filled with any or a combination of some of the following: down, feathers, hair, cotton batting, foam rubber, etc.

Mediterranean style Commercial term for 20th-century furniture designs and motifs based upon countries touching the Mediterranean Sea, manufactured from about 1960 on. Ideas were drawn from French Provincial, Italian Renaissance, and especially Spanish influences, offering vigorous lines, deep moldings, metal ornamentation, molded as well as grilled panels, intricate carving, curved legs, spindles, and caning.

mission Massive oak furniture which had its origin in the Spanish-oriented southwestern U.S. Upholstered pieces, usually leather, use hand-hammered copper nailheads.

mock-up Sample piece produced to show a design idea or to display at wholesale furniture markets. Many mock-ups of case pieces have only an outer shell, without drawers or other inside parts.

modern In furniture and design, a broad term for work that is not imitative of any past tradition, but rather developed for today's needs, with today's materials and techniques. Modern is no single style, but it is a number of expressions of a search for original designs free of classic references, simple, functional, easily maintained, yet aesthetically pleasing.

modesty panel Panel of cane, wood, or other materials, fixed into the exposed back of a kneehole desk to shield the user's legs. Also called *kneehole panel* or *knee-space panel.*

modular furniture A 20th-century concept in furniture design. Correlated pieces are designed to a given set of dimensions (module) and also to fractions of that module. The fractions and modules can be stacked or butted together, and units can be added or taken away as needed to serve various purposes, including seating, storage, display, and shelving.

moiré A waved or watered effect on fabric, especially rep or corded silks and synthetics. The fabric is pressed between engraved cylinders which emboss the grained design onto the material.

molding A shaped strip, usually of wood, fastened to a surface to give variety of contour. Cornices, flat panels, and columns, for example, are often varied with moldings having different profiles.

Morris chair A large, straight-lined, 19th-century easy chair named for English designer William Morris, with loose cushions and an adjustable back. Late 19th-century ancestor of today's recliner.

mortise A hole cut in a piece of wood which receives a tenon projecting from another piece of wood. It is used in cabinet joinery.

mortise-and-tenon joint A method of joining two pieces of wood. The projecting tenon of one piece fits into the open shape (mortise) of the other. Often used to join stretchers to leg posts or seats to the back posts of chairs, as a glued joint.

motif The distinctive feature of a design or ornament, or the theme of a style or period.

mottle A wood grain effect produced by short, irregular, wavy fibers across the face of the wood as cut.

mounts See HARDWARE.

Murphy bed Originally, a fall-down bed hidden away in a closet or in a covered recess in a wall. Later, the term for many sophisticated space-saving beds consisting of a rigid frame with a mattress that fits into a closet, bookcase, or architectural recess when not in use.

muslin A plain-weave fabric which may be bleached or unbleached. It is used as undercovering on upholstered pieces to tie in the stuffing and padding materials prior to putting on the final upholstery fabric.

N

nap Fibers raised on the surface of a fabric to create a downy or fuzzy appearance.

Naugahyde A trademark name for vinyl upholstery and wall-covering fabrics produced by the United States Rubber Company.

needlepoint A dense cross-stitch embroidery done on net, heavy canvas, or coarse linen. It resembles a coarse tapestry. From the 15th century on, used as an upholstery covering for chairs, sofas, etc.

neoclassic Classic as revived or "new classic," a term for the several later styles using the shapes and motifs of ancient Greece and Rome.

nested tables A series of small tables, graduated in size, so that one can be set inside the other.

night stand Occasional table, sometimes with cabinet, drawer, or shelf, used beside a bed to hold such items as a lamp, clock, or telephone. Also called a *night table* or *bedside table*.

nonwoven A class of fabrics produced by the bonding or interlocking of fibers, or both, but not understood to include felt. The nonwoven sheet is made by mechanical, chemical, thermal, or solvent means, or with an adhesive, or any combination of these, as distinct from weaving, knitting, or tufting.

nylon A protein-like chemical that can be manufactured as fibers, in sheet form, or as bristles. Upholstery fabric produced from nylon is tough, elastic, and strong. Provides high degree of abrasion resistance, dries quickly, and is easy to care for.

O

oak One of the most important woods used for furniture making. It may be sawed, either plain or quartered, the latter being generally preferred for fine work, because of the striking pattern produced. Oaks are divided into over fifty species, but the differences in the wood are not great. They are all hard, durable, and very similar in grain. *Red oak* and *white oak* are two commonly used varieties. Because it is porous, oak should be treated with a filler before applying stain or varnish.

occasional furniture Term applied to small furniture items such as cocktail tables, end tables, sofa tables, night stands, chests, commodes, and pull-up chairs, designed to permit varied uses in a room. Includes *occasional chairs* and *occasional tables*.

oil finish A wood finish accomplished by repeated polishing with boiled linseed oil. A low, satin-like luster is achieved, and the wood is made fairly resistant to stains from heat and water.

olefin An extremely light synthetic fiber, soil resistant and an excellent insulator, used to produce outdoor carpets and sturdy upholstery fabrics resistant to abrasion, pilling, and aging. Sensitive to heat and susceptible to shrinkage.

onlay Surface decoration of wood appliquéd on wood, in the manner of sheathing or veneer, with shapes cut out. Also called *overlay*. Contrast to INLAY.

open back A chair back that has an unupholstered opening between the rails and side splats, or a decorative open-frame back.

open stock Furniture that is regularly kept in stock and is usually available for immediate delivery. Not custom-made or specially finished. It is possible to buy parts of suites rather than complete groups from open stock.

Oriental Furniture style with Far Eastern design features. Woods of contrasting colors are used (usually teak, bamboo, walnut and/or rosewood) with geometric designs and sleek, uncluttered lines.

ormolu Gilded brass, copper, or bronze, especially popular as an ornament to French furniture of the 17th and 18th centuries.

ottoman Low upholstered seat without arms or back, often used as a footstool. Similar to a *hassock*.

outdoor furniture Patio, terrace, or porch furniture made to withstand the elements. Metal, glass, and plastics are favorites for outdoor tables, chairs, and lounges, as well as redwood and cypress wood. Molded fiberglass and polyvinyl chloride are especially well suited to outdoor use.

oval back Type of chair with oval-shaped back frame, upholstered or open, used by Hepplewhite and in Louis XVI chairs.

overlay See ONLAY.

oxbow front Curved front, concave in center and convex at the ends, found in Chippendale and other 18th-century cases. Also called *yoke front*.

P

pad foot A flattened disklike foot often found under a cabriole leg.

parquetry Type of marquetry consisting of geometric patterns, generally of different colored woods. Used in floors and furniture.

Parsons table Rectangular table developed by Frank A. Parsons, Parsons School of Design, New York. Produced as an occasional and dining table. Table is unique in that square legs are situated on four corners.

particle board Panels manufactured by bonding

wood particles with synthetic resins under heat and pressure. Used as the core for many plywood panels, as panels to be printed (engraved), or other uses in furniture construction. Depending on the size of wood particles, this product is also called *fiberboard, hardboard,* or *chipcore.*

parting rail A wood divider between drawers on front of case pieces. An important structural element; may be an important design feature when exposed.

party set Informal dining furniture, traditionally in lower price brackets, usually composed of a table and four to six chairs, made from a variety of materials.

patina Softening of color and texture of a surface through age, wear, or rubbing. Originally a coating on old metal, acquired through exposure or acid treatment, the term now also refers to the gloss on wood.

patio furniture See OUTDOOR FURNITURE.

pattern In wood, the design of grain appearing when the wood is cut the long way rather than across the annual rings, which is called the *figure.*

paw foot Furniture foot carved to resemble an animal's paw, most often that of a lion.

pecan Hardwood from south-central U.S., used for furniture and veneer. Reddish-brown with occasional darker streaks in heartwood, and creamy white sapwood, with a distinct pattern and pores larger than hickory or walnut, close grain, very heavy and strong.

pecky lumber Wood having channeled or pitted areas or pockets of disintegration, as sometimes found in pecan, cedar, and cypress.

pedestal Tall, generally narrow column on a base, designed as a support often for an object of art, but also for a piece of furniture.

pedestal desk Desk with drawers on both sides of kneehole. Also called *kneehole desk.*

pedestal table Table supported by a heavy column (or columns) with spreading feet or base.

pediment Decorative architectural hood or top of a cabinet; usually triangular, rounded, or with broken apex and finial.

peg Wooden dowel, pin, or spike used to hold furniture parts together, sometimes deliberately exposed to emphasize the construction.

Pembroke table Small, rectangular occasional table with wide drop leaves and a single drawer.

pendant A hanging ornament in various shapes, usually functioning as hardware on furniture.

Pennsylvania Dutch Name used for rural peasant styles developed by settlers in Eastern Pennsylvania, mostly German and Swiss. They simplified designs from their countries of origin, but added designs in bright colors depicting fruit, flowers, and animal motifs, as well as circular geometric hex signs and hearts.

period A roughly defined time when a particular influence or style prevailed. These styles usually started before and lasted past the time of the designated period. Often there are transitional periods when the incoming and outgoing styles mix and blend.

Phyfe, Duncan Most famous of Early American cabinetmakers (1768–1854). Almost always referred to by his full name, he was Scottish born, but worked in Albany and New York. His early furniture was influenced by the Adam brothers, Hepplewhite, and Sheraton, but is remembered also for his own departures. His early work was almost entirely in mahogany. Later he used Empire and Directoire ideas, working in rosewood with much brass adornment. Lyre and plume motifs are frequent in his fine carved ornament, along with oval medallions and acanthus motif. Chair legs often curved outward to the side, tables were supported on lyre-shaped bases or finely carved pillars.

pick See FILLING YARN.

piece dyed Fabric dyed after it has been woven or knitted. The opposite of yarn dyed.

piecrust table Tripod table with circular top and a scalloped, molded rim which looks like a crimped piecrust edge, associated with Chippendale.

pie match See SUNBURST.

pierced work Ornamental woodwork in which portions of the background are cut or chiseled out, leaving an openwork design. It is similar in appearance to fretwork. Pierced work was a popular form of decoration for chair backs.

pier glass and table Tall, narrow, decorative mirror hung above a small console table, originally placed between windows.

pilaster Flat column applied vertically to the surface of a piece of furniture. Can be for strength or a design element.

pile Cut or uncut loops that stand up on the face of a fabric, making it thick and three-dimensional, in contrast to flat-woven cloth. Examples are velvet, velveteen, plush, corduroy, and frieze.

pine Abundant in supply, this soft wood does not swell or shrink appreciably and is easy to work. Used mostly in construction of Early American,

Provincial, and rustic furniture. *Knotty pine* is used extensively for paneling, plywood, cabinets, and doors.

pit grouping See SECTIONAL FURNITURE.

plain weave A basic weave in which the warp and weft are the same size and alternate under and over each other in a regular manner. Used to make muslin, taffeta, etc. The other basic weaves are *satin* and *twill.*

platform bed A mattress set on top of a wood or plastic platform or pedestal. Sometimes, the mattress is recessed into a frame on the top of the platform, and there is a shelf that may go partially or completely around the perimeter. In other designs, the mattress may appear to float over a base that is recessed below it.

platform rocker Rocking chair whose motion derives from a mechanism in the base rather than from curved runners.

plush A long-pile velvet. Deeper and lusher than velvet or velour, it may be of silk, mohair, or synthetic fibers. Used as an upholstery fabric. Velvet pile is usually less than 1/8-inch thick, and plush pile is longer than 1/8-inch.

plywood Structural material made of very thin layers of wood bonded together with the grain of each layer, or ply, at right angles to that of the next. Often, the center layer is thicker and more porous than the others and is called the *core*. The crisscross effect gives strength to plywood which is sold in panels.

polyester A man-made fiber produced from coal, air, water, and petroleum elements. Has the following characteristics: strength, crease resistance, shrink resistance, quick drying, dyes well, shape retention, high stretch, abrasion resistance, minimum care.

polyfoam A synthetic resin that simulates latex foam rubber and is used for upholstered furniture, pillows, mattresses, etc. Firmness, resilience, and density can be varied. Also called *polyurethane foam.*

polystyrene Rigid plastic material that is injection molded. Used for decorative panels, trays, drawer fronts and drawers, corner blocks, and structural parts.

polyurethane As a lightweight filling material it is the same as polyfoam. It can also be made very firm; the rigid foam is used for decorative furniture parts and even chair legs and frames.

post Vertical strip or upright member of framework of a piece of furniture: upright corner section of a case; upright of a poster bed; projecting part that anchors a drop pull to a cabinet; and the upright of dining-room chairs.

print Surface having a pattern imposed with ink or dye by means of stencils, rollers, blocks, or screens. Applies both to fabric and wood.

Provincial See COUNTRY.

pull Handle to open drawers or doors of cabinets.

Q

Queen Anne The furniture and interior styles of England during reign of Queen Anne (1702–1714). English furniture developed a simple, curved line. Called *The Age of Walnut* for its favored wood. Moving away from earlier Dutch influences of the time of William and Mary, cabinetmakers developed and refined the club foot and the cabriole leg, ornamenting its knee, and repeating versions of its curve. They preferred restrained ornament, with some use of the scallop-shell motif, and the broken-C curve. Developed the chair without stretchers, many cabinets for books and china, as well as secretaries.

queen-size mattress Mattress that is usually 60 inches in width and 80 inches in length. Commonly referred to as a *5/0.*

quilted fabric Two layers of fabric with padding between the layers, held in place by stitches that usually follow a definite pattern.

R

rabbet joint A joining technique for supporting shelving or drawer bottoms in vertical units. It is used to stiffen or reinforce the vertical member. The edge of the vertical piece of wood fits into a groove in the horizontal piece. Also called a *dado joint.*

rail The horizontal strip of a frame or a panel. The horizontal tie bar in the framing of a piece of furniture, such as the top of a chair back, or a stretcher rail.

random match In veneering or decorative surfacing, a casual, unmatched effect with no attempt at a symmetrical or repetitive pattern.

rattan The long, solid, round stems of a species of palm native to India and southeast Asia. In larger diameters, used for furniture framing; smaller diameters used for weaving. Depending on the size and construction, rattan is also called *peel cane, reed,* or *wicker.*

rayon Generic term for man-made fibers composed of regenerated cellulose derived from trees, cotton, and woody plants. It is characterized by high absorbency, bright or dull luster, pleasant feel or hand, good draping qualities, ability to be dyed in brilliant colors, and superior strength in high tenacity types. Used extensively for blends with other fibers.

recessed stretcher In furniture, the cross stretcher that unites with the two side stretchers rather than with the front legs. This creates a set-back which allows room for the sitter's heels.

recliner Lounge chair that adjusts to various positions; usually incorporates an automatic footrest.

redwood A handsome uniformly reddish-brown softwood which takes paint and stains well. Used mostly for outdoor furniture. Native to the western U.S., especially California.

reed See *rattan.*

reeding Rows of beading or semicylindrical convex moldings used in close parallel lines. When concave moldings are used, it is called *fluting.*

refectory table Long, narrow, heavy dining table, often with low, heavy stretchers, and bulbous legs.

Regency, English The period in Great Britain (1811–1830) during which the Prince of Wales was regent and then became George IV. Furniture design made direct use of Roman, Greek, and Egyptian elements. English Regency coincides with Directoire and Empire styles in France, and with early Biedermeier in Germany, as well as Duncan Phyfe's work in America. All combined a classic simplicity in outline with elegant decoration. Chinese motifs and lacquer remained popular, as did Roman and Egyptian ornament, bronze and gilt. Cabinets and bookcases followed architectural forms, sofas were like Roman beds, tables often elaborately inlaid; woods were dark. Favored fabrics included damasks, velvets, and brocades.

relief Three-dimensional ornament or shape projecting from flat surface upon which it was worked, by modeling or carving, either slightly, as in *low relief,* or considerably, as in *high relief,* which is closer to sculpture in the round.

rep A plain-weave fabric with a heavy filler thread giving the fabric a corded effect, a definite crosswise rib.

repeat A single complete unit of the pattern that is repeated on a fabric. As a measure, repeat means the distance from a point in the pattern to the same point in the next example of the pattern unit.

residential furniture Furniture designed mainly for use in a person's private home.

Restoration Period See JACOBEAN.

reverse box match A decorative veneer technique similar to a reverse diamond match, but angled to create a cross-patterned center with right-angled patterns going off in four directions.

reverse diamond match Four wedges of wood or veneer set together to form an X at the center with consecutively smaller V's radiating out from the center in all four directions. Also referred to as a *butterfly match.*

rib fabrics A general term for knit or woven fabrics with a straight raised cord or ridge effect across the length or width of fabric; may also be diagonal. The rib is generally repeated at close regular intervals.

rim Raised border or edge of a table top or the top of a cabinet.

ripping Cutting wood with the grain, i.e., in the direction the grain runs. Opposite of *cross-cutting,* which is sawing wood across the grain.

rocker A unique American chair developed in the Colonial period, its legs mounted on curved runners permit a rocking motion. Also called a *rocking chair.*

rococo Eighteenth century European style of elegant, elaborate, and complicated decoration based on natural forms, including flowers, fruit, leaves, shells, and rocks. Originating in France as an outgrowth of the Baroque style, this decor swept over all Europe. It expressed pleasure and exuberance, using much carving and gilt and very light colors.

roll-top desk Desk whose tambour lid front rolls up to open and down to cover the writing surface.

rosewood Heavy, dark, multi-streaked, brown wood, often used as an inlay on fine furniture. There are many varieties, of which the most popular is *Brazilian rosewood.*

rotary-cut veneer A slice of veneer made by cutting a log in a circular manner around the circumference. It is similar to the unwinding of a roll of paper. A bold, variegated grain is produced since the cut follows the log's annual growth rings.

router Tool or machine that cuts mortises, dovetails irregularly shaped holes, grooves, and makes carvings.

runs In wood finishing, defects in a dried film caused by excessive amount of material applied unevenly.

rush Long stem of marsh-growing plant, a variety of sea grass, used to weave chair seats.

S

saddle seat A scooped-out seat which resembles the contour of a saddle. The seat is convex from the sides and back to a raised central ridge. Often found in Windsor chairs with thick pine seats.

sample A furniture prototype constructed to show to prospective buyers, usually at wholesale furniture markets.

sander Machine that smooths surface of piece of wood by rubbing it with a coated abrasive.

sanding In wood finishing, process of smoothing the surface of wood, after its shaping and again after its assembly into a piece of furniture, by even rubbing, by hand or machine, with a coated abrasive.

sapwood Outer layers of growth in a tree, exclusive of bark, usually lighter in color than the heartwood.

sateen Strong, lustrous, satin-weave cotton fabric. May be bleached, dyed, printed, or made with woven patterns. Also spelled *satine*.

satin *(1)* One of the three basic weaves. The others are *plain weave* and *twill*. *(2)* The resulting fabric, made of silk, man-made fibers and others, in a satin weave, made with more threads on the face than on the back. The more usual type has more warp yarns visible on the surface; another has more filling yarns. In either case, the result is a very smooth, generally lustrous surface with a thick, close texture and a dull back. Has a wide variety of uses, including upholstery.

satin, antique A fabric with tiny slubs that appear to be irregularities. Some versions use thicker slub yarns. The amount of slubbing can be controlled to create either a heavy-textured look or a delicate, random effect. Used extensively for drapery and upholstery in all-cotton, cotton blended with rayon, acetate, nylon, and/or all-silk.

satinwood A highly figured, close-grained, hard, durable wood native to Ceylon and the East Indies. It is light yellow to golden brown in color with a lustrous satinlike quality. A favorite wood in the Louis XV and Louis XVI periods, and was also favored by Adam, Chippendale, and Sheraton for inlay and veneering. Hepplewhite used satinwood as a background for painted medallions.

sawbuck table Rectangular table on X-shaped

supports, developed in the 17th century, now generally a rustic outdoor version in redwood or pine. Also see TRESTLE TABLE.

Scandinavian modern Style of 20th-century furniture evolved by designers of Sweden, Norway, Denmark, and Finland, marked by respect for materials, simplicity, concern for purpose, and for comfort. Entirely without applied ornament, and restrained in line, it stresses wood craftsmanship. Favored woods are walnut, teak, and rosewood. Oil-rubbed finish is a main characteristic.

scoop seat A slightly concave seat, dipped to accommodate the contour of a seated person. It is found in classic chairs, and reappears in the late 18th century in Sheraton's work and the Empire style. A variation appears in presentday contour and molded plywood chairs. Also called a *drop seat*.

Scotchgard A trademark name for a flourochemical process applied to fabrics to make them resistant to stains from dirt, water, or oil.

scroll An S or C-curved ornamentation. A spiraling and convoluting line, like a rolled piece of paper, makes the scroll.

scroll foot A flattened scroll at the end of a cabriole leg.

seasoned lumber Wood that has been dried in the air or in a kiln to improve its durability for furniture construction, and to control warping and checking. Also see KILN-DRIED.

secretary A desk surface with a space for writing appliances which is combined with a drawer base below and a bookcase cabinet above.

sectional furniture Referring generally to upholstered furniture, one piece of a group of complementary sections which can be grouped in a variety of arrangements or used separately. When the separate pieces form a U-shape, the grouping is called a *pit grouping*.

self-covered seat deck Area under the loose cushions on a piece of upholstered furniture which is covered in the same fabric as the rest of the piece. Also called *self-covered deck*.

selvage Finished edging along both lengthwise sides of a woven or knitted fabric or carpet to prevent unraveling.

semainier Tall, narrow seven-drawer chest. Introduced in Louis XV period, with one drawer for each day of the week.

serpentine front Undulating front surface, generally convex in the center, concave on either side.

serpentine stretcher   Curved shaped X-stretcher.

serving table   Side table with drawers for silver for use in a dining room. The larger units are similar to buffets, and many contain cabinet space. The top surface is used to hold food, platters, and service pieces for use at the dining table. Also called a *server.*

settee   Long seat with side arms and back, sometimes upholstered.

Shaker furniture   Extremely simple, sturdy, well-designed wood (chiefly pine) furniture made in the mid-19th century by the Shakers, a religious sect, in their independent rural communities in the Eastern U.S., especially Maine and New York. Few turnings, and no inlays, carving, or veneer were permitted, nor any type of decoration beyond an occasional red stain.

sheen   In wood finishing, degree of luster of a dried film.

shell   *(1)* In furniture making, the frame or basic construction. *(2)* Ornament in shape of one of a number of shells, including especially the scallop, but also the snail and others, which appears in many styles.

Sheraton, Thomas   English cabinetmaker of the late Georgian period (1751–1806). His best designs were noted for proportion, refinement, elegance and dignity, with many perpendicular lines. Favored motifs included the lyre, urns, reeding, fluting, pendants, and latticework; preferred wood was mahogany, but he also used satinwood, tulipwood, and rosewood, especially for inlays. Innovations were the first dual-purpose furniture, twin beds, and dome-topped desks and dressing tables. Most chairs had square backs with carved openwork and underbracing. Legs were slender and tapered.

shield back   Shape of a chair back popularized by Hepplewhite in mid-18th century England. The chair back resembles a shield-shaped frame with a tapered point at the center bottom. The frame would sometimes have a splat of carved feathers, ribbons, a sheaf of wheat, etc.

shott, shot, shute   See FILLING YARN.

sideboard   Originally an open-shelf dining-room piece, literally a side board or boards, now a piece with cabinet and/or drawers below, and sometimes open shelving above for the display of plates and silver.

side chair   Small chair without arms, generally a term for dining chairs other than those for the host and hostess.

side pleat   See KNIFE PLEAT.

side rail   In a bed, a board that joins the headboard and footboard and supports boxspring and mattress.

silent valet   Skeleton-like wood or metal framework designed to hold a man's complete change of clothing; usually also containing a jewelry tray. Often combined with a chair.

silk   A natural fiber extruded from the silkworm as it spins its cocoon. Silk may be used alone as a fiber or blended with other natural or synthetic fibers. It has a fine hand, drapes beautifully, and takes a brilliant dye.

simulated finish   Wood treatment with stains and varnishes producing appearance of wood different from one actually used, e.g., a simulated fruitwood finish on maple.

sinuous wire spring   Upholstered furniture spring manufactured in a zig-zag or S-shape with both ends fastened directly to the upholstered furniture frame. Also called *sinuous arc.*

skirt   Fabric valance around the base of an upholstered chair, couch, etc., to hide the legs and wood construction of the seat. The skirt may be pleated, shirred, or tailored (fitted and plain). Also see APRON.

slat   A horizontal bar connecting the upright members of a chair back.

slat back   Type of high, open chair back, having horizontal slats, sometimes carved or shaped, popular in 18th century England and America. Also see LADDER BACK.

sleigh bed   Bed with large scroll-like footboard and headboard, similar to old-style sleigh fronts, popular in French Empire period.

sling chair   A 20th-century canvas (or leather) and metal-rod chair. The wrought-iron base is shaped like two bent butterfly paper clips with two peaks in the front and two higher peaks in the back. The canvas cover or sling has four pockets which fit over these peaks. The sling makes a concave sweep from the back peaks to the front peaks.

slip cover   A removable fitted cover made to protect upholstery fabric, or to cover worn upholstery, or to provide a change for a new season. May be made of cotton, linen, chintz, silk, or synthetics. The idea of slip covering became popular in the Louis XV period.

slip match   A veneering pattern created by joining the veneer sheets side by side so that the figure is repeated over and over in a continuous manner.

slipper chair   Low, armless boudoir chair, sometimes upholstered, so called because it was used when putting on shoes.

slipper foot A club foot with a more pointed and protruding toe. It was a popular furniture foot in the Queen Anne period in England.

slip seat A seat that can be lifted out from the frame of a chair and be readily re-covered.

snack table Small, portable, lightweight occasional table used for informal food service to one person; often foldable for storage, and sold in a set.

sofa Long upholstered seat, usually for three or more people, sometimes with two arms and a back.

sofa bed A sofa whose back drops down; becomes parallel with the seat, and makes a sleeping surface. Also called *jack-knife sofa bed*.

sofa sleeper A convertible sofa with a concealed sleeper unit (mattress, etc.) beneath the seat. May vary in size from a love seat (48-inch sleeping area) to a standard 7-foot or longer couch which usually opens to a 54-inch or 60-inch sleeping surface.

sofa table An oblong table with flaps, or dropleaves, at the short ends which are supported by hinged brackets, similar to a Pembroke table. A drawer is in the longer side of a table frame. Today, also the name given to a variety of long narrow tables approximately the same height as the back of a sofa.

softwood Wood from one of the nonporous trees such as the pine, with needle-like, scale-like, or coniferous leaves.

solid Term for furniture made entirely from solid wood. Pieces so constructed usually have greater weight and less grain figure than those made partially from plywood and veneer. Solid wood is also used for turned parts, such as legs, and for carved parts.

solution dyed Synthetic fiber dyed by adding color to the chemical liquid from which the fiber is formed.

spade foot A rectangular, tapered foot often found in Hepplewhite designs and also in Sheraton's work. It is generally separated from the rest of the leg by a slight projection.

Spanish furniture Spanish design in the 16th, 17th and 18th centuries. Moorish influences persisted, notably in use of tooled and colored cordovan leather for furniture covers, seats, and decorations, as well as in brilliant colors, geometric motifs, inlay, and gilding. Spanish versions of Italian and French Renaissance forms tended to heaviness and some crudity of outline. Essentially rectangular and

heavy, chair backs and seats were often covered in leather or rich fabric, especially velvet, with wide arms, and later, high backs and posts with finials. Favored wood was walnut, but chestnut, oak, and others were used, as were inlays of ebony and raised relief designs of boxwood. Use of iron, both ornamental and structural, increased.

spindle Slim turned rod used in chair backs, headboards, etc.

spiral turning Twisted, screwlike turning.

splat Vertical, flat central member of an open chair back, rising from seat to top rail between two posts, to form back rest. Also spelled *splad*.

split spindle Spindle turning cut in half lengthwise, thus creating two half-round moldings. Used to decorate flat surfaces.

spool turning Turning resembling a row of spools or buttons, a mid-19th century American motif in mass-produced furniture.

spoon back (1) High chair back, resembling a spoon, to fit the body's contour, used in Dutch, William and Mary, and Queen Anne styles. (2) Later, in early 19th century, an upholstered chair with low arms rising from the front legs and forming one piece with a back rail.

spring In upholstery and bedding, a device, usually of wire, to give resilience to a piece.

stacking furniture Cabinets, shelves, and drawer units designed to be placed one atop another to create a free-standing wall system. Also chairs and stools designed to fit one atop the other for space-saving and storage.

staining In wood finishing, process of applying coloring matter to the outer surfaces of wood to enhance characteristic grain, provide uniform overall color, or to imitate or match other cabinet woods.

step table Two-tiered, rectangular occasional table with the smaller surface above, suggesting a pair of steps.

stile (1) Vertical member of a door in a cabinet which frames a panel. (2) Vertical member of a mirror frame. (3) The outer uprights of some panelback chairs. Also see UPRIGHTS.

stock dyed Fiber dyed before it is spun into thread or yarn.

storage bed A platform bed with storage below. The mattress is placed on a base fitted with drawers or cabinets. Storage space can also be concealed in the headboard, usually with doors in front or with lift-lid top.

storage wall A series of modular units which can be set up in a variety of combinations as a wall, or against one. May surround the head of a bed.

stretcher Crosspiece that braces legs of chairs, tables, etc. Made of wood or metal.

strié A fabric with an uneven color or streaked effect produced by using warp threads of varying tones. It is possible in this manner to produce a two-toned effect in taffeta, satin, or corded upholstery fabrics.

studio couch A seating device that converts into a sleeping unit by means of removable cushions or bolsters and retractable springs. An informal bed unit. A studio couch with an auxiliary set of spring and mattress kept, trundle-bed fashion, under the main spring and mattress, can convert into two twin beds.

stump Front support of a chair arm.

style The unique characteristics of design. A furniture style includes the motifs, techniques, and materials typical of a certain period of time or a particular designer.

suite Set of matched furniture, coordinated to be used together for a particular room, such as a headboard, night tables, dresser, and chest of drawers, all made in the same decorative style, ornamented in the same manner, and finished in the same color.

summer furniture Furniture used outdoors, or as odd pieces in the home, made mainly of aluminum, wicker, steel, redwood, wrought iron, rattan, bamboo, plastic, or fiberglass. The category of furniture is known as *summer and casual furniture.*

sunburst A figured wood grain in which rays radiate outward from a central point. This effect is often created through veneer inlaid in this pattern. Also referred to as a *pie match.*

swatch A small sample of cloth or material. Also called a *clipping* or *cutting.* Used as a specimen of the color, pattern, and texture of a fabric, as an aid to making choices, a sales tool.

swing-leg table See GATE-LEG TABLE.

swivel chair Chair with revolving seat and stationary base. Also made as a rocker.

T

tambour Sliding cover made of thin, flexible wood strips mounted on a heavy canvas or liner which slides in a pair of horizontal, vertical, or curved grooves to make a rolling or sliding door, as in a roll-top desk.

tapestry A fabric with a design woven in during the manufacturing, making it an essential part of the fabric structure.

Taslan A trademark name for DuPont's textured, air-bulked yarn.

T-cushion A seat cushion for a chair or sofa which is wider in front than at the back because the arms of the upholstered unit do not extend to the front of the seat. The two rectangular projections of the cushion (the crosspiece of the T) fill up the space between the end of the armpiece and the front of the chair or sofa seat. A sofa with two cushions will have only one projection or ear on each cushion.

tea cart Small, movable, wheeled cabinet with table top for serving; often with drop leaves, tray, and drawer. Now also used as a *bar cart,* or for barbecue service outdoors. Also called *tea wagon.*

teak Hardwood from Southeast Asia, especially Burma and Indonesia, used for furniture. Tawny yellow to dark brown, often with lighter streaks, sometimes with mottled and fiddleback grain. Strong, tough, oily wood.

tea table Small table with gallery around top, either round or rectangular.

tenon In joinery, a projection cut on a piece of wood shaped to fit into a cavity, or mortise, in another piece. Also called a *tongue.*

tester The top or canopy of a four-poster bed, made either of wood or fabric.

tête-à-tête An S-curved sofa for two. A 19th-century design in which the seated persons sit shoulder to shoulder, but facing in opposite directions.

texture The feel and the appearance of the tactile effect of the surface of a material, e.g., smooth, rough, fuzzy. Also grain in wood.

textured fabric Fabric characterized by some unevenness of surface.

textured yarn Any filament yarn that has been reprocessed to modify or otherwise alter its basic physical characteristics. This is done to obtain stretch; bouclé, pebble, or crepe effects; to get lighter, bulkier, more resilient fabrics; and to increase the cover, agreeable hand, or opacity of fabric.

ticking Closely woven fabric used to cover mattresses, box springs, pillows, and cushions, often with a stripe design.

tier table   A pedestal or tripod table with a series of graduated surfaces, the uppermost being the smallest.

tilt-top table   Small tripod or pedestal-based table with hinged top which can either be held horizontally or dropped vertically when not in use.

tongue-and-groove   Flush wood joint in which a long, straight projection (the tongue) of one board fits into a corresponding groove in another.

top rail   Uppermost cross piece of a chair back, joining the two end uprights. Also top cross piece on case goods.

traditional   In interior decoration, a term usually applied to a style of a bygone age, in contrast to a contemporary or modern style.

transitional   Style category that usually has a blending of traditional and contemporary design motifs.

trapunto   A type of quilting that gives a raised relief effect to a stitched design. The design is usually outlined with single stitches, and then filled from behind. Often used to embellish the pillow backs of upholstered pieces.

tray   Type of "inside" drawer behind a door or doors, usually without hardware.

tray table   Small folding stand, with removable tray at top, for serving.

tray-top table   A small table with a low gallery or skirting around three or all four sides.

trestle table   Long, narrow table supported by two heavy uprights joined by a stretcher rather than by four legs, or pedestal supports. A *sawbuck table* is one supported by X-shaped trestles, developed in the 17th century.

tri-fold mirror   Mirror style, usually placed on a dresser top, with a large center section and two side panels that are hinged. Also called *tri-plex* or *wing mirror.*

tripod table   Small table mounted on a pedestal terminating in three outward flaring legs, popular in 18th century.

trundle bed   A pullout bed on casters somewhat smaller than the bed under which it is set. Similar to a *hideaway bed.*

tub chair   A late 18th-century English easy chair with a rounded back and wide wings, similar to a barrel chair, but wider, taller, and more enveloping.

tub front   See BLOCK FRONT.

tubular furniture   Contemporary furniture with structural parts made of plastic or metal rods or tubes including the chair and table legs, chair arms, and back rests. Outdoor furniture is often made of PVC plastic or aluminum tubes with plastic webbing or plastic-covered pillows.

Tudor-Elizabethan   English period (1485–1603) during which new Renaissance forms combined with the established Gothic. Generally, furniture was massive, with straight lines, and elaborately carved. Beds were huge, bedposts highly ornate; chairs and tables had underbracing. Features included bulbous melon turnings, Tudor rose, carved acanthus leaves, linenfold motif, etc.

tufting   An upholstery technique. The covering fabric and the padding are tied back in a definite pattern, creating little "pillows" between the depressions. The tieback process is usually fastened with self-covered buttons. Tufting makes the upholstery fabric conform to the curves of the unit.

turning   An ornamental or structural element of furniture produced by rotating a wood dowel on a lathe, and shaping the dowel with cutting tools into a series of nodules, swellings, disks, etc.

tuxedo sofa   A clean-lined, simple, upholstered sofa with thin sides that flare out slightly. The upholstered sides are the same height as the sofa back, creating a continuous line. Can be finished with a skirt.

tweed   A rough-surfaced, textured material with a homespun effect. The yarn is usually dyed before weaving, and it is often woven in two or more colors to obtain a pattern: plaid, check, or herringbone.

twill   (1) One of the three basic weaves. The others are *satin* and *plain weave.* (2) A strong, durable fabric woven with filling threads crossing the warp in a staggered pattern, producing an effect of parallel diagonal lines, which can be varied in size and shape.

twin-size mattress   Mattress that is usually 30 inches in width and 74 inches in length. Referred to as a *3/3.*

U

underbracing   Arrangement of stretchers or braces under chairs, tables, and chests used to strengthen and reinforce the units.

upholstery   Process and technique of covering, padding, or stuffing a framework for a seating unit. Also the materials used in this operation. In ancient cultures, a skin or leather was nailed on a frame. Later, cushions were used for more comfort.

uprights In chair construction, the outer vertical posts, or stiles, that extend up from the back legs of the chair and support the chair back. These vertical members are braced and connected by the top rail. The uprights can be turned, straight, or shaped, depending on the period and the style of the furniture.

V

vanity, vanity table A dressing table.

vat dyeing A dyeing process that gives a permanent fast color. Each fiber of the fabric has the colors of the vat chemically induced and fixed into it. The fastness will vary from color to color. Used mainly for cotton, rayon, linen, and some blended fibers.

velour A soft pile upholstery fabric, generally woven in a satin weave or plain weave, resulting in a short, thick pile. Also some fabrics with a nap finish. The term *plush* is used interchangeably for velour construction.

velvet Fabric with a thick, soft pile formed of loops of the warp thread, either cut at the outer end or left uncut. Pile may be of several lengths in jacquard effects, and of different colors. Background may be plain, twill, or satin weave. Velvet can be made of wool, silk, cotton, nylon, etc.

velveteen Cotton or rayon pile fabric with short, nappy surface. Filling threads are cut after weaving. Pile is not as erect as that of velvet; it slopes slightly, making surface more lustrous. Used for upholstery and drapery.

veneer Thin slice of wood used to resurface a coarser, less decorative wood or particle board. Veneer is produced from a log that has been sliced, shaved, sawn, or peeled by rotary cutting, each way of cutting producing a different grain effect or figure in the resulting veneer sheets. These are applied and matched or combined in different ways to produce decorative patterns.

veneer matching See BOOK MATCH, BOX MATCH, BUTT MATCH, CENTER MATCH, CHECKERBOARD MATCH, DIAMOND MATCH, FOUR-WAY MATCH, HERRINGBONE MATCH, RANDOM MATCH, REVERSE BOX MATCH, REVERSE DIAMOND MATCH, SLIP MATCH, SUNBURST, and V MATCH.

Victorian English and American design trends during whole of Queen Victoria's long reign in England (1837–1901) are usually divided into three periods: *Early Victorian,* 1837–65; *Mid-Victorian,* 1865–1880; *Late Victorian,* 1880–1901. The first era saw the debasement of Empire and Sheraton furniture often with Gothic decoration. In the second, Louis XVI and then Renaissance styles were revived. The last period brought the manufacture of combination furniture and designs made under patents from the government. Commercial designers freely drew their inspiration from many previous styles, shape and ornamentation elaborated so much that the origins of designs became unrecognizable. In general, carving was heavy and curved, and scale was exaggerated. Chairs with oval or horseshoe-shaped backs, heavily overstuffed seats, button tufting, and plush upholstery were popular.

vinyl Nonwoven plastic material capable of being embossed or printed to give a wide variety of finishes. Often made to resemble leather. Supported vinyls, used as upholstery fabric, are laminated to a fabric back and are produced in various weights. Unsupported vinyls have no fabric backing and are used for seat covers, outdoor furniture, etc.

V match Veneer cut and butted together to form a decorative pattern in which the wood grain radiates from a center line to form a pattern resembling a series of V's set one over the other. Also called an *angle match.*

W

wale *(1)* A row or chain of loops running lengthwise in knitting. *(2)* A ridge formed by a row of tight loops running lengthwise in woven fabric.

wall system Series or combination of wall-hung or free-standing cabinets, shelves, drawers, desks, and bar units, permitting different arrangements as desired. Provides usable storage, display, or work space up or around the wall.

walnut Hardwood grown through Asia, Africa, Europe, and America. A widely used furniture wood, it has strength, beauty, durability, and attractive graining. Ranging from a soft, light brown to deeper tones, it has a great variety of figures and is easy to work.

wardrobe Cabinet in which to hang clothes.

warp *(1)* Threads that run the length of the fabric, through which the filling yarns *(weft)* are passed in weaving. *(2)* In furniture or woodworking, the twisting or bulging of a piece of wood, which can be caused by a certain change in the moisture content of the wood.

water bed Mattress formed by the injection of water into a plastic container. *Flotation sleep systems,* including frames, etc., have been developed.

weave The process of making fabrics by interlacing warp threads (the lengthwise threads) with the weft or filler threads (horizontal or across-the-fabric threads). Different patterns and textures are possible depending on the type of loom, the weaving pattern, and yarns used.

webbing Strips of tightly woven burlap, linen, plastic, nylon, rubber, elastic, or metal used in upholstery construction as a reinforcement and support for springs and cushions. In some seats of outdoor furniture, the webbing forms the finished seat or back rest.

weft See FILLING YARN.

Welsh dresser Sideboard, or hutch, with doors and drawers below, and open shelves above, often receding, for dinnerware display.

welting Fabric-covered cord, sewn into the edge seams of upholstery, where a firm, defined edge is needed as a box-shaped cushion. Strengthens and gives a finished appearance to the seams.

whatnot A tier or tiers of open shelves used to display curios.

wicker Strong woven matting of willow, reed, or rattan, cut into different diameters and used to construct furniture, often for outdoor use.

William and Mary King and Queen of England (1689–1702). The Baroque style from the Low Countries, birthplace of King William, influenced English design under these monarchs. Oriental imports grew, and French cabinetmakers were encouraged. A new English style, more simplified and comfortable, evolved. Cabinet work was often arched; rectangular double-arched backs, extensive upholstery, including needlework, lacquer, and marquetry, were features. Beds were tall; highboys and lowboys appeared, as did the turned foot, cabriole leg, and outward-flaring arm. Walnut was the wood of the time.

Windsor chair An 18th-century chair with bentwood back frame and numerous turned spindles, pegged turned legs, and wood or rush seat. The spindles were originally made in a shop near Windsor Castle in England, hence the name. Its greatest development came in America, where it was lightened and became more graceful. Versions include *bow-back, fan-back, writing-arm,* and others. English versions usually have a splat.

wing chair Large upholstered chair with side pieces projecting from the high back, originally designed as protection from drafts.

wing mirror See TRI-FOLD MIRROR.

woof See FILLING YARN.

wool A natural fiber from the fleece of sheep or hair from goats. The surface of the wool fiber makes it possible to felt wool. It is warm, resilient, and is used for upholstery fabric, carpets, and other household uses.

wrap group Modular case pieces designed so as to provide study, storage, display, or other space up and around the walls of a room. Term is used mainly with bedroom furniture.

wrought iron Malleable iron that has been worked, bent, and twisted to form both the decorative and structural parts of furniture. Wrought iron has been used for hardware, for decoration, and strength on much period furniture down through history. Also used for outdoor and casual furniture.

X

X-stretchers Crossed stretchers used to connect and reinforce the four legs of a chair or other piece of furniture. Various styles use shaping, turning, or other decoration of these stretchers as important design elements.

Y

yarn An assemblage of fibers, either natural or man-made, discontinuous or continuous, twisted together to form a continuous strand which can be used in weaving, knitting, or otherwise made into textile material.

yarn dyed Yarn dyed before it is woven or knitted.

yoke front See OXBOW FRONT.

INDEX